THE BALLETS OF MAURICE RAVEL

The Ballets of Maurice Ravel

Creation and Interpretation

DEBORAH MAWER
Lancaster University

ASHGATE

© Deborah Mawer, 2006

Deborah Mawer has asserted her moral right under the Copyright, Designs and Patents Act, 1988, to be identified as the author of this work.

Published by
Ashgate Publishing Limited
Gower House
Croft Road
Aldershot
Hants GU11 3HR
England

Ashgate Publishing Company
Suite 420
101 Cherry Street
Burlington
Vermont, 05401–4405
USA

Ashgate website: http//www.ashgate.com

British Library Cataloguing in Publication Data
Mawer, Deborah, 1961–
    The Ballets of Maurice Ravel: Creation and Interpretation.
    1. Ravel, Maurice, 1875–1937 – Criticism and interpretation. 2. Ballets – History and criticism.
    I. Title
    781.5'56'092

US Library of Congress Cataloging in Publication Data
Mawer, Deborah, 1961–
    The Ballets of Maurice Ravel: Creation and Interpretation / Deborah Mawer.
      p. cm.
    Includes bibliographical references (p.) and index.
    1. Ravel, Maurice, 1875–1937. Ballets. 2. Ballets – History and criticism. I. Title.
    ML410.R23M39 2006
    781.5'56'092–dc22
                                                              2005014109

ISBN-10: 0-7546-3029-3

This book is printed on acid-free paper.

Typeset by Saxon Graphics Ltd, Derby

Printed and bound in Great Britain by MPG Books, Bodmin, Cornwall

For my parents and Alexander

Contents

List of figures

Acknowledgements

In a book on a wide-ranging topic such as this, there are many individuals and organizations whose assistance needs to be properly acknowledged; in various ways, the book is the result of collaborative activity. Special thanks are due to Lynn Garafola, Stephanie Jordan, Richard Langham Smith, Simon Morrison and Nigel Simeone, whose generosity extended to reading substantial portions of the manuscript and offering valuable feedback. From a balletic perspective, I am also grateful for contact, correspondence and useful advice from John Craxton, George P. Lynes II, Nigel Stewart and others. From a musical perspective, the support and advice of colleagues, including Robert Orledge, Jean-Michel Nectoux, Roger Nichols, Roy Howat and Nicholas Baragwanath, has been much valued.

During the research stages across 2000–03, I have been particularly appreciative of the efficient staff response at the Bibliothèque Nationale de France, especially the Bibliothèque-Musée de l'Opéra under its director Pierre Vidal and the Département de la Musique under Catherine Massip, without the resources of which this book would have been impossible. Other informative, helpful people included Francesca Franchi at the Royal Opera House Archives, staff at the Theatre Museum, the Victoria and Albert Museum, The New York Public Library for the Performing Arts, Stockholm DansMuseet and Paris Opéra. Helen Clish organized access to materials from the Rare Books Archive and Jack Hylton Archive at Lancaster University. Staff assisted at John Rylands Library, University of Manchester, the Cambridge University Library and Wimbledon School of Art (Theatre). Additionally, contacts at Durand/BMG and Heugel/United Music Publishers tracked down elusive ballet scores.

I have been fortunate in being able to test out ideas from this project in a newly designed final-year musicology course at Lancaster University during the session 2002–03. The course used its topic of balletic collaboration, performance and interpretation as the vehicle for assessment through group presentation and discussion. Student feedback was very helpful in identifying ideas that needed further clarification and in raising awkward but thought-provoking questions! Music research students with strong interests in ballet, Helen Minors, Emily Turfus and Laura Halsey, made particular contributions. Beyond music, colleagues in art and dance within the Lancaster Institute for the Contemporary Arts offered encouragement.

At Ashgate Publishing, I should like to thank Rachel Lynch, succeeded by Heidi May, for backing this project from its inception. Ashgate's generosity in respect of illustrative music examples and photographs, its flexibility of approach and steadily growing list of twentieth-century French music and inter-arts titles made it the first-choice publisher for this enterprise. For efficient steering of the book script through to publication, I am grateful to senior desk editor Kirsten Weissenberg and to my trusted copy editor in Cambridge, Lucy Carolan.

Most of all, I want to express thanks for the support of my husband, Ronald Woodley, not only in a practical sense, but also in offering (un)certain insights and suggestions, especially with regard to tricky corners in the French translations.

Crucially, this project could not have been brought to fruition without financial assistance from various organizations. Generous funding from the British Academy enabled an intensive research trip to Paris during Summer 2002, followed up by a further visit assisted by Lancaster University in Summer 2003. Research leave from the Arts and Humanities Research Board has proved invaluable in enabling the writing of this book across 2003–04, and a second small grant from the British Academy in 2003 has made possible the acquisition of photographs and permissions, essential to delivering the interdisciplinary subject-matter.

While I am most appreciative of this collective body of support, the responsibility for what follows remains uniquely mine.

orchestral score © 1921 Editions Durand S.A.; and *Boléro*, orchestral score © 1929 Editions Durand S.A., are reproduced by kind permission of Editions Durand S.A., Paris/BMG.

Note on the text

All references are given in full at their first citation in the footnotes, with short titles thereafter. The most important published sources of Ravel ballet literature are listed in the Select bibliography, together with the main manuscript sources consulted. This bibliography does not include performance reviews or newspaper articles (other than those by Ravel, or interviews with him), minor articles, music scores, or literature offered in footnotes simply as further reading. Unless otherwise indicated, footnote references relate to the most recent edition of any text detailed in the bibliography.

References to frequently mentioned archival sources are given in abbreviated form in the footnotes, as follows:

B de l'A	Bibliothèque de l'Arsenal (Arts du Spectacle), Bibliothèque Nationale de France, Paris
BL	British Library, London
B-MO	Bibliothèque-Musée de l'Opéra, Bibliothèque Nationale de France
BNF	Bibliothèque Nationale de France
BNF Mus	Département de la Musique, Bibliothèque Nationale de France
FR	Fonds Rouché, Bibliothèque-Musée de l'Opéra
FM	Fonds Montpensier, Département de la Musique
HRC	Humanities Research Center, University of Austin at Texas
ROHA	Royal Opera House Archives, Covent Garden, London
ROLC	Robert Owen Lehman Collection, The Morgan Library, New York
TML	Theatre Museum, Victoria and Albert Museum, London

The Appendix listing is compiled from many sources, but special acknowledgement should be made of Martha Bremser (ed.), *International Dictionary of Ballet*, 2 vols (Detroit and London: St. James's Press, 1993).

Translated materials are provided in English within the main text and French in footnotes for verification purposes. Unless otherwise stated, English translations have been undertaken by the author.

Musical references employ a mixture of bar numbers and rehearsal figures depending on the available editions of a work. Generally, bar numbers are used for piano scores and rehearsal marks for full orchestral/ballet scores.

Consequently, a shorthand system has been devised for orchestral references: Fig. 1^{-1} refers to the bar preceding rehearsal figure 1; Fig. 1 denotes the full bar with this attached label; Fig. 1^{+1} refers to the bar following rehearsal figure 1. In respect of music examples, the relevant edition or version (with publication date) is cited at its first occurrence. Subsequent examples do not restate a source unless following a change of edition.

In musical discussion the sign '/', as in F/F♯, indicates modal 'mixture': the presence of alternative pitches used in a flexible, inflected manner. Separation of pitches by commas indicates a neutral, basic listing, such as for scalic or chordal components. Separation of pitches by means of '–' indicates a voice-leading progression: directed linear movement from one pitch to another. Modes are referenced in the same way as major or minor scales: hence C major, C aeolian or E phrygian.

Introduction

This book aims to offer a dedicated study of Maurice Ravel's ballets and, following Ravel's example, it seeks to situate the music within its broader cultural context. Apart from being the composer of at least six main works that may be termed ballets, Ravel wrote three scenarios and made a major contribution to a fourth, as well as writing reviews and articles on ballet. Additionally, he enjoyed drawing and produced, for instance, the frontispiece to the piano version of *Le Tombeau de Couperin*. Ravel's aesthetic perspective upon the arts was a holistic one. In the spirit of the Symbolist poets, he sought interconnections – even an artistic synaesthesia, rather than compartmentalization. Such an aesthetic stance was distinct from his compositional practice, which was an intensely personal matter.

A common problem when dealing with ballet is that the contributions of the collaborators are regarded in isolation.[1] In Ravel's case, one frequently hears *Boléro* or the Second Suite from *Daphnis et Chloé* in the concert hall, but relatively rarely is that music placed in the context of attendant scenario, dance and design. Similarly, scholarly emphasis has favoured Ravel's output as a whole,[2] or particular ballet companies taken as a whole.[3] However, given Ravel's increasing popularity – not least (ironically) through abstracting ballets from their fuller artistic contexts, but also through the appearance of *The Cambridge Companion to Ravel*,[4] the new Peters Edition of the piano music[5] and affordable

---

[1] This concern is shared by Nicholas Cook, *Analysing Musical Multimedia* (Oxford: Clarendon Press, 1998), v. While there is an aesthetic/stylistic context for each choreographer or designer of which one must be respectfully aware, such contexts can be outlined only briefly, with suggestions for further reading.

[2] See Gerald Larner, *Maurice Ravel* (London: Phaidon, 1996), or Roger Nichols (ed.), *Ravel Remembered* (London and Boston: Faber & Faber, 1987).

[3] See Lynn Garafola, *Diaghilev's Ballets Russes* (New York: Oxford University Press, 1989), Lynn Garafola and Nancy Van Norman Baer (eds), *The Ballets Russes and its World* (New Haven, CT: Yale University Press, 1999), or Bengt Häger, *Ballets Suédois*, trans. Ruth Sharman (London: Thames & Hudson, 1990).

[4] Deborah Mawer (ed.), *The Cambridge Companion to Ravel* (Cambridge: Cambridge University Press, 2000).

[5] *Ravel's Piano Music – A New Edition*, a series edited by Roger Nichols, includes *Le Tombeau de Couperin* (London, Frankfurt, New York: Edition Peters [1995]).

Dover editions covering a range of works,[6] a research project on Ravel's ballets is timely. Furthermore, whilst there is considerable interest in artistic interplay in early twentieth-century Paris, Ravel's ballets have not yet enjoyed sufficient attention. The previous dedicated volume on the composer's staged works, embracing ballet and opera, was that by his friend and pupil Alexis Roland-Manuel in 1928,[7] and so this present volume aims to fill a striking gap in Ravel literature; comparatively speaking, there is no such gap in Stravinsky studies and the situation has recently been remedied for Prokofiev's ballets.[8] Paradoxically, even if this is seemingly a study of just one genre, it is a book about Ravel's music more broadly because of his predilection for compositional remodelling. Ravel's ballet music often began life as piano repertory, which was then orchestrated and expanded again for the stage; the importance to Ravel of dance in music leads him to extend his boundaries.

Numerous questions emerge. What was the nature of the 'poietic', collaborative relationships for these ballets, and what were Ravel's collaborative strengths and weaknesses? (For explication of poietic–esthesic matters, see Chapter 1.) By extension, how were conflicting demands resolved: issues of autonomy in music and dance versus the need for collaborative fusion? Apart from the wealth of material on Serge Diaghilev, what information about figures such as Michel Fokine, Natalia Trouhanova, Ida Rubinstein, Jacques Rouché, Rolf de Maré and Jean Börlin might enhance historical and interpretative understanding of Ravel's ballets? From an 'esthesic', interpretative stance, how do the six main musical pieces work within the context of the other balletic elements? Is the music so enhanced or diminished and what are the overall relations within a supposed composite art-work: is the whole greater than the sum of its parts? How successful a ballet composer was Ravel, and what is the status and significance of his ballet music? These varied questions and issues underpin the text, which in turn attempts some answers.

A book dealing with this type of complex topic cannot hope to be comprehensive, but rather to extend outwards from music to create an appropriate overview and means for readers to pursue areas of interest further. The subject presents as a jigsaw puzzle. Sadly many pieces, especially relating to dance, were lost years ago. Others will not be examined because the project needs realistic boundaries and to reflect the author's

---

[6] Maurice Ravel, *Four Orchestral Works* (New York: Dover, 1989) and Maurice Ravel, *Le Tombeau de Couperin and Other Works for Solo Piano* (New York: Dover, 1997).

[7] Alexis Roland-Manuel, *Ravel et son œuvre dramatique* (Paris: Librairie de France, 1928). Given its publication date, this book does not include *Boléro*.

[8] Stephen D. Press, *Prokofiev's Ballets for Diaghilev* (Aldershot: Ashgate, 2005).

skills.[9] With a couple of exceptions, this book does not engage with music sketches or music manuscripts because these tend not to relate directly to balletic creation and collaboration, and because they merit detailed study in their own right. Similarly, this project is not concerned with dance notation, which is a highly specialized skill. The main approach to dance and design is historical, and while reference is made wherever possible to more recent, available videos, there is little dance movement analysis. After a work's premiere, references to subsequent productions are necessarily selective, but these have still allowed the presentation of previously untrawled or untranslated material. A balance has been sought between providing a 'factual' history of Ravel's ballets and exploring lines of interpretative enquiry.

The research mainstay of this scholarship consists of primary and early secondary Parisian sources. Beyond are other materials that could constitute the bases for further dedicated studies, with scope for fruitful collaboration between musicologist and dance researcher, which this book can only outline: the English production and reception history of Ravel's ballets, with emphasis upon Frederick Ashton, Ninette de Valois and the Royal Opera House Archives; detailed manuscript study of Ravel's scores at the Humanities Research Center in Texas and at The Morgan Library in New York. New York also offers the perfect location, with significant institutional resources pertaining to the New York City Ballet, The New York Public Library for the Performing Arts and George Balanchine Foundation, for detailed examination of Balanchine's championing of Ravel's music.

In order to establish Ravel's relations within a complex collaborative network, Chapter 1 outlines the historical and cultural context, introducing the main characters and companies with whom Ravel worked during his balletically active years, 1909–29, as well as the composer's aesthetic writings on ballet and opera. This chapter airs, briefly and accessibly, the historical and critical/interpretative approaches that are employed in discussion of the ballets. Approaches of Stephanie Jordan and Daniel Albright prove especially relevant.[10]

---

[9] Nicholas Cook adopts a similar music-plus approach in *Analysing Musical Multimedia*, vi. Although my main background is in musicology and music analysis/interpretation, balletic interest extends from childhood training and considerable experience of viewing productions, through to writing a monograph that focuses on Milhaud's ballet, *La Création du monde* – Deborah Mawer, *Darius Milhaud: Modality and Structure in Music of the 1920s* (Aldershot: Ashgate, 1997, repr. 2000) – and chapters on 'Ballet and the apotheosis of the dance' and 'Musical objects and machines', in Mawer (ed.), *The Cambridge Companion to Ravel*, 140–61, 47–67.

[10] Stephanie Jordan, *Moving Music: Dialogues with Music in Twentieth-Century Ballet* (London: Dance Books, 2000); Daniel Albright, *Untwisting the Serpent: Modernism in Music, Literature and Other Arts* (Chicago and London: University of Chicago Press, 2000).

Chapters 2–7 cover each main balletic undertaking, with some works grouped thematically in and between connected chapters so as to explore childhood (*Ma Mère l'Oye* and briefly *L'Enfant*), waltzing (*Valses nobles* and *La Valse*) and neoclassicism (*Le Tombeau de Couperin* and 'Fanfare' from *L'Eventail de Jeanne*). Structurally, the main pre- and postwar waltzes are pulled together to form a central backbone. These chapters play out the book's 'Creation and interpretation' subtitle. Each chapter introduces its main parameters and commences poietically, examining the musical evolution and collaborative processes of the original creations from documentation such as letters, scenarios and programmes. A particular concern is with the creative challenge for Ravel and Fokine presented by the finale of *Daphnis*.

Esthesic, interpretative readings follow on or become interpolated, with primary focus upon the music – especially melody and rhythm – linked to lighter treatment of other disciplines. Portions of each work are selected for critical treatment in connection with 'themes' such as Greekness and emotional antitheses (*Daphnis*), neoclassicism (*Le Tombeau*), or Spanishness, machines and sexuality (*Boléro*). Readings are supported by varied sources relating to chosen productions so as to highlight both plurality and the potency of the music. Greatest emphasis is given to works originally envisaged as ballets by Ravel: *Daphnis et Chloé* (1912), *Boléro* (1928) and *La Valse* (1929), but since Ravel also questions traditional boundaries of genre in his opera-ballet hybrid *L'Enfant et les sortilèges*, it would be perverse not to accommodate this work within a balletic canon.

Chapter 8 adopts a broader perspective, summarizing the main findings, setting out Ravel's collaborative strengths and weaknesses, mentioning uncompleted ballet projects, overviewing the performance tradition and offering conclusions on the special status of the ballets.

There are various ways to read this book. It is possible to read through the broadly chronological chapters in order, or to select any individual chapter, but the existence of chapter themes and topical subheadings listed in the Contents means that one can choose non-linear routes through the text. In this manner, the reader may trace Ravel's association with the Ballets Ida Rubinstein; productions by Frederick Ashton or George Balanchine, including their contrasting readings of *La Valse*; or designs of Jacques Drésa or Léon Leyritz for more than one ballet. Equally, s/he may select themes that bypass chronology and run within and across chapters, pertaining to several works: portrayal of foreign national identity ('Russianness' and 'Spanishness'), musical evolution, or critical reception. More concealed ideas include exoticism, machines, destructive dance endings, and 'objets sonores' in respect of waltzes, fanfares or conjuring up the 'antique'.

This book aims to attract a broad readership of musicians, both professionals and students, as well as dance scholars and amateur ballet-/concert-goers. In seeking to promote accessibility, it avoids unnecessarily technical language; the few required musical symbols are given in the Note on the text, above.

Chapter 1

Cultural and critical backdrop

In collaboration with some of the greatest contemporary ballet directors, choreographers, dancers and designers, Maurice Ravel provided musical scores, plus certain scenarios, for a broad range of ballets. These ballets offer a distinct and sizeable contribution to the audio-visual feast consumed in Paris both before and after the First World War, essentially across the years 1909–29, which mirrors the existence of the Ballets Russes itself. This varied repertory includes *Ma Mère l'Oye* (Mother Goose), *Valses nobles et sentimentales* (retitled *Adélaïde ou Le Langage des fleurs*), *Daphnis et Chloé*, *Alborada del gracioso*, *Le Tombeau de Couperin*, *La Valse*, *L'Enfant et les sortilèges* (an opera-ballet), 'Fanfare' for *L'Eventail de Jeanne* and *Boléro*.

With these Ravel ballets as its focus, this book seeks to view ballet ideally as a composite artistic genre whose status despite the challenges, even compromises, of collaboration should be upheld alongside that of opera. Puns aside, ballet should not be seen as a 'Cinderella' art-form. Its lack of verbalized text does not hinder the development of detailed scenarios, and can increase artistic freedom, so that one balletic facet may complement, and sometimes create judicious tension with, another. The whole, in theory at least, should be greater than the sum of its parts: to study or experience ballet music as an abstracted symphonic suite is to miss the point. Nonetheless, questions of musical autonomy versus collaborative issues are highly germane, and are aired below.

Historical context and collaborative ballet network

In the ballet world of the earlier nineteenth century France had been centre stage, thanks particularly to Marie Taglioni (1804–84) who made her Paris Opéra début in 1827; contemporaneously, ballet became interpolated within operatic productions. Taglioni was reputedly the first to utilize work *sur les pointes* as an expressive device. Ironically, in terms of French identity, this Parisian star was half-Italian and half-Swedish, and her greatest glory was the Scottish-inspired tragedy *La Sylphide*,[1] choreographed by her father and

---

[1] The music was by Jean Schneitzhoeffer. In opposition to later perceptions that privileged the distant east and south, Scotland of the Sir Walter Scott era was viewed as a northern exotic, replete with kilts.

premiered at the Opéra on 12 March 1832, which came to symbolize Romantic ballet.[2] In turn, the supernatural story staples of French Romantic ballet, with their simulated flights of fairies and sylphs, are at some level echoed in Ravel's *L'Enfant et les sortilèges*. Another hugely popular work, still a mainstay of current repertory, was the tragic *Giselle* premiered on 28 June 1841, with music by Adolphe Charles Adam to a scenario by Théophile Gautier. It was closely tailored to the choreographic requirements of Jules Perrot and Jean Coralli, who sought to showcase the talents of Carlotta Grisi (while Romantic ballet adored and promoted the ballerina, standards of male dancing lagged behind). By the late 1840s, the heyday was already over and a slow decline ensued, even if this was halted temporarily by the comedy *Coppélia*, to the music of Léo Delibes and choreography of Arthur Saint-Léon, premiered on 25 May 1870.[3]

As France's balletic fortunes were waning, those of Russia were in the ascendant. Indeed, Taglioni and *La Sylphide* had appeared in St Petersburg by 1837, with Fanny Elssler soon after. Other French citizens chose to develop their careers in a Russia that was briefly culturally sympathetic and distant from European unrest epitomized by the Franco-Prussian War of 1870, with Perrot and Saint-Léon bringing productions to St Petersburg. The greatest French émigré was arguably Marius Petipa (1818–1910),[4] whose brother had first danced Albrecht in *Giselle*. Petipa was hugely influential in his long-held appointment at the Maryinsky from 1869, formulating his own set principles that favoured lavish and intricate large-scale constructions: complex plots, multiple scene changes and magnificent costumes. The prima ballerina, usually imported, still constituted the focal point, with fixed formulae for solos, *pas de deux*, and the *corps de ballet* in their national dances. It was Petipa who choreographed to great acclaim Tchaikovsky's *La Belle au bois dormant* (The Sleeping Beauty) Op. 66 (1888–9),[5] a ballet which launched the celebrated teacher Enrico Cecchetti (1850–1928) as the Bluebird. This work, premiered at the Maryinsky in 1890, with a young Igor Stravinsky reputedly present, was amongst the first by a composer of serious orchestral music, a tradition

---

[2] For a classic text, see Ivor Guest (with Foreword by Dame Ninette de Valois), *The Romantic Ballet in Paris* (London: Pitman, 1966; 2/1980). For a recent, collective account, see Rebecca Harris-Warrick, Noël Goodwin and John Percival, 'Ballet', in *The New Grove Dictionary of Music and Musicians*, ed. Stanley Sadie, 29 vols (London: Macmillan, 2001), vol. II, 565–96.

[3] This work's lasting popularity is evident by its being toured to the diminutive eighteenth-century Grand Theatre in Lancaster by the Vienna Festival Ballet in March 2004.

[4] See Tim Scholl, *From Petipa to Balanchine: Classical Revival and the Modernization of Ballet* (London and New York: Routledge, 1994).

[5] Tchaikovsky's musical triumphs *Swan Lake* (1875–6) and *The Nutcracker* (1892) were both compromised early on by mediocre productions.

that Ravel would continue in France. Other Petipa highlights included *Don Quixote* (1869) and *La Bayadère* (1877), both to music of Léon Minkus. This latter ballet explored exotic mélange based upon an Indian tale of a warrior and temple dancer, and was a choreographic *tour de force*. Additionally, the Hungarian-inspired *Raymonda*, to Alexander Glazunov's score, was premiered in 1898.

And so Russia, having benefited from French expertise, definitely had the edge, although Petipa's ideas themselves became dated. While musical quality improved, the plots lacked dramatic unity, with the *corps de ballet* remaining 'outside', and the dancing leaving much scope for increased expression and imagination. But nowhere was the problem of conservative, formulaic ballet more acute than in France. Fundamental change was needed to espouse a forward-looking aesthetic that embraced modernism – a ballet fit for the twentieth century. Consequently, the stage was most appropriately set for a group of dynamic Russian émigrés who sought the artistic freedom,[6] opportunities and cultural cachet of Paris just after the *fin de siècle*. And thus Franco-Russian cross-fertilization worked in reverse.

Cue the dynamic but ruthless impresario Serge Diaghilev (1872–1929), who in creating the Ballets Russes became a catalyst for ballets by Stravinsky, Rimsky-Korsakov, Reynaldo Hahn, Ravel, Prokofiev, Erik Satie, Francis Poulenc, Darius Milhaud and many others in the first two decades of the twentieth century.[7] Diaghilev had also been the founder of a magazine entitled *Mir Iskusstva* (The World of Art), which acted as a vehicle across 1898–1904 to publicize avant-garde views on ballet in Russia, including his own 'Complicated questions' about artistic aesthetics. Joint editorship of the magazine was assumed by Diaghilev, Léon Bakst (1866–1924) and Alexandre Benois (1870–1960). Bakst, the pseudonym of Lev Rosenberg of Jewish origin, was to become famous for his astonishingly prolific, eclectic Russian designs, contributing half of the entire sets and costumes for the prewar Paris seasons, as well as being

---

[6] Political unrest had been evident since the assassination of Tsar Alexander II in 1881, with renewed anti-Semitism in its wake, but increasingly alarming signs appeared, especially the major bloodshed of January 1905. See Richard Taruskin, *Stravinsky and the Russian Traditions: A Biography of the Works through Mavra*, 2 vols (Oxford: Oxford University Press/University of California Press, 1996), vol. I, chapters 8 and 9.

[7] This Ballets Russes account builds on that in Mawer, 'Ballet and apotheosis of the dance', 141–2. For essential reading, see Garafola, *Diaghilev's Ballets Russes*, and Garafola and Van Norman Baer (eds), *The Ballets Russes and its World*. For more specific angles, see Lynn Garafola, 'Dance, film and the Ballets Russes', *Dance Research*, 16/1 (Summer 1998), 3–25, or Cyril Beaumont, *The Diaghilev Ballet in London* (London: Putnam 1940, 2/1945; A. & C. Black, 3/1951).

active in producing scenarios.[8] As Robert Hansen has commented, 'In the public imagination no designer was more strongly associated with the Ballets Russes.'[9] Additionally, Bakst acted as a teacher, in 1906 setting up a small art school that numbered among its pupils the young Marc Chagall who, fifty years on, would also be involved with Ravel's music. Meanwhile Benois, the spokesperson for *Mir Iskusstva*, was another highly respected painter, art historian and writer,[10] especially sensitive to music. He was convinced that 'it was the music which provided ballet with its centre of gravity. The moment had arrived when one listened to the music and, in listening to it, derived an additional pleasure from seeing it ... this is the mission of ballet.'[11]

Michel (Mikhail) Fokine (1880–1942), a product of the Imperial Ballet, also came to the fore as a result of his 'liberating' reformist views.[12] He was significant as a choreographer, dancer and writer, publishing memoirs and articles of a manifesto nature. He worked too as a teacher, including among his pupils in Stockholm around 1913 the young Jean Börlin, who would later choreograph Ravel's *Le Tombeau de Couperin*. Like Benois, Fokine was very interested in music and benefited from musical training. His main balletic creed may be summarized as seeking a stylistic flexibility tailored to thematic requirements and period; balletic movement rather than mimed story-telling should communicate dramatic expression and the *corps de ballet* should play an integral part. (For detail, see Chapter 3.)

---

[8] On Bakst, see Alexander Schouvaloff, *Léon Bakst: The Theatre Art* (London and New York: Sotheby's Publications, 1991) and Irina Pruzhan, *Léon Bakst: Set and Costume Designs; Book Illustrations; Paintings and Graphic Works*, Eng. trans. Arthur Shkarovski-Raffé (Harmondsworth and New York: Penguin Books/Viking, 1987). For an early text, see André Levinson, *Bakst, The Story of the Artist's Life* (London: Bayard, 1923; repr. New York: Benjamin Blom, 1971) or Arsène Alexandre and Jean Cocteau, *The Decorative Art of Léon Bakst*, trans. Harry Melvill (London: Fine Art Society 1913; repr. New York: Dover, 1972). On the sumptuous artistic feast, see Alexander Schouvaloff, *The Art of Ballets Russes: The Serge Lifar Collection of Theater Designs, Costumes and Paintings at the Wadsworth Atheneum* (New Haven, CT and London: Yale University Press, 1997).

[9] Robert C. Hansen, *Scenic and Costume Design for the Ballets Russes* (Ann Arbor, MI.: UMI Research Press, 1985), 22.

[10] See *Alexandre Benois, 1870–1960, Drawings for the Ballet* [exhibition catalogue] (London: Hazlitt, Gooden & Fox, 1980); Benois, *The Russian School of Painting* (New York, 1916); Benois, *Memoirs*, trans. Moura Budberg, 2 vols (London: Chatto and Windus, 1964); Benois, *Reminiscences of the Russian Ballet*, trans. Mary Britnieva (London: Putnam, 1941); Benois, 'The origins of the Ballets Russes' [unpub.], in Boris Kochno, *Diaghilev and the Ballets Russes*, trans. Adrienne Foulke (London: Penguin Press, 1971), 2–21.

[11] Benois, quoted in Jordan, *Moving Music*, 3.

[12] See Garafola, 'The liberating aesthetic of Michel Fokine', in *Diaghilev's Ballets Russes*, 3–49; and Jordan, 'Liberation movements', in *Moving Music*, 30–36.

In Paris, although the Opéra kept a smallish company, indigenous ballet no longer reflected the golden age of *Giselle*; Diaghilev neatly seized on the West's growing fascination with the 'East' – the exoticism of the Russian Steppes – by persuading Anna Pavlova (1881–1931), Tamara Karsavina (1885–1976), Vaslav Nijinsky (1888–1950), his younger sister Bronislava Nijinska (1891–1972) and Fokine to showcase their talents. On 18 May 1909, inventive dances from Borodin's *Prince Igor* and Tcherepnin's *Le Pavillon d'Armide* first performed to a most receptive public, especially impressed by the male dancers' technique, led to Diaghilev's establishment of a permanent touring company, starring Karsavina and Nijinsky. As *premier danseur*, Nijinsky became legendary for gravity-defying leaps, but his career ended early with a tragic descent into mental illness.[13]

Amongst early productions was the beautiful Fokine/Benois *Les Sylphides*, previously choreographed in St Petersburg as *Chopiniana*, which took up where Romantic 'ballet blanc', with full-length white net skirts, had left off, except that it was innovatively plotless. This work's re-branding sought to outdo its nineteenth-century referent, *La Sylphide*. A little later, Rimsky-Korsakov's exotic *Shéhérazade*,[14] Stravinsky's *L'Oiseau de feu* (The Firebird) and *Petrushka*, with Fokine and Benois, strongly affected Ravel who had already been approached amongst the first major Western composers to provide the score for *Daphnis et Chloé* – one of several Greek projects, inspired ultimately by Isadora Duncan (1878–1927), that also included *Cléopâtre* and *Narcisse*. And so Ravel came into contact with the legendary Ballets Russes, this powerhouse of theatrical design and forward-looking choreography. The troupe's defining achievements occurred across 1912–13: Nijinsky's ground-breaking choreography for Debussy's *Prélude à l'Après-midi d'un faune* whose masturbatory gestures, even if exaggerated by the press, scandalized its spectators, followed by the violently awesome *Le Sacre du printemps* (The Rite of Spring),[15] which sparked a public riot during its premiere at the new Théâtre des Champs-Elysées on 29 May 1913. (For Ravel's views, see p. 20 below.)

Ballet was no longer boring, but Diaghilev's volatility meant that in parallel with unprecedented success ran fundamental ruction. Fokine walked out after the strife of *Daphnis* and was appointed Maître de Ballet of the

---

[13] Insight into his distressing state of mind is afforded by the unexpurgated version of his diary: Vaslav Nijinsky, *The Diary of Vaslav Nijinsky*, trans. Kyril Fitzlyon, ed. and introduced by Joan Acocella (London: Penguin Books, 2000).

[14] Another work which celebrated the exotic, though in ways which today seem at best stereotypical and at worst inherently racist, was *Le Dieu bleu* by Reynaldo Hahn with designs and costumes by Bakst.

[15] On *Le Sacre* as a 'Figure of Consonance among the Arts', see Albright, *Untwisting the Serpent*, 104–08.

Stockholm Royal Opera, producing there his *Les Sylphides*, *Shéhérazade* and *Cléopâtre*. Nijinsky too set up his own breakaway troupe in 1914, for which Ravel produced an orchestration of Schumann's *Carnaval* and a re-orchestration of *Les Sylphides*. The incorporation of new blood included the choreographer Léonide Massine (1896–1979), who was involved in the triumphs of Satie's *Parade* (1917), Stravinsky's *Pulcinella* (1920) and Prokofiev's *Le Pas d'acier* (1927).

Through the 1920s, the Ballets Russes inevitably lost some prewar iconoclasm; there were fewer innovations and more revivals. Witness the production of Tchaikovsky's *La Belle au bois dormant* at the Alhambra Theatre, London in November 1921, although the move was arguably innovative in introducing this extended work to a Western audience. Equally, one should not oversimplify, since June 1923 was still to see Stravinsky's astoundingly percussive and rhythmic *Les Noces*, choreographed in constructivist fashion by Nijinska (see Chapter 5). Other Nijinska creations included Stravinsky's *Renard* (1922), Poulenc's *Les Biches* and Milhaud's zany divertissement *Le Train bleu* (1924), while the Stravinsky/Balanchine *Apollon Musagète* (1928) offered a special late supper: Balanchine, also involved in the choreography of *L'Enfant*, was to become a crucial interpreter of Ravel's music. Since the Ballets Russes troupe was catalysed essentially by one man, the original company effectively died with him in 1929; at Diaghilev's bedside in Venice were Serge Lifar, Boris Kochno and Ravel's friend Misia Sert. Nonetheless, a younger 'cousin', Colonel de Basil's Ballets Russes de Monte Carlo (1932–52),[16] emerged to uphold something of the legacy.

The second Russian troupe with which Ravel came in contact in the 1920s was the Ballets Ida Rubinstein. Unsurprisingly, some personnel were in common with the Ballets Russes,[17] including the colourfully dramatic Ida Rubinstein (1885–1960) herself: 'A sphinx, an enigmatic being, of inflexible nature, constrained to suppleness by her iron will'.[18] Rubinstein, the stage-name of Lydia Horwitz, was a Russian Jewish dancer who had starred in the Ballets Russes production of *Cléopâtre* in 1909–10 and appeared in *Shéhérazade*. And whatever she lacked in classical tech-

---

[16] See Vicente García-Márquez, *The Ballets Russes: Colonel de Basil's Ballets Russes de Monte Carlo, 1932–1952* (New York: Knopf, 1990).

[17] Diaghilev also turned upon Rubinstein, becoming increasingly jealous and vitriolic in his criticism and referring to her troupe with sneering anti-Semitism as the 'Ballets Juifs'. See Michael de Cossart, *Ida Rubinstein (1885–1960): A Theatrical Life* (Liverpool: Liverpool University Press, 1987), 125, and 'Ida Rubinstein and Diaghilev: a one-sided rivalry', *Dance Research*, 1/2 (Autumn 1983), 3–20.

[18] René Dumesnil, 'Souvenirs sur Ida Rubinstein', *Le Monde* (26 October 1960): 'Un sphinx, un être énigmatique, nature inflexible, contrainte à la souplesse par sa volonté de fer'.

nique,[19] she made up for through captivating beauty, unusual height, acting/miming skills and a larger-than-life personality (involving amorous liaison with Romaine Brooks). Moreover, Rubinstein enjoyed the funds necessary to translate her ideas into action, mounting *Antigone* to sets by Bakst in St Petersburg and the Fokine/Bakst *Salomé* to music by Glazunov in 1908; according to Benois, both Bakst and Fokine adored Rubinstein.[20] The production of Gabriele d'Annunzio's *Le Martyre de St Sébastien* to Debussy's music at the Théâtre du Châtelet in 1911 constituted an early highlight, and in 1919 Rubinstein reproduced and danced Florent Schmitt's *La Tragédie de Salomé*, previously featured with Ravel's *Adélaïde* in Natalia Trouhanova's *Concerts de danse* in April 1912.

In the opening 1928–9 season, the impressive list of works commissioned by, and starring, Rubinstein included Honegger's *Les Noces de Psyché et de l'Amour*, Stravinsky's *Le Baiser de la fée*, Milhaud's *La Bien-aimée*, Auric's *Les Enchantements d'Alcine*, Henri Sauguet's *David* and Ravel's *Boléro*. Nijinska had been secured as the main choreographer, with Massine undertaking two projects and Fokine assuming a late production of *Boléro* in 1934; her approach strived to maximize the autonomy of dance. Benois was now Rubinstein's chief designer, Bakst having died in 1924. Other balletic links were forged by the fact that the young Englishman Frederick Ashton (1904–88) was a member of the *corps de ballet*. For Ashton, 'She [Rubinstein] was an enigmatic personality of compelling appearance … Only the very best collaborators would do to produce her concept of beauty.'[21]

And so Russians remained a most potent force in Parisian ballet. Implicit in the background however, underpinning Rubinstein's success at the Opéra but also seeking to re-build a French theatrical school, was a second, crucial catalyst, Jacques Rouché (1862–1957). Rouché was an erudite, visionary thinker, who undertook research and training in Germany and Russia and articulated his progressive views in articles and monographs, and through editorship from 1907 of *La Grande Revue*.[22] As Diaghilev, his interest was

---

[19] Rubinstein won the respect of André Levinson, who saw her as 'a supreme paradox' of tall elegance and concluded that 'I have no idea how to express my admiration for the intelligent and haughty dilettantism of that remarkable artist'. (Levinson quoted in Cossart, *Ida Rubinstein*, 89.) But others caricatured her as 'Ida Rubinstein, who could not dance' (Richard Buckle with John Taras, *George Balanchine, Ballet Master: A Biography* (London: Hamish Hamilton, 1988), 54). Benois countered, 'But *how* she walked.' (Benois, *Memoirs*, vol. II, 241.)

[20] Benois, *Memoirs*, vol. II, 243. See too Louis Thomas, 'Le peintre Bakst parle de Madame Ida Rubinstein', *Critique des idées et des livres* (25 February 1924), 87–104.

[21] Frederick Ashton, 'Miss Rubinstein', *The Times* (21 October 1960), 15.

[22] See Jacques Rouché, 'Mise en scène en crise, ou crise de mise en scène? Ce que j'ai fait au Théâtre des Arts. Ce que je fais et veux faire à l'Opéra', *Excelsior*, n.d.: Dossier d'artiste, Jacques Rouché (B-MO); Rouché, 'Souvenirs', *Revue des deux mondes* (1 November 1951), 116; Rouché, *L'Art du ballet dès origines à nos jours* (Paris: Editions de Tambourinaire, 1952).

founded upon art and, like Fokine within dance, Rouché argued for the fullest stylistic exploration in staging, while disapproving of violent contrast between décor and costumes.[23] (Thanks to Rouché much of the primary source material for this study survives, archived subsequently within the Fonds Rouché at the Bibliothèque Nationale de France.) Through the inter-war and war years (1915–44), Rouché offered a strong directorship of the Opéra that did much to rekindle opera and ballet in France, encouraging new approaches to training, including Dalcrozean eurhythmics in the early 1920s alongside more rigid, established traditions.

From his prewar years as Director of the Théâtre des Arts in the Batignolles district of Paris (see Figure 2.1, p. 51), Rouché fostered new French talent, especially in artistic design: Jacques Drésa (theatrical pseudonym of André Saglio), René Piot and Maxime Dethomas. Rouché gave Ravel his early 'break' with *Ma Mère l'Oye* in 1912 (see Ravel's enthusiastic response below); he also supported Russo-French initiatives, putting on the *Concerts de danse* of Trouhanova, another of Diaghilev's discarded artists, later in 1912. This four-work extravaganza included designs by Rouché protégés and choreography by the ex-Bolshoi reformer Ivan Clustine (1860–1942) who, à la Fokine, favoured costumes that reflected their subject-matter.[24] Paul Dukas's *La Péri* was premiered at this event, having also been abandoned by Diaghilev, despite Bakst's wonderful Persian costume designs. Through the 1920s, Rouché's support of events large and small continued, including the delightful if wholly inconsequential French *divertissement*, *L'Eventail de Jeanne*, to which Ravel contributed.

The third influential director relevant to Ravel's activities was the Swede Rolf de Maré (1888–1964),[25] who founded the Ballets Suédois (1920–25). De Maré had suffered a childhood of ill-health, but consequently developed much perseverance and determination. When Fokine shared an idea to tour the Stockholm Royal Opera ballet, de Maré ventured further, proposing a Swedish ballet company with a Swedish choreographer. In return, de Maré helped Fokine set up his dance school near Copenhagen,[26] but Fokine must

---

[23] Jacques Rouché, *L'Art théâtral moderne* (Paris: Cornelly, 1910, new edn 1924), 1, 10. On incidental music and lighting, see 58, 61–2.

[24] Ivan Clustine came to France in 1906, becoming Maître de Ballet at the Opéra across 1912–14. His salary was to be 10,000 French francs in the first year, rising to 12,000 in the second and third years. In 1914, he went to the United States and was closely associated with Pavlova until her untimely death: Dossier d'artiste, Ivan Clustine (B-MO).

[25] De Maré set up the Archives Internationales de Danse (AID) in Paris; for related newspaper clippings of the early 1930s consult Dossier d'artiste, Rolf de Maré (B-MO). See also Alexandrine Troussevitch, 'Les Conférences des Archives de la Danse', *Revue musicale*, 146 (May 1934), 393–4. The main Ballets Suédois collection is now held at the Stockholm DansMuseet.

[26] Häger, *Ballets Suédois*, 8–9.

have resented having his idea and protégé Börlin taken over. Indeed the mainstay of de Maré's company was the *premier danseur* and choreographer Jean Börlin (1893–1930), whose stylistic principles represented an extension of those of Fokine (see Chapter 6), although he was also influenced by early contact with Duncan and Emile-Jaques Dalcroze. Sadly, Börlin was to die very young in New York, working on a Metropolitan Opera commission. Meanwhile, the leading female dancers were Jenny Hasselquist (1894–1978) and Carina Ari (1897–1970), and the experienced administrator was Jacques Hébertot (1886–1970), then director of the Théâtre des Champs-Elysées. Like Diaghilev and Rouché, de Maré too commissioned many important works: Milhaud's *La Création du monde* (1923) with Fernand Léger's bold cubism; Satie's extraordinary *Relâche* (1924)[27] with scenery by Francis Picabia; and a cinematographic entr'acte by René Clair. Having forged Parisian contacts from 1910 onwards, he also employed Jean Hugo, Pierre Bonnard and Pierre Laprade, the set painter Georges Mouveau and costumier Muelle. Repertory ranged from the avant-garde *Sculpture nègre*, the expressionist *Maison de fous*, the surrealist *Les Mariés de la Tour Eiffel*[28] and primitivist Milhaud/Paul Claudel *L'Homme et son désir* (1918), through to the Swedish folk-inspired *Nuit de Saint-Jean*, Cole Porter's popular American ballet *Within the Quota* and Ravel's neoclassical miniature, *Le Tombeau*. Arguably, the most far-reaching of these exerted a reciprocal influence upon the late Ballets Russes.

Although choreographic and design extensions to this intricate, incestuous, collaborative framework are theoretically endless, selected figures may be mentioned. Within Rouché's extended tenure at the Opéra, the disciplined Russo-French dancer Serge Lifar (1905–86) became Maître de Ballet (1929–44). Lifar had previously been involved in Ballets Russes productions at the Opéra, such as the 1924 revival of *Daphnis* and, as *premier danseur*, assumed the title role in the Prokofiev/Balanchine *Le Fils prodigue* (1929). His major prewar creative success was with *Icare* (1935), an extraordinary, experimental ballet initially without music, a privileging of dance over music doubtless influenced by his early teacher, Nijinska. Regarding Ravel's music, Lifar worked with *Adélaïde* and *Boléro*, as well as producing the famous *Pavane pour une infante défunte* at the Opéra on 31 December 1944, coupled with Jolivet's *Guignol et Pandore*. Following accusations, later dropped, of German collaboration in the Second World War, Lifar resumed his role at the Opéra in 1947; he remained there until 1958, the date of his last connection with *Daphnis*. While Lifar was admired as a most striking dancer, who raised the male status and propelled modern French

[27] On *Relâche* as a 'Figure of Dissonance among the Arts', see again Albright, *Untwisting the Serpent*, 220–25.

[28] *Les Mariés* is regarded as another inter-arts 'dissonance': ibid., 278–87, 289–91.

ballet, he was seen as a difficult and vain man.[29] Apart from his practical work, Lifar was an articulate writer, producing several volumes including a biography of Diaghilev.[30]

Also associated with the Ballets Russes was the colourful, idiosyncratic Russian dancer and choreographer Massine.[31] Following early successes mentioned above and initial contact with Ravel's *La Valse* in 1920, he joined Colonel de Basil's troupe and later emigrated to the United States. He became known to the general public through the famous ballet film *The Red Shoes* (1948) and, a couple of years later, finally choreographed *La Valse*, though not wholly successfully; the two works were connected via the figure of Lermontov (see Chapter 5). During the war years he had also choreographed *Aleko* (1942), to the music of Tchaikovsky and décor of Chagall.

Marc Chagall (1887–1985),[32] taught by Bakst, was a versatile, prolific Russo-French painter of Hasidic Jewish heritage, who also sculpted and later worked with stained glass and ceramics. His colossal status is evidenced by the stature of galleries worldwide that house his works: the Guggenheim Museum, the Royal Academy of Arts and Tate Gallery London, the State Russian Museum and Chagall Museum in Nice. Chagall was a vivid colourist, employing musical imagery such as Yiddish folk fiddlers, and Biblical emblems, especially angels. In Paris around 1910, he was connected with Fauvism and knew André Derain, who later designed Massine's *La Valse*; he also had links with Apollinaire and Cubism. He lived through much change and persecution, from which he sought escape – living in the United States through the Second World War – but essentially his personal style overrode external influence. He produced work to accompany other art-forms, illustrating Gogol's *Dead Souls* for the Parisian publisher Vollard, as well as La Fontaine's *Fables* and an edition of the Bible. In this spirit Chagall engaged with the Stravinsky/Fokine *L'Oiseau de feu* for the New York City Ballet in 1949 and, in the later 1950s, Ravel's *Daphnis* contemporaneously with his major lithographic project on the myth. Other commissions included the Chagall Windows for the Hadassah Hospital synagogue in Jerusalem (1960–61) and mosaics and tapestries for the Israeli Knesset.

---

[29] See Buckle, *George Balanchine*, 54, or Pierre Michaut, 'The dance at the Paris Opera', *The Dancing Times* (September 1938), 633–7: 632.

[30] See Serge Lifar, *Serge de Diaghilev: sa vie, son œuvre, sa légende* (Monaco: Editions du Rocher, 1954); *La Danse: les grands courants de la danse académique* (Paris: Denoël, 1938); *Histoire du ballet russe* (Paris: Nagel, 1950). See too André Levinson, *Serge Lifar: destin d'un danseur* (Paris: Grasset, 1934) and Dossier d'artiste, Serge Lifar (B-MO).

[31] See Léonide Massine, *My Life in Ballet*, ed. Phyllis Hartnoll and Robert Rubens (London: Macmillan, 1968); Vicente García-Márquez, *Massine: A Biography* (London: Nick Hern, 1996); Dossier d'artiste, Léonide Massine (B-MO).

[32] Extensive literature includes Gianni Pozzi et al., *Chagall*, Masters of Art series (New York: Peter Bedrick Books, 2001).

Two characters essential in this balletic framework relevant to Ravel are 'Sir Fred' and 'Mr B'. Ashton had been an early pupil of Massine, and had danced in the Ballets Ida Rubinstein for the Parisian premieres of *Boléro* and *La Valse*. His long choreographic career from 1926 to 1973 included much sensitive interpretation of Ravel's music: *Pavane* and *Valses nobles* (*Valentine's Eve*) from the 1930s, *Daphnis* and *La Valse* in the 1950s. Ashton thus played a unique role in popularizing Ravel's ballets in England, giving them a new English 'accent'.[33] Ashton's exact contemporary George Balanchine (1904–83), born Balanchivadze (of Georgian origin) in St Petersburg, spent much time in the United States. His first creations for the Ballets Russes were several opera-ballets including *L'Enfant*, premiered in 1925 and variously re-choreographed. As Ballet Master of the New York City Ballet, Balanchine created a highly acclaimed version of *La Valse* and choreographed a large proportion of Ravel's music for the 1975 centenary celebrations.[34] His special strength was a deep musical knowledge embedded in immensely imaginative choreography. Richard Buckle tells light-heartedly how Mr B would move from the ordinary to the extraordinary: 'Choreography is a bit like cooking – a matter of doing something different (or the same only better) with the same old ingredients. Balanchine puts together a few classical steps: very neat, very nice, you think – then suddenly the thing flowers.'[35] Within thriving research on Balanchine, a fascinating account of his collaboration with Stravinsky has recently appeared,[36] but the story of association with Ravel's music should also be heard.

Finally, mention must be made of Maurice Béjart (b. 1927),[37] who started out at the Monnaie de Bruxelles with his Ballets du XXe Siècle and then moved on to work with his Béjart Ballet Lausanne. From a Ravelian

---

[33] See David Vaughan, *Frederick Ashton and his Ballets* (London: A. & C. Black, 1977) and more recently the insightful, revealing work by Julie Kavanagh, *Secret Muses: The Life of Frederick Ashton* (London: Faber, 1996). See too the dedicated issue of *Dance Now*, 3/3 (Autumn 1994). Much primary source material is available at the ROHA, together with the Dossier d'artiste, Frederick Ashton (B-MO).

[34] See [George Balanchine,] *Choreography by George Balanchine: A Catalogue of Works*, ed. Leslie George Katz, Nancy Lassalle and Harvey Simmonds (New York: Eakin Press Foundation/Viking, 2/1984). See also information furnished by the invaluable George Balanchine Foundation.

[35] Richard Buckle, 'Balanchine comes to town', *Sunday Times Magazine* (22 August 1965).

[36] Charles M. Joseph, *Stravinsky and Balanchine: A Journey of Invention* (New Haven, CT and London: Yale University Press, 2002). See too extensive research by Jordan, including on the Stravinsky/Balanchine *Agon*: Stephanie Jordan, *Music Dances: Balanchine choreographs Stravinsky* (New York: The George Balanchine Foundation, 2002; video).

[37] For an early biography, see Roger Stengele, *A la recherche de Béjart* (Brussels: J. Verbeeck Editeur, 1968).

perspective, interest is focused upon variant readings of *Boléro* from 1961 onwards, re-gendered as with Stravinsky's *Le Sacre*. In the spirit of Ida Rubinstein, Béjart's personality has always been set firmly centre stage.[38] His audacious and unconventional interpretations, influenced by varied cultural and mystic concerns, have evinced extreme reactions: for some he has been revolutionary, for others showy and opportunist. For some time now, however, his work has achieved the respectability of admission to the canon of the Parisian establishment and his creations draw huge crowds at the Opéra.[39]

Ravel's writings on stage works: ballet and opera

Ravel's rich writings, comprising production reviews, interviews, articles and letters, on theatre, dance and design, reflect upon past and contemporary practice, so relating to the historical contextualization outlined above. Up to a point, they also constitute a theorizing of the composer's own practice and an exposition of his aesthetic creed in relation to the composite arts of the stage. As such, these materials provide an apposite starting-point for later discussion on which types of critical approach are likely to be conducive to his ballets.

Ravel is knowledgeable and uncompromising about the jaded state of ballet in France (and to a lesser extent in Russia) before and around the turn of the century. His view, bluntly articulated, anticipates the now well-founded perception of a lack of invention and acute need for reform: 'For a half-century, the art of choreography had stopped evolving', so forcing other artistic collaborators to distance themselves.[40] Similarly, reviewing d'Indy's *Fervaal* at the Opéra in 1913, Ravel is painfully aware of problems of qualitative mismatch between operatic component elements. Although his assessment of d'Indy's music is predictably guarded, Ravel still believes it far outshines the composer's misguided literary attempts at a libretto in the spirit of his nineteenth-century German hero, Wagner.[41] As for the décor of

---

[38] For more information, see four extensive box files on Béjart at the B-MO, labelled by decade.

[39] Béjart's *Concours* was received most enthusiastically at the end of the 2002 Paris Opéra season.

[40] Ravel, 'Nijinsky, maître de ballet', unpublished article reproduced in Marcel Marnat, *Maurice Ravel* (Paris: Fayard, 1986), 699–700: 699: 'Depuis un demi-siècle, l'art chorégraphique avait cessé d'évoluer.' For part of the MS, see plate 15 in Arbie Orenstein (ed.), *A Ravel Reader* (New York: Columbia University Press, 1990).

[41] Ravel, '*Fervaal*', *Comœdia illustré* 5/8 (20 January 1913), 361–4. While aware of his literary limitations, Ravel was perhaps more indulgent with his own scenarios than those of others (accepting that ballet texts were not for direct public consumption).

MM. Delmas and Muratore: while it strives to be less constrained, the fact that these artists make such evident effort for mediocre result simply confirms the sorry theatrical state of affairs.

Despite his criticism of these continuing endemic problems, Ravel cannot hide his innate enthusiasm for theatrical work, especially in relation to his own practice. Even if his early *La Cloche engloutie* was destined to remain unfinished, the experience had whetted his appetite. In a light-hearted letter of 1906, the composer exclaims: 'It is enthralling to make a work of theatre ... in this damned job there are some wonderful moments.'[42] Dance, embodying music and movement, constitutes perhaps the single most important concept for Ravel's compositional practice. From pure music, the concept extends through folk dance to classical dance within ballet. Ravel's beloved Pays Basque thrives on refined dance, inspired by the subtle Pyrenean light: 'The people feel it; they are agile, elegant, and their joy is not vulgar. Their dances are nimble, with a restrained voluptuousness.'[43] Exceptionally, such authenticity may be transferred to the concert hall. Reviewing the Concerts Lamoureux in 1912, Ravel appreciates the dances in a ballet-cum-lyric drama entitled *Le Miracle* by Georges Hüe, a figure subsequently written out of musical history. Having previously heard the work staged at the Opéra, Ravel delights in re-experiencing qualities of 'candour' and exquisite orchestral sonority that had first struck him within 'these dances of cheerfully popular mien, in ingenious and varied rhythm'.[44]

As a French artist, Ravel plays his part in effecting reform within stage productions, mischievously pointing up shortcomings at the Opéra-Comique by comparison with Rouché's innovative Théâtre des Arts (where his own apprenticeship had begun).[45] His critique concentrates initially on Camille Erlanger's opera *La Sorcière* (The Witch) and, in a mixed musical review, he perceives 'Wagner's formidable example' in distorting the French vocal writing. Ravel is particularly 'embarrassed' because the treatment of theatrical décor and production is completely at odds with his own aesthetic convictions. He acknowledges the décor's 'ingenious and picturesque qualities', but in his view it also lacks the crucial quality of 'style'. With innate conservatism in upholding the past over the present, Ravel suggests that a lesson could be learnt from the great nineteenth-century painters. He argues

---

[42] Letter from Ravel to Maurice Delage (12 June 1906), in Arbie Orenstein (ed.), *Maurice Ravel: lettres, écrits, entretiens* (Paris: Flammarion, 1989), 84–5: 'C'est passionnant, de faire une œuvre de théâtre ... dans ce bougre de métier il y a des moments admirables.'

[43] Letter to Ida Godebska (19 July 1911), in Orenstein (ed.), *A Ravel Reader*, 126.

[44] Ravel, 'Concerts Lamoureux', *Revue musicale de la S.I.M.*, 8/3 (March 1912), 50–52: 52: 'ces danses d'allure gaiement populaire, d'un rythme ingénieux et varié'.

[45] Ravel, '*La Sorcière* à l'Opéra-Comique', *Comœdia illustré*, 5/7 (5 January 1913), 320–23. Note Ravel's contributions to a journal that emphasized the visual dimension.

against false complication, which, he jibes rather snobbishly, 'may yet satisfy the taste of many amateurs', and advocates, à la Fokine, the need to temper style in accordance with the period and national identity being evoked through the music.

By contrast, at the Théâtre des Arts Ravel applauds Piot's boldly coloured scenery, which possesses a 'beauty' highly prized in his own artistic aesthetic. The design constructed by Mouveau for a production of the 'sublime' third act of Mozart's *Idomeneo* in Ravel's view represents the best seen at that theatre and on any Parisian stage for an extended period. Nonetheless, Ravel is sufficiently perceptive to see that, even in this enlightened forum, fundamental change takes time: 'as long as these superfluous little distractions in all corners of the stage destroy the line of the plot, lyric art, lowered today to the level of pretentious entertainment, will not be able to rediscover its sublime path'.[46] Ravel also cautions against attempts at verisimilitude in respect of gesture, echoing contemporary visual principles of Drésa (see Chapters 2 and 4). Finally, this extended review critiques the Persian tale *La Source lointaine,* with moderately interesting music by Mme Armande de Polignac (1876–1962). More significantly, Ravel makes informed criticism of dance: 'The principal performer is Mlle Napierkowska: there is no-one unaware of her supple grace and elegance of arm movements, which one does not often see even among dance artists.'[47] Such dancing clearly conformed to Ravel's consistent values of refinement and beauty. The scenery by M. Doucet is revered for its 'very rare sensitivity to colour'. Although Ravel sees the décor and costumes as a simple scaling-up of Persian miniatures, 'their interpretation creates no flaw'. In this way, Ravel applies his own striving for perfection to other domains.

Ravel's support of judicious reform is further emphasized by a piece dedicated to the second series of musical productions at the Théâtre des Arts, a venue for which he had now acquired a special affection. With unqualified high praise, this was 'successful in all respects' since it was unified by the Ravelian prerequisite of good 'taste'.[48] Ravel is aware of the far-reaching experiments in Germany and Russia on theatrical décor, which were researched by Rouché and adapted in his theatrical practice. He castigates mainstream directors for being content to tinker with an outmoded illusionary approach, and views Rouché's theatre as the brave exception: 'a gigantic

---

[46] Ibid., 323: 'tant que ces petites agitations superfluées à tous les coins de la scène détruiront la ligne de l'action, l'art lyrique, abaissé aujourd'hui au rang d'un amusement prétentieux, ne pourra retrouver sa route sublime'.

[47] Ibid.: 'L'interprète principale est Mlle Napierkowska, dont personne n'ignore la grâce souple et une élégance des mouvements du bras que l'on n'observe pas fréquemment, même chez les artistes chorégraphiques.'

[48] Ravel, 'Au Théâtre des Arts', *Comœdia illustré*, 5/9 (5 February 1913), 417–20: 417.

effort is being attempted on a single minuscule stage',[49] with young painters allowed to experiment and even make a few mistakes. But when they do err, their innovative research into colour or style still remains noteworthy for Ravel.

A music-hall/circus style adaptation of a piano duet suite by Gabriel Fauré is highly germane to the notion of refashioning within Ravel's own practice: '*Dolly* ... brought into question again the appropriateness of transporting works of absolute music to the stage.'[50] Unsurprisingly, Ravel raises no objection, providing that the ubiquitous if little-defined 'taste' prevails; indeed, he confesses with sardonic humour that 'Certain composers, myself included, have devoted themselves to profaning their own music.' On musico-choreographic relations in the 'Lullaby', Ravel perceives excessive tension: 'there is too evident a contrast between this gracious, slow, *sotto voce* melody, and the angry foot-stamping of a little girl, the pirouettes and face-slapping of two Pierrots'.[51] This comment gives a broad indication as to where Ravel sets his boundaries of acceptable 'dissonance'. Elsewhere, the stage action is so well adapted to the music that, paradoxically, it feels as if the music had been composed to illustrate the action. For Ravel, this seems to have constituted the ideal music–dance relationship: a balanced reciprocity; similarly, the strikingly illustrative music of his *Ma Mère l'Oye* could subscribe to this inversional theory.

Ravel was in no doubt about the artistic primacy of the early years of the Ballets Russes, whatever his personal difficulties with Diaghilev. In a balanced, probing critique, he reviews the 1913 revival of Musorgsky's powerful tragedy *Boris Godunov*,[52] the opera whose premiere in Paris of 1908 had been instrumental in establishing Diaghilev's name in the West. A later review of Stravinsky's lyric tale *Le Rossignol* also acknowledges the Russian achievement, observing the reactionary machinations of the French press, who end up turning a collective 'pirouette' when a work once berated for its innovation is grudgingly admitted to the canon.[53] This, Ravel notes, is what had already occurred with Stravinsky's *Le Sacre*; he then sides with Emile Vuillermoz in declaring *Le Rossignol* a masterpiece straight away. The composer also extols the exquisitely 'harmonious' Asiatic costumes and décor of Benois, his friend and eventual collaborator, 'whose moderation pertains

---

[49] Ibid., 420: 'un effort gigantesque est tenté sur une seule scène minuscule'.

[50] Ibid., 418: '*Dolly* ... a remis en question l'opportunité de transporter à la scène les œuvres de musique pure.'

[51] Ibid., 419: 'il y a un contraste trop évident entre cette mélodie gracieuse, lente, assourdie, et les trépignements rageurs d'une petite fille, les pirouettes et les gifles de deux Pierrots'.

[52] Ravel, 'Boris Godounoff', *Comœdia illustré*, 5/17 (5 June 1913), n.p.

[53] Ravel, 'Les Nouveaux Spectacles de la saison russe', *Comœdia illustré*, 6/17 (5 June 1914), 811–14.

perhaps to his French origin'. This closing comment must be met with a wry smile: even Ravel cannot avoid the odd nationalistic *faux pas*.

Further insights into the Ballets Russes are contained in a short, well-expressed unpublished article, entitled 'Nijinsky, maître de ballet', which probably dates from the War years. Moving on from a criticism of later nineteenth-century ballet, Ravel explains that from the theatrical power houses of St Petersburg and Moscow emerged exceptional figures to 'renew the art of the Dance'. He refers to works of the 1909–12 Paris seasons choreographed by Fokine: *Shéhérazade*, a strong musical influence upon *Daphnis*; *Prince Igor*; *Daphnis* itself; and *Les Sylphides*, which re-evokes 'all the gracious beauty of romantic ballet'. Fokine is perceived as a strong, versatile choreographer, an evolutionary figure (rather like Ravel), but not the revolutionary that is Nijinsky. Even Fokine's choreography for *Petrushka* is not truly modernist, whereas Nijinsky's *L'Après-midi* certainly is: 'at his very first attempt, Nijinsky had realized modern ballet'.[54] Ravel is however sensitive again to issues of compatibility and wholeness regarding balletic components: the contrast between Debussy's soft-edged, fluid music and Nijinsky's hard-edged, angular choreography is too great to achieve 'cohesion'. Such oneness is seen to occur soon after with the pro-Dalcrozean achievement of *Le Sacre*, so meeting with Ravel's approval (if not that of Jean Cocteau who saw the 'parallelism' as a failure).[55]

Ahead of contemporaries such as Debussy, Ravel immediately recognizes the significance of *Le Sacre* for music, for choreography and as a synthesized whole.[56] He marvels at the intimate music–dance collaboration and relates specific musical features – sound-blocks, ostinato, melodies and forceful sonorities – to what he perceives as their respective dance counterparts, namely dance groups, repeated movements, 'plastic' lines and gestures: 'all these concentrated elements seized you from the start, transported you without respite into splendid and terrible regions, from where, brusquely, you were propelled, panting with a religious anguish'.[57] Furthermore, for Ravel, all significant choreographic work after *Le Sacre* stemmed from it.

---

[54] Ravel, 'Nijinsky, maître de ballet', in Marnat, *Maurice Ravel*, 700: 'dès son premier essai, Nijinsky avait réalisé le ballet moderne'.

[55] See again Albright, *Untwisting the Serpent*, 106.

[56] On reconstructing *Le Sacre*, see Millicent Hodson, *Nijinsky's Crime against Grace: Reconstruction Score for the Original Choreography of Le Sacre du printemps* (Stuyvesant, NY: Pendragon Press, 1996).

[57] Ravel, 'Nijinsky, maître de ballet', 700: 'tous ces éléments concentrés vous saisissaient dès le début, vous transportaient sans repos en des régions splendides et terribles d'où, brusquement, vous étiez précipités, haletants d'une angoisse religieuse'. Ravel's critique is entirely consistent with Albright's view of dissonant music co-existing consonantly with dance: see below.

But ballet history is as fluid as dance itself, and the heyday of the Ballets Russes too comes and goes. By 1922, Ravel believes Diaghilev's troupe has peaked and that contemporary ballet is again declining.[58] A decade later, during his own distressing decline, he strives poignantly to uphold something precious for the next generation in an article within which he sees traditional lyric theatre as increasingly abandoned, in danger of dying, but as a spectacle that must yet be revived.[59]

Fairly consistent, however, across a broad time-span from 1912 through to the early 1930s, is Ravel's aesthetic creed on stage works and the arts. This holistic view strongly supports audio-visual and literary combination: 'Poets, musicians and painters must all come together to restore to us the grandeur and the completeness of theatrical emotion.'[60] Ravel skilfully walks a tightrope, promoting closeness of association but avoiding naivety in overstating similarities. When asked about impressionism, he does not recognize the quality in music, despite *Daphnis*, and retorts: 'Painting, *ah ça c'est autre chose*! Monet and his school were impressionists. But in the kindred art there is no counterpart of this.'[61] Thus Ravel's neat balancing act views music as a 'kindred art', which is yet something else in relation to painting. Slightly paradoxically, Ravel does perceive a Chabrier–Manet connection that goes deeper than their respective major influences within music and art. This notion involves receiving the same kind of emotional 'impression' from both artists and links with his sensitivity towards synaesthesia: Ravel claims to experience in Manet's *Olympia* the transposed 'soul' ('l'âme') of Chabrier's *Mélancolie*.[62] Such a conviction may be related specifically to Ravel's composing of *La Valse* as a 'poème chorégraphique pour orchestre',[63] and more generally to his 'visualization' within musical composition. As Stravinsky considers form in his *Octuor*, so Ravel confides that, compositionally, 'During this [gestational] interval, I come gradually

---

[58] C.v.W, 'The French Music Festival: an interview with Ravel', Ravel, *De Telegraaf* (30 September 1922), in Orenstein (ed.), *A Ravel Reader*, 423–4.

[59] Ravel, 'Les Aspirations des moins de vingt-cinq ans: la jeunesse musicale', *Excelsior* (28 November 1933).

[60] Ravel, '*La Sorcière* à l'Opéra-Comique', 323: 'Poètes, musiciens et peintres, tous doivent concourir à nous restituer la grandeur et la plénitude de l'émotion scénique.'

[61] Ravel, 'Take jazz seriously!', *Musical Digest*, 13/3 (March 1928), 49–51.

[62] Ravel, 'Mes souvenirs d'enfant paresseux', *La Petite Gironde* (12 July 1931), 1: 'Il me semble toujours retrouver en elle l'âme de la *Mélancolie* de Chabrier simplement transposée sur un autre plan.' Although the authenticity of this article has been questioned, Ravel's essential authorship has been strongly supported by François Lesure. By the late 1890s Ravel had styled himself 'the little symbolist'; see Arbie Orenstein, *Ravel: Man and Musician* (New York: Columbia University Press, 1975; Dover, 2/1991), 22.

[63] *Daphnis* too was styled a 'symphonie chorégraphique', though not in Ravel's score.

to see, and with growing precision, the form and evolution which the subsequent work should have as a whole.'[64]

Such holistic notions lead to Ravel's most important statement on artistic singularity: 'For me, there are not several arts, but one alone. Music, painting, [dance] and literature differ only as far as their means of expression. There are not therefore different kinds of artists, but simply different kinds of specialists.'[65] It may be attractive to see in this creed parallels with a Wagnerian *Gesamtkunstwerk* ('total art-work') philosophy, but this could only be a superficial association and one fundamentally abhorrent to Ravel's French cultural heritage. Fully cognizant of Wagner's 'prodigious invention', 'profound musicality' and orchestration skills, Ravel still had little time for the epic self-aggrandizing, even fanatical, conception so alien to his own miniaturized craft.[66] More fruitful connection could be forged between Ravel's statement and Charles Baudelaire's sensory, symbolic sonnet, *Correspondances*, published in *Les Fleurs du mal* (1857), which Ravel knew well: 'Comme de longs échos qui de loin se confondent / Dans une ténébreuse et profonde unité, / Vaste comme la nuit et comme la clarté, / Les parfums, les couleurs et les sons se répondent.'[67]

In articulating his creed, Ravel distinguishes between being a practitioner and an informed observer: although he is a musician and has not been trained to write or paint, he claims that he still reads and looks at paintings professionally as though he were such a practitioner. (Thus he usefully perceives a separation between artistic message and technique.) Certainly, his published criticism goes some way to support this stance. Ravel's artistic statement may be thought to embody more of a semantic than a real argument, but it nevertheless establishes the seriousness of inter-arts ventures from the composer's stance and presents him as a strong advocate of artistic synthesis. Overall, Ravel's writings reveal that he has his finger largely on the pulse and

---

[64] Ravel, 'Contemporary music', *The Rice Institute Pamphlet*, 15 (April 1928), 131–45, repr. in Orenstein (ed.), *A Ravel Reader*, 40–49: 46. 'Evolution' and 'wholeness' are also central.

[65] Ravel, 'Mes souvenirs d'enfant paresseux', 1: 'Pour moi, il n'y a pas plusieurs arts, mais un seul. Musique, peinture et littérature ne différent qu'en tant que moyens d'expression. Il n'y a donc pas diverses sortes d'artistes, mais simplement diverses sortes de spécialistes.'

[66] See Ravel, '*Parsifal*', *Comœdia illustré*, 6/8 (20 January 1914), 400–03; also, Louis Laloy, 'Wagner et les musiciens d'aujourd'hui: opinions de MM. Florent Schmitt et Maurice Ravel – Conclusions', *La Grande Revue*, 13/9 (10 May 1909), 160–64.

[67] Charles Baudelaire, *Selected Verse*, trans. Francis Scarfe (Harmondsworth: Penguin Books, 1967), 36–7: 'Like prolonged echoes which merge far away in an opaque, deep oneness, as vast as darkness, as vast as light, perfumes, sounds, and colours answer each to each.'

that, besides music, he is especially well informed about artistic design.[68] While accepting that the composer is not necessarily the best or only arbiter of his music/art-work once it is released into the public domain, Ravel's views remain highly pertinent from both poietic and esthesic stances.

Creative–interpretative (poietic–esthesic) interactions

There is a vast literature on critical approaches to music, let alone dance,[69] design and combinations thereof. The approach here therefore must be selective, flexible and generally compatible with, if not uncritical of, Ravel's perceptions. This book, however, is not intended to be overly theoretical; rather, it concentrates on observing some theoretical notions 'in action' within the music and resulting composite works. In circumscribed and accessible formalist music analysis, the focus will be upon Ravel's melody and rhythm, supplemented by discussion of harmony, form, orchestration and sonority, and the overall critical approach will be loosely founded upon Jean-Jacques Nattiez's theories, in exploring 'poietic' and 'esthesic' dimensions.[70]

These terms may be roughly equated with the more familiar synonyms 'creative' and 'interpretative', although they do connote a richer field of meaning: 'poietic' as relating to something being constructed, made, composed, written, choreographed or designed; '[a]esthesic' as relating to the experiential side of the thing having been made (hearing, seeing, reading, sensing, perceiving, interpreting). The idea is to examine process as well as

---

[68] Ravel showed promise in drawing from 1885, with several charcoal sketches of sea and river scenes preserved in the Ravel Estate and referenced as photographs in the BNF (for instance, Cliché B.N.: 85 C 172990 and Cliché: C 71738). At Montfort-L'Amaury from 1921, he designed Greek-style friezes and other effects for his home.

[69] See Janet Adshead-Lansdale and June Layson (eds), *Dance History: An Introduction* (London and New York: Routledge, 2/1994); Ann Dils and Ann Cooper Albright (eds), *Moving History/Dance Cultures: A Dance History Reader* (Middletown, CT: Wesleyan University Press, 2001); Sondra Horton Fraleigh and Penelope Hanstein (eds), *Researching Dance: Evolving Modes of Enquiry* (London: Dance Books, 1999); and the journals *Dance Research* and *Discourses in Dance*. Dance analysis generally goes beyond the scope of this book, but the reader may be interested to consult the following: Janet Adshead (ed.), *Dance Analysis: Theory and Practice* (London: Dance Books, 1988); Susan Leigh Foster (ed.), *Choreographing History* (Bloomington: Indiana University Press, 1995), or Foster (ed.), *Corporealities: Dancing, Knowledge, Culture, and Power* (London and New York: Routledge, 1996).

[70] Jean-Jacques Nattiez, *Music and Discourse: Toward a Semiology of Music*, trans. Carolyn Abbate (Princeton, NJ: Princeton University Press, 1990). For a useful collective text, exploring music and meaning in social context, see Derek B. Scott (ed.), *Music, Culture, and Society: A Reader* (Oxford: Oxford University Press, 2000).

product, especially what can be gleaned of creative/collaborative processes for Ravel's ballets. In her influential book, *Moving Music*, Stephanie Jordan does not make much play of this aspect but concentrates on interpretation, arguing that 'examples of the collaborative process are already well documented and a commission or style doesn't necessarily produce a particular kind of work'.[71] For Ravel, however, this does not quite hold true: such processes are not well documented, and relations between process and product are interesting precisely because supportive collaboration need not equate with a strong product, or tense collaboration with a poor one.

The poietic–esthesic approach also points up the phenomenon of positioning. These perspectives are not neutral or impartial: 'producer' and 'receiver' inevitably adopt some sort of ideological stance and it is crucial to be aware of the potential for bias. The present study is hermeneutic not scientific and, despite one's striving towards a 'factual' objectivity, subjectivity will remain: the important thing is to recognize and celebrate the differences. It employs a wide range of sources, focusing upon primary and early secondary sources from Parisian archival locations, with distinctions between the two varying between disciplines, primary source definitions tending to be slightly stricter in music than dance.[72] And while there is a continuum from those involving heavy bias through to those that are relatively impartial, there are very few that could be termed absolutely 'neutral'.

Sources that may involve significant subject-positioning by their authors, dependent upon personal agendas and motives, include collaborators' and performers' memoirs (which may involve 'ghosting', translation, abridging, inaccuracies across time), essays, articles, performance reviews, artistic statements and letters. One needs to be sensitive to likely re-positioning in respect of private and public utterances: the most honest, unpublished records versus sanitized, even propagandist, published ones. (In other words, can hidden assumptions be exposed to deconstruct a given position?) Additionally, photographers adopt physical as well as ideological positions, with pre-determined camera angles and posed subjects, which in turn influence photographs and ballet films/videos – each in this way just 'a translation of the ballet';[73] so, too, microphone position and sound techniques affect music recordings – each again a single 'translation'. Editing processes create further interference.

More neutral sources tend to have greater 'factual' content, such as playbills, tickets, programmes (though these cannot reflect late changes), booking forms, contracts, financial accounts (but even these can incorporate

---

[71] Jordan, *Moving Music*, xi–xii.

[72] See June Layson, 'Dance history source materials', in Adshead-Lansdale and Layson (eds), *Dance History*, 18–31.

[73] Jordan, *Moving Music*, 101.

inaccuracies, or 'colouring'), invoices for costumes and so on. Another imbalance concerns the paucity of dance sources, in comparison with those for music: in the absence of much original choreographic notation, whether after Rudolph Benesh or not, the researcher is more reliant upon potentially coloured memoirs and reviews, both of which tend to reveal little about precise steps or use of dance space.

In the approach to ballet, there is much overlap between basic categories of process, that is, many creative and interpretative layers and interactions. At a simplified theoretical level, one might identify on the creator/producer side: the director as catalyst, the scenario writer(s), composer, choreographer, designer and lighting specialist. Thus there are already multiple views of the emerging collaborative art-work. From an opposing stance, the art-work is perceived, and so also affected, by many different individuals or groups with their own experiences: performers, audience or spectators (amateur or professional), newspaper and journal critics writing within national cultural contexts (for example French, Russian, English), musicologists, dance and art scholars, and general historians. But the reality is much less clear-cut: complex interactions occur so that flexibility of approach is essential. Interpretative stances are embedded in the initial creation, such as in a composer's response to a ballet's mythical or historical subject-matter, and even within his/her composition. Some aspects of a composition may be deemed structural and immutable; others may involve the composer as merely the first interpreter. (See Toscanini on *Boléro* in Chapter 7.) Creation also occurs in performance and subsequent productions, especially in relation to choreography and dancing. A music or dance historian acts both as 'chronicler' and interpreter;[74] any notion of the author as invisible is a construction, even a sleight-of-hand.

Nattiez's approach positions in the middle of these interactions a 'material trace', superseding the more problematic term 'neutral trace'. Nicholas Cook is, however, still sceptical as to whether this is much more than the 'score in drag';[75] a balletic extension would be the more rarely found choreographic notation in drag, and any case for this being neutral is harder to make. Choreographers' scores are often notated by a third party and their trace leaves much more open to interpretation than a musical score. Other traces include the scenario text, costumes and sets, stage and lighting directions. But by their very nature these are seldom definitive: variant scenario texts may exist, including different translations; discrepancies may occur

---

[74] June Layson, 'Historical perspectives in the study of dance', in Adshead-Lansdale and Layson (eds), *Dance History*, 4.

[75] Nicholas Cook, 'Theorizing musical meaning', *Music Theory Spectrum*, 23/2 (October 2001), 170–95: 181. Ravel's music scores embody variant texts that may reflect external influence, e.g. the non-choral version of *Daphnis* demanded by Diaghilev.

between musical texts, whether manuscripts or early editions; alternative costume sketches or drawings may remain.

All these sources involve signs or codes, comprising 'signifiers' (particular artistic features or cues) and 'signifieds' (meanings or conventions, as interpreted by producers and receivers).[76] Questions arise as to whether these meanings spring entirely from socio-cultural construction or whether they are somehow intrinsic. A third way, proposed by Cook, places 'constraints upon the number of meanings any given music can support under any given circumstances'.[77] With reference to readings of Beethoven's Ninth Symphony by Donald Francis Tovey and Susan McClary, Cook argues that it may be possible to accommodate opposing views within a larger-scale interplay between musicology and theory/analysis. Jordan too talks of 'music as meaning, affect, and rhetoric', of gendered readings of tonality including McClary's and, with reference to Carolyn Abbate after Roland Barthes, of multiple narrative voices in nineteenth-century opera – sometimes 'unsung', dissonant interpretative texts that may disrupt a work, yet may not necessarily be obvious to its creator.[78]

Many would argue that such traces can only be raised to the status of a composite work by activation through rehearsal and performance(s), which involves individuals who are simultaneously interpreters and, in some sense, creators: conductors and musicians; ballet-masters, principal dancers and *corps de ballet*; costumiers, scenery painters and lighting technicians. This is part of Cook's argument in music,[79] and is one even more pertinent to ballet: by foregrounding the performative within balletic ontology, dance theory has for some time run ahead of mainstream musicology. Performance is not subservient to musical or other notations. Multiple performances may lead to widely differing interpretations and vice versa. Most profoundly, re-choreographing and re-designing may result in an interpretation divergent enough to constitute a new work; thus, in time, there may emerge a complex of related works.

Relations between balletic elements

Crucially, there is interaction between the diverse elements that make up a ballet and enable it to work (or not). Recent influential sources on such

---

[76] See Nattiez, *Music and Discourse*, 4.

[77] Cook, 'Theorizing musical meaning', 195.

[78] Jordan, *Moving Music*, 65, 71–2.

[79] Cook, 'Theorizing musical meaning', 179; Nicholas Cook, 'Between process and product: music and/as performance', *Music Theory Online*, 7/2 (2001), 1–31: 15–20. See too Matthew Butterfield, 'The musical object revisited', *Music Analysis*, 21/3 (October 2002), 327–80: 331–2.

interrelationships have included Jordan's *Moving Music*, although this does not discuss design, and the American literary critic Daniel Albright's versatile and ingenious *Untwisting the Serpent*, bringing together music, art and literature.[80] How then does one approach disciplines/media which are fundamentally different, but which must, paradoxically, be intricately entwined to constitute an artistic whole? The problem is compounded by the confusing existence of some shared terminology. Certain terminological meanings across music and dance are broadly equivalent and offer a common currency: 'patterns of climax and dénouement, the hierarchy of structural units (phrase, periods, paragraphs, and so on), concepts of return as a method of closure (with a refrain or in an ABA structure)'[81] and rhythm, yet others such as 'dynamics' and 'accentuation' are more problematic and differentiated.[82] Ravel himself was aware of this phenomenon in the discussion of 'impressionism' quoted above. The elements must be sympathetic and thematically directed, sometimes via a scenario, yet there are arguably more differences than similarities, and this is how they create a multidimensional, multi-layered experience. 'The excitement of watching ballet is that two very different things – dancing and music – fit together, not mechanically but in spirit', writes the critic Edwin Denby, whose stance echoes that of Alexandrine Troussevitch: 'It will not be a matter of concordances of signs, but concordances of spirit.'[83]

For the benefit of musicians, an aside on dance and the relatively young discipline of dance research may be apt. Dance within ballet has traditionally been an ephemeral art of expressive bodies in motion, with its own set of codes relating to gesture, facial expression and body language. Generally, there is less notation than for music and less preservation for posterity, though passing down of celebrated choreographies, such as those 'after Fokine', may occur largely through dancers' physical memories. Choreography as a practised livelihood has often created a reluctance to have works notated since this compromises control, sometimes even ownership or employment. Witness Nijinska in correspondence with Rouché: she expresses irritation about the 'inscription' of a ballet, then to be shown to

---

[80] Additional sources include Judith Mackrell's user-friendly, if theoretically diluted, *Reading Dance* (London: Michael Joseph, 1997), while Joseph, *Stravinsky and Balanchine* also offers a possible model.

[81] Jordan, *Moving Music*, 73.

[82] See Anne Hutchinson Guest and Valerie Preston-Dunlop, 'What exactly do we mean by dynamics?', *Dance Theatre Journal*, 13/2 (Autumn–Winter 1996), 28–38.

[83] Eric Denby, 'A note to composers' (1939), quoted in Jordan, *Moving Music*, 3; Alexandrine Troussevitch, 'La Chorégraphie et ses rapports avec la musique', *La Revue musicale*, 15 (May 1934), 340–48: 348: 'Il ne s'agira pas de concordances de signes, mais de concordances d'esprit'.

Albert Aveline, and is sceptical whether such a score could enable a faithful rendition by others.[84] Dance scores have not traditionally been seen as a ticket to immortality, and yet Fokine protested about unfaithful copies of his work – some limited notation of his does exist, such as a set of storyboard sketches for *Le Dieu bleu*.[85] Notators and researchers of choreology, such as Ann Hutchinson Guest, are a specialized subset of the dance community, although interestingly some information was filtering through to musical circles by the late 1920s.[86] Furthermore, the community has been divided on the merits of reconstructing 'dead' ballets. Lynn Garafola notes attractively that 'Balanchine liked to compare ballets to butterflies: both died when their day was over.'[87] She makes the point, even if visual artists might beg to differ, that 'Ballets … aren't collectibles. Unlike paintings, which can survive virtually untended in basements or storage vaults, ballets exist only as long as they are performed.'[88] How can one recapture the immediacy, feeling and phenomenological experience of a premiere in isolation from the socio-cultural context that occasioned it? There is however a compelling academic and practical impetus to bring 'lost' ballets back to a performable state. The last few years have witnessed impressive reconstructions of Nijinsky's choreographies for *Le Sacre* and *L'Après-midi*, whose idiosyncratic notation had lain undeciphered for forty years in the British Library.[89]

Without getting inappropriately embroiled in dance movement analysis or art criticism, one may consider a few basic shared attributes of dance, music and art. Both music and dance exist in moving time, at localized and larger-scale levels, but neither need restrict itself to linear or chronological readings. Although Ravel's music is often teleological, or goal-directed, this is not the only way that time operates; the phenomenon can be manipulated,

---

[84] LAS Nijinska, 9 (letter, 4 May 1928; B-MO).

[85] See Garafola, *Diaghilev and the Ballets Russes*, plate 10.

[86] See Valentin Parnac, 'Notation de danses', *La Revue musicale*, 9 (March 1928), 129–32.

[87] Lynn Garafola, 'Ten years after: Peter Martins on preserving Balanchine's legacy', *Dance Magazine* (May 1993), 38–42: 42.

[88] Garafola, 'Ten years after', 40; see also Clive Barnes, 'Reconstructions: dead ducks do not fly', *Dance Magazine* (August 1999 [online]) and Ramsay Burt, 'Re-presentations of re-presentations: reconstruction, restaging and originality', *Dance Theatre Journal*, 14/2 (1998), 30–33.

[89] See Alexandra Carter, 'The Case for Preservation', *Dance Theatre Journal*, 14/2 (1998), 26–9; Jill Beck (ed.), *A Revival of Nijinsky's Original L'Après-midi d'un faune* (Chur, Switzerland: Harwood Academic, 1991 [video]); and Hodson, *Nijinsky's Crime against Grace*. Potentially, 'parallelism' may cause problems if a reconstruction 'keys' choreography to the rhythms and metres of a musical score, rather than recreating a music–dance counterpoint. I am grateful to Simon Morrison for this observation.

so creating new inflections of artistic meaning. As Judith Mackrell comments: 'It is rhythm ... that allows choreographers to play with Time – to drive it forward, freeze it or make it race.'[90] Similarly, time in music can be speeded up, compressed, presented in slow motion, or even frozen. In both domains, cinematic flashbacks can replay time and events with the benefit of hindsight. Furthermore, localized uncoupling of time between music and dance can be most effective, highlighting periods when the domains are 'in step'.[91] More than one rate of time, or movement, can go on in music or dance at any moment, so creating complexes. Up to a point, designs also exist in time to punctuate a paced sequence of scenes whose tableaux lead the eye in patterns of movement, with their inherent dramatic action directed by the scenario. And of course the scenario narrative has a temporal dimension that need not conform to linear progression.

Dance and art exist within space and in order to animate space: 'Space isn't simply a neutral area where the dance takes place. Like the stillness between movements, it's part of the dance itself.'[92] At a basic level, dance may be seen to mediate between music and art; between time and space. While dance foregrounds the moving body, a balletic backdrop may complement with painted figures, nominally fixed in space and temporarily removed from time. Furthermore, albeit less central, space is still relevant to music: ballet musicians are playing within physical space, even if unseen in the pit; aurally, their sounds are spatially organized; linguistically, textures are often defined as having wide or close chordal spacing; and visually, space exists in scoring on the page. Examples of these effects of playing with time and space can all be observed in the practice of Ravel and others in the chapters that follow.

Although, esthesically speaking, no element should weakly shadow another, poietically some function more as sources than others. For Ravel's ballets, music generally precedes dance even though it may postdate the scenario and be contemporaneous with design. Music is frequently the source of emotion: 'I cannot move, I don't even want to move, unless I hear music first.'[93] And as Jordan has acknowledged, 'We rate musicality as one of the supreme attributes of the dancer and choreographer'.[94] Moreover, if the dance or design works well with the music there is a good chance that the whole will coalesce. If not, the whole is unlikely to work.

---

[90] Mackrell, *Reading Dance*, 176.
[91] See Jordan, *Moving Music*, 75.
[92] Mackrell, *Reading Dance*, 171. On notions of related space, see examples of Cook's 'conceptual integration network', in 'Theorizing musical meaning', 183–5.
[93] Balanchine, quoted in Jordan, *Moving Music*, 3.
[94] Jordan, *Moving Music*, ix.

Is it heretical to suggest that, in this Ravelian context, some elements may be more equal or autonomous than others? Design models, costumes and sets clearly do not enjoy autonomy. Similarly, dance, even though it creates its own musico–rhythmic patterning, cannot stand alone. Yet it is possible – if undesirable – to present the ballet music without dance: indeed, the best musical performances were often to be achieved by orchestras in the concert hall rather than in cramped opera-ballet pits where conductors scrambled to find sufficient rehearsal time amid conflicting theatrical demands. Ravel seems at times – in a Symbolist spirit – to have experienced dance movement through the domain of music; and a kind of synaesthesia is also implicit in utterances such as that of Balanchine: 'Music must be seen!', although this was meant in terms of being 'visualized' choreographically.[95]

In seeking to express relations between music and other balletic components, one may select, for the sake of argument, three points/states along a theoretical continuum from diversity to unity: minimal, moderate or maximal correspondence. 'Correspondence(s)' maintains the Symbolist association of its French equivalent, *correspondances*. No state is theoretically superior to another, and such states will be fluid and ever-changing through a work. An excess of either extreme might prove detrimental to the overall effect and preclude notions of wholeness. There is also an associated historical progression from a favouring in the early twentieth century of closely corresponding elements for (Ravelian) extended classical ballet through to a celebrating of divergence within overt manifestations of modernism – primitivism, surrealism and modern dance – which may achieve cohesion through a dialectical playing out of oppositions or complementations.

Interestingly, many esthesic theories that relate music and other arts have resorted to musical metaphor: counterpoint, harmony, consonance and dissonance. Albright proposes re-nuanced theories of consonance and dissonance as a means of redressing the balance, previously tipped towards counterpoint, in favour of vertical inter-arts events – especially dissonant 'transmediating chords'. More abstract terms include contrast, conflict, disjunction, opposition, fusion and synthesis. Ironically, since ballet performance makes no recourse to visible verbal texts, the problem of relations seems compounded by words. It may be unhelpful to overuse expressions such as 'mirror' or 'reflect', which can be interpreted as exaggerating similarity or subjugating one medium to another, but one should not be overly prescriptive. There can be occasions when these descriptors are appropriate.

To illustrate theoretical extremes, Albright presents the diametrically opposed philosophies of the eighteenth-century separatist Gotthold Ephraim

---

[95] Balanchine quoted in Antoine Livio, 'Balanchine et Stravinsky: 40 ans d'amitié', *Ballet Danse, L'Avant-scène, Le Sacre du printemps* (August–October 1980), 124.

Lessing and the Roman 'synthesizer' Horace.[96] Up to a point, Lessing's stance is upheld by the eminent film critic Claudia Gorbman, while Ravel acts as a twentieth-century embodiment of Horace. To acknowledge that various things go on simultaneously, or (as a character from a Margaret Atwood novel put it), in 'another dimension of space',[97] and have their own distinctive voices is unproblematic. The difficulty comes when comparing what some may view as chalk and cheese. Gorbman and others have sought to avoid this problem by distancing themselves from a similarity–difference axis, favouring the idea of a 'mutual implication' that results in a *combinatoire* of expression', as a realization of meaning.[98] For the various arts invoked in ballet, this would need to be re-couched as a 'multiplex of expression'. The concept exhibits some similarity with that of the music theorist Eugene Narmour (preceded by Leonard B. Meyer), who considered musical 'implications' that might subsequently be realized.

For his part, Albright argues that artists who favour divergence, or 'dissonance' as he terms it, may find that 'the impression of realness, *thereness*, is heightened, not diminished'.[99] (Ravel's intention too was to avoid a phoney realism, but this was sought via consonance and fantasy.) At the most differentiated, or in Gorbman's view 'disparate', end, one might experience collage or juxtaposition of the unrelated. Equally, elements could act in contradiction, one undermining the other in dramatic intrigue. Disjunction or 'fissures' may emerge, relating to Abbate's 'unsung', dissonant narratives. New layerings and meanings, especially ironic ones, may be revealed; conversely, the result may simply be diffuse. Gorbman's esthesic 'disparate media' are certainly very different from Ravel's 'kindred arts', experienced through composing music and scenario and even conceptualizing staging, yet her 'mutual implication' idea may throw light on specific productions.

In respect of the pro-synthesis position and the time–space agenda – applicable to Ravel – Albright concedes that 'If time and space are part of the same system, then a painting and a poem may be conceived as the same thing, reconstituted on different axes', although he still cautions against taking things too far, which may inadvertently point up their differences.[100] But the esthesic result usually still requires overall unity; as Jordan has emphasized, 'This is one "whole" experience, music and dance inextricably combined.'[101]

---

[96] Albright, *Untwisting the Serpent*, 8–10.

[97] Margaret Atwood, *The Blind Assassin* (London: Virago Press, 2001).

[98] Claudia Gorbman, 'Narrative film music', *Yale French Studies*, 60 (1980), 189–90. See too Gorbman, *Unheard Melodies: Narrative Film Music* (Bloomington: Indiana University Press, 1987), a text also referred to by Cook, 'Theorizing musical meaning', 188–9.

[99] Albright, *Untwisting the Serpent*, 7.

[100] Ibid., 6–7.

[101] Jordan, *Moving Music*, 65.

While Albright points out that a highly mimetic, self-replicating composite art may appear as calculating or deceptive – 'mere *trompe-l'œil, trompe-l'oreille*'[102] – one should acknowledge that this phenomenon fascinated those who, like Ravel, conjured with Symbolist equivalences. Other effects of close imitative relations, or paralleled actions, may be to suggest 'security', 'triumph', even humour.[103] One aspect may lead another (astray) in an unequal partnership, which may or may not be appropriate. At its best, close correspondence may produce an intense intimacy; at its worst, it may become predictable and boring.

Where further balancing and blending between extremities is concerned, Albright engages with Adorno's *Philosophie der neuen Musik*,[104] suggesting that in a modernist context a compensation process tends to operate whereby, if the music exhibits internal dissonance, then relations between that music and its associated arts tend to be consonant, and vice versa. And even if this theory is not always borne out in Ravel's ballet productions, it is well worth keeping in mind. Albright's establishing of inter-arts 'figures' of consonance, dissonance and complexes thereof is attractively flexible, although such dynamics of tension and resolution arguably still hold as much applicability to counterpoint or polyphony through time as to harmony.

Some have discarded the term 'counterpoint' on the assumption that it is synonymous with its imitative subset; nonetheless counterpoint as combined melodies may promote the idea of clearly identifiable and individualized voices, coming and going in time, that exhibit awareness of the other's existence – an expressive 'combinatoire'. These voices may enjoy elaborate interplay and a precarious balancing between autonomy, or integrity, and the necessary level of 'interdependence' (Jordan), or power sharing (Kalinak).[105] It is the quality of dialectical interplay that ensures that the entity is worth more than a straight totalling of its components. Such an idealized middle situation is well expressed by Jordan: 'Music and dance are seen as interactive, interdependent components or voices, each working upon the other, so that the whole experience becomes more than the sum of its parts.'[106] Regarding effect/affect, one collaborating composer has argued that when balletic elements are working together really well the nature of

---

[102] Albright, *Untwisting the Serpent*, 12.

[103] Jordan, *Moving Music*, 75.

[104] Albright, *Untwisting the Serpent*, 29.

[105] Kathryn Kalinak, *Settling the Score: Music and the Classical Hollywood Film* (Madison, WI: University of Wisconsin Press, 1992), 29–31.

[106] Jordan, *Moving Music*, ix. Troussevitch, 'La Chorégraphie', 346, expresses a similar ideal, especially apt for Ravel's miniaturism: 'An art-work is a minuscule thing which contains a great thing.' ('Un œuvre d'art est une chose minuscule qui contient une grande chose.')

their interaction ceases to matter: 'In a successful piece, the effect of the music on the dance and vice versa is not important; we become affected overridingly by the combined experience.'[107]

The following chapters experiment with suitable language to express the relations found in particular loci. No one creed is adhered to slavishly since this is not primarily a theoretical book, or one with any particular belief-system to promulgate. Moreover, flexibility is essential since the ballets explored travel a long way, historically and aesthetically, from the premiere of *Ma Mère l'Oye* to Béjart's reading of *Boléro*. Nonetheless, for all the differences and qualifications, particular attention is paid to Ravel's own views in conjunction with those of Jordan and Albright.

---

[107] Christopher Best, 'Why do choreographers and composers collaborate?', *Dance Theatre Journal*, 15/1 (1999), 28–31: 30.

Chapter 2

Childhood fantasy and exoticism:
Ma Mère l'Oye and *L'Enfant*

An important part of Ravel's compositional identity in ballet is bound up with themes of childhood fantasy and associated exoticism, illustrated by *Ma Mère l'Oye* (Mother Goose, 1908–10) as the main focus, and by *L'Enfant et les sortilèges* (The Child and the Sorcery, 1920–25) as a subsidiary concern. Ravel's love of the fairytale has long been acknowledged,[1] and his interest in confected exoticism, especially the chinoiserie of *Ma Mère l'Oye*, is evidenced by the picturesque yet wholly artificial 'salon chinois' that he created in the early 1920s at his home in Montfort-L'Amaury.[2]

On the large scale, two approaches to writing ballet music are revealed. In the closing years of the Belle Epoque, Ravel's first balletic excursion, *Ma Mère l'Oye*, represents a refashioning or new facet of an existing work, even though significant new music was created with the 'Prélude', 'Danse du rouet' (Dance of the Spinning Wheel) and interludes; by contrast, *Daphnis et Chloé* was initially conceived as ballet. Despite Russo-French collaboration being essential for the substantive development of Parisian ballet, this chapter shows that there was also a forward-looking indigenous French perspective, masterminded by Rouché.[3] The more obscure personnel involved in *Ma Mère l'Oye* were Jacques Drésa (1869–1929) and Jeanne Hugard, whose sympathetic, amicable collaboration from Ravel's stance set an initial gold standard, or its own fairytale, in creating a synthesized balletic whole, albeit as a modest, circumscribed project which has not enjoyed the same impact as *Daphnis*, *Boléro*, or *La Valse*.

Ravel's exploration of childhood continues in the heyday of the 1920s in his masterly *L'Enfant* to the libretto of Sidonie-Gabrielle Colette

---

[1] See René Chalupt, 'La Féerie et Maurice Ravel', *La Revue musicale*, 19 (December 1938), 128–34; Pierre G. Bréant, 'Le Fantastique comme attirance', *Musical*, 4 (June 1987), 52–61.

[2] Ravel's house is a child's treasure trove of mechanical trinkets and ornaments, including ships in glass bottles and the smallest cat in the world; see too p. 138.

[3] For a fascinating account of Rouché's activities at the Théâtre des Arts and Opéra, see Lynn Garafola, 'Forgotten interlude: eurhythmic dancers at the Paris Opéra', *Dance Research*, 13/1 (Summer 1995), 59–83. Rouché's *L'Art théâtral moderne* was contemporaneous with *Ma Mère l'Oye*.

(1873–1954). Although *L'Enfant* is typically regarded as opera, of arguably higher status, it is an opera-ballet hybrid, aptly classified by Ravel as a 'fantaisie lyrique'. While *Ma Mère l'Oye* is about children's stories and adventures, *L'Enfant*, with the benefit of Colette's script, offers a complex psychological portrayal of the child from within.[4] Whereas the former presents an ordered, traditional image of childhood, with children sometimes vulnerable (lost in the forest), the latter focuses on the destructive child rebel flouting authority, who gradually grows up a little to discover compassion and conscience. The incidental mother of *Ma Mère* becomes a central force in *L'Enfant*, as she was in Ravel's life. This idea can be related to psychoanalytic perceptions whereby fantasy 'turns upon the nature of infantile containment – upon the image of a child held within the environment or sphere of the mother's voice', as an intense experience, whether negative or positive.[5]

Additionally, both works thrive on imagination and invoke exoticisms: Laideronnette, the 'pagodes' and 'négrillons' in *Ma Mère*; the personified 'Tasse Chinoise' (Chinese Cup) and 'La Théière' (Teapot – Black Wedgwood) in their jazzy, zany and mechanistic foxtrot in *L'Enfant* (Fig. 28 [music score]).[6] Further common elements include books, spells, birdsong, nocturnal episodes and fantastical gardens. (*L'Enfant*'s nocturnal Garden Scene projects a literal exoticism, 'outside' the Child's restricted experience.) The idea of the works as connected texts across an extended time-span is supported by a joint production of Opéra National de Lyon given by a team of youngish collaborators on 21–23 March 2000.[7]

Ravel's deep pleasure in fairytale and intricate toy mechanisms was a manifestation of part of his artistic persona that thrived on subtle exploration of the child-like: a most sophisticated naivety. Indeed, something of the child remained within the man. For Benois in the happy, early summer of 1914, 'dear Maurice' was still the impish schoolboy, flying delightedly around on the high-speed merry-go-round at Ciboure.[8] Over a decade later, according to violinist Hélène Jourdan-Morhange (1892–1961), the attractive trait remained:

---

[4] For a strong reading, which highlights the Freudian psychoanalytic approach of Melanie Klein, see Richard Langham Smith, 'Ravel's operatic spectacles: *L'Heure* and *L'Enfant*', in Mawer (ed.), *The Cambridge Companion to Ravel*, 188–210: 199–210. Such psychoanalytic concerns of Klein, Freud and Jacques Lacan are developed further in a biographical *tour de force*: Julia Kristeva, *Les Mots: Colette, ou la chair du monde* (Paris: Fayard, 2002); Eng. trans. Jane Marie Todd (New York: Columbia University Press, 2004).

[5] Kaja Silverman, *The Acoustic Mirror: The Female Voice in Psychoanalysis and Cinema* (Bloomington and Indianapolis: Indiana University Press, 1988), 72.

[6] Maurice Ravel, *L'Enfant et les sortilèges* (Paris: Durand, 1925).

[7] For programme, see PRO C. 41 (B-MO).

[8] Benois, *Reminiscences of the Russian Ballet*, 366.

Ravel was a child when he was thrilled with a new suit and proudly showed off his gloves in the latest fashion: a child again when he shouted from as far away as he could to one of our girl friends who had come to meet him getting off the boat at New York, "You must see the amazing ties I've brought!"[9]

As late as 1931, Ravel was recalling his musical childhood with affection and artistic insight in the article-interview entitled 'Mes souvenirs d'enfant paresseux', which nicely echoes the opening directions for *L'Enfant* who, as the curtain rises, is 'en pleine crise de paresse' (Fig. 1 [score]).

Apart from the light-hearted enthusiasms, there were more serious concerns. Ravel's diminutive physical stature, at just 1.61 metres, presented a constant challenge for one who took such pride in his appearance and was a factor in his easier relationship with children than adults. Three small waist-coats, shades of brown, gold and black with paisley and fleur-de-lys patterns, displayed in his house could belong to children. In his lack of marital relations, his overly close relationship with his mother (whose portrait hung above his piano), his dislike of and detachment from officialdom (all the unanswered letters hidden behind a panel at Montfort-L'Amaury!), and possibly in his collaborative difficulties with Colette, there was something of a Peter Pan figure. The world of childhood offered escape or sanctuary, while opening doors on imagination and exoticism. Sociologically, Ravel's experience maps very neatly on to a study that correlated child and adult personality traits: 'Men with a history of childhood shyness are described in adulthood as bothered by demands, withdrawing when frustrated, and showing a reluctance to act ... Our most striking discovery ... is their delay in marrying, becoming fathers, and establishing stable careers.'[10]

Although there are differences, not least between the French and Scottish cultural backgrounds, comparison with James M. Barrie (1860–1937) and his *Peter Pan or the Boy who Would not Grow Up* (play, 1904; *Peter and Wendy* [novel], 1911) throws up some striking similarities suggestive of a character type.[11] One may identify to some degree with Dan Kiley's popular

---

[9] Hélène Jourdan-Morhange, 'Mon ami Ravel', *La Revue musicale*, 19 (December 1938), 192–7: 193. 'Ravel était un enfant quand il se réjouissait d'un complet neuf et montrait avec orgueil des gants à la dernière mode: un enfant encore, lorsqu'il cria du plus loin qu'il put à une de nos amies venue l'accueillir à la descente du bateau, à New-York. – "Vous allez voir les cravates épatantes que j'ai apportées!"'

[10] Avshalom Caspi, Glen H. Elder Jr, Ellen S. Herbener, 'Childhood personality and the prediction of life-course patterns', in Lee N. Robbins and Michael Rutter (eds), *Straight and Devious Pathways from Childhood to Adulthood* (Cambridge: Cambridge University Press, 1990), 13–35: 24.

[11] Writings on Barrie and *Peter Pan* extend from early appreciation – J. A. Hammerton, *Barrie: The Story of a Genius* (New York: Dodd, Mead and Co, 1929) – to recent psychological studies – Kathleen Kelley-Laine, *Peter Pan: The Story of Lost Childhood* (Rockport, MA: Elements Books, 1997).

psychological observation of a syndrome, wherein Peter Pan denotes 'the alienation of men failing to confront the emotional realities of the modern world', supposedly caused by overly strong women, especially mother figures.[12] Ravel and Barrie were broad contemporaries, active either side of the First World War and dying in the same year – neither living to see postwar Europe. Certainly, parallels exist in terms of their personal relations. Like Ravel, Barrie was, in different circumstances, intensely – even obsessively – fond of his mother and conscious of his small stature and boyish looks. Ostensibly as an avuncular presence, but probably equally as a would-be child, Ravel befriended the Godebski children associated with *Ma Mère l'Oye* and Barrie the Llewelyn Davies children (one of whom was called Peter) who inspired the novel version of *Peter Pan*, just a year before the production of Ravel's ballet. (In similar vein, some six years later, Colette's libretto for *L'Enfant* was inspired by her actual daughter.)

While hardly unique in doing so, both Ravel and Barrie employed exoticism in their respective works to enhance the magic of childhood fantasy: for Barrie, Tiger Lily epitomized the exotic, to some extent legitimising a subtle sexuality; for Ravel, in addition to creating a more generalized exotic aura, the equivalent was the character Laideronnette. On this complex issue of sexuality, both creators hung on to vestiges of childhood and found developing adult sexual relations challenging; even though Barrie did get married, it was not successful. Both men have been regarded as slightly detached observers or 'outsiders', with Alfred Cortot perceiving Ravel as 'a somewhat distant young man'.[13] It is an acknowledged consequence of childhood shyness that men may often present as 'normatively "off-time" in their transitions to age-graded roles',[14] a notion for which Peter Pan offers the ultimate, impossible example.

By way of a balletic link, both *Peter Pan* and *Ma Mère l'Oye* (as *Mother Goose*) were later choreographed and reinterpreted by Jerome Robbins (1918–98): the former at the Winter Garden Theatre, New York on 20 October 1954,[15] and the latter as part of the Ravel centennial celebrations with the New York City Ballet on 22 May 1975: 'Robbins imagines some children in

---

[12] See Jacqueline Rose, *The Case of Peter Pan, or the Impossibility of Children's Fiction* (London: Macmillan, 1984, rev. 1992), xiv, with reference to Dan Kiley, *The Peter Pan Syndrome: Men who Have Never Grown Up* (New York: Dodd and Mead, 1988).

[13] Cortot quoted in Orenstein, *Ravel: Man and Musician*, 18.

[14] Caspi et al., 'Childhood personality', 25.

[15] See Jody Sperling with Lynn Garafola, 'Works choreographed and staged by Jerome Robbins', in Lynn Garafola with Eric Foner (eds), *Dance for a City: Fifty Years of the New York City Ballet* (New York: Columbia University Press, 1999), 189–206: 195.

an attic, with a grandmama who reads some stories. The children prefer to enact them, while distorting them to their liking.'[16]

Fairytale sources and musical evolution

As children's piano pieces for four hands, *Ma Mère l'Oye* was conceived across 1908–10, the first piece appearing in September 1908, with the others following at the request of Jacques Durand in April 1910.[17] Ravel's statement on the work emphasizes the principle of *dépouillement* – a removal of inessentials – significant for his longer-term aesthetic, and the esteem in which he held his young family friends: 'The plan to evoke in these pieces the poetry of childhood naturally drove me to simplify my approach and strip my writing to essentials … the work was written at Valvins for the pleasure of my young friends Mimie and Jean Godebski.'[18]

Thus in 1910, dedicated to the children of his good friends Ida and Cipa Godebski, Ravel published a suite of five titled movements, the middle three of which were headed by fairytale quotations, already indicating programmatic or impressionistic intent.[19] In the event, because of remaining technical difficulties, the work was first performed at a concert of the Société Musicale Indépendante on 20 April 1910 by Jeanne Leleu (a pupil of Marguerite Long) and Geneviève Durony. That Ravel greatly appreciated their efforts is evident in a letter to Leleu: 'When you become a great virtuoso … you will perhaps have a very sweet memory of having given an artist the really rare joy of having heard a rather special work interpreted exactly

---

[16] Antoine Livio, 'Dans le monde: New York', *dp* (October 1975), 6, in George Balanchine, Dossier d'artiste, B-MO. 'Robbins imagine des enfants dans un grenier, avec une mère-grand qui lit des histoires. Les enfants préfèrent les vivre, en les déformant à plaisir.' For more, see Lincoln Kirstein, *Thirty years: Lincoln Kirstein's The New York City Ballet* (New York: Knopf, 1973, 2/1978; London: A. & C. Black, 1979), 256–7; consult also the Jerome Robbins Trust and Foundation, and Jerome Robbins Dance Division, The New York Public Library for the Performing Arts.

[17] The piano duet MS (18 pp.; signed and dated April 1910) was held by Mme Alexandre Taverne and remains in the Ravel Estate.

[18] Alexis Roland-Manuel, 'Une esquisse autobiographique de Maurice Ravel', *La Revue musicale*, 19 (December 1938), 17–23: 21. 'Le dessein d'évoquer dans ces pièces la poésie de l'enfance m'a naturellement conduit à simplifier ma manière et à dépouiller mon écriture … l'ouvrage fut écrit à Valvins à l'intention de mes jeunes amis Mimie et Jean Godebski.' Valvins was the Godebski riverside country home near Fontainebleau.

[19] Also in 1910, Jacques Charlot produced a solo piano transcription; see Ravel, *Le Tombeau de Couperin and Other Works for Solo Piano*.

as befitted it. A thousand thanks for your child-like and thoughtful performance.'[20]

This miniature comprises an arch structure, framed by a slow opening and close (see Table 2.1): 'Pavane de la Belle au bois dormant' (Pavane of Sleeping Beauty in the wood) and 'Le Jardin féerique' (The fairy garden). Moving inwards, the meandering, melancholic 'Petit Poucet' (Little Tom Thumb) is balanced by an expressive, emotive waltz 'Les Entretiens de la Belle et de la Bête' (Conversations of Beauty and the Beast) – the first of several balletic waltzes across Ravel's career. The exotic core is provided by

Table 2.1 *Ma Mère l'Oye*: fairytale sources and (re-)ordering of movements

Piano duet	Ballet score	Fairytale source
-----	Prélude [fanfare]	-----
-----	Ier tableau, Danse du rouet et scène	Charles Perrault, *Histoires ou contes du temps passés avec des moralités* [Mother Goose Tales] (*Contes*, 1697)
I. Pavane de la Belle	IIme tableau, Pavane	Perrault, *Histoires*[a]
II. Petit Poucet	IVme tableau, Petit Poucet	Perrault, *Histoires*
III. Laideronnette	Vme tableau, Laideronnette	Comtesse d'Aulnoy, *Serpentin vert* (*Les Contes des fées*, 1697–8)
IV. Les Entretiens	IIIme tableau, Les Entretiens	Marie Leprince de Beaumont, *Magazin des enfants, Contes moraux* (1757)
V. Le Jardin	[VIme]Apothéose, Le Jardin	Main source: Perrault, *Histoires* (ending of 'La Belle au bois dormant')[b]

[a] 'La Belle au bois dormant' is also found in the later Brothers Grimm: Jacob Grimm (1785–1863) and Wilhelm Grimm (1786–1859), *Dornröschen* (*Sleeping Beauty* or *Rose-d'épine*). See *Dornröschen* (Mainz: Jos. Scholz, 1912).

[b] Charles Perrault, 'La Belle au bois dormant', *Histoires ou contes du temps passé des moralités*, in *Contes*, ed. Gilbert Rouger (Paris: Editions Garnier, 1967), 97–107: 101–3.

---

[20] Letter to Jeanne Leleu (21 April 1910), in Marguerite Long, *Au piano avec Maurice Ravel* (Paris: Julliard, 1971), plates 4 and 5. 'Quand vous serez une grande virtuose … vous aurez peut-être un souvenir très doux d'avoir procuré à un artiste la joie bien rare d'avoir entendu interpréter une œuvre assez spéciale avec le sentiment exact qui y convenait. Merci mille fois pour votre exécution enfantine et spirituelle.'

a central march: 'Laideronnette, Impératrice de pagodes' (The Ugly Little Girl, Empress of the Pagodas).

The piano original is reduced to skeletal essentials: the opening stately 'Pavane', with its tiny ternary outline, AA'BAA' across 20 bars, presents a wistful melody in an A aeolian mode (A, B, C, D, E (F/F♯), G) which leads towards the middle of each bar. A hymn-like finale, based in a 'happily-ever-after' C major with a 'sharpened' central portion, to some extent shares this reductive approach. Such stripping is over-zealous in its effect on texture and the work gains much through its later orchestral enrichment.

Despite this pragmatic limitation, exotic touches are evident even in the first version: fragments of haunting birdsong near the end of the wandering C minor scalic and metrically irregular 'Petit Poucet' (bars 51–4). High chromatic appoggiaturas of songbirds (prima, RH) are answered by minor-third cuckoo 'sighs' (prima, LH), interspersed by silence (Example 2.1). The former were later orchestrated for solo violin, with harmonic glissan-dos, and the latter for flute, supported by string trills. In this way Ravel illustrates the quotation of the famous Charles Perrault (1628–1703) that prefaces his music: 'He thought he would easily find his way by means of the bread that he had scattered everywhere he had been; but … birds had come and eaten everything.'[21]

Exoticism is most obviously embedded in the energetic and, at times, very forthright 'Laideronnette'. Mechanical mock-Chinese (or Javanese) pentatonic figurations of semiquavers and quavers are supported by penta-tonic harmonization below, favouring gamelan-like fourths, fifths and major seconds (Example 2.2). Both treble and bass run their phrases across the barlines in playful parodistic vein. Even the modality on F♯ is as distant as possible from the work's C-based tonic. Superficial intertextual association

Example 2.1 *Ma Mère l'Oye* (piano duet, 1910): bird song in 'Petit Poucet' (bars 51–4)

---

[21] Perrault, 'Le Petit Poucet', *Histoires ou contes*, 187–98: 190–91. 'Il croyait [re]trouver aisément son chemin par le moyen de son pain qu'il avait semé partout où il avait passé; mais … les oiseaux étaient venus qui avaient tout mangé.' Perrault also produced adaptations of classic folk tales such as *Bluebeard* and *Little Red Riding Hood*.

Example 2.2 *Ma Mère l'Oye*: pentatonicism in 'Laideronnette, Impératrice
          des Pagodes' (bars 9–13, reduction)

with Debussy's 'Pagodes' from *Estampes* (1903) is almost inevitable. Thus
Ravel revivifies an episode from the obscure tale of 'Laideronnette' (made
ugly by a witch's spell) by Marie-Catherine, Comtesse d'Aulnoy
(1650–1705), ripe with musical imagery: 'She undressed and climbed into
the bath. Straight away, pagodes and pagodines [tiny make-believe people]
began to sing and play instruments: some had theorbos made from a walnut
shell; some had viols made from an almond shell; for it was necessary to
proportion the instruments properly to their size.'[22] The sparse writing of the
slower-moving middle section of this ternary design (bars 65–137; Figs.
9–14 of ballet score) again apes a harmonic reduction and cries out for the
woodwind/percussive treatment and visual representation that Ravel could
surely already imagine.[23] Fig. 9 would come to mark the masked appearance
of the Empress, 'en chinoise de Boucher', followed at Fig. 11 by that of the
Green Serpent.

Ravel's orchestration of the suite ensued in 1911, after a little more
coaxing from Durand, followed by the ballet version towards the end of the
year (see Table 2.1).[24] The orchestral forces require just 32 players but, as
would become a technical hallmark, Ravel achieves so much with economical means. The composer's basic double woodwind includes cor anglais and

---

[22] Comtesse d'Aulnoy, *Serpentin vert*, in *Les Contes des fées* (Paris, 1697–8); quotation
heading 'III. Laideronnette': 'Elle se déshabilla et se mit dans le bain. Aussitôt pagodes et
pagodines se mirent à chanter et à jouer des instruments: tels avaient des théorbes faits d'une
coquille de noix; tels avaient des violes faites d'une coquille d'amande; car il faillait bien
proportionner les instruments à leur taille.'

[23] Although Rouché suggested the ballet idea towards the end of 1911, Ravel must already
have had a strong extra-musical impetus from the fairytale quotations.

[24] The orchestral suite MS (38 pp.) is held in the Carlton Lake Collection, HRC, and was
published by Durand, 1912. The full ballet score is available on hire (Durand, 1912), with an
annotated duration of 28 minutes; a piano reduction of the ballet version, again by Charlot,
was also published in 1912. For a complete ballet CD recording, see, for example, Ravel,
Orchestral Works (Hamburg: Teldec Classics–Ultima, 1997; 0630-18959-2), performed by
The St Paul Chamber Orchestra, cond. Hugh Wolff (duration: 23′ 30″).

contrabassoon, supplemented by two horns, but his scintillating, magical timbres are secured particularly by means of percussion: timpani, tam-tam, xylophone, keyed glockenspiel, celesta and harp. String effects assist, with muted tones, tremolos, pizzicatos and harmonics. Such use of timbre is broadly analogous to Drésa's use of colour in his costumes and sets, discussed below.

So 'Laideronnette' maximizes its Eastern promise with glockenspiel, celesta and harp to punctuate the section marked 'Danse' (Fig. 3), and these same instruments clinch the apotheosis of the finale with their ecstatic glissandos (Fig. 5). This early idea of a dance apotheosis would reach its zenith in *La Valse*. Equally, the dialogue of 'Les Entretiens' between the melodious treble voice of Beauty and deep, but uncertain, chromatic bass of the would-be handsome Beast is enhanced by instrumental characterization on clarinet and contrabassoon respectively. The developing intensity of their relationship is symbolized by thematic combination (Example 2.3). Ravel thus transcribes musically the lines of Marie Leprince de Beaumont (1711–80) that head this Gymnopédian waltz in F:

'When I think of your good heart, you do not appear to me so ugly.' – 'Oh! Lady, yes! I have a good heart, but I am a monster.' … The Beast had disappeared and she just saw at her feet a prince more handsome than Love who thanked her for having broken his spell.[25]

Example 2.3 *Ma Mère l'Oye* (piano ballet score, 1912): thematic combination in 'Les Entretiens de la Belle et de la Bête' (bars 107–110)

---

[25] Marie Leprince de Beaumont, 'Les Entretiens de la Belle et de la Bête', in *Magazin des enfants, Contes moraux* [Children's Treasury of Moral Tales] (Paris, 1757); quotation heading 'IV. Les Entretiens': '"Quand je pense à votre bon cœur, vous ne me paraissez si laid." – "Oh! dame, oui! j'ai le cœur bon, mais je suis un monstre." … La Bête avait disparu et elle ne vit plus à ses pieds qu'un prince plus beau que l'Amour qui la remerciait d'avoir fini son enchantement.' For a very different cultural-societal 'take', see Jean Cocteau's film, *La Belle et la Bête* (1946).

Appropriately enough, given its fantasy and idiosyncrasies, Ravel dedicated a copy of *Ma Mère l'Oye* to Erik Satie: 'grandpapa of "The Conversations", and others'.[26]

In addition to orchestrating existing material, Ravel's balletic fashioning involved reordering and creation of more music in an impressively short few weeks, following Rouché's request.[27] Reordering focused on the middle movements, with 'Les Entretiens' brought forward to precede 'Laideronnette', to be separated by 'Petit Poucet'. The reasoning for this must relate partly to the similar storylines of the first two items, effectively different presentations of the same moral principle of looking beyond the surface.[28] Beauty and the Beast, as a disguised prince, is well known; the lesser-known 'Laideronnette' goes one better in that both the title character and the amorous Green Serpent have been rendered incognito by curses. In the Comtesse d'Aulnoy's story, at the lifting of curses, a princess and king are revealed who, having fallen in love, inevitably marry. In turn, this story constitutes an appropriate final dream for Sleeping Beauty – a tale within a tale. It is also the case that 'Laideronnette' builds to a strong, extrovert climax, appropriate towards the ballet's conclusion, whereas 'Les Entretiens' develops an intimate interlude, more suitable earlier on.

Ravel's creation of new material focused upon the opening 'Prélude', a first tableau ('Danse du rouet'; see below), and five interludes to facilitate scene changes and smooth musical joins between tableaux (full ballet score: pp. 27–8, 32–5, 49–51, 58–61, 85–8).[29] Undoubtedly the most dramatic, memorable interlude is that which comprises a free percussive cadenza for harp, with celesta, thence to a flute flourish, to create a stunning, shimmering evocation of moonlight, immediately preceding 'Laideronnette' (Example 2.4).

Where beginnings are concerned, the mysterious 'Prélude', marked 'Très Lent', starts perversely but successfully with Ravel's concluding motive from 'Le Jardin féerique' (Fig. 5), thus substantiating the arch structure. This material uses Ravel's favoured technique for conveying myth – whether dealing with 'genuine' or falsified antiquity: a repeated play of rising fifths (with falling sevenths) in flutes, balanced by a muted hunting horn fanfare,

---

[26] Orenstein (ed.), *Maurice Ravel: lettres*, 513.

[27] It was not always Rouché taking the initiative: Ravel had written to Rouché in August 1910 proposing D.-E. Inghelbrecht as conductor for the Théâtre des Arts. (Rouché had in fact appointed Grovlez.)

[28] On fairytale psychology, see Maire Luise von Franz, *An Introduction to the Psychology of Fairy Tales* (Zurich: Spring Publications, 2/1973) and Jack Zipes (ed.), *The Oxford Companion to Fairy Tales: The Western Fairy-Tale Tradition from Perrault to Pratchett* (New York: Oxford University Press, 2000). See the overtly psychoanalytic interpretations of Bruno Bettelheim, *The Uses of Enchantment: The Meaning and Importance of Fairy Tales* (London: Thames & Hudson, 1976, rev. edn Penguin, 1991).

[29] The ballet score figures replicate those of the orchestral score (where applicable), restarting at Fig. 1 for each movement.

Example 2.4 *Ma Mère l'Oye*: opening of harp cadenza preceding 'Laideronnette'

featuring the inverted falling fourth. Muted string harmonics complete the timbral palette (Example 2.5). Comparison can be made with treatment of fifths in *Daphnis*, and this fanfare assists in surmising what might have been found in the lost equivalent for *Adélaïde* (Chapter 4); similarities exist too with the postwar 'Fanfare' for *L'Eventail de Jeanne* (Chapter 6). The fifth motive is transferred to horns (Fig. 2), thence to clarinet and bassoon in a reprise (Fig. 5^{+3}). This idea recurs at the close of the first tableau (Figs. 27–8) and much later, in the interlude that precedes the finale, combined thematically with the second phrase from the 'Pavane' (ballet score, p. 87). Meanwhile, imitative play of the fanfare motive between horns leads to exquisite whispers of upper woodwind sound, echoes of *L'Oiseau de feu*, supported by divided tremolo strings (Fig. 1; reprise at Fig. 6^{+2}), at about doubled tempo. When this latter material returns, combined with fanfares, at the 'Très modéré' preceding the finale, the dawn chorus depiction is explicit in the score: 'Petit jour. Chants d'oiseaux' (ballet score, p. 86).

Ravel's attention to detail on a small canvas is superb: fine gradations of dynamic with swift surges to *forte*, single and double grace-notes, accentuations, slurrings modified by staccatos, flute tremolo and vibrato markings. On its second hearing, building to the curtain rise, this material

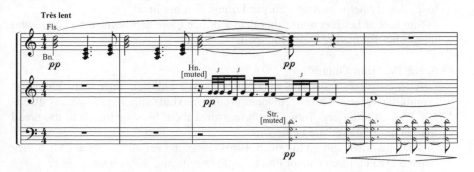

Example 2.5 *Ma Mère l'Oye* (ballet, 1912): 'Prélude' (bars 1–4)

pregnant with expectation reaches a sumptuous yet foreboding peak, secured by lush harp flourishes, which leads seamlessly into the first tableau (Fig. 9).

Ravel's derived scenario

Alongside the development of his musical material, Ravel had worked swiftly on his accompanying scenario, closely derived from the fairytale sources. (It is impossible in this context not to make a superficial association with Tchaikovsky's fairytale ballet *La Belle au bois dormant*.) A concise version of this scenario is offered in a catalogue of Ravel's works, published in 1954:

Scene I. 'Dance of the spinning wheel'
An enchanted garden. An old woman is seated at her spinning wheel. Princess Florine enters, skipping with a rope. She stumbles and falls against the spinning wheel, whose spindle pricks her. The old woman calls for help. Gentlemen and maids-of-honour run up. They try vainly to revive the Princess. They then recall the fairies' curse. Two ladies-in-waiting prepare the Princess for her century-long night.

Scene II. 'Pavane of the Sleeping Beauty'
Florine falls asleep. The old woman stands up. She throws off her shabby cape and adopts the sumptuous clothing and charming features of the Good Fairy.
Two little Negroes appear. The fairy entrusts them with guarding Florine and the task of entertaining her slumber.

Scene III. 'Conversations of Beauty and the Beast'
Beauty enters. She takes her mirror, powders her face. The Beast enters. Beauty notices him and stops petrified. She rejects, horror-stuck, the declarations of the Beast who falls to his knees, sobbing. Reassured, Beauty trifles with him coquettishly. The Beast falls down, faint with despair. Touched by his great love, Beauty helps him up again and offers him her hand.
She sees at her feet none other than a prince more handsome than Love, who thanks her for having ended his spell.

Scene IV. 'Tom Thumb'
A forest, night falls. The woodcutter's seven children enter. Tom Thumb is crumbling a piece of bread. He looks around him but cannot make out any dwelling. The children cry, Tom Thumb reassures them by showing them the bread that he has scattered along the way.
They lie down and go to asleep. Birds come and eat all the bread. When they wake up the children cannot find a single crumb, and they go away sadly.

Scene V. 'Laideronnette, Empress of the Pagodas'
A tent draped in Chinese style. Male and female 'pagodins' enter. Dance. Laideronnette appears, dressed in the Chinese style of Boucher.[30] The Green Serpent slithers amorously nearby.
'Pas de deux', then general dance.

Scene VI. 'The Enchanted Garden'
Dawn. Birdsong.
Prince Charming enters, guided by a Cupid. He notices the sleeping Princess. She awakens at the same time that day is dawning.
All the ballet characters gather around the Prince and the Princess, united by Cupid.
The Good Fairy springs up and blesses the couple.
Apotheosis.[31]

---

[30] François Boucher (1703–70) produced decorative paintings on mythological or pastoral subjects. Such eighteenth-century allusion is broadly consistent with the fairytale sources.

[31] *Catalogue de l'œuvre de Maurice Ravel* (Paris: Fondation Maurice Ravel, 1954):

1er Tableau. – 'Danse du rouet'
Un jardin de féerie. Une vieille femme est assise à son rouet. La princesse Florine entre, sautant à la corde. Elle trébuche et va donner sur le rouet dont le fuseau la blesse. La vieille appelle à l'aide. Les gentilshommes et les demoiselles d'honneur accourent. Ils essayent vainement de ranimer la Princesse. On se rappelle alors la malédiction des fées. Deux dames d'autour viennent la préparer pour sa nuit séculaire.

2e Tableau. – 'Pavane de la Belle au bois dormant'
Florine s'endort. La vieille s'est redressée. Elle rejette sa cape sordide et paraît sous les vêtements somptueux et les traits charmants de la fée Bénigne.

Deux négrillons se présentent. La fée leur confie la garde de Florine et le soin de distraire son sommeil.

3e Tableau. – 'Les Entretiens de la Belle et de la Bête'
Entre la Belle. Elle prend son miroir, se poudre. Entre la Bête. La Belle l'aperçoit et reste pétrifiée. Elle repousse avec horreur les déclarations de la Bête qui tombe à ses genoux, sanglotant. Rassurée, la Belle se joue de la Bête avec coquetterie. La Bête tombe évanouie de désespoir. Touchée par ce grand amour, la Belle la relève et lui accorde sa main.

Elle ne voit plus à ses pieds qu'un prince plus beau que l'amour, qui la remercie d'avoir terminé son enchantement.

4e Tableau. – 'Petit Poucet'
Une forêt, le soir tombe. Entrent les sept enfants du bûcheron. Petit Poucet émiette un morceau de pain. Il interroge les alentours et ne découvre aucune habitation. Les enfants pleurent, Petit Poucet les rassure en leur montrant le pain qu'il a semé le long de leur chemin.

Ils se couchent et s'endorment. Les oiseaux passent et mangent tout le pain. A leur réveil ils ne trouvent plus une miette et s'éloignent tristement.

5e Tableau. – 'Laideronnette, impératrice des pagodes'
Une tente drapée à la chinoise. Entrent pagodins et pagodines. Danse. Paraît Laideronnette, en Chinoise de Boucher. Serpentin Vert rampe amoureusement à ses côtés.

Pas de deux, puis danse générale.

Even from this functional, matter-of-fact scenario various observations may be made: Ravel's idea of dream tales enveloped in a larger tale is explicit. Neat conflation occurs between Beauty who is Sleeping and the one who encounters the Beast, similarly between a prince 'more handsome than Love' and Prince Charming 'guided by a Cupid'. The arch structure, already evident musically, is reinforced by Ravel's bringing forward the garden as the initial setting, then returning to it for the final tableau (he would revisit it in the Garden Scene of *L'Enfant*). As is typical of the fairytale subject-matter, the scenario thrives on deceptive appearances and their potential for dramatic irony or misunderstanding: the old woman in Scene I is revealed as the Good Fairy in Scene II; the bread strewn by 'Petit Poucet' represents illusory security and, musically, the misleading, twisting lines create aural deception. Furthermore, the idea of the hidden or masked accords strongly with part of Ravel's aesthetic identity; the scenario itself exists as a concealed text, not for public view.

Apart from the Good Fairy, other instances of symbolism include that of Cupid as a catalyst for, and personification of, love. In the language of hyperbole and fantasy, the Princess's awakening symbolizes a simultaneous global release from darkness as dawn breaks, together with the potential for love. Comparison may be made with the final tableau of *Daphnis*. As with all good children's tales, the story combines tragi-comic elements: the pathetic naivety of the lost children in the forest; the spinning wheel mishap followed by the impotent rushing around of the courtly entourage. Other oppositions, so clearcut in children's eyes, include goodness/evil, beauty/ugliness, day/night, dream-world/reality. (For more, see Chapter 3.) Apart from Scene/tableau V, with overtones of the Garden of Eden and sexuality safely enclosed beneath the cover of chinoiserie, the exotic element is apparent in Ravel's introduction of two black boys – ('négrillons') – influenced perhaps by the contemporary staging of Rimsky-Korsakov's *Shéhérazade* or Hahn's *Le Dieu bleu*. 'Négrillon' translates unacceptably today as 'piccaninny' or 'Negro boy' and, while there is no reason to believe that Ravel endorsed racism, his use of the term indicates how profoundly societal attitudes have changed.

6e Tableau. – 'Le Jardin féerique'

Petit jour. Chants d'oiseaux.

Entre le Prince Charmant, guidé par un Amour. Il aperçoit la Princesse endormie. Elle s'éveille en même temps que le jour se lève.

Tous les personnages du ballet se groupent autour du Prince et de la Princesse unis par l'Amour.

La fée Bénigne surgit et bénit le couple.

Apothéose.

One can question the overly pragmatic tone of Ravel's scenario, the clichéd ensemble finale with rather lame re-entry of the Good Fairy, and the isolated, dramatically weak, forest episode. Additionally, the ending of the 'Conversations of Beauty and the Beast' reproduces almost verbatim the quotation of Mme Leprince de Beaumont. But to be fair, the scenario was necessarily written very rapidly and Ravel recognized his literary limitations: 'everything is joined together by an argument, doubtless fragile, but sufficient for my intentions to be understood.'[32]

Even for this miniature, there are variant scenario sources and the issue arises as to whether any one is definitive. Essentially, there is an evolutionary process at work, but it would be falsely simplistic to latch on to one version. The primary source is Ravel's initial manuscript (A), followed by that in the first production, as notated in a 1912 programme (B), and that consolidated in publication of Ravel's 1912 ballet scores (C).[33] The concise version above, sanctioned by the Maurice Ravel Foundation, could constitute source D, but one could also refer to the 1915 programme with yet further variants.[34]

There is little purpose in comparing linguistic minutiae, yet it is germane to summarize the main issues and developments. Source A consists of Ravel's original scenario, accompanied by headed notes/listings and a letter to Rouché. The three-page scenario (fol. 3r and v; fol. 4r), handwritten on yellow squared paper in dark purple ink, adopts a note-like style and was seemingly written at speed. Generally, this manuscript is more detailed than later sources; it reveals Ravel's heavy involvement in the staging of *Ma Mère l'Oye* and that significant changes occurred in this domain through collaboration and production.

Ravel's initial theory (source A) was that the tale-within-a-tale should be conveyed physically on stage by a huge book, carried with difficulty by four 'négrillons'. In gilt script would be the title *Les Contes de Ma Mère l'Oye*. In his letter to Rouché, where he comments that the outline needs filling out, Ravel quotes from the scenario: 'The book is placed vertically at the back of the stage.' He continues by explaining this device for minimizing scene

---

[32] René Bizet, '*Ma Mère l'Oye*: c'est un petit ballet très original de M. Maurice Ravel', *L'Intransigeant* (28 January 1912): 'le tout est relié par un argument, fragile sans doute, mais suffisant pour qu'on comprenne mes intentions.'

[33] (A): LAS Ravel, 1 (B-MO); (B): Théâtre des Arts, *Ma Mère l'Oye, Pupazzi, Jeannine* [saison 1911–12] (Rec. Yf58f), BNF Mus. This programme probably corresponds to a series of fifteen performances, coupled with Florent Schmitt's *Les Pupazzi* and B. Grasset's *Jeannine*, which commenced on 23 May 1912; see 'Théâtre des Arts, saisons 1912 et 1913' (FR, Th. des Arts, Arch. R4 [fol. 16]). (C): solo piano reduction and orchestral hire score (Paris: Durand, 1912); Ravel's scenario is carefully overlaid on the music.

[34] *Ma Mère l'Oye* programme (March 1915), B-MO.

changes: 'When opened, it [the book] takes the place of the décor. An opening would be made *always on the same side* which would show for the first page a door, for the second a forest, for the third the [Chinese] tent scene.'[35] Each new story would be signalled by one of the 'négrillons' turning over a page.

By the time of source B, the large book idea has been shelved for practical reasons in favour of a less literal approach: 'She [the Good Fairy] goes to kiss the sleeping princess on the forehead and gives her The Stories of *Mother Goose* for her dreams.'[36] Interestingly, however, in source C, over which Ravel had greater control, the pendulum has swung back in the other direction. Ravel has recognized the need for compromise, but he has no intention of losing his decorative notion altogether: 'She [the Good Fairy] disappears. The little black boys approach the princess and bow ceremoniously. They unfurl a banner on which is inscribed the title of the first Story to be presented: "The Conversations of Beauty and the Beast".'[37] Thus these different versions create a documentary trace, the modifications within which generally point to collaborative intervention, discussed below. Such subtleties would be hidden if the 1954 version were regarded as unequivocally definitive.

Another development across the scenarios concerns renumbering of scenes/tableaux and a redesignating of the start of Scene II: in source A, the 'Pavane' was subsumed within the opening scene; by source C, it has become a scene in its own right. A third issue involves the number of personnel to execute the scenario. Essentially, source A proposes ambitious requirements that are then cut down, not least because of the tiny stage dimensions of the Théâtre des Arts (see Figure 2.1): four 'négrillons' and two Cupids in source A are later reduced to two and one, respectively. The number of maids-of-honour within the 'coryphée' – a class of dancers in French ballet who perform in small groups but are distinct from and better paid than the *corps de ballet* – varies from two to 'a simple quadrille', with some numerical alterations made in blue crayon upon pencil markings in Ravel's notes. Ravel's intention of bringing the full cast back on stage for an ensemble finale was one of very few points of issue between himself and Drésa, detailed below.

------

[35] LAS Ravel, 1; letter to Rouché (n.d. [1912]), reproduced in François Lesure and Jean-Michel Nectoux (eds), *Maurice Ravel* [exhibition catalogue] (Paris: Bibliothèque Nationale, 1975), 33. 'Le livre est posé verticalement au fond de la scène. Ouvert, il tient lieu de décor. Une ouverture serait pratiquée toujours du même côté qui représenterait, pour le 1er feuillet une porte, soit pour le 2e un fourré, pour le 3e l'entrée de la tente.' Ravel's scenario indicates that this tent features Chinese lanterns.

[36] (B): 'Elle va baiser au front la princesse endormie et lui donne comme rêves: Les Contes de la *Mère l'Oye*.'

[37] (C): 'Elle disparaît. Les négrillons s'avancent vers la princesse et s'inclinent cérémonieusement. Ils déroulent une banderole sur laquelle est inscrit le titre du 1er Conte que l'on va représenter: "les Entretiens de la Belle et de la Bête".'

Figure 2.1   The former Théâtre des Arts, renamed Théâtre Hébertot. Private
collection.

The composer's thoughtfulness is evident in the source A notes; he lists the
many children's roles including Petit Poucet and his six brothers, 'pagodes'
[*sic*] and 'pagodines', cupids, birds and fairies. Acknowledging the genre as
a 'ballet-pantomime', he questions which leading roles are to be female and
which male. Prince Charming is an interesting case in point: despite pantomime precedents, Ravel originally meant the character to be played by a
man. Furthermore, he wonders whether Prince Charming and the Green
Serpent might be played by one man, although he appreciates potential
problems of swift costume changes, since that for Prince Charming in the
final tableau must be 'magnificent'. In practice, both the premiere and 1915
productions used women, as occurred too with the Green Serpent; for cast
details, see Appendix. Ravel also ponders whether Prince Charming's role,
among others, should be danced or mimed and plans to discuss this with the
'maître de ballet'. At the point where the masked Beast, hand in hand with
Beauty, is transformed into the handsome prince, Ravel comments in paren-
thesis that this should involve 'grands enlèvements' (high supported lifts) if
the role were to be danced.

Additionally, sources A/B clarify that Ravel's enchanted garden was to be in
'eighteenth-century English style', contemporary with the notated fairytales,

featuring 'box hedges cut into globes, tied with garlands',[38] an original formality of setting to be re-adopted in *Adélaïde* (Chapter 4). Meanwhile, most sources
concur about the exotic, frightening disguise of Laideronnette, herself afraid to
display her ugliness: 'an [eye] mask of black velvet, a tulip in her hand', typically symbolizing a declaration of love.[39] Fondness for floral symbolism also
peaks with *Adélaïde*. Interestingly, sources A/B are explicit about a 'Scène
d'amour' with the Green Serpent, later downplayed as a 'Pas de deux' (sources
C/D: Fig. 13). Small details relating to the first tableau include modifying stage
directions from left to right for the old woman sitting at her wheel (sources A
and C) and changing the equipment on which the princess pricks her finger
from 'fuseau' (A/B: 'spindle') to 'quénouille' (C/1915 programme: 'distaff')
and back again (D).

Musical literalism in portraying scenario: 'Danse du rouet'

This new opening scene offers an apt locus for a brief look at Ravel's portrayal
of his scenario (source C), which constitutes a musical narrative. For the
spinning wheel being worked by the old lady in the garden, Ravel adopts the
classic 6/8 metre, an Allegro tempo marking and swirling chromatic passage-
work to project aurally the fast circular movements of the wheel and long
line of the thread (Example 2.6).[40] Such semiquaver motion in compound

Example 2.6 *Ma Mère l'Oye* (piano ballet score, 1912): 'Danse du rouet'
            (Fig. 9; bars 1–4)

---

[38] Sources A/B: 'Un jardin de féerie XVIIIᵉ siècle anglais. Buis taillés en boules, reliés par des guirlandes.'

[39] Sources A, B and C: 'un loup de velours noir masquant son visage, une tulipe à la main'; 'un loup' translates as a mask or wolf.

[40] For the fairytale source and its prediction, see Perrault, 'La Belle au bois dormant', 97–107: 98. 'The Princess will pierce her hand on a spindle; but instead of dying, she will only fall into a deep sleep which will last a hundred years, at the end of which the son of a King will come to wake her up.' ('La Princesse se percera la main d'un fuseau: mais au lieu d'en mourir, elle tombera seulement dans un profond sommeil qui durera cent ans, au bout desquels le fils d'un Roi viendra la réveiller.')

metre is shared by Ravel's early 'Chanson du rouet' (1898), indicative of a certain mechanical 'objet sonore', previously modelled by Schubert in 'Gretchen am Spinnrade' (D.118). At another level, these fleeting, nervous figurations create appropriate unease. Similarly, at the indication 'La Princesse Florine entre, sautant à la corde' (Princess Florine enters, skipping with her rope), a new layer of literal depiction is superimposed on the spinning music (Fig. 10). Florine's sprightliness is conveyed by staccato descents and leaps in the woodwind, articulated by rests; strings are fittingly pizzicato, with quadruple stopping in violins suggesting adventurous playful antics on stage. Chromaticism and tremolos persist to maintain instability. Further games ensue, since 'Puis elle joue au volant' (Then she plays 'shuttlecock' [badminton]); once more Ravel skilfully superimposes his sonic images, so neatly conflating and playing with time and words (Example 2.7). (Although 'volant' can mean 'wheel', it is convincingly interpreted as 'shuttlecock' in the annotated hire score held at United Music Publishers.) For this solo game, Ravel requires harp (plus celesta) and viola glissandos, the latter ending in a sky-high harmonic followed a rest – the fall of the shuttlecock.

The lead-up to mishap features four bars of mildly clashing major-second intervals, oscillating with their semitonal neighbours, strengthened by offbeat accents (Fig. 23). An effective touch as Florine stumbles and is pierced by the spinning wheel is that Ravel reduces the sound to *pp* – an inverted climax, her fall conveyed by descending pizzicato triplet quavers, then exaggerated in slowed-up motion by the reduction to duplets to dovetail with the metrical

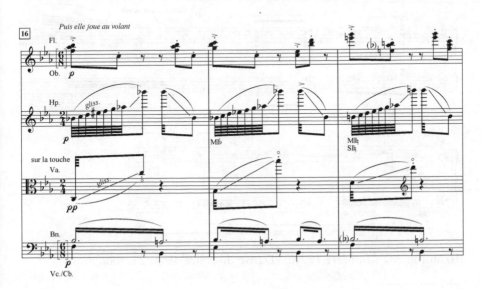

Example 2.7 *Ma Mère l'Oye* (ballet, 1912): 'Danse du rouet' (Fig. 16, reduction)

change to 2/4 (Example 2.8). Only after Florine's fall is the sound level dramatically raised for the old woman's anguished cries for help: accented descending violin portamentos (Fig. 24[+1]). The extent of literalism in Ravel's musical response to the detailed action of his scenario may be surprising, but the effect is wholly compelling. Such literalism is child-friendly because it is a child-like approach.

Balletic collaboration (Drésa and Hugard)

Even a small-scale venture requires collaboration with many other artists and performers. Beyond his double contribution in providing music and scenario plus ideas on staging, Ravel collaborated with Rouché as theatre director, Drésa as designer, Georges Mouveau as stage decorator,[41] Hugard

Example 2.8 *Ma Mère l'Oye*: 'Danse du rouet' (Fig. 24, reduction)

---

[41] Mouveau, one of Les Apaches, worked at the Théâtre des Arts and followed Rouché to the Opéra.

as choreographer with Léo Staats as general ballet-master, Gabriel Grovlez as conductor,[42] and Mme Ariane Hugon and 'Caryathis'[43] as leading dancers.

Ravel was clearly very taken by Drésa's approach to design for *Ma Mère l'Oye* and put his seal of approval on it in a letter of early January 1912: 'I don't know how to tell you how delighted I am with the sketch of the décor, which I have just seen at Mouveau's house. It has enchantment, and, most especially, it is proper décor.'[44] Indeed, Ravel acted on his delight soon after by requesting to Rouché that he and Drésa work together again on *Adélaïde*.

Although thrilled with the basic design, Ravel still feels able to raise a staging issue upon which he and Drésa do not see eye to eye. This point demonstrates Ravel's remarkably detailed engagement in matters beyond music and his negotiating skills, making light of his question despite its concerning a significant detail: 'I had believed, first of all, that the backcloth was [to be] divided into two planes.'[45] Tactically, Ravel then gets Mouveau on side, explaining that while Mouveau has informed him that this is not what Drésa now intends, his own thoughts are endorsed by Mouveau. Indeed Mouveau corresponded accordingly with Drésa: 'Take Ravel's word for it. The yellow backcloth on one plane and in front of this backing the cut-out green plane is all that's needed for the scenery, which will be charming, if you really want my opinion.'[46] (That Mouveau would have had to intercept the machinist already progressing with Drésa's instructions suggests that these modifications may not have occurred.) Ravel continues in his gentlemanly attempt to persuade Drésa, explaining that the book idea has been superseded. His new idea, developed from his letter to Rouché (in line with scenario source C), is that

---

[42] Gabriel Grovlez (1879–1944) was a respected pianist-conductor and composer who in March 1906 had introduced Ravel's *Sonatine* to its Parisian public. From 1911 to 1913, he was music director of the Théâtre des Arts. Autograph letters from Grovlez to Rouché are held in a Dossier d'artiste, Gabriel Grovlez (B-MO).

[43] 'Caryathis', or 'Caryatis', was the stage-name of Elise Jouhandeau, née Toulemon.

[44] Letter from Ravel to Drésa (January 1912), in Orenstein (ed.), *Maurice Ravel: lettres*, 121. 'Je ne saurais vous dire combien me ravit l'esquisse du décor que je viens de voir chez Mouveau. C'est de la féerie et, surtout, c'est du décor.'

[45] Ibid.: 'j'ai cru, tout d'abord, que le rideau de fond était décomposé en 2 plans.'

[46] Letter from Mouveau to Drésa (January 1912): 'Croyez en Ravel. Le fond jaune sur le plan et devant ce fond le plan vert découpé c'est tout le succès d'un décor qui sera délicieux si vous voulez bien m'en croire.' On simple hanging scenery involving a back-cloth and cut-cloths, see Vladimir Polunin, *The Continental Method of Scene Painting*, ed. Cyril W. Beaumont (London: C. W. Beaumont, 1927; repr. Dance Books, 1980), 14.

having presented the banner, on which the text of the story is inscribed, to the princess and the public, the "négrillons" will go towards the back of the stage, and will bring down – or at least, will make a show of this – the drop curtain which will come down *in front of* that of the opening décor.[47]

This process would continue for subsequent scenes, with these drop curtains raised before the finale, back in the enchanted garden. It is unclear whether these precise arrangements operated, since the remaining stage photograph, from a Théâtre des Arts performance reproduced in *Comœdia illustré* of 20 March 1913, is of the last scene (Figure 2.2). Ravel's final negotiating ploy with Drésa is to discard another idea – an ingenious 'tunnel' in which to hide Florine – about which he was less bothered and whose impracticality was presumably apparent.

Figure 2.2   Jacques Drésa's set for *Ma Mère l'Oye*, final scene (1912/13): 'Prince Charming and Sleeping Beauty in the Wood' (from *Comoedia illustré*, 20 March 1913). By permission of the Bibliothèque Nationale de France.

---

[47] Letter from Ravel to Drésa (January 1912): 'les négrillons, après avoir présenté à la princesse, et au public, la banderole sur quoi est inscrit le livre du conte, iront vers le fond, et amèneront – ou du moins, en feront le simulacre – la toile de fond qui descendra <u>devant</u> celle du 1er décor' (the emphasis is Ravel's).

Drésa too was a force to be reckoned with and, like Ravel, he moved beyond his strict brief. In correspondence with Rouché on 2 February 1912, Drésa, having watched the previous evening's performance, declares his disquiet about one aspect of the scenario.[48] The final 'apotheosis' is well managed by its performers, but the subsequent cramped appearance on stage of all other personnel, in or out of character – Petit Poucet leaping onto an armchair – 'instantly spoils' the care taken thus far. Drésa does not mince his words: 'In these circumstances, I strongly urge you to forbid *any* of the artists who are not in the last tableau to come back at the end of the show.'[49] Certainly, the extant photograph of the staged finale shows only characters actively involved (see Figure 2.2).

Substantial aesthetic accord existed between Ravel and Drésa: neither sought illusion or fake realism, but both favoured impressionistic qualities or unreality. Nevertheless, Ravel's art involves a curious paradox since his evocation of a fictitious world includes elements of highly plausible sonic mimicry: the spinning wheel, birds and meandering paths (see pp. 52–4 above). A letter from Drésa to Rouché, referring to a contemporary production of Molière's *Le Sicilien ou L'Amour peintre* acts as a manifesto for Drésa's art.[50] This document opens boldly by claiming that painting is not meant to give '*the illusion* of nature'. On the contrary, painting offers 'an *impression* of life and light' whereby a passing glimpse or sense is created of the place imagined by the artist. Drésa regards the pursuit of *trompe-l'œil* not as positively child-like but as negatively 'infantile'. Similarly, he regards replicating precise tones as 'absurd'.[51]

Part of the reason for Drésa's stance against attempts at theatrical realism is that as soon as actors or dancers come on stage, the incongruity or 'dislocation' between the living and the fake real is uncomfortably apparent. Thus faithfully copied cathedrals, or (for *Ma Mère l'Oye*) palaces or forests, would be reduced to 'lamentable parody'.[52] Another reason for Drésa's avoiding 'real' colours in his décor is that he wants to set in foreground relief the play of his vibrant, picturesque costumes. Consequently, he favours colder tones of blues and greys to help the décor recede. Interestingly, like Ravel, Drésa too specifically admires François Boucher. He finishes by describing the sort of compromise necessary in *Ma Mère l'Oye*, which is that if the plot demands a represention of foliage, then one should give 'a

[48] LAS Saglio [Drésa], 3: Pièce 19 (5) (FR, Th. des Arts, Arch. R8 (4)).

[49] Ibid.: 'Dans ces conditions je vous demande avec insistance d'interdire <u>complètement</u> le retour de <u>tous</u> les artistes qui ne sont pas du dernier tableau à la fin du spectacle' (the emphasis is Drésa's).

[50] LAS Drésa [André Saglio], 4 [4 fols, n.d.] (B-MO).

[51] LAS Drésa, 4 [fol. 1].

[52] LAS Drésa, 4 [fol. 2].

sufficient impression', which still avoids the pretence of 'a puerile attempt at simulating reality'.[53]

Examples of Drésa's work are found in photographs of the final staged scene and two watercolours from the collection of *Comœdia illustré*;[54] other small costume sketches appear in the 1912 programme. The photographed set, presumably from the subsequent performance of 5 March 1913[55] and captioned as 'Prince Charming and Sleeping Beauty in the Wood', has an impressionistic quality: delicate *pointilliste* treatment, with several arch-like structures suggested – the gaps between trees in the enchanted garden (see Figure 2.2). Its intimacy, unavoidable in the Théâtre des Arts, accords with Ravel's miniaturist aesthetic. Equally, the design's conception and scale do not dwarf the stage figures of five women and three children: two little Negro boys in plumed hats and decorative coats with sashes and ribboned cuffs and hems (more seventeenth- than eighteenth-century), and a tiny girl Cupid in headdress and tutu. Two female dancers are identified as Mlle Ariane Hugon and Mlle Henriette Quinault, and, in pantomime tradition, Prince Charming is played by a woman.[56] All costumes have a courtly grandeur: the two ladies-in-waiting are hatted and wear full-skirted dresses, with braiding at the shoulders and ribboned edging to the petticoat layers. The dancers adopt a classical symmetry: one Negro boy on the far left and one on the right, four figures across the centre – the ladies-in-waiting flanking Prince Charming and La Belle/Florine who link arms – with Prince Charming holding the hand of Cupid (in front), balanced by the Good Fairy (behind).

Drésa's cartoon-like watercolour images, catalogued as 1912, represent the draped, striped Chinese tent, with Laideronnette and Serpentin Vert beneath a large, central circular design (Figure 2.3) and a stately interior space, with double doors, ornate wall patternings and a small full-skirted female figure, presumably La Belle (Figure 2.4). Additionally, simple line drawings, signed by Drésa, are found in the 1912 programme for La Belle, Florine and one of the 'négrillons'. La Belle is depicted in a grand ensemble of a full-skirted, flouncy-sleeved dress and dramatic headdress, whereas Florine is much more girl-like with her skipping rope and modest head attire.

Drésa's achievement, and Rouché's role as catalyst, was noted implicitly by André Boll in a collected volume to which Hugard also contributed. Beyond the Diaghilev 'revolution' and the importing of foreign ideas into France,

---

[53] LAS Drésa, 4 [fol. 4].

[54] See also Roland-Manuel, *Maurice Ravel et son œuvre* (Paris: Durand, 1914), 16.

[55] See the 1912–13 listing of performances of *Ma Mère l'Oye*, *Les Aveux indiscrets* and *Le Feu* (*3ᵉ entrée des Eléments*) (FR, Th. des Arts, Arch. R 4 [fol. 18]).

[56] Since photograph captions and roles do not match, it is unclear which dancer adopts which role. Mlle Hugon danced Florine in 1912 and probably plays the equivalent 'La Belle' here. Mlle Quinault originally played La Belle, but seemingly plays Prince Charming here.

Figure 2.3   Jacques Drésa's watercolour sketch (1912) for 'Laideronnette' (from *Comoedia illustré*). By permission of the Bibliothèque Nationale de France.

one should not forget the credit due to Jacques Rouché from his direction of the Théâtre des Arts. This effort, devoted almost exclusively to dramatic works, nevertheless allowed some shows whose kinship with ballet was evident: shows such as *Ma Mère l'Oye* and *Le Sicilien, Les Dominos* and *Le Festin d'Araignée* [The Feast of the Spider].[57]

More explicitly, Raymond Cogniat was in no doubt about the 'extremely brilliant career' that awaited Drésa and his peer Dethomas.[58]

Typically, in seeking to view Ravel's music within its artistic context, it is the dance component that proves most elusive, and the work of Jeanne (Jane) Hugard 'de l'Opéra', as titled in the 1912 programme, remains the

---

[57] André Boll, 'Le décor de ballet', in *Les Spectacles à travers les âges: musique, danse* (Paris: Editions du Cygne, 1932), 265–72: 272: 'on ne saurait oublier l'apport dû à Jacques Rouché lors de sa direction au Théâtre des Arts. Cet effort, consacré presque exclusivement en faveur d'œuvres dramatiques, comportait néanmoins des spectacles dont la parenté avec le ballet était évident. Spectacles comme *Ma Mère l'Oye* et *le Sicilien, les Dominos, le Festin de l'Araignée*.' Two of these – *Le Sicilien* and *Les Dominos* – were plays with incidental music. Louis Laloy's *Les Dominos* used music by Couperin, while the ballet-pantomime *Le Festin de l'Araignée* Op. 17 was composed by Albert Roussel (1869–1937) and premiered by Grovlez on 3 April 1913.

[58] Raymond Cogniat, *Les Décorateurs de théâtre*, Cinquante ans de spectacles en France (Paris: Librairie Théâtrale, 1955), 41.

Figure 2.4 Jacques Drésa's watercolour sketch (1912) for 'Les Entretiens' (from *Comœdia illustré*). By permission of the Bibliothèque Nationale de France.

most intangible of all.[59] It is difficult to get much impression about Hugard's choreographic contribution, or even about her as a person. Most of what can be gleaned comes implicitly from contemporary reviews that consider dance and staging, but do not mention Hugard by name, or from Ravel himself who was clearly most enthusiastic about his experience of dance, as concept and practice, in his first balletic collaboration:

> I wanted everything to be danced as much as possible. Dance is an admirable art, and never have I had better insight into it than through watching Mme Hugard devise the steps. Mlle Hugon, who will play the princess, has herself found some of the most graceful figurations, amongst others a danced interpretation of 'The awakening of Sleeping Beauty in the wood', which is exquisite.[60]

---

[59] Hugard was on the Opéra payroll in 1932, and probably much earlier; see Garafola, 'Forgotten interlude', 79. Hugard is credited as playing Florine in this 1912 programme (source B).

[60] Bizet, '*Ma Mère l'Oye*': 'J'ai voulu que tout soit dansé, autant que possible. La danse est un art admirable, et jamais je ne m'en suis mieux aperçu qu'en voyant Mme Hugard régler les pas. Mlle Hugon, qui jouera la princesse, a elle-même trouvé quelques-unes des plus gracieuses, entre autres une interpretation dansée du "Réveil de la Belle au bois dormant", qui est exquise.'

Interestingly, in the same volume as Boll's essay is a chapter entitled 'Du ballet classique' by Jane Hugard.[61] Although the piece does not offer specific information about *Ma Mère l'Oye*, it allows us to gauge Hugard's approach to early twentieth-century repertory. In a damning indictment of the status quo, it calls for reform at the Opéra, so confirming the strong motivation behind the independent ventures of the Théâtre des Arts. Hugard claims that around 1900 most ballerinas had a remarkably poor musical background and were hardly familiar with basic musical notation, including rhythms or scales. Dance training was crude and inartistic: 'rhythmically, they [ballerinas] knew only the barbaric striking of the traditional stick of their ballet-masters who would try in this way to make rhythm "enter" and "leave" the feet of their *sujets* while deafening their ears. Dance thus became an art of "horse-training"'.[62] Hugard describes the humdrum existence of the girls, whose mornings consisted of exercises and endless waiting, followed by afternoon rehearsals and evening performances, day after day. She muses: 'As for dreaming about Art and about their Art? … Who would inspire within them the creation of a soul? … Not for a tinker's tuppence, our "girl from the Opéra"!'[63] And so, depressingly, there is no prospect of bettering their position from that of 'a "little rat" in a hole' ('un "petit rat" dans son trou').

Limited further insight into the dancers' perspective for *Ma Mère l'Oye* is found in the extensive memoirs of Elise Jouhandeau ('Caryathis'), the original dancer of Serpentin Vert. Jouhandeau recounts the sheer youthful joy she experienced straight after the premiere as she bumped into Rouché while crossing the wings backstage, 'still fully imbued with the fervour of her role'.[64] She also offers a personal view on interaction with Ravel, explaining how she went off to thank him for flowers received from him as a gift. For Jouhandeau, this was a 'M. Maurice Ravel, whose serious and humble face, like that of an El Greco ascetic, intimidated me. He seemed

---

[61] Jane Hugard, 'Du ballet classique: le caractère et l'évolution classique', in *Les Spectacles à travers les âges* (Paris: Editions du Cygne, 1932), 208–12. Hugard wrote works on dance (antique, religious, circus and masque), plus poetry and fiction.

[62] Ibid., 210: 'elles ne connaissaient, du rythme, que les frappements barbares du traditionnel bâton de leurs maîtres de ballet qui essayaient[,] ainsi, de faire "entrer" et "sortir" le rythme des pieds de leurs sujets en en assourdissant leurs oreilles. La danse devenait alors un art de "manège"'.

[63] Ibid., 211. 'Quant à songer à l'Art et à leur Art? … Qui aurait suscité en elles l'éclosion d'une âme? … Pas pour quatre sous romanesque, notre "demoiselle d'Opéra"!'

[64] Elise Jouhandeau, *Joies et douleurs d'une belle eccentrique*: *l'altesse des hasards* (Paris: Flammarion, 1954), 87: 'encore tout imprégnée de la ferveur de son rôle'. On Caryathis and the exotic dancer, Djemil Anik, who played the Good Fairy, see Garafola, 'Forgotten interlude', 62–4, 77.

detached from everything outside.'[65] And so one finds further corroboration of the view supporting a parallel with J. M. Barrie that Ravel could appear distant in his relationships.

Despite that perception, Ravel's stance on the collaborative process-cum-product was wholly positive, as evidenced by an effusive thank-you letter to Rouché, the dedicatee of the ballet score 'en amicale reconnaissance'. Ravel praises Rouché's modernist philosophy for 'this Théâtre des Arts, which these days, alone in France, brings us something new',[66] and expresses his unqualified joy, exceeding expectation, in having a theatre work produced just as intended. In establishing artistic relations, he invokes musical and literary metaphor: 'the sumptuous and delicate harmony' of Drésa's work acted as a commentary upon his own 'musical fantasy'. As for Hugard, Ravel perceives 'an intelligent and astute collaborator', who created sensitive, elegant work because, revealingly, she responded exactly to his instructions. Ravel's view of successful collaboration was essentially one where his conception was mirrored elsewhere, rather than perhaps a geuninely balanced partnership whose path evolved. (That Hugard was too straightlaced was opined by José Bruyr who thought her interpretation of the child-like too 'well-behaved' ('bon enfant').)[67] The excellent contributions of Grovlez and the orchestra are also recognized. A nice final touch concerns Ravel's language in thanking his performers: 'All my interpreters, children big and small, brought to their roles, however modest, an artistic conscience which delighted and profoundly touched me.'[68] There is a touch of the Peter Pan here and a clear understanding that presenting a *divertissement* on childhood themes demands as much seriousness of purpose as any adult tragedy.

The premiere and its critical reception

Although the premiere of *Ma Mère l'Oye* definitely took place within a mixed programme including Alfred de Musset's *Fantasio* and Laloy's *Les*

---

[65] Jouhandeau, *L'Altesse des hasards*, 87: 'M. Maurice Ravel, dont le visage grave et humble, comme celui d'un ascète de Greco, m'intimida. Il semblait détaché de tous les dehors.'

[66] Letter from Ravel to Rouché (1 February 1912); typed copy of autograph, B-MO: 'ce Théâtre des Arts qui, seul en France, nous apporte actuellement quelque chose de neuf'. (See Chapter 1.) Not everyone had such a positive view of this theatrical troupe, which was thought by Piot to lack discipline: see Garafola, 'Forgotten interlude', 64–5.

[67] José Bruyr, *Maurice Ravel ou le lyricisme et les sortilèges* (Paris: Editions Le Bon Plaisir, 1950), 133.

[68] Letter from Ravel to Rouché (1 February 1912): 'Tous mes interprètes, grands et petits enfants, ont apporté à leurs rôles, même modestes, une conscience artistique qui m'a ravi et profondément touché.'

Dominos at the Théâtre des Arts in the Parisian suburb of Batignolles, confusion surrounds the precise date. While the original intention was to present the premiere on Sunday 28 January 1912 – and this is the official date given on the scores and in at least one newspaper review[69] – Ravel's own testimony in a letter, documentation in the Fonds Rouché and René Bizet's interview for *L'Intransigeant*, itself dated 28 January, support Monday 29 January.[70] Ravel's letter to the singer Mme Paule de Lestang explained that unfortunately the premiere had had to be postponed by a day thereby giving him a clash of engagements; however, it is possible that a Sunday dress rehearsal effectively constituted an 'avant-première' (preview) and this may be why the earlier date has stuck.[71]

Essentially, *Ma Mère l'Oye* was afforded an enthusiastic press, with music and design highly praised and other elements more variably received. A detailed, balanced account which acts as a barometer of public opinion is provided by the eminent critic Emile Vuillermoz; a second, thought-provoking review by the composer-critic Reynaldo Hahn displays some envy and bias. By way of introduction, Vuillermoz considered that Ravel had successfully negotiated the dangers of dealing with a childhood fairy-tale topic.[72] Similarly for Hahn, who wasted no love on Ravel,[73] this issue was well handled by his fellow composer even if he could not resist a little jibe at Rouché's theatre: 'nothing is less naive, less childish, less "Stories of Mother Goose" than this attractive ballet of M. Ravel, put on by M. Drésa and presented … in a little temple consecrated to decadence'.[74] '[T]he essential principle', Hahn noted with implicit superiority, 'is to

---

[69] 'Le septième concert d'abonnement' [undated newspaper clipping], FM (BNF Mus).

[70] Letter from Ravel to Mme Paule de Lestang (26 January 1912), in Orenstein (ed.), *A Ravel Reader*, 129. Within 'Lettres de lancement–programmes 1910–13', a typed schedule for the Théâtre des Arts, 1910–13, states unequivocally 29 January for *Ma Mère l'Oye* (FR, Th. des Arts, Arch. R4 [fols. 13/14]).

[71] See Louis Peltier, 'Avant-première': Dossier d'œuvre, *Ma Mère l'Oye* (B-MO). Undated letters to Rouché (LAS Grovlez, 1; LAS Grovlez, 4) reveal that the use of many deputizing musicians in the matinée (because of concert clashes) necessitated an extra Sunday morning rehearsal. If Rouché could not grant this, Grovlez could accept no responsibility for the consequences. This correspondence may explain the postponement. (An earlier letter from Grovlez to Rouché (5 January 1912) discusses the 'amusing' possibility of Ravel and Schmitt appearing on the same playbill in February 1912; see too Chapter 4.)

[72] Emile Vuillermoz, 'Les Théâtres: *Ma Mère l'Oye.–La Lépreuse*', *Revue musicale de la S.I.M.* (15 February 1912), 55–9: 56.

[73] Marnat, *Maurice Ravel*, 327.

[74] Reynaldo Hahn, review in *Comœdia* (2 February 1912): 'rien n'est moins naïf, moins enfantin, moins "Contes de Ma mère l'Oye" que ce joli ballet de M. Maurice Ravel, monté par M. Drésa et donné … dans un petit temple consacré à la décadence.'

obtain, through complication, quasi-childish effects of simplicity'.[75] Drésa would doubtless have taken issue with this, although Hahn admitted that everything was undertaken tastefully 'to avoid anything that smacked of crude theatrical mirages'. For Vuillermoz, Drésa's achievement was clear-cut: 'The decorative part of the spectacle is of a refined nature ... Drésa dazzled us.'[76]

With a certain canny insight, Hahn saw 'Ravel the musician' as aesthetically slightly at odds with 'Ravel the librettist' and Drésa. His comments marry up with the paradox, identified earlier, of Ravel's literalism within fantasy: 'Imitation, banished from the theatrical illusion, continuously drives the orchestra ... If there is excessive simplicity in the staging, there is perhaps in the orchestration an excess of minutiae and "pointillism".'[77] Hahn had to concede, however, Ravel's genius for special sonorities that were 'seductive', 'fertile' and inventive. For Vuillermoz, the matter was once more unequivocal: 'Musically, *Ma Mère l'Oye* is a complete delight.'[78] A critic for the *Monde musical* added weight to the argument expressed earlier about how much the liberated orchestral music gains over the piano original; he appreciated the literal use of 'les bois' for the 'Pavane of Sleeping Beauty in the woods', plus harmonics and glissandos, and upheld a composer's right to transform his work.[79]

As for Ravel's 'vague', 'mundane' scenario, Vuillermoz understandably thought this of a lesser order than the music. He also harboured reservations about the choreographic dimension ('la réalisation plastique'), and thus implicitly about Hugard, fearing that Rouché's reaction against theatrical convention equated to a loss of professionalism:

His [Rouché's] very legitimate disdain of cold technique, of classical dance, leads him instinctively to call on the impulsiveness of an unsophisticated amateurism which has its charm at times but which cannot be applied more widely without damage. Doubtless this approach is very well-bred, the scorn for the polish of the professionals and their servile adherence to rhythm and metre is

---

[75] Ibid.: 'le principe essentiel est d'obtenir, par la complication, des effets de simplicité quasi puérile'.

[76] Vuillermoz, 'Les Théâtres', 57: 'La partie décorative du spectacle est d'un art raffiné. ... Drésa nous a éblouis.' In 'Avant-première', Louis Peltier commented perceptively on Drésa's contrasting of cold and warm colours, and his introduction of black, in Japanese style.

[77] Hahn, *Comœdia* review: 'L'imitation, bannie de l'illusion théâtrale, anime sans répit l'orchestre ... S'il y a excès de simplicité dans la mise en scène, peut-être y a-t-il, dans l'orchestration, un excès de minutie et de "pointillisme".'

[78] Vuillermoz, 'Les Théâtres', 56: 'Musicalement *Ma Mère l'Oye* est un ravissement complet.'

[79] A. M., '*Ma Mère l'Oye* de Maurice Ravel au Théâtre des Arts', *Monde musical* (15 February 1912).

positively aristocratic, but, really, some of the house performers are too blue-blooded. They do pile it on![80]

The correspondent for the *Monde musical* was more equivocal, invoking the topical Jean d'Udine, a free-thinking eurhythmic enthusiast after Emile-Jaques Dalcroze who influenced Caryathis: 'As for knowing whether this ballet is "danceable", whether M. Ravel danced it before writing it, ask Jean d'Udine what he thinks about it.'[81]

In performance, the musical coup was well secured by Grovlez who held, according to Vuillermoz, the 'magician's wand' of Ravel, and by the orchestra's polished performance of a difficult score. For the general public, the dancing of Hugon and other attractive dancers and mime-artists, together with the costumes and sets, was seen to offer 'a perceptible pleasure'; moreover, all these main interpreters (Hugon, Anik, Caryathis, Couperant, Quinault, Delaunay and Sandrini) were felt to have properly understood and implemented Ravel's ideas.[82] In short, *Ma Mère l'Oye* had found 'universal favour' and constituted 'the triumph of the elegant, aristocratic, smiling and slightly ironic art of Ravel'.[83]

Selected later productions (Leyritz and Bolender)

Subsequent productions of *Ma Mère l'Oye* occurred during the First and Second World Wars. These included a matinée on 11 March 1915 at the Palais du Trocadéro,[84] still conducted by Grovlez. On this occasion, choreography was not by Hugard but by Staats, who returned with Rouché to the

---

[80] Vuillermoz, 'Les Théâtres', 57. 'Son dédain, très légitime, de la froide technique, de la danse classique l'a conduit tout naturellement à faire appel au primesaut d'un amateurisme ingénu qui a parfois son charme mais qui ne saurait se généraliser sans dommage. Sans doute ce parti-pris est de bonne compagnie, ce mépris du professionel à grand air et dédaigner d'obéir servilement au rhythme et à la mesure est assez grand seigneur, mais, vraiment, certains interprètes de la maison ont le sang trop bleu. Ils exagèrent!' Nijinsky's wonderfully ambiguous response was reputedly: 'It's like dancing at a family-party.' (Alexis Roland-Manuel, *Maurice Ravel*, trans. Cynthia Jolly (London: Dobson, 1947), 65.)

[81] A. M., '*Ma Mère l'Oye*'. 'Quant à savoir si ce ballet est "dansant", si M. Ravel l'a dansé avant de l'écrire, demandez à Jean d'Udine ce qu'il en pense.' See for instance Jean d'Udine, 'Lettre ouverte à M. Albert Bertelin', *Le Courrier musical*, 15/3 (1 February 1912), 62–7, and Garafola's account in 'Forgotten interlude', 62. Vuillermoz, 'Les Théâtres', 56, also alludes to 'cette mystérieuse gymnastique'.

[82] A. M., '*Ma Mère l'Oye*'; Peltier, 'Avant-première'.

[83] Vuillermoz, 'Les Théâtres', 56, 57: 'le triomphe de l'art élégant, aristocratique, souriant et un peu ironique de Ravel'.

[84] *Deuxième Matinée, Théâtre National de l'Opéra* (11 March 1915), Carton 2238 (Rouché gift, B-MO).

Opéra, officially assuming the post of 'maître de ballet' in late 1915.[85] Once more, the roles of Prince Charming and Serpentin Vert were taken by women: Mlle G. Franck and Mlle Delsaux respectively, while La Bête was played by M. Raymond. Mlle Barbier, previously a maid of honour, was La Belle. As before, minor changes are apparent in the scenario for this performance, which was reproduced in the programme. (In the later 1920s, Ninette de Valois was instrumental in bringing *Beauty and the Beast* to England and Ireland: see Appendix.) On 11 June 1942, during the Occupation of Paris, the Opéra-Comique put on a production by Ravel's artist friend Léon Leyritz (whose *Boléro* had appeared at the Opéra in December 1941; see Chapter 7), with choreography by Constantin Tcherkas and conducted by Roger Désormière. Leyritz created white and gold gouache designs for various accessories (Sleeping Beauty's bed and footstool and the spinning wheel); costume designs are preserved for the seven children of 'Petit Poucet', the Pagodines in 'Laideronnette' and for Beauty and the Beast.[86] Additionally, watercolour sketches remain to illustrate the fixed scenery and three drop curtains ('rideaux volants'), in the spirit of Ravel's intentions, together with a photograph of the staged scene (Figure 2.5).[87] This photograph captures Leyritz's set in action framed by three imposing columns, beneath one of which sleeps the Princess on a simple bed. At the rear hangs a dark backcloth of high trees with a palatial château depicted to the viewer's right; meanwhile in the foreground, children wander around looking up in perplexed bewilderment.

In the United States, *Mother Goose* was created by Todd Bolender (b. 1914) for the American Concert Ballet in 1943, with a new version of the *Mother Goose Suite* presented by the newly founded New York City Ballet at the City Center of Music and Drama on 1 November 1948. John Martin was captivated by this 'completely enchanting little work, characterized by delicacy of imagination and beautiful taste'.[88] To save funds, attractive costumes designed by Derain some time earlier for a work of Balanchine were recycled, but seemingly to good effect.[89] Bolender returns to the original

---

[85] Garafola, 'Forgotten interlude', 62.

[86] A poster bill, accessory and costume designs are preserved at the B-MO (Esq. O.C. 1942; D. 216, O.C. 4.).

[87] This 'photo de scène (Le Petit Poucet)' of Leyritz's décor is referenced as Opéra-Comique, 1942, in Lesure and Nectoux (eds), *Maurice Ravel*, 33 and elsewhere (but is captioned as Opéra, 1939, in the file Ravel (M) 1, BNF Mus). Another stage photograph, dated 1942, appears in Cogniat, *Les Décorateurs de théâtre*, 96. On built scenery consisting of angled 'flats', see Polunin, *The Continental Method of Scene Painting*, 1.

[88] John Martin, 'City Ballet unit gives 2 novelties: new version of Bolender work and a Balanchine selection', *New York Times* (2 November 1948).

[89] Nancy Reynolds, 'Listening to Balanchine', in Garafola with Foner (eds), *Dance for a City*, 153–68: 160, 220 n. 5.

Figure 2.5   Léon Leyritz's staged set for *Ma Mère l'Oye*: 'Petit Poucet' (Opéra-Comique, 1942). By permission of the Bibliothèque Nationale de France.

suite formula and links the episodes by means of 'a middle-aged woman, "The Spectator", who sits in a corner of her drawing room and remembers herself as a young girl' – a device similar to that later employed by Robbins (see pp. 38–9 above). This non-dancing role was strongly played by Beatrice Tompkins. In fact, Martin suggests, Bolender's interpretation conveys more a nostalgic memory of youth itself than any particulars of *Mother Goose*. In addition, youthful lovers congregate in the garden and a new exoticism enters with an 'Oriental Prince'. A special highlight is secured by the climactic unmasking of the Beast. Bolender works in a sensitive, subtle way that maintains the necessary 'vitality'; he and Marie-Jeanne, as the young girl, skilfully avoid 'that tenuous sentimentality that so often reduces these fragile Ravel items to meaninglessness'.[90] Such efforts were well supported by the other leading performers and musically by the orchestra under Leon Barzin.

Postlude: *L'Enfant et les sortilèges*

Although this hybrid work, premiered in Monte Carlo on 21 March 1925, is more opera than ballet – since its sung text by Colette is crucial – it remains an important contribution to the dance repertory. Here Ravel returns to the theme of childhood (as he would do once more with his contribution to *L'Eventail de Jeanne* – see Chapter 6), but there is a marked contrast between the innocent, carefree, prewar *Ma Mère l'Oye* and the tougher, neoclassically parodistic, postwar *Enfant*. The two-part *Enfant*, totalling fifty minutes, is approximately twice the size of its sibling piece and required a compositional gestation of five years in contrast to the swift balletic incarnation of *Ma Mère l'Oye*.[91] Both works interpolate characterizations of the waltz – another important theme in Ravel's œuvre, to be extensively discussed in Chapters 4–5 – but *L'Enfant* demonstrates a significant progression: compare the early Satie-esque 'Les Entretiens' with the extended 'Tempo di Valse lente' (Fig. 105). While both serve to develop their respective dramatic situations, the fluidity, mood changes and wry sophistication of the latter example are remarkable: the drawled American inflection of The Dragonfly (Example 2.9; Fig. 107), the Bat's crazy speeding waltz with flapping wings (Fig. 113), parodistic hints of *La Mer* for tree frogs emerging from a small-

---

[90] Marie-Jeanne's superb performance was firmly endorsed by J. M., 'City Ballet does Balanchine work: Troupe in first performance of *Divertimento* – Bolender *Mother Goose* offered', *New York Times* (3 November 1948).

[91] The vocal score MS (75 pp.), marked 'divers lieux 1920–25' is held in the ROLC, and the orchestral MS (164 pp.) in the Carlton Lake Collection, HRC. Durand published both versions in 1925.

Example 2.9 *L'Enfant et les sortilèges* (ballet, 1925): 'Danse des Libellules' (Fig. 107, reduction)

scale cousin 'la mare' ('the pond'; Fig. 117), self-parody reminiscing on ghostly wisps of *La Valse* in the 'Dance of the Tree Frogs' (Fig. 122^{+5}) and the languorous apotheosis (Fig. 132) as The Child with his caged Squirrel experiences loneliness amid the wildlife.

A thorough study of the multi-dimensional *L'Enfant* would be worthy of a small book in its own right; the present discussion is necessarily more circumscribed and will confine itself to three salient figures in the work's history: Colette, Balanchine and Kylián. Despite Ravel's apparent thriving on the interaction for *Ma Mère l'Oye*, he was revealed in *L'Enfant* as a much less communicative partner. As Richard Langham Smith comments, 'It would be nice to think of text and music in *L'Enfant* as one of the great collaborations of the 1920s; in fact it was rather the reverse.'[92] Ravel had first encountered Colette during the Belle Epoque at one of the lavish cultural soirées held by Mme René de Saint-Marceaux, where he reputedly played for Isadora Duncan, but for Colette the composer remained reserved, fitting the image that Caryathis had conveyed: 'Could I say that I really knew my illustrious collaborator, the composer of *L'Enfant et les sortilèges*? … Looking for attention, he feared criticism … Perhaps secretly timid, Ravel maintained a distant manner, a dry tone.'[93] Colette remarks on Ravel's appearance: the ties that Jourdan-Morhange remembered,[94] the copious hair and sideburns that exaggerated his large head in comparison with his slight body; shades once again of Peter Pan, Barrie and social awkwardness.

In 1915 Rouché, ever the catalyst, had requested a libretto for what Colette termed a 'féerie-ballet' (fairytale ballet),[95] which astonishingly she produced in little over a week, breaking off temporarily from *Chéri*. Roughly contemporary with *Ma Mère l'Oye*, Colette's theatrical enthusiasms had also involved sexually explicit dance routines in Parisian shows, such as *La Chair*. Rouché had mentioned Ravel as a possible collaborator, while underlining that he could not be hurried. In practice, owing to the war, his emotional crisis following his mother's death in 1917 and prior commitments, Ravel did not begin work until 1920. Meantime, Colette felt 'a hermetic silence'; she wondered whether Ravel was working and tried to comprehend

---

[92] Langham Smith, 'Ravel's operatic spectacles', 201. For a detailed introduction to Colette, despite a slip about the musical ending of *L'Enfant*, see Judith Thurman, *Secrets of the Flesh: A Life of Colette* (London: Bloomsbury, 1999).

[93] Colette, 'Un salon de musique en 1900', in Colette et al., *Ravel par quelques-uns de ses familiers* (Paris: Editions du Tambourinaire, 1939), 115–24: 115–20. 'Puis-je dire que j'ai vraiment connu, mon collaborateur illustre, l'auteur de *L'Enfant et les sortilèges*? … Recherchant l'attention, il craignait la critique … Peut-être secrètement timide, Ravel gardait un air distant, un ton sec.'

[94] In the 1930s especially, Jourdan-Morhange ('Moune') acted effectively as an intermediary between her beloved Ravel and Colette, with whom she was also very close. See Thurman, *Secrets of the Flesh*, 376.

[95] Colette, 'Un salon de musique', 120.

his internalized creative process: 'the slow frenzy which possessed and isolated him, unconcerned with the hours and days'.[96]

Mechanical hitches compounded the problem: Ravel did not receive Colette's libretto before 1918 since his first copy was lost in the wartime post.[97] In February 1919, he explained to Rouché that he needed to contact Colette about her 'danced opera', but had lost his address book![98] A week later he duly apologized to Colette for being 'such a faltering collaborator'; more positively, he sought modifications: extending the squirrel's dialogue and incorporating ragtime and black American references for the Teapot. Colette encouraged these ideas and complimented Ravel on *Ma Mère l'Oye*, but she still referred to the new project by its provisional title, *Divertissement pour ma fille*, inspired by her young Bel-Gazou. Ravel countered that since he had no daughter this would not do and so, as a fundamental change, the Child became masculine although the mezzo-soprano role is still sung/danced by a female, simulating pantomime tradition. One small detail concerned the precise sounds for the duetting Cats, Ravel in all seriousness deliberating the merits of 'mouain' over 'mouaô',[99] though in practice he explored a range of subtly modulating inflections.

Apart from a light-hearted, appreciative letter from Ravel of 16 March 1925, preceding the premiere, this was about it, and so Colette – who had never heard any music before the opening night – could not help feeling offended, even though she had already gained an idea of Ravel's character and composition methods.[100] Ravel may have found working with such a high-powered, sexually extrovert and adventurous woman as Colette off-putting; equally, he may have felt that being presented with a long-finished libretto of a first-rate novelist amounted to a *fait accompli*. Yet for all their differences, these contemporary modernists shared affinities for childhood fantasy, nature and feeling, such that curious telepathic forces shaped the work: 'Ravel and Colette ... shared a private wavelength.'[101]

For the young Balanchine, *L'Enfant* also marked the first contact with Ravel's music that would lead to a new interpretation of *La Valse* in 1951 and the centennial balletic extravaganza with the New York City Ballet in 1975. For *L'Enfant* alone, this phenomenally productive choreographer of

---

[96] Ibid., 121: 'la lente frénésie qui le possédait et le tenait isolé, insoucieux des jours et des heures.'

[97] Orenstein, *Ravel: Man and Musician*, 78.

[98] Letter from Ravel to Rouché (20 February 1919), in Orenstein (ed.), *Maurice Ravel: lettres*, 171. The genre has evolved into 'l'opéra-dansé'.

[99] Colette, 'Un salon de musique', 121.

[100] Even students such as Roland-Manuel never saw Ravel compose, although they sometimes saw him orchestrate; see Barbara L. Kelly, 'Maurice Ravel', in *The New Grove Dictionary of Music and Musicians*, ed. Stanley Sadie, 29 vols (London: Macmillan, 2/2001), vol. XV, 864–78: 868.

[101] Thurman, *Secrets of the Flesh*, 340.

legendary status would create four interpretations across his career, accepting that most credit for the initial concept was due to Raoul Gunsbourg.[102] Balanchine's presence as the new ballet-master for the Ballets Russes from January 1925, superseding Nijinska, also preserved an indirect link between Ravel and Diaghilev after their estrangement over *La Valse* in 1920. Charles Joseph explains that 'During his first year with the company, he [Balanchine] produced a dozen ballets for opera productions, including Ravel's *L'Enfant et les sortilèges*'; Ravel's participation at the piano for some rehearsals was recalled by Alexandra Danilova.[103]

Interaction between sung and danced parts in *L'Enfant* is complex and has varied from one production to another. The Dragonfly, for instance, is a sung part, but in the first production it was complemented by a group of four dancing Dragonflies. The Squirrel and the Shepherd and Shepherdess also manifested themselves doubly: their danced personas included the illustrious Danilova and Tcherkas, who went on to choreograph *Ma Mère l'Oye*.[104] Meanwhile, the role of the Ashes, 'grey, undulating, mute' (Fig. 48), toying with the vociferous Fire, was danced by the young Alicia Markova. Interplay between dance and sung text enabled, at least theoretically, the creation of visually captivating groups of dancers whose collective 'voice' could be projected by a solo singer: a feature developed in Balanchine's 1946 production.

Lightness of approach was crucial in transporting the spectator to a world of childhood, and this facet was intrinsic to Balanchine's choreographic style, as de Valois explained: 'The quality he could put into an opera ballet was absolutely extraordinary. But he was always very funny. He took … all the opera ballets as a huge joke; he wasn't the least bit pompous.'[105] Kochno also believed that Balanchine preserved a childish aspect within his personality.[106] Dance and humour combined to secure the magic of a child's view:

---

[102] [Balanchine,] *Choreography by* George Balachine, 347.

[103] Joseph, *Stravinsky and Balanchine*, 47; Buckle, *George Balanchine*, 33. On Diaghilev and *L'Enfant*, see also Chapter 5, n. 11.

[104] According to [Balanchine,] *Choreography by George Balanchine*, 72, dancers were first credited in a programme of 15 February 1926. This same source carries a synopsis of *L'Enfant*: 'A naughty child, confined to his room, smashes the teapot, mistreats his pet squirrel, tears the wallpaper, assaults the fireplace, the clock, his school books. The objects come to life, assert themselves, rebuke him. Transported into a magic garden, the child is confronted by animals and trees that in the past have suffered from his cruelties; they attack him. During the fray a small squirrel is injured; moved to compassion, the child dresses its wound. The animals are astonished; when in despair the child cries out for his mother, they assist him, and lead him to her.'

[105] John Drummond, *Speaking of Diaghilev* (London and Boston: Faber & Faber, 1997), 224–5. Although the prefix 'opera-' generally raises a work's status, for some it has a diminishing effect.

[106] Buckle, *George Balanchine*, 33.

inanimate objects coming to life, the illusion of fecund flying night-life projected by flightless human dancers – realizations of the impossible.[107] Moved
by the premiere, Colette observed Ravel's different reaction: 'The moonlit
brilliance of the garden, the flight of the dragonflies and of the bats … "It's
amusing, isn't it?" said Ravel' (Example 2.9; Fig. 107).[108] And so the two
male creators donned their pleasurable Peter Pan hats. This fantasy image is
beautifully preserved in a photograph of Ravel dwarfed by the masked and
winged female dragonflies on either side of him (Figure 2.6).

Balanchine's next version of 20 November 1946, for the Ballet Society,
New York, worked with a translation of the libretto entitled *The Spellbound
Child*, by Lincoln Kirstein and Jane Barzin; Barzin's husband Leon conducted.[109] Although the Child was apparently sung and danced by a single
male, Joseph Connolly, most roles were doubly performed with a dancer on
stage and the singer in the orchestral pit. Such concealed singing had its
source in score designations such as 'behind the stage' for the chorus of
Tree Frogs (Fig. 101). But inevitably the logistics of dealing with a large
cast and Colette's giant personified objects on a very shallow stage caused
difficulties, as Bolender and Buckle observed.[110] In the penultimate interpretation (supported by Jerome Robbins), presented on 15 May 1975 within
the Ravel Festival by the New York City Ballet and conducted by Ravel's
best-known pupil Manuel Rosenthal, a similar fusion was achieved by the
dancers and six off-stage singers. Once more, the title role was danced and
sung by a single male performer, Paul Offenkranz.[111] Subsequently, to overcome some staging problems a dedicated televised version of *The Spellbound
Child*, in Catherine Wolff's translation, was broadcast on 25 May 1981.
This version was directed and produced by Emile Ardolino and Judy Kinberg
for the PBS series 'Dance in America'. The film was rehearsed in New York

---

[107] For more illusion in *L'Enfant*, see Carolyn Abbate, 'Outside Ravel's tomb', *Journal of
the American Musicological Society*, 52/3 (Fall 1999), 465–530: 515.

[108] Colette, 'Un salon de musique', 122: 'L'éclat lunaire du jardin, le vol des libellules et
des chauves-souris … "N'est-ce pas, c'est amusant?" disait Ravel.' The many reviews from
February 1926 (FM: France–Compositeurs: Ravel, BNF Mus) say little about choreography:
'M Génin chante et danse agréablement le fox-trot' and, confusingly, 'Sous l'ingénieuse
direction de Mme Virard, le corps de ballet bondit, tournoie et se livre à des véritables prou-
esses clownesques' (Henry Malherbe, 'Chronique musicale, *L'Enfant et les sortilèges*',
Le Temps (3 February 1926)). Doubts as to whether Balanchine choreographed the premiere
have been countered by recollections of Danilova and Markova (Alice Marks); see Buckle,
George Balanchine, 338n.

[109] [Balanchine,] *Choreography by George Balanchine*, 174. Tanaquil LeClercq danced
the Princess prior to her success in the leading role of *La Valse*; similarly, Barbara Karinska
executed the costumes for both works.

[110] Buckle, *George Balanchine*, 161–2.

[111] [Balanchine,] *Choreography by George Balanchine*, 268.

Figure 2.6   Ravel and two dragonflies from *L'Enfant et les sortilèges*
(Eugene Steinhof production, Vienna, 1929; from *L'Art vivant*,
1 May 1929). By permission of the Bibliothèque Nationale de
France.

and shot in Nashville, Tennessee, where special effects were introduced,
with animation to push forward the narrative.[112] Choreography was by
Balanchine in association with Kermit Love, who also took responsibility
for designs, costumes and puppets.[113] Dancers from the New York City

---

[112] Buckle, *George Balanchine*, 306.
[113] [Balanchine,] *Choreography by George Balanchine*, 281. For a photograph of
Balanchine with puppets, see the George Balanchine Foundation website: http://balanchine.

Ballet joined forces with students of the School of American Ballet; as before, the singers were concealed. Manuel Rosenthal conducted the orchestra.

Finally, the Czech-born Jiří Kylián (b. 1947), an exceptional choreographer of the next generation, offers an ingenious and wholly engaging danced account of *L'Enfant*.[114] Already explicit in the score at several points, such as the 'stuffy and grotesque dance' in laboured Bachian style for two chairs (Fig. 17), or the 'Ballet of little characters, who express, through dancing, the sorrow of not being able to join up again' for the pastoral figures torn off the wallpaper (Fig. 56), dance is here writ large, with the result that one realizes how eminently danceable is Ravel's whole score and how vividly dance befits childhood imagination. After all, children love to dance and hate to sit still.

So the Armchair and Easy Chair sidle up, pop out their heads, manœuvre lazily on wheels, and embrace as they play out their precious, mock-Baroque musical antics. Dance clinches this grotesque humour. And the eclecticism of Kylián's dance movements complements Ravel's own musical eclecticism,[115] while his suppleness of invention enhances a full range of musico-dramatic situations: comedy, contests, fantasy, a gathering of multicoloured exotic tree frogs, flying insects, a fireplace of flickering flames. Similarly, it seals the expression of diverse emotions: the Child's anger and defiance (with percussive dance counterpoint of stamping and table-banging; Figs 2–3),[116] his empathy with the Princess (fluid emulative movements), his fear as supernatural forces run out of control (enclosed body language), the voluptuousness of mating cats (acrobatic rolling, intertwining). Ingenuity of staging is demonstrated by a multipurpose device: a bell-shaped lattice cage functions as a whalebone skirt for a monstrous, tyrannical Mother, as the Squirrel's and later the Child's prison, more playfully as a climbing-frame,

---

org/06/index.html (accessed 29 March 2004).

[114] Maurice Ravel, *L'Enfant et les sortilèges*; libretto by Colette, choreography/staging by Jiří Kylián, performed by the Nederlands Dans Theater (Virgin Classics [VHS video, VVD 382], 1986; RM Arts/BBC/WDR [DVD], 2001). 51 minutes' duration; educational use only.

[115] Carolyn Abbate considers Ravel's wide-ranging allusive styles that animate 'dead' objects, rather like the Child's broken toys, as contributing to a kind of *tombeau*. But although adults simulating playing with toys fits neatly with a Peter Pan image, the *tombeau* idea overplays the extent to which these styles were ever 'real'. See Abbate, 'Outside Ravel's tomb', 473.

[116] The Child is played by Marly Knoben. His/her musical defiance may be inferred from the opening harmonic solecisms in irregular metre (recast from Act II of the unfinished *La Cloche engloutie*): empty triads missing their thirds, consecutive fifths and second inversions (bare fourths). These incomplete constructions also convey expectancy and a certain primitivism.

a dancing roundabout and, thrown on its side, as a cradle for Squirrel and Child. Additionally, the use of masks for the Prince, for the manic maths figures and for the insects accords well with Ravel's fondness for disguise.

While Kylián's interpretation is weird and witty and is strongly supported by John Macfarlane's scenery and vibrant costumes, by turns translucent and lustrous, the musical performance supplied by the Parisian Orchestre National and Choeur de la RTF, conducted by Lorin Maazel, is also exemplary. Together, they secure the most exquisite melting into the nocturnal Garden Scene (Fig. 100). As with *Ma Mère l'Oye*, astonishing sonorities can be achieved in performance, and Maazel succeeds in maximizing the impact of Ravel's imaginative percussion: the swanee whistle ('flûte à coulisse') to depict the owl, magical harp harmonics and wind-machine rustlings.[117] Maazel also fully exploits Ravel's notated vocal effects:

Example 2.10 *L'Enfant et les sortilèges*: exotic incantation of the Tree Frogs (Fig. 110⁺³, reduction)

---

[117] Elsewhere Ravel requires the rare 'luthéal', a celesta, whip, wood-block, cranked rattle, and even a cheese-grater!

the menacing, nasal incantation of the tropical Tree Frogs (Example 2.10; Fig. [101] 110), the Trees' portamentos (Fig. 104) and the primitive and awesome bestial cries (Fig. 136⁻³), anticipating *Boléro*, which are transformed at the revelatory point into quasi-religious half-spoken chant (Fig. 140).[118] Such extraordinary sound-worlds realized through performance look forward, sometimes to electronic sound, at other times to the elemental primitivism of Carl Orff's *Carmina Burana* (first heard in 1937, the year of Ravel's death).

For opera purists this danced interpretation may have overstepped its mark and subjugated its singers, who once again are invisible, creating the effect of a voice-over, film soundtrack or disembodied Greek chorus in its own dimension of space. But *L'Enfant* is not pure opera; it is a fluid genre that leaves interpretative scope for maximizing either the balletic or the operatic, or for steering a middle course.[119] Where dance is maximized, the spectator does not usually expect to see the orchestral musicians so why not adopt a similar policy for the singers? Ravel had already sanctioned off-stage singing. (Conversely, Kylián's recent ballet *One of a Kind*, given in Paris on 6 February 1999, enjoys confounding this expectation with a blend of taped and live music performed on stage.) Kylián's approach is compelling in its clean presentation of visual movement (generally inaudible) combined with sound (invisible throughout); most importantly, his creative imagination is wholly sympathetic to and supportive of Ravel's aesthetic of childhood fantasy.

Although dance was deemed to be the weak element in the premiere of *Ma Mère l'Oye*, both these evocations of childhood gain from the three dimensions of a staged performance. Ravel's sumptuous orchestral scores are enhanced by design and dance, especially in Kylián's delicious interpretation of *L'Enfant*. Where opera is concerned, it would be sacrilegious to ask whether the music was enhanced or diminished in staged production since it is accepted that the whole exists only as an integrated work-concept. One might do well to remember this when listening to an abstracted suite of ballet music.

---

[118] On the animals' achievement of speech, see Abbate, 'Outside Ravel's tomb', 512.

[119] The latter policy was evident in an Opera North production during May 2002, featuring a talented young mezzo-soprano, Claire Wild, as the Child, choreography by Amir Hosseinpour and staging by Nigel Lowery; its most controversial aspect was the cats' raping of the Child. *L'Enfant* continues to thrive at the Opéra, with a revival of the 1998 production coupled by Zemlinsky, *Der Zwerg* (The Dwarf) presented on 24 October 2001. Gaële Le Roi played the Child with Felicity Palmer as Mother and musical direction by James Conlon.

Chapter 3

Greekness and myth in
Daphnis et Chloé

Daphnis et Chloé (1909–12) was one of Ravel's grandest compositional undertakings and an undeniable musical *chef d'œuvre:*[1] a one-act ballet in three scenes lasting more than 50 minutes and featuring a large orchestra with magnificent percussion, a chorus and lavish visual tableaux. Although best known in its orchestral suite format and notated first – as was Ravel's norm – in piano score, *Daphnis* was commissioned by Diaghilev and the Ballets Russes[2] and envisaged from the start as ballet. The 1912 programme classified it as a 'symphonie chorégraphique': solo dances alternate with more extended *corps de ballet* sections commenting, chorus-like, on the main action, and leitmotif-type treatment identifies characters and situations. If the result is a narrative ballet arguably a little short on dramatic action, *Daphnis* has nevertheless enjoyed varied balletic interpretation across the decades of its existence.

This venture was undoubtedly Ravel's most high-profile collaboration, yet it was not without almost catastrophic setbacks and angst. The issue of averting unsatisfactory endings is echoed in the work itself, with both Ravel and the choreographer, Fokine, struggling to achieve the bacchanalian conclusion. In turn, the frenzied ending of *Daphnis* represents the beginning of a large-scale trajectory of increasingly destructive music–dance endings, taken up again in *La Valse* and finally *Boléro*.[3] While coverage here

---

[1] As early as 1925, Goddard asserted that 'In the large expanse of *Daphnis and Chloé* there is not one [orchestral] effect that fails'. (Scott Goddard, 'Maurice Ravel, some notes on his orchestral method', *Music & Letters*, 6 (1925), 291–303: 291.)

[2] In comparison with the positive experience of *Ma Mère l'Oye*, the collaborative process with Diaghilev and the Ballets Russes was often a difficult one. Notwithstanding these tensions, Ravel also orchestrated music for Ballets Russes-related projects before and after the First World War: Musorgsky's *Khovanshchina*, re-orchestrated jointly with Stravinsky in 1913; sections of Schumann's *Carnaval* and Chopin's music used in *Les Sylphides* for Nijinsky's troupe in 1914; and Chabrier's *Menuet pompeux* in 1919 (see Chapter 7).

[3] Jankélévitch expresses this powerfully: 'dance, that is to say stagnation, movement on the spot, the whirling action, which, instead of being unleashed on the world, surges back on itself, finds its finality within itself'. (Vladimir Jankélévitch, *Ravel* (Paris: Editions Rieder, 1939; Editions du Seuil, ed. Jean-Michel Nectoux, 3/1995), 156.)

concentrates upon the premiere, the more successful Opéra production of 1921 (still involving Fokine) is also included, together with the English inflection achieved through the Ashton/John Craxton production of 1951, starring Margot Fonteyn. The balletic identity of *Daphnis* also enables one to take on board art of the stature of Chagall in his 1958–9 productions with Lifar and George Skibine.

Within a context of late nineteenth- and early twentieth-century Atticism in the arts, special treatment is given to differing creative and interpretative views on the portrayal of Greek legend, whether literal, archaic, imaginary, or filtered through an eighteenth-century lens. Essentially, the mixture comprises classicism and opulent exoticism.[4] As a connected concern, the classical dramatic idea of emotional and character antitheses is revisited.

Underpinning this agenda is an issue of elusiveness: in portraying Greek myth, the balletic origins of *Daphnis* become ironically the source of myth and mystery themselves. As Lynn Garafola has confided, '*Daphnis et Chloé* is a most mysterious ballet. We know a certain amount about it, mainly related to Ravel, but very little about what it looked like choreographically or how it was danced.'[5] On the one hand, all Ravel's ballets present as jigsaws with significant missing pieces so that one should be careful not to overstate this specific instance: the star-studded cast of *Daphnis* has ensured better documentation than for more unsung collaborations. On the other hand, mystery is intrinsic; in the Symbolist spirit of synaesthesia, *Daphnis* explores correspondences between the real world and dream-like imagination, between the mortal coil and immortal world of the gods, between natural and supernatural, *trompe l'œil* and *trompe l'oreille* (see too Chapter 5). The French critic Danielle Cohen-Lévinas considers equivalence, mimesis and morphology in *Daphnis* to the extent that the piece – especially its music – appears as a semblance of, or substitution for, itself: 'The work no longer offers a definitive face, but rather its likeness.'[6] Simon Morrison also considers *Daphnis* as a 'lost work' or 'missing ballet'.[7] Certainly, its

---

[4] For a reading that highlights exoticism and fragility, see Lawrence Kramer, 'Consuming the exotic: Ravel's *Daphnis and Chloe*', in *Classical Music and Postmodern Knowledge* (Berkeley: University of California Press, 1995), 201–25.

[5] Personal correspondence (6 February 2003). On the problematics of seeking to reconstruct the past, see Drummond, *Speaking of Diaghilev*, Part I: *The Project*.

[6] Danielle Cohen-Lévinas, '*Daphnis et Chloé* ou la danse du simulacre', *Musical*, 4 (June 1987), 88–95: 91: 'L'œuvre n'offre plus un visage répertoriable, mais son simulacre.' For more on this text and an introduction to *Daphnis*, see Mawer, 'Ballet and the apotheosis of the dance', 143–9.

[7] Personal correspondence (8 May 2003). During the production period of this present book, Morrison's own powerful reading of *Daphnis* has appeared: Simon Morrison, 'The origins of *Daphnis et Chloé* (1912)', *19th Century Music*, 28/1 (Summer 2004), 50–76.

ontology is fascinating, and it is a work that almost did not happen: myth upon myth.[8]

Dramatis personae **and collaborative intrigue**

The long-delayed premiere at the Théâtre du Châtelet on 8 June 1912 involved celebrated personnel: Diaghilev as impresario and linchpin, Fokine, Bakst as designer, Ravel himself, the phenomenal title-role dancers Nijinsky and Karsavina and the incomparable Pierre Monteux as conductor.[9] But before detailing poietic interactions between collaborators and considering the emergent product, it is useful to summarize the main collaborative issues that brought the project dangerously close to disaster.

An initial barrier was the language incompatibility which complicated the working through of the ballet's scenario between Fokine and Ravel. A frustrated Ravel exclaimed to Mme de Saint-Marceaux:

> I've just had an insane week: preparation of a ballet libretto for the next Russian season. Almost every night, I was working until 3 a.m. ... Fokine doesn't know a word of French, and I only know how to swear in Russian. Despite the interpreters, you can imagine the flavour of these discussions.[10]

A few months after the premiere, Ravel confided to Rouché that these difficult negotiations over the text for *Daphnis* had made him most cautious about repeating the exercise elsewhere.[11]

Another issue for Ravel concerned the nitty-gritty of contractual arrangements. He sought Michel Calvocoressi's help in drawing up an alternative royalty agreement, not least because of his claim of measurable input into the scenario: the *status quo* would have meant that in the event of *Daphnis* being produced by the Opéra, monies were split equally between the then ballet-mistress, Mme Stichel, Fokine and himself. An understandably

---

[8] For a superb overview of the mythic phenomenon, see Robert A. Segal, *Theorizing about Myth* (Amherst, MA: University of Massachusetts Press, 1999).

[9] For an 'authentic' digitally re-mastered recording, listen to Pierre Monteux, London Symphony Orchestra and Chorus of the ROH, Covent Garden; Ravel, *Daphnis et Chloé*, complete ballet (London: Decca, 1959, reissued 1996; DECCA 448 603-2).

[10] Letter to Mme René de Saint-Marceaux (27 June 1909), in Orenstein (ed.), *A Ravel Reader*, 107 (spelling modified).

[11] Letter to Rouché (7 October 1912), in Marnat, *Maurice Ravel*, 350. Inauspicious association continued: in September 1918, Ravel recounted wryly to Mme Fernand Dreyfus about his brother's Russian rabbits, Daphnis and Chloé, who seemed incapable of consummating their fractious relationship. (Orenstein (ed.), *A Ravel Reader*, 182.)

uncompromising Ravel declared, 'Now, *under no circumstances* would I allow my work to be performed on those terms.'[12]

Ravel was now in his mid-thirties, yet he was relatively inexperienced in collaboration and in delivering a large-scale commission; Fokine, on the other hand, at just thirty was precocious in this respect, having started his essays on ballet reform nine years earlier. The composer's inexperience may partly explain his notable *faux pas* in letting Gabriel Pierné (1863–1937), principal conductor of the Orchestre Colonne, perform the First Suite – 'Nocturne', 'Interlude' and 'Danse guerrière' ('a very considerable fragment of my ballet')[13] – on 2 April 1911, in advance of the balletic premiere and in what would be the same venue. (Note incidentally Ravel's unquestioning claim to ballet ownership.) While the opportunity for Ravel to have his music performed by one of the strongest Parisian symphony orchestras was too tempting to resist, this action was guaranteed to incur the wrath of Diaghilev, who had commissioned the score in 1909 and was still awaiting it well into 1912. For his part, Ravel was still struggling to complete the first act – the conclusion of the third tableau was particularly problematic, resulting in two different endings of 1910 and 1912 discussed below – while a second act was never composed. (Moreover, he had several other compositional projects, including his other early ballets and *L'Heure espagnole*, first produced at the Opéra-Comique in May 1911.) The situation was compounded by Diaghilev's unprofessional behaviour in permitting, supposedly at Bakst's suggestion, the original *Daphnis* sets to be deployed in the 1911 season for another Greek ballet, *Narcisse*, to music by Tcherepnin.[14] To avoid repeating himself, Bakst was then forced to ignore some of Fokine's stage directions for *Daphnis*, positioning the Nymphs on the opposite side, level with the tree canopy rather than in the grove. And even this position was reached only after Diaghilev had been dissuaded from recycling *Narcisse* costumes in *Daphnis*.

Tensions were undoubtedly most severe between Fokine and Diaghilev: in heartfelt if melodramatic language Fokine declared *Daphnis* 'the most sorrowful work of my entire life' and claimed that Diaghilev sought to sabotage his work.[15] Although Fokine was the official ballet master and from early April 1912 was in possession of Ravel's final score, he felt with good reason that he was being compromised because of Diaghilev's increasing obsession with Nijinsky. Diaghilev's protégé, indeed lover, was concurrently choreographing his first ballet to Debussy's *L'Après-midi*

---

[12] Extensive letter to Michel-Dimitri Calvocoressi (3 May 1910), in ibid., 115–16.

[13] Letter to Gabriel Pierné (June 1910), in ibid., 117.

[14] For detail, see Michel Fokine, *Memoirs of a Ballet Master*, trans. Vitale Fokine (London: Constable, 1961), 201, or Schouvaloff, *The Art of Ballets Russes*, 79–80.

[15] Fokine, *Memoirs*, 202.

(which, like *Daphnis*, missed its deadline and had to be replaced by *Le Spectre de la rose*). Fokine was denied sufficient rehearsal time because of the demands of *L'Après-midi*, which astonishingly required some 120 rehearsals. Hence tensions also surfaced between Fokine and Nijinsky who was to dance the role of Daphnis. Diaghilev then tried to call off the performance altogether, threatening Ravel's publisher Durand with cancellation,[16] and employing the dubious technique of using Fokine's wife to try to persuade Fokine to give up. The production was postponed from 5 to 8 June and, as the final blow, Diaghilev apparently sought to stage it merely as a curtain-raiser half-an-hour earlier than the usual performance time to minimize the audience. Since it was put on at the very end of the 1912 season, it could have only two performances (and had merely three in 1913). Diaghilev's spite was such that the company of dancers was not allowed to present Fokine with the customary bouquet on stage after the premiere. Unsurprisingly, Fokine quit the company straight afterwards, although this was not to be the end of his involvement with *Daphnis*.[17] He would dance as Daphnis briefly on the 1914 London tour and in the Opéra production of 1921.

Against this disharmonious backdrop, that *Daphnis* took place at all may be viewed as miraculous and a testimony to Fokine's tenacity and Ravel's perseverance. (Ironically, Ravel did still dedicate his score to Diaghilev, if only to maintain appearances.) At face value, the human problematics of *Daphnis* provide a textbook example of all that could possibly go wrong with balletic collaboration. On closer inspection, however, there were areas of aesthetic common ground and occasional compromise, especially between Ravel and Fokine. Despite difficulties, this relationship seemingly enjoyed some warmth beyond a shared loathing of Diaghilev, and even if Fokine was more forthcoming and positive about it than Ravel, the composer commented a little later that 'One cannot forget ... *Daphnis et Chloé*, where Michel Fokine organized the tumult and fury of Asiatic dances and brought the friezes of Greek temples to life marvellously.'[18]

---

[16] See Durand's account, primarily supporting Ravel: Jacques Durand, *Quelques souvenirs d'un éditeur de musique*, 2 vols. (Paris: Durand, 1924), vol. II, 16.

[17] For detail, see Tamara Karsavina, *Theatre Street: The Reminiscences of Tamara Karsavina* (London: Heinemann, 1930, rev. edn Constable, 1948).

[18] Ravel, 'Nijinsky, maître de ballet', in Marnat, *Maurice Ravel*, 699. 'On ne peut oublier ... *Daphnis et Chloé*, où Michel Fokine ordonna le tumulte et la furie des danses asiatiques, anima merveilleusement les frises des temples grecs'.

Fokine–Ravel scenario

The main credit for freely adapting a scenario on *Daphnis*, thus 'reading' myth, should go to Fokine, who presented a two-act version to the Imperial Maryinsky Theatre in St Petersburg around 1907. Fokine exerted some artistic licence regarding this date, stated as '1904', so as to underplay the influence of the revolutionary Hellenist, Isadora Duncan.[19] Nonetheless, Ravel insisted that as the French speaker and writer of scenarios for *Ma Mère l'Oye* and *Adélaïde* he too had considerable input: 'We spent (I say *we*, because I worked on it also) many nightly hours writing the libretto, which I later retouched.'[20] Ravel's input seemingly reduced physicality – dramatic violence and overt sexuality[21] – while increasing the child-like, idyllic innocence. Bakst, acting partly as interpreter between Fokine and Ravel, also wanted to be seen as contributing to the scenario. In a letter to his wife in summer 1909, he commented light-heartedly: 'Because of Diaghilev I can be sure of not sitting on a sand dune ... and with Fokine and Ravel we have put together an interesting libretto.'[22] One way or another consequential changes occurred, with, according to Calvocoressi, 'Fokine eventually casting the libretto into shape to Ravel's satisfaction'.[23]

As was the case with *Ma Mère l'Oye* and *Adélaïde*, there are several scenario sources, varying in their detail of treatment and transliteration of names: *La Grande Saison, programme officiel des Ballets Russes*, 1912 (source A); the 1913 orchestral score and Fokine's 1912 libretto, both published by Durand and largely consistent with one another (B); the 1954 Ravel catalogue (C) and Fokine's memoirs (D).[24] The original story of *Daphnis* is Longus's Greek pastoral romance, probably written in the Second Sophistic period, which Ravel loved reading in its idiosyncratic sixteenth-century

---

[19] Scholl, *From Petipa to Balanchine*, 59–60. Ravel too indulged in creative re-dating, stating that *Daphnis* was begun in 1907, before work on the scenario: [Roland-Manuel,] 'Une esquisse autobiographique', 22. This date does not tally with Calvocoressi's account: see n. 103.

[20] Letter to Calvocoressi (3 May 1910), in Orenstein (ed.), *A Ravel Reader*, 116.

[21] Despite Ravel's sexual distancing (Chapter 2), he was amused by the innuendo intrinsic to his previous operatic venture, *L'Heure espagnole* (1907–9): see letter to Ida Godebska (20 January 1908), in ibid., 92. Such notions were evidently much less appropriate to Ravel in ballet.

[22] Bakst letter (17 June 1909), quoted in Schouvaloff, *Léon Bakst*, 76. Although Bakst and Fokine were not personal friends, they were strong colleagues and Fokine rated Bakst highly as a painter. See Schouvaloff, *Léon Bakst*, 51.

[23] Michel-Dimitri Calvocoressi, *Musicians Gallery* (London: Faber & Faber, 1933), quoted in Nichols (ed.), *Ravel Remembered*, 187.

[24] Source A: *Programme officiel des Ballets Russes* (Paris: Brunhoff, 13 May–10 June 1912): Fonds Rondel 12522, B de l'A; B: Fokine's 'livret', B-MO; C: *Catalogue de l'œuvre de Maurice Ravel*, 18; D: Fokine, *Memoirs*, 197–9.

French translation by Jacques Amyot (1513–93). There exists also a cor-
rected eighteenth-century translation by Paul-Louis Courier, with illustrations by Ravel's acquaintance Pierre Bonnard.[25]

A suitable flavour of the Fokine–Ravel scenario may be obtained from
selected extracts of the full version presented in Ravel's score. The opening
stage directions read:

> A meadow at the edge of a sacred wood. In the far distance, some hills. On the
> right, a cave, at the entrance of which, carved out of the rock itself, are depicted
> three Nymphs, in archaic sculpture. A little way further back, on the left, a large
> rock vaguely assumes the shape of the god Pan. On the second level, sheep
> graze. A clear afternoon in springtime. At the rise of the curtain the stage is
> empty.
> Enter youths and young girls, carrying baskets of gifts destined for the Nymphs
> [Fig. 3]. Little by little the stage fills up [Fig. 4]. The crowd bows down in front
> of the altar of the Nymphs. The young girls cover the base with garlands of
> flowers.[26]

The narrative as developed in the ballet concerns the developing love from
platonic beginnings between a shepherd and shepherdess, Daphnis and
Chloé. *En route*, Daphnis has to negotiate various feats (mirrored in reality
by the collaborative trials): to compete with an inadequate clumsy suitor, a
goatherd called Dorcon, and to avoid succumbing to Lyce[n]ion and her
seductively discarded veils – the erotic legitimized via the exotic (see
Chapter 2). Lastly, however, he must rescue Chloé from her pirate abductors
and their leader Bryaxis; he meets his major challenge thanks only to the
divine intervention of Pan, the shepherd-god of Arcadia. The story ends
with blissful reunion and varying degrees of sexual fulfilment depending on
the artists involved.

---

[25] Longus, *Les Pastorales de Longus ou Daphnis et Chloé*, trans. Jacques Amyot, rev.
Paul-Louis Courier, ill. Pierre Bonnard (Paris: A.Vollard, 1902); see too Longus, *Daphnis
and Chloe*, Eng. trans. G. Thornley (London: Heineman, 1916). Ravel, Bonnard and Laprade,
who would design *Le Tombeau*, had been invited on a yacht cruise in 1905 with Alfred and
Misia Edwards.

[26] (B): 'Une prairie à la lisière d'un bois sacré. Au fond, des collines. A droite, une grotte,
à l'entrée de laquelle, taillées à même le roc, sont figurées trois Nymphes, d'un sculpture
archaïque. Un peu vers le fond, à gauche, un grand rocher affecte vaguement la forme du
dieu Pân. Au second plan, des brebis paissent. Un après-midi clair de printemps. Au lever du
rideau la scène est vide.
Entrent des jeunes gens et des jeunes filles, portant des corbeilles de présents destinés
aux Nymphes. Peu à peu, la scène se remplit. La foule s'incline devant l'autel des Nymphes.
Les jeunes filles entourent les socles de guirlandes.'

Fokine–Ravel collaboration and aesthetic connection

According to Fokine's recollections, he was introduced to Ravel by Diaghilev, probably in 1909, and was thrilled that someone of Ravel's stature was to compose the music for 'my *Daphnis* ballet'; note Fokine's ownership here.[27] Although Fokine wanted Ravel to enjoy full creative freedom in initiating the musical composition and had great faith in the potential originality of the music, he nevertheless looked for collaborative intimacy when working through the dramatic action: 'It was essential for me to have him feel exactly as I did at each moment of this romance of a shepherd and a shepherdess on the Isle of Lesbos. It was equally important that we both should understand the meaning of each dance in the same way.'[28] Fokine surely sought greater control than Ravel desired, yet there was a valuable meeting place over aesthetic. Ravel's attitude to the necessary modernizing of dance is apparent from Chapter 1, while Fokine presented his reforming ideas in explanatory notes which accompanied his early submission of the *Daphnis* outline to the Russian theatre authorities:

> The dance should explain the spirit of the actors in the spectacle. More than that, it should express the whole epoch to which the subject of the ballet belongs.
>
> For such interpretative dancing the music must be equally inspired … it is necessary to create a form of music which expresses the same emotion as that which inspires the movements of the dancer …
>
> The ballet must no longer be made up of 'numbers', 'entries' and so forth. It must show artistic unity of conception. The action of the ballet must never be interrupted to allow the *danseuse* to respond to the applause of the public.
>
> In place of the traditional dualism, the ballet must have complete unity of expression, a unity which is made up of a harmonious blending of the three elements – music, painting, and plastic art … there shall be but one thing – the aspiration for beauty.[29]

Fokine's ideas point up the importance of historically plausible dance and costume style. The days of stereotypical formulae were over; music and dance must coexist as equal partners within a supportive complex, an idea

---

[27] Fokine, *Memoirs*, 195. Calvocoressi too recalled an early meeting at Diaghilev's apartment in the Hôtel de Hollande; see Nichols (ed.), *Ravel Remembered*, 187.

[28] Fokine, *Memoirs*, 196. The original location was Sicily.

[29] Cyril W. Beaumont, *Michel Fokine and His Ballets* (London: Dance Books, 1996; orig. pub. London: C. W. Beaumont, 1935), 23–4. Fokine published later versions of these reforms in 'The new Russian Ballet', *The Times* (6 July 1914), 6, and the Russian journal *Argus*, 1 (1916); see Beaumont, *Michel Fokine*, 144–7, 135–43, respectively. According to Simon Morrison, earlier drafts are found in the Mikhail Fokine Collection, Russian National Library, St Petersburg (RNB fond 820/2) and in the Kadletz Collection, State Theatre Library, St Petersburg (GTB no. 19996).

with which Ravel firmly concurred. Although *Daphnis* preserves a traditional 'pantomime' section enacting Pan's love for Syrinx (around Fig. 172)
and there were unintended noisy hiatuses for scene changes in the premiere,
both Fokine and Ravel aimed for continuous music and action rather than
old-fashioned 'numbers'. This principle of continuous movement is well
embodied in one of Bakst's costume sketches for Chloé: she is depicted
barefoot in a flowing veiled garment, fleeing from the brigands with what
looks like a voluminous scarf flying out behind, creating an overall circularity (see too Figure 3.1).[30] Fokine's discussion of 'unity of expression' and
'harmonious blending' matches Ravel's perception of shared artistic purpose
and bonds between types of specialist (Chapter 1), accepting that similarity
of emotive, expressive effect between music and dance is distinct from their
technical means. Ravel too felt very strongly about pursuing aesthetic
beauty.

In any collaboration there must be room for dissent.[31] According to
Fokine, during various meetings there was only one major difference of
opinion between Ravel and himself. This is doubtless a view through rose-
tinted spectacles after the event, but it is still revealing to note which disa-
greement Fokine chose to highlight. For the pirates' initial attack (Fig.
61ff.), he wanted a direct, bloodthirsty killing of shepherds, abduction of
women and cattle rustling. Ravel favoured the less literal approach of a
sudden lightning strike. In practice, violence is minimized in Ravel's portrayal with just three bars of 'Très animé' for Chloé's abduction (Fig. 67⁻⁴);
nevertheless, the confrontational 'Danse guerrière' (Fig. 92ff.) proves highly
effective in prolonging dramatic tension. Fokine's account of this fracas is
interesting for the light that it throws upon the collaborative process:

> I yielded, realizing that this was the way he felt at that moment, and that, proba-
> bly due to my limitations in the French language, I was unable to inspire him to
> create musically that violent, gruesome picture which was so vivid in my imagi-
> nation. I later came to reproach myself for not having insisted on this point ... It
> is far better to appear to be a stubborn, uncooperative character; it is even better
> to have a quarrel ... than to depart from one's convictions if one believes them
> to be the truth.[32]

---

[30] Undated, unsigned costume design for Tamara Karsavina as Chloé [1912]: Ella Gallup
Sumner and Mary Catlin Sumner Collection, Wadsworth Atheneum, Hartford, CT. See
Schouvaloff, *Léon Bakst*, 153, or *The Art of Ballets Russes*, 81. Bakst's sensitivity to movement was attested to as early as 1913; see Alexandre, 'Appreciation', in *The Decorative Art
of Léon Bakst*, 1–17: 3.

[31] See Philip Flood, 'In the silence and stillness', *Dance Theatre Journal*, 13/4 (1997),
36–9: 38.

[32] Fokine, *Memoirs*, 199. See also Best, 'Why do choreographers and composers
collaborate?'.

Figure 3.1   Tamara Karsavina as Chloé (1914). Photograph by E. Otto
              Hoppé. By permission of the Theatre Museum, London;
              © V & A Images.

This extract shows that Fokine, too, was frustrated by the language difficulties. Clearly, on occasion he perceived in Ravel's response 'a lack of virility',[33] which he considered necessary for portraying the ancient world –though even he was shocked by the explicit sexuality of Nijinsky's *L'Après-midi*, which shared the stage with *Daphnis*.

The challenge of endings for Ravel and Fokine

Both Ravel and Fokine had to overcome their respective challenges to create an exciting, triumphant 'Danse générale' to clinch closure after the main scenario action (Fig. 199ff.) – the start of Ravel's exhilaration–destruction trajectory through to *Boléro*. The concluding portion of the scenario reads: 'A group of young girls dressed as *bacchantes*, shaking tambourines. Daphnis and Chloé embrace [s'enlacent] tenderly. A group of young men invades the stage. Joyful tumult.'[34] Whatever Ravel's inhibitions, the text leaves scope for wild orgiastic treatment: the antique 'bacchantes' may be interpreted as drunken and promiscuous female revellers and *s'enlacer* in respect of Daphnis and Chloé may read as 'to intertwine' voluptuously. This question of effecting endings illustrates nicely the differences between musical and choreographic method; as Philip Flood notes, 'Artists must recognise their differences in making work in order to plan ahead. The act of music composition is primarily a solitary activity'.[35] So it was for Ravel, a painstaking, lonely activity on a time-scale of years rather than months.

Ravel had completed his first piano score of *Daphnis* by May 1910, but its conclusion did not satisfy him and he struggled for another two years to perfect his musical vision.[36] Essentially, the original version, workable by

---

[33] Fokine, *Memoirs*, 200. Ravel's distancing from heterosexuality has raised inevitable questions about his orientation. See Philip Kennicott, 'Ravelation', *Dance Magazine* (April 1990), 68–9: 68. For a fascinating hermeneutic reading of Ravel's possible homosexuality, see Benjamin Ivry, *Maurice Ravel: A Life* (New York: Welcome Rain Publishers, 2000; repr. 2003). The balance of evidence still favours a more asexual existence, with occasional, customary recourse to female prostitutes.

[34] (B): 'Entre un groupe de jeunes filles costumées en bacchantes, agitant des tambourins. Daphnis et Chloé s'enlacent tendrement. Un groupe de jeunes hommes envahit la scène. Joyeux tumulte.' (Figs. 194–6, 1912 version.) In the ensemble finale, Daphnis and Chloé come to the fore (Fig. 204), and then Dorcon (Fig. 206).

[35] Flood, 'In the silence and stillness', 38.

[36] The early piano MS (47 pp.), in the Ravel Estate, is signed and dated 1 May 1910, although contractual reasons may have influenced this date. Also in 1910, Durand released prematurely some uncorrected proofs, and I am very grateful to Nigel Simeone for access to a copy. A second MS (186 pp.), in ink and pencil, signed and dated 5 April 1912, is held in the HRC and this formed the basis of the orchestral edition published in 1913. A second piano reduction, with small variants in scenario text, was published by Durand and, confusingly, bears the 1910 date although it postdates the premiere.

the standards of a lesser artist, but not in comparison with Stravinsky's new *L'Oiseau de feu*, took insufficient risk and would have approximated to conventional responses that Fokine also wanted to avoid: it was quite short and in regular triple metre.[37] After all, as Flood argues, 'The real danger in making work jointly is that creative originality will be rubbed out … leading to a product that is weak, dull, compromised and ineffectual.'[38]

Ravel's reworked ending in the 1912 manuscript was much more extensive and, as Larner has noted, 'immeasurably more dangerous',[39] in its celebration of fast 5/4 metre, arranged as 3 + 2, amid disorientating chromaticism ('Danse générale', Fig. 199ff.). (For Ravel, chromaticism connotes excitement or instability and is used to warn the title roles of potential sexual threat: Daphnis in Lyceion's dance (Fig. 58ff.) – a Wagnerian characterization of a dangerous woman – and Chloé in the pirates' 'Danse guerrière' (Fig. 92ff.).) Ravel admitted that part of the creation – presumably the dotted fourth motive combined with chromaticism – was that of Rimsky-Korsakov: 'I was in a bad mood over it, so much so that I put Rimsky's *Shéhérazade* on the piano and tried, very humbly, to write something like it.'[40] But, since this was a Ballets Russes commission, following *Shéhérazade* in the same programme, such intertextuality was hardly inappropriate.

Forward propulsion, almost a tripping sensation, is embedded in the musical fabric rather than being superimposed by tempo changes as in the original. This principle is intensified near the close by reducing the beats in the bar from five to three (Fig. 218), and finally to two (Fig. 221), for progressively shorter time-spans. This 5/4 metre itself constitutes a diminution of the 7/4 patterning that first occurs in a much earlier portion of the 'Danse générale' across Figs 17–29. If these two portions (Figs. 17–29 and 199–221) are regarded end-on, the pattern of metric diminution can be seen more clearly: 7 (3 + 2 + 2), 5 (3 + 2), 3, 2. Ravel's basic revisionary technique of compressing beats within bar-units (2 × 3/4; 1 × 5/4), while expanding overall dimensions and imagination, is illustrated by aligning the openings of the 1910 and 1912 versions (Example 3.1). Additionally, dynamic markings are more varied in the final version, including stabbing *sforzando* gestures followed by dynamic fading, rather than the overused 'hairpin' gestures of the original.[41] Ravel's awesome wordless chorus, in the spirit of Debussy's 'Sirènes' from *Nocturnes*

---

[37] See Jacques Chailley, 'Une première version inconnue de *Daphnis et Chloé* de Maurice Ravel', *Mélanges d'histoire littéraire offerts à Raymond Lebègue* (Paris: Nizet, 1969), 371–5, and Orenstein, *Ravel: Man and Musician*, 215–6.

[38] Flood, 'In the silence and stillness', 38.

[39] Larner, *Maurice Ravel*, 132.

[40] Recounted by Manuel Rosenthal in Nichols (ed.), *Ravel Remembered*, 44.

[41] The 'hairpin', or what one might frivolously term the 'Ravel swell', is nonetheless a characteristic feature of the composer's mature style, comprising a crescendo followed immediately by a diminuendo.

Example 3.1 *Daphnis et Chloé*: comparison of 1910 and 1912 piano versions
(a) 'Danse générale' (1910; p. 93)
(b) 'Danse générale' (1912; Fig. 199)

(1899), also justifies its inclusion much more effectively in his revision (Fig. 218ff.) than in his first effort, when it reappeared too late. The full effect is triumphant and ecstatic, even orgiastic.

To return, after an extended solo musical journey, to Flood's discussion of time-scales: 'The choreographer, on the other hand, works in a studio with a group of dancers, making the piece in real time, giving out movement material that is developed to a greater or lesser degree by the performers.'[42] In Fokine's case, the time-scale for this intense and highly physical work was almost impossibly short, which compounded the challenge received from Ravel to choreograph a risk-taking conclusion in 5/4 metre.

Karsavina's memoirs reveal the pressure to which Fokine was subjected: 'Fokine was too maddened, working against time, to give me much attention; on the morning of the performance the last act [scene] was not yet brought to an end.' Such an account might be thought exaggerated, but Fokine's description is similar, with apparently twenty pages of music to be choreographed in three days.[43] Parallels are evident between Ravel's desperate working with Rimsky's *Shéhérazade* on his piano and Fokine's even more frenzied work with his frazzled dancers hours before the premiere. In attempting to master the primitivist 5/4 rhythms, Karsavina explains how she and Ravel initially counted their way through the passage at the back of the stage although, disconcertingly, she presents the formula as an inverted

---

[42] Flood, 'In the silence and stillness', 38.

[43] Fokine, *Memoirs*, 209–10.

2 + 3 grouping: '123 – 12345 – 12'.[44] More generally, Karsavina indicates Ravel's helpful involvement in the production process; unlike Caryathis (see Chapter 2), she considered that 'There was nothing Olympian about Ravel.' According to Lifar's testimony, if numbers failed words assisted: a chanting – cursing perhaps – of 'Ser-gei Dia-ghi-lev' bridged dance and musical metre (note, however, that stress on the 'ghi' of the surname is necessary to preserve the metric subdivision).[45]

As for Fokine, he claimed not to resent Ravel's awkward 5/4 and 7/4 metres, regarding them as naturally conceived expressions that served the joint work. After all, Fokine's approach sought to avoid slavish replication between music and dance, supporting part of Nijinsky's *L'Après-midi* against critical claims that one domain should merely mirror the other:

> Many feel that the dance movements must exactly correspond with the movements in the music. I call this 'rhythmomania' and I am of the opinion that the music can express a gamut of agitation going on in a person's soul and that the person can at the same time express the entire storm without any movement, frozen in a position.[46]

For the ending of *Daphnis*, Fokine came up with what he claimed was a one-off incremental staging method whereby he sent two bacchantes dashing across the stage singly, then as groups of two, three and so on until he had constructed 'an entire group with interwoven arms reminiscent of Greek bas-reliefs'.[47] As if part of a mosaic, each dancer needed only to memorize his/her brief, distinctive sequence of steps, but collective effects were achieved with one mass arriving at the far-side rear stage and another emerging from the front wing. Fokine's satisfaction at having clinched this ending and therefore the ballet is palpable: 'The entire ensemble lurched together in a whirlpool of a general dance, and – the biggest part of the most difficult finale was ready!'[48] Diaghilev questioned the artistic merit of Ravel's chorus (although his real motivations in 1914 were financial); Fokine on the other hand was in no doubt about this operatic contribution, representing the dancers' joyous whoopings: 'in the finale it accompanied the dance with wild outcries. In high leaps, everyone disappeared into the

---

[44] Karsavina, *Theatre Street*, 238–9. These evocative memoirs were supposedly concluded on the day of Diaghilev's death: 20 August 1929.

[45] Lifar, *Serge de Diaghilev*, 239.

[46] Fokine, *Memoirs*, 209. Jordan interprets 'rhythmomania' as a jibing reference to Dalcroze, despite some Dalcrozean characteristics within Fokine's approach: *Moving Music*, 30.

[47] The momentum and tension thus created parallels instrumental growth principles as later used by Ravel in *Boléro*.

[48] Fokine, *Memoirs*, 210.

wings. This bacchanal aroused the enthusiasm of the audience.'[49] The premiere was basically successful, even if the restricted rehearsal time inevitably impacted upon the production's refinement; the high stature of the
music, however, was not in question, whatever the small-minded quibbles
of Pierre Lalo or Arthur Pougin.[50]

'The past is a foreign country':[51] Ancient Greekness in *Daphnis et Chloé*

As Christopher Best observes, 'The definitive test of a successful collaboration must be the strength of the work itself, not how sweet and amicable [or
otherwise] the working relationships between its creators prove to be.'[52]
Exploration of Greekness in *Daphnis* is a good way to put it to that test.

If any past connotes a 'foreign country', then the situation is compounded
in portraying Ancient Greece. Treatment of Greekness in *Daphnis* involves
geographical and temporal distancing: an exotic far-away land of sun and sex
on the very edge of Europe in a bygone age. Geographical positioning is
complicated; Fokine's question 'shall Greeks dance the French way?'[53] shows
that he recognized the dangers of Franco-centrism, but inevitably this is a
Greece viewed from St Petersburg and Paris. Temporal positioning involves
points across a spectrum: myths emerge from ancient Greek beginnings and
are notated in the civilization of Classical Greece (c. 500–400 BC); Longus's
Daphnis as Fokine's source supposedly appears around AD 200; Ravel's
translation by Amyot occurs in the sixteenth century, followed by Courier in
the eighteenth. Finally, from its period of composition during the Belle
Epoque the work embodies a 'searching for the golden age'[54] of a nostalgic
Arcadia, subsequently reproduced and further experienced in the twenty-first
century. Artistic responses to the past may be polarized as attempts to imitate/
revive, via broad emulation, through to efforts to distort/rewrite, and these are
inflected eclectically by knowledge (itself not neutral), personal experience
and aesthetic. The approaches of Ravel, Bakst and Fokine, postdating
Duncan's 'revivals', may be positioned inside this framework.

For the musical evocation of Greece, Fokine had hoped to hear reconstructed ancient sounds, but during his discussions with Ravel he learned

---

[49] Ibid., 214.

[50] Pierre Lalo, 'La Musique', *Le Temps* (11 June 1912), 3; Arthur Pougin, 'Semaine théâtrale', *Le Ménestrel*, 24 (15 June 1912), 187–9.

[51] David Lowenthal, *The Past is a Foreign Country* (Cambridge: Cambridge University
Press, 1985).

[52] Best, 'Why do choreographers and composers collaborate?', 31.

[53] From Fokine's early 'manifesto', quoted by Garafola, *Diaghilev and the Ballets
Russes*, 8.

[54] Lowenthal, *The Past is a Foreign Country*, 21.

that information was scant and therefore 'no resurrection is possible'.[55] With time, it seemed less important: Ravel found other solutions. Although his folk-inspired *Cinq mélodies populaires grecques* (1904–6) and his harmonization of the three-step *Tripatos* (1909) were broadly contemporary with *Daphnis*, his involvement in *l'affaire grecque* was more by accident than by design.[56]

Nonetheless, a powerful sonic image of Greekness is heard in the slow opening mechanism of stacked bare fifths with a derived melodic fifth idea later to become closely associated with Daphnis and Chloé. While for Ravel the hollow fifth is always invested with antique association, a non-specific symbol of the past, this complex creates the ultimate locus as an awe-inspiring, spacious primordium. The rainbow-like spectrum reproduces *en bas-relief* one of the Greek ecclesiastical modes, A lydian ('Introduction', through to Fig. 1). All seven pitches are invoked, commencing with the low fundamental: A–E–B–F♯–C♯–G♯–D♯ (Example 3.2). In particular, the tritone from bass to treble (A–D♯), the *diabolus in musica*, is well suited to conveying the supernatural world of Pan and his Nymphs. Further play with the opening perfect fifths includes rotation, inversion about a pivot on G: C–G–D, within the Daphnis–Chloé leitmotif heard on horn (Example 3.3; Fig. 2⁻³). This action simulates a physical motion in space, a half-revolution pivoting on one foot: a synaesthetic working through of choreographic potential in the music that befits a 'symphonie chorégraphique'.[57] In addition, the lower fifth C–G may be associated with Daphnis and the higher G–D with Chloé.

In and following this Introduction, Ravel's handling of the Greek subject-matter involves, as in *Ma Mère l'Oye*, a notable literalism or close corre-

Example 3.2 *Daphnis et Chloé* (ballet, 1913): 'Introduction' (bars 1–7, reduction)

---

[55] Fokine, *Memoirs*, 195.

[56] In his extended letter to Calvocoressi of May 1910, mentioned above, Ravel felt the need to check the names of Lyceion and Lammon and certain story details with his friend – who became thus at some level another collaborator.

[57] See Mawer, 'Musical objects and machines', 49.

Example 3.3 *Daphnis et Chloé*: solo horn theme (Fig.2^{-3})

spondence in projecting the scenario through musical narrative.[58] This happens overtly with the wordless chorus – marked 'Behind the stage' but more often placed in a stage box – offering a haunting and aptly unintelligible Greek-style commentary, oscillating initially between the pitches B and A.[59] At the entry of young people bearing baskets of gifts (Fig. 3), the music suggests anticipation with ascending scalic string triplets marked *pp*, increased focus being denoted by the removal of mutes and supported by a gradual accelerando. At the initial climactic point when the crowd bows before the Nymphs' altar (Fig. 4), the music too climaxes: *fortissimo*, with massed scintillating sonority.

Although Ravel was not at all religious, he expresses convincingly the pagan ritual of the processional 'Danse religieuse' (Figs. 5–15), as a mysterious, serene hymn to the fecundity of nature. Again his approach to ancient Greekness is to lay bare its scalic ingredients as a kind of 'back to basics', uplifted by sumptuous, impressionistic orchestration, which resonates with the broadly contemporary exoticism of Rimsky-Korsakov and Borodin, and a sensuous, almost tactile, crescendo. This dance utilizes melodic fragments that are focused initially upon a mixolydian mode, B, C♯, D♯, E, F♯, G♯, (A); the effect of this emphasis upon the supertonic heard over a tonic pedal on A is to highlight the modal legacy and make the music sound 'older' (Example 3.4). In time, this A–B–A relationship is projected across the work. As earlier, there is a musical literalism to Ravel's scenario depiction, achieved partly through the leitmotif technique. Following its initial airing, the melodic fifth idea returns on E–A (Fig. 10) to mark Daphnis's appearance with his sheep at the back of the set. When Chloé joins him, the musical completion is achieved by an immediate transposition down a further fifth – D–G – which is balanced by being heard in a higher register.

As musical materials become formed beyond their primeval beginnings, Ravel's debt to eighteenth-century classicism becomes increasingly evident

---

[58] Virginia Christian perceives a 'story which is … intricately linked to the music': Virginia Christian, '*Daphnis et Chloé*', in Bremser (ed.), *International Dictionary of Ballet*, vol. I, 339–41: 340.

[59] In an Ashton revival of May 2004, this church-like chorus maintained a presence that at times subjugated the orchestral thematic material.

Example 3.4 *Daphnis et Chloé*: 'Danse religieuse' (Fig. 5, reduction)

through repetition, sequence and regular phrasings. As he later explained, what he wanted to create was 'a vast musical fresco, less concerned about archaism than about faithfulness to the Greece of my dreams, which marries quite readily with that imagined and depicted by French artists at the end of the eighteenth century'.[60] Cocteau talked of the eighteenth-century artistic attraction to *Daphnis*, of 'innumerable pictures which reproduce its leading incidents from the elaborate modesty of Daphnis's bath, while Chloé slyly looks on, to the suggestive entanglement of the four feet overhanging the edge of the grotto – the typical galanteries, which were such a sheer delight'; and in turn parallels have been mooted between the rococo paintings of Boucher and Ravel's consciously naive, idyllic image.[61] Moreover, Ravel himself had invoked Boucher in his previous scenario for *Ma Mère l'Oye*.

Ravel's striking visual metaphor, mixing ancient fresco and painting of the second classical period, evokes a Greece rather different from that realized by the prolific designer. Bakst's depiction of Greekness was part of a larger prewar contribution which included projects at the Maryinsky Theatre, the St Petersburg production of *Antigone* for Rubinstein, and the Ballets Russes creations of *Cléopâtre* and *Narcisse* (effectively Bakst's first interpretation of *Daphnis*: see p. 82). His approach (like Dresa's: see p. 57 above) was to eschew traditional attempts at illusion, and in common with Ravel, Benois and Fokine he supported synaesthetic artistic connections: 'The sole and essential function of décor was the creation of visual poetry.'[62] He so loved ballet that, given the chance, he would have trained as a choreographer.[63] Bakst's work is steeped in orientalism, from Russia and warmer climes, but the artist with whom he identified most readily was the tragically short-lived Art Nouveau illustrator, Aubrey Beardsley (1872–98).

---

[60] [Roland-Manuel,] 'Une esquisse autobiographique', 21: 'une vaste fresque musicale, moins soucieuse d'archaïsme que de fidélité à la Grèce de mes rêves, qui s'apparente assez volontiers à celle qu'ont imaginée et dépeinte les artistes français de la fin du XVIIIᵉ siècle'. See also André Mirambel, 'L'Inspiration grecque dans l'œuvre de Ravel', *La Revue musicale*, 19 (December 1938), 112–18.

[61] Jean Cocteau in Alexandre, *The Decorative Art*, 46; Kennicott, 'Ravelation', 68.

[62] Hansen, *Scenic and Costume Design*, 23.

[63] Schouvaloff, *Léon Bakst*, 229.

So Bakst brought to *Daphnis* a view of ancient Greece infused by the luxuriant exoticism of the Steppes, but influenced also by a trip he had made to Greece in 1907. His interpretation of the opening stage directions, used for Scenes I and III, results in a set whose foreground features strong vertical groupings of 'pencil' cypresses (so typical of Corfu) surrounding a central meadow or grove, with a background of rocky outcrops (Figure 3.2).[64] This use of 'massive verticals … that both isolated and weighed on the drama'[65] was a hallmark which may be compared with Ravel's architectural verticals – the importance of chord and cadence, especially relating to the modal progression A–B–A, to articulate strategic arrival-points in the score. (The harmonic palette of *Daphnis*, with added sevenths, ninths and unresolved appoggiaturas, has been a source of fascination since the 1920s.)[66] Such verticality relates nicely to Albright's theory of focusing on 'transmediating chords' (see p. 30), essentially concordant here.

Further details of the set include three nymphs who inhabit trees to the left of centre, appearing rather congested, and a small Greek shrine at a curious backwards angle[67] in the far distance on top of a mountain. Despite these shortcomings – and one should remember that Bakst was not aiming for simulated realism – even the conservative André Levinson found much to praise: 'I know nothing in the entire work of Bakst that is equal to these tender, fresh, damp greens of the meadow and of the forest where the two children walk about displaying the charming torment of love that knows nothing of itself.'[68] Vuillermoz developed this stance, regarding the set as one of 'the most seductive' that Bakst had produced; for all that, its Russian inflection is a little chilly – though one would hardly go as far as the miserable Lalo, who saw it as incomprehensibly 'sad, cold and without light'.[69]

For Scene II, Bakst's brief was quite different, the score directions reading as follows:

---

[64] Bakst's set design painting is preserved in the Musée des Arts Décoratifs, Paris. He also produced a modified set for the 1921 Opéra revival (Cliché: C 60953 B.N. Opéra).

[65] Garafola, *Diaghilev's Ballets Russes*, 34.

[66] Alfred Casella, 'L'Harmonie', *La Revue musicale*, 6 (April 1925), 28–37: 32–3.

[67] Bakst's idiosyncratic perspective was criticised by Benois: Hansen, *Scenic and Costume Design*, 29. The third dimension is the first of 'Les Problèmes plastiques' discussed by Cogniat, *Les Décorateurs de théâtre*, 21–8: 21–2.

[68] André Levinson, *Bakst: The Story of the Artist's Life* (New York: Benjamin Blom, 1923; reissued 1970), 179–80. He had been less complimentary about a 1913 production with Bakst's sets, at the Théâtre des Champs-Elysées, which exhibited 'a harsh, motley, polychromatic style' and lack of intimacy: André Levinson, *Ballet Old and New*, trans. Susan Cook Summer (orig. pub. St Petersburg: Svobodnoe iskusstvo, 1918; New York: Dance Horizons, 1982), 59.

[69] Emile Vuillermoz, 'Les Théâtres, la grande saison de Paris', *Revue musicale de la S.I.M.* (1912), 62–8: 67; Pierre Lalo, 'La Musique', 3.

Figure 3.2   Léon Bakst, *Daphnis et Chloé*: Scene I (programme, 1912). By permission of the Bibliothèque Nationale de France.

A faint glimmer. We are at the pirate camp. A very uneven coastline. In the back-ground, the sea. On the right and left, a view of rocks. A trireme is revealed, close to the coast. In places, cypress trees. Pirates, running here and there, weighed down with booty, can be seen. Torches are carried, which finish by lighting up the stage fiercely.[70]

In response, Bakst's scene was arid, even desert-like – Levinson's 'grim and desolate face of Hellas'; such refined antithesis, developed below, is also voiced by Cocteau: 'the least terrifying of storms succeeded by the most perfectly formed of rainbows form an ideal framework for scenery which is suave and grim by turns'.[71] Fierce orange for the jagged and hostile coastal cliffs is matched aurally by the bold rhythmic outline of Ravel's 'Danse guerrière', in the style of the 'Polovtsian Dances' from Borodin's *Prince Igor*. The pirate camp, with its smoking fire, is situated on the left side of the tableau close to the moored ship (Figure 3.3). On contemporary paints, Diaghilev's stage-painter Vladimir Polunin is informative, cautioning that French colours, initially so intense, soon fade and go patchy. Bakst's orange could be produced from an earth colour (ochre, sienna), or from strong, heavy 'red lead'.[72] Bakst's technique received effusive early appreciation, with embedded musical imagery, from Arsène Alexandre: 'he realises an "orchestration" of colour in unison with the true colour of music. Does he wish to show us the divine haze of Greece shimmering in the sun, or to call up the glowing, poisoned splendours of the East?'[73] Such impressionistic qualities compare with Ravel's orchestral practice, which at this time thrived on rich, exotic musical colour to create a dream-like atmosphere.

Where costumes were concerned, while Bakst did imitate the essentials of classical Greek attire as an academic reconstructive quest, his 'take' on the past was modified by his use of bold colours and a circular floral hallmark.[74] Nevertheless, predominantly white tunics, 'chitons', were used for the title roles, certainly on the 1914 London tour (see again Figure 3.1), where

---

[70] (B): 'Une lueur sourde. On est au camp des pirates. Côte très accidentée. Au fond, la mer. A droite et à gauche, perspective de rochers. Une tryrème se découvre, près de la côte. Par endroits, des cyprès. On perçoit les pirates, courant ça et là, chargés de butin. Des torches sont apportées, qui finissent par éclairer violemment la scène.'

[71] Levinson, *Bakst*, 179; Cocteau in Alexandre, *The Decorative Art*, 46.

[72] Polunin, *The Continental Method of Scene Painting*, 18–19.

[73] Alexandre, *The Decorative Art*, 7–8.

[74] Hansen, *Scenic and Costume Design*, 29; Garafola, *Diaghilev's Ballets Russes*, 17. For reproductions of Bakst's costume designs, see Schouvaloff, *Bakst*, 155 [Maiden]; Cyril W. Beaumont, *Ballet Design: Past and Present* (London: Studio, 1946), 78; and *Catalogue principally of Diaghilev Ballet Material* (London: Sotheby & Co., 1968), 7, 17.

Figure 3.3   Léon Bakst, *Daphnis et Chloé*: Scene II (programme, 1912). By courtesy of the Rare Books Archive, Lancaster University Library.

Beaumont recalled that 'Fokine [as Daphnis] wore a shorter white tunic, and danced with a long slender white wand.'[75]

Indeed, Fokine himself wished to revivify the ancient styles of dancing depicted in rotation on Attic vases,[76] or on temple friezes, as Ravel had noted. This more literal approach to Greekness is nicely summed up by Lowenthal: 'Would-be travellers long to experience an exotic antiquity, to live in times superior to today, to know what actually happened in history.'[77] In turn, this need to know what happened becomes an issue for today: the lack of choreographic information for *Daphnis*, part of its myth, is a problem raised by Garafola (see p. 80 above). Limited information is forthcoming in reviews, but the main reliance has to be upon Fokine's testimony.[78]

From his *Memoirs* one learns that Fokine reconstructed 'groups, poses, lines, and movements based on the study of Greek sculpture and painting',[79] with use of interlocked arm gestures, observed from bas-relief. Additionally, he distinguished between sophisticated movements for some characters, supposedly deriving from Classical Greece, and more primitive 'archaic poses' for others. All dancers wore leather sandals (such as the one that Chloé loses at Fig. 67) or were barefoot, which directly affected the steps, precluding work *sur les pointes*. The mysterious, remote nymphs moved in a stylized manner in flattened profile reminiscent of bas-relief – a technique borrowed by Nijinsky in *L'Après-midi*, though frustratingly for Fokine, given the overshadowing effect of *L'Après-midi*, Vuillermoz perceived the influence as reversed.[80] In turn, the Greeks had borrowed this concept from the Egyptians, while Fokine's playing with two-dimensional effects anticipates video art. Furthermore, Fokine looked to produce collective sculptural effects through aleatoric means, trusting to the improvisational imagination

---

[75] Beaumont, *The Diaghilev Ballet in London*, 87. This crook is alluded to in Gross's sketches: Valentine Gross, *Nijinsky on Stage*, intro. Richard Buckle (London: Studio Vista, 1971), 117–18, 121. Given the time-lapse before Beaumont's recollections of 1940, there is scope for error.

[76] Serge Lifar quoted in Roger Nichols, *Ravel* (London: Dent, 1977), 80.

[77] Lowenthal, *The Past is a Foreign Country*, 21.

[78] Russian readers receive a fuller account than the abridged English translation of Fokine, *Memoirs*. According to Morrison, there is further visual evidence in St Petersburg: three early sets of photographs (Files 13/6, 13/7 and 13/8) of Fokine and his wife in Greek-style costumes, housed in the Mikhail Fokine Archive, State Theatre Library. Morrison considers that the images in 13/6 and 13/8 resemble those reproduced in *Comœdia illustré* (5 June 1912), although the Fokines only danced the title roles briefly in 1914 (on tour in Monte Carlo, and in London when Vera Fokina alternated with Karsavina) and 1921. In 13/7, 'Fokine's costume consists of sandals, white tunic, headband, and sash. The décor includes French patio doors, a Russian floor carpet, and an Indian silk sari – true cosmopolitanism.' I am grateful to Simon Morrison for this information.

[79] Fokine, *Memoirs*, 213.

[80] Vuillermoz, 'Les Théâtres', 68.

of his dancers within defined bounds.[81] Also germane to Fokine's stance is Lowenthal's observation that '[o]nce morally instructive, the past has become a source of sensate pleasure';[82] certainly, Fokine sought to recreate a pleasurable decadence, embracing the sensuous and, more problematically for Ravel, the sensual.

A digest of critical opinion suggests that, in contrast with Ravel's perfectionism, the haste behind the choreography was apparent and that Fokine could have strengthened his characterization of movements and, for Samazeuilh, of wilder 'whirlwinds' ('tourbillons').[83] Levinson's barbed critique of Nijinsky's 1913 revival offers more choreographic detail: incensed by a perceived desecration of antiquities, he decried 'These dancing Hellenes, barefoot or in sandals, throwing their knees up high, sauntering around in pairs or forming sculptural groups and processions in simulation of ritual mime, are intolerable, like any vulgarization of great art and almost inscrutable sacred objects.'[84] More positively, Fokine was seen as sensitive to beauty – an echo of his notes on ballet aesthetic – and the free scenario provided sufficient pretext for the choreographic variety in which he excelled.[85] In this admirable performance, 'the pirates and shepherds tread suavely or stamp furiously upon the marvellous "resonating carpet" (thus spake Erik Satie) that Ravel spread under their musicianly feet'.[86]

Fokine was the artist most concerned to pursue the 'resurrection', almost Christ-like, of a dead civilization, so illusion might be seen to apply at least within the choreographic dimension. In this respect, as Garafola points out, it is important not to adopt an implicit superiority: 'Today, naturalism has fallen into disrepute, and when we speak of this scientific off-spring of realism, the tone is apt to be disparaging. Yet in its time naturalism was a galvinizing imaginative force that hurtled the artist into the real worlds of slums, brothels, and vaudeville theaters.'[87] In practice, authenticity in relation to the past is unattainable, yet, as Ravel remarked, in the search for originality 'something will never emerge more distinctly than in your unintended

---

[81] Fokine, *Memoirs*, 214.

[82] Lowenthal, *The Past is a Foreign Country*, 51.

[83] Gustave Samazeuilh, 'Les Ballets Russes, Théâtre du Châtelet', *Le Courrier musical* (15 June 1912), 364–5; Lalo, 'La Musique', 3.

[84] Levinson, *Ballet Old and New*, 60.

[85] Vuillermoz, 'Les Théâtres', 67; Samazeuilh, 'Les Ballets Russes', 365.

[86] Vuillermoz, 'Les Théâtres', 68: 'les pirates et les bergères piétinent suavement ou furieusement le merveilleux "tapis resonant" (Erik Satie dixit) que Ravel étendit sous leurs pieds musiciens'.

[87] Garafola, *Diaghilev's Ballets Russes*, 9.

unfaithfulness to a model'.[88] So, Ravel and Bakst looked mainly to construct personal images of Greece that thrived on fantasy and *fin-de-siècle* orientalism, although Ravel's image can be both elemental and mediated by classicism, and Bakst's costumes do have a reconstructive aspect.

While one should not underplay the differences,[89] the three responses to the Greek theme are partly unified by their early twentieth-century Russianness – including that of Ravel, under the guise of Rimsky-Korsakov and Borodin. Choreography, music and flowing costume design also unite in celebrating movement.[90] In promoting a mixture of dream-world and perceived reality, they also mirror Daphnis's uncertainty early in the third scene as to whether his experiences were dreamed or real. Following the premiere, Louis Schneider in *Comœdia* praised Bakst's sets that did not sum up the story-line but rather established its contrasting character and meaning: 'Thus the painter with his palette has realized the triptych dreamt of by the choreographer and the composer.'[91] So Schneider upholds the role of complementation in fashioning a whole, an idea introduced in Chapter 1. Similarly, the experienced Vuillermoz was convinced that through the methodical construction of its different collaborators 'The synthesis of *Daphnis et Chloé* was … absolutely complete.'[92]

Antitheses of emotion and character

As an offshoot of classical Greek drama, the idea of antitheses or oppositions, with some subsequent dialectical resolutions, may help to interpret further artistic interactions in *Daphnis*, including those relating to performance. Within the ballet are embedded various oppositions and more ambiguous relations of emotion and character, sometimes built up into structural complexes: characters within the original myths have been subject to much psychoanalysis. Indeed the highly diverse nature of the dances for the main characters was recognized by Samazeuilh and others from the premiere onwards, while for Beaumont, recollecting 1914, what remained vivid were

---

[88] Ravel quoted by Roland-Manuel, 'Des valses à *La Valse*', in Colette et al., *Maurice Ravel par quelques-uns de ses familiers*, 141–51: 145: 'ce quelque chose n'apparaîtra jamais plus clairement que dans votre involontaire infidélité au modèle'.

[89] Lifar arguably overplayed them: Lifar, *Histoire du ballet russe*, 215.

[90] See Garafola, *Diaghilev's Ballets Russes*, 39.

[91] Quoted in Schouvaloff, *Léon Bakst*, 149. This inter-arts view resonates with Alexandre, *The Decorative Art*, 8: 'His general colouring, always broad and simple … allows an infinite play of modulations, and seems itself to vary in tone, in sympathy with the poem and the music.'

[92] Vuillermoz, 'Les Théâtres', 66. 'La synthèse de *Daphnis et Chloé* fut … très complète.'

strongly contrasting *corps de ballet* moments: the serene 'Danse religieuse' and brutal 'Danse guerrière'.[93] Quasi-symbolist contrasted pairings that were mentioned earlier include natural/supernatural and dream-world/reality. Other antitheses pertain to location (lush meadow/arid desert), to time (day/night) and crucially to people: crowd/individual, exhilaration/despair, power/powerlessness, elegance/gaucheness, sophistication/primitivism and promiscuity/chastity. (These latter oppositions were well articulated in Ashton's revived choreography of 2004: Lyceion's sexuality was highlighted by Marianela Nuñez in her voluptuous entwinement with the naive Daphnis, played by Federico Bonelli, while Bryaxis's attempted rape of the innocent Chloé was implicit in tearing off her dress.)

Such oppositions may be fashioned into complexes, as illustrated by the pitting of the violent, rustic dance of the collective pirates (Example 3.5; Fig. 92ff.) against the vulnerable, refined solo dance of Chloé (Fig. 132ff.), her hands bound by rope. For the first, 'dissonant' state, Bakst's set for Scene II, introduced earlier, creates the hostility and Ravel plays the virility game, employing a relentless punctuating 2/4 metre at a loud dynamic, marked 'Animé et très rude'. This locus was where Fokine chose his risky, but appar-

Example 3.5 *Daphnis et Chloé* (piano version, 1912): 'Danse guerrière' (Fig. 92)

---

[93] Samazeuilh, 'Les Ballets Russes', 365; Beaumont, *The Diaghilev Ballet in London*, 87–8. These episodes remained amongst the most powerful episodes in a 2004 production, especially black-clad pirates brandishing fire torches and executing the bravura *grand jeté*.

ently effective, improvised group staging. Beaumont's testimony for 1914 points up the unified violent vision: 'a thrilling scene of quarrelling and discord, of savage fighting and wrestling, admirably phrased to the music and set against a background of orange-brown cliffs and a burning blue sky'.[94] In the antithetical second state, Chloé's poignant sophistication in her 'Imploring dance' receives special characterization in Ravel's halting waltz (Example 3.6; Figs. 133–9), with unusual built-in *tempo rubato* – a classic instance of 'music as an emotional metaphor'.[95] (For more on the waltz, see Chapters 4–5.) The approach marries with Fokine's quest for polarized dance styles, which for Chloé and Daphnis were based on the '*plastique* of the period of Greece's prime'.[96] This raises the question of how exactly Fokine achieved his aims. Levinson considered that only Maurice Emmanuel approximated a convincing reading of *orcheisthai* movement from ancient Greek art sources. There was more common ground with 'modern' ballet, he argued, than often supposed, including *attitudes*, *battements* and *fouettés*; in contrast to Fokine's interpretation, some movements were on full *pointe* using a precursor of the *pointe* shoe. Rather than being entirely naturalistic, Greek dance still involved 'artifice' and semi-nudity was not the order of the day.[97] Whatever their authenticity, Fokine's musico-choreographic strategies received exquisite realization in Karsavina's dancing (Figure 3.1): 'she is forever grace, a flower or smile personified; from all of her being wafts a scent of youth, of charm and seduction whose impression on the spectator is irresistible'.[98] Subsequently these oppositions are deconstructed through the will of Pan, with Chloé's beautiful anguish transferred to the pirates and mutated into ugly terror, aided by the formidable wind-machine, and the

Example 3.6 *Daphnis et Chloé* (ballet, 1913): 'Danse suppliante de Chloé' (Fig. 133)

---

[94] Beaumont, *The Diaghilev Ballet in London*, 88.

[95] Jordan, *Moving Music*, 65.

[96] Fokine, *Memoirs*, 213.

[97] Levinson, *Ballet Old and New*, 65–7.

[98] Pougin, 'Semaine théâtrale', 189; 'elle est toujours la grâce, la fleur et le sourire en personne; de tout son être s'échappe un parfum de jeunesse, de charme et de séduction dont l'impression sur le spectateur est irrésistible.'

pirates' exhilaration ultimately restored to Chloé and Daphnis in the blissful
finale.

The polarized dances of Dorcon and Daphnis, embedded in the dancing
competition for Chloé's affections, offer a progression from the ridiculous
to the sublime. (Ironically, a real dancing competition was also unfolding
between Nijinsky and Fokine, with Diaghilev completing that triangle.)
There is even onomatopœia to the names of Daphnis and Dorcon, the latter's brusque sounds suggesting a rough manner. Interestingly, their opposed
dance treatments resonate with eighteenth-century treatises which related
dance movements to social status and politics: 'From the Regular or Irregular
Motion of the Body, we distinguish the handsome Presence, and Deportment
of the fine Gentleman, from the awkward Behaviour of the unpolish'd
Peasant.'[99] Dorcon's aptly titled 'Danse grotesque' (Example 3.7; Fig. 32ff.)
shares the artless 2/4 metre of the pirates. The old chestnut of comic, gruff
bassoons present a prosaic melody that begins with a pompous concluding
fourth gesture, stopping the movement in its tracks, and is followed by
running quavers that would better serve as an opening. When the phrase
does stop, it lands on a dissonant 'bum note'. The constant pedal on
E implies that this heavy-footed dancing never leaves the ground, while
harmonic mismatch with the melody creates further humour. The caricature
is completed by loud off-beat belches (Figs. 33–4) and unseemly semiquaver scuttling to resume position at phrase endings (Figs. 36–7). At 'Pesant'
(Fig. 40), 'the crowd imitates ironically the gauche gestures of the goatherd', with slithering glissandos and an instance of the music quoting and
parodying itself that disintegrates into 'general laughter' (Example 3.8; Fig.
41), conveyed by reiterated staccato chords and hiccupping grace-notes.

Example 3.7 *Daphnis et Chloé*: 'Danse grotesque de Dorcon' (Fig. 32,
          reduction)

---

[99] John Weaver, *Anatomical and Mechanical Lectures upon Dancing* (1721), quoted by
Richard Leppert, 'On music and dance', in Derek B. Scott (ed.), *Music, Culture and Society:
A Reader* (Oxford: Oxford University Press, 2000), 100–02: 101.

Example 3.8 *Daphnis et Chloé*: 'un rire général' (Fig. 41, reduction)

To maximize the character's clumsy appearance, Fokine explains that 'In the dances of Darkon [*sic*] and the nymphs I used more archaic poses ... for the composition of Darkon's part, I utilized more angular positions.'[100] (Such angularity and awkwardness is preserved visually by economical, yet surprisingly evocative, sketches undertaken by Valentine Gross, later Hugo, in the darkness during rehearsals for *Daphnis*. In one sketch, Dorcon is depicted with his right arm raised, displaying an inelegant flat hand as a symbol of his painful labouring of the obvious (Figure 3.4).)[101] The original performer of this role was Adolph Bolm, and Vuillermoz's critique usefully reminds one that effective comedy relies upon impeccable timing: 'Bolm triumphed in a boldly-drawn buffoon dance where he maintained a truly heroic rhythmic precision.'[102] (Much more recently, Martin Harvey triumphed in a 2004 production, with 'he-man' gestures, mock poses after Rodin's 'Le Penseur' and vacuous thrusting.)

While Bolm was a fine executant of existing ideas, Nijinsky supposedly catalysed Ravel's musical exploration in *Daphnis*. Ravel's first jottings for Daphnis's dance (piano score, pp. 26ff.) were thought to be 'inspired by the memory of a wonderful leap sideways which Nijinsky ... used to perform in a *pas seul* in *Le Pavillon d'Armide* ... they were intended to provide the opportunity for similar leaps – the pattern characterized by a run and a long pause, which runs through Daphnis's dance'.[103] His fellow dancer Lydia Sokolova (stage-name of the less exotic Hilda Munnings) recalled this

---

[100] Fokine, *Memoirs*, 213.

[101] Gross, *Nijinsky on Stage*, 110–11.

[102] Vuillermoz, 'Les Théâtres', 68. 'Bolm triompha dans une danse bouffonne hardiment dessinée où il affirma une précision rythmique réellement héroïque.'

[103] Calvocoressi, *Musicians Gallery*, quoted in Nichols (ed.), *Ravel Remembered*, 187. If Ravel's first music was in response to Nijinsky's dancing of *Le Pavillon*, this corroborates other evidence favouring a likely compositional start-date of 1909. A more light-hearted perspective was given in the 1912 programme, in which 'Le Kanguroo [*sic*]: M. Nijinsky' was one of a series of cartoons, entitled 'Buffonneries Parisiennes', reproduced from *Excelsior* of May 1912. This kangaroo image was still relevant to the reconstructed Ashton reading after Fokine, performed by Bonelli at the Royal Opera House in 2004.

Figure 3.4   Valentine Gross, sketch of Dorcon (Adolph Bolm, 1912). By
permission of the Theatre Museum, London; © V & A Images.
© ADAGP, Paris and DACS, London 2004.

astonishing propulsion in *Le Spectre* and asserted that even in his time,
'Nijinsky had been such a myth'[104] – that word again. Nijinsky's power and
athletic technique were legendary; his wife Romola exclaimed that 'His
legs were so muscular that the hard cords stood out on his thighs like
bows.'[105]

For Daphnis's 'Graceful and agile dance' (Example 3.9; Fig. 43ff.), Ravel
employs an elegant 6/8 metre with lilting triplets, and focuses on the treble
register. Daphnis's singable regular phrases, played on flute, could be
derived from a folksong; his half-close (bars 2–3) makes effective use of the
concluding fourth that Dorcon 'mishandled'. A classical model, perhaps
Schubertian, is alluded to in the balancing of an initial F major with its

[104] Lydia Sokolova, *Dancing for Diaghilev*, ed. Richard Buckle (London: John Murray,
1960), 52. See too Nandor Fodor, 'The riddle of Nijinsky', *The Dancing Times*, 333 (June
1938), 268–9.

[105] Romola Nijinsky, *Nijinsky* (London: Victor Gollancz, 1933, repr. 1937), 93.

Example 3.9 *Daphnis et Chloé*: 'Danse gracieuse et legère de Daphnis'
(Fig. 43)

poignant *alter ego* F minor (Fig. 44) – Daphnis may find happiness with
Chloé, yet his intrinsic sadness remains (in the original story he is abandoned by his mother and ends by committing suicide). Daphnis's sophistication is indicated timbrally by the subtle sonority: strings playing *sur la
touche* (on the fingerboard) and ethereal flute harmonics (Fig. 44). Bars 3–4
of each grouping project a pair of leaps synaesthetically via a spring-board
of rising string and harp glissandos – Calvocoressi's 'run' – then suspended
in space with a pause over a quaver rest.[106]

It is interesting to compare Nijinsky's interpretation of Daphnis with the
later characterization by Fokine himself. While Nijinsky was not conven-
tionally handsome and could appear emotionally detached, even sanctioning such disengagement – 'I make myself dance from the outside',[107] Fokine
was physically attractive and benefited from detailed musico-choreographic
understanding. Sokolova had articulated the difference convincingly in discussing *Le Spectre*: 'Fokine danced with a complete understanding of the
music and of the steps he had invented to go with it. Nijinsky had been
sexless – an elfin thing. Fokine dancing with Karsavina was very much the
lover.'[108] Similarly, while she found Nijinsky's performances of Daphnis
hard to read, Sokolova perceived in Fokine's elegant dancing of the role a
fitting 'gentleness', deep insight into artistic communication and his sheer
pleasure in the doing.

Selected interwar productions

Fokine's dancing offers a point of continuity with the predominantly French
productions of the interwar years. *En route*, there was Ravel's further angst
regarding Diaghilev's decision to present merely the cut-down 'budget'

---

[106] See Nichols, *Ravel*, 79; Cohen-Lévinas, '*Daphnis et Chloé*', 92; and Mawer, 'Ballet
and the apotheosis of the dance', 146.

[107] Fodor, 'The riddle of Nijinsky', 269.

[108] Sokolova, *Dancing for Diaghilev*, 52–3.

version of *Daphnis* without the chorus for its UK premiere at Drury Lane on 9 June 1914.[109] Nevertheless, this occasion began the popularization of Ravel's ballets in England, preparing the ground for Ashton's post-Second World War production of *Daphnis*. British interest in Greekness too was long-lived. Schools of Revived Greek Dancing, such as the Ginner Mawer School with the author's namesake Irene Mawer, still flourished in London through the late 1920s and 1930s.[110]

Where the continuing Parisian vogue for Greekness was concerned, the Opéra production of *Daphnis* on 20 June 1921, restaged and danced by Fokine with his wife and conducted by Philippe Gaubert, was a much less fraught affair than the premiere. With its symbolic status and its thematic décor the Opéra provided an apt venue, the Greekness of *Daphnis* according with the sculptural groupings complete with lyre and pipes, on the façade of the Opéra Garnier.[111]

In a letter to Rouché of spring 1921 Ravel voiced his pleasure at Bakst's contribution to the new production: 'I'm entirely in agreement with your opinion on the subject of Bakst's décors and costumes. The second, particularly, is one of his most beautiful.'[112] In May and June 1921, Bakst also wrote to Rouché, asking for a dedicated evening in the theatre to pay proper attention to the lighting. Regarding his collaboration with Fokine and portrayal of the archaic, he explained that 'In agreement with M. Fokine, it will be necessary to have wigs with *glued-down threads* (my invention) for all the dancers to wear – this will give them that striking *archaic head* which the painters liked so much in *L'Après-midi d'un Faune*.'[113] And where correspondence between Fokine and Ravel was concerned, even the contrary critic Louis Vuillemin found that 'The gestures and steps, group entrances,

---

[109] Hence the infamous Ravel–Diaghilev correspondence in *The Times*, repr. Beaumont, *The Diaghilev Ballet in London*, 85–7.

[110] See Clifford K. Wright, 'Dancing in Ancient Greece and Rome', and 'Ginner Mawer Display', *The Dancer* (July–August 1928), 463–7, 496–7.

[111] For his enjoyment at Montfort-L'Amaury, Ravel produced mock-Greek designs: a chair-back with a goddess playing double pipes, a black and white geometric frieze around his dining room walls; he also displayed a Greek vase decorated with figures and a lyre.

[112] Letter to Rouché (16 March 1921): LAS Ravel 5, quoted in Lesure and Nectoux (eds), *Maurice Ravel*, 37. 'Je suis tout à fait de votre avis au sujet des décors ainsi que des costumes de Bakst. Le second, particulièrement est l'un de ses plus beaux.' For Bakst's costumes, see D. 216, 76 (B-MO).

[113] Letter to Rouché (17 May 1921): MS, Archives Nationales, AJ[13] 1208 (Bakst); quoted in Lesure and Nectoux (eds), *Maurice Ravel*, 37. 'D'accord avec M. Fokine, il faudra avoir les perruques en fils collés (mon invention) que porteront tous les danseurs et danseuses – ce qui leur donnera cette frappante tête archaïque dont les peintres aimaient tant dans *L'Après-midi d'un faune*'. Note Bakst's ownership of the wig idea (complete with emphasis through underlining) and the continuing comparison with *L'Après-midi*.

[and] general dances truly complement the symphonic episodes.'[114] Fokine was back in the Parisian limelight, and *Daphnis* stayed in the repertory for several years.

Other 1920s revivals included that by the Ballets Russes at Monte Carlo on 1 January 1924, danced by Anton Dolin (1904–83) and Sokolova with choreography (according to the poster) 'd'après Fokine', undertaken by the company's *régisseur*, Sergei Grigoriev (1883–1968). Garafola comments that 'He [Grigoriev] had a remarkable memory and kept detailed notebooks (with diagrams) about the ballets he rehearsed', but even so, 'he had to do some filling in ... his "own unaided memory" was not entirely sufficient.'[115] In fact Dolin stated that Nijinska had a subsidiary role in the reconstruction,[116] before taking her version 'after Fokine' to the Teatro Colón in Buenos Aires, 1927. In the same year there was a significant Opéra revival starring Carlotta Zambelli and Albert Aveline, but despite the personal credentials, these refashioned performances did not really gel or last.

An Opéra production by Lifar – who had played a brigand and a Greek in 1924 – took place around 1934, shortly before Ravel's death. Critical response was again mixed. Jean-Louis Vaudoyer acknowledged Ravel's masterly score, credited Rouché with bringing this work back into the repertory and praised Lifar as Daphnis: 'He is certainly the only dancer of these times who is able to present himself in a role where memory evokes Nijinsky without this memory being altered or betrayed.'[117] The other dancers apparently fared less well, lacking Lifar's stature and connection with tradition. For Henry Bidou however, Lifar was merely mediocre, his real skills resting with original invention as displayed in his contemporary fantasy, *Icare*

---

[114] Louis Vuillemin, *La Lanterne* (21 June 1921). 'Gestes et pas, entrée de groupes, danses générales, sont véritablement complémentaires des épisodes symphoniques.' For another supportive review, see A. R., '*La Péri* et *Daphnis et Chloé* à l'Opéra', *Comœdia* (21 June 1921).

[115] Personal communication (6 February 2003); Sergei L. Grigoriev, *The Diaghilev Ballet, 1909–1929*, trans. Vera Bowen (Harmondsworth: Penguin Books, 1960), 196. Some Grigoriev manuscripts are preserved in the Music Division, The Library of Congress, Washington, DC. On the restoration of Bakst's sets, whose ultramarine and other deep colours had faded, see Polunin, *The Continental Method of Scene Painting*, 72.

[116] Drummond, *Speaking of Diaghilev*, 237–46. I am grateful to Lynn Garafola for making this point. Newspaper clippings relating to Nijinska's productions are preserved at the Library of Congress.

[117] Jean-Paul Vaudoyer, 'Critique Théâtrale' (28 November 1934), *Daphnis et Chloé*, Dossier d'œuvre, B-MO. 'Il est certainement le seul interprète de ce temps qui puisse se montrer dans un rôle où le souvenir évoque Nijinsky sans que ce souvenir soit altéré ou trahi.' For Lifar as Daphnis, see Serge Lifar, *Lifar on Classical Ballet*, trans. D.M. Dinwiddie (London: Allan Wingate, 1951), plate 24.

(1935).[118] Both reviewers thought the scenario did not fully serve the musical score and that adaptation was needed. Moreover, new designs had become inevitable after Bakst's death; a most unhappy subscriber, while conceding Lifar's status, deplored 'The sad, horrible, miserable evening! *Daphnis* passed in a fog, Longus plunged into grime, Ravel's music illustrated by funeral daubings ... Bakst's décor no longer exists.' His substantive point was that the original production worked as a fusion, supporting Vuillermoz's assessment, and that one could not subsequently keep some elements but not others: 'Is it necessary to teach those in charge ... that it is impossible, in *Daphnis*, to cut dance off from décor, because the fusion is too complete, too deliberate, too premeditated?'[119]

Selected productions after the Second World War

From this point Ravel is a silent partner in further interpretation of his music. Effectively, this is equivalent to present-day practice since, for reasons of finance and choreographic control, most ballet companies work to pre-existing music rather than commissioning new scores. What strikes the spectator is the sheer diversity of choreography and art that Ravel's *Daphnis* has engendered from the English-accented Greek classicism of the Ashton/Craxton production (1951), through the unmistakable painting of Chagall for two choreographic productions (1958–9), to modern, sexually explicit, productions such as that of Graeme Murphy for the Sydney Dance Company (1982) which might have won Fokine's admiration if not Ravel's.[120] The New York City Ballet has also put its signature to *Daphnis*, with choreography by John Taras (1975). All this implies that beyond its immediate composer relationship the music has universal qualities; that it has the flexibility to reach out to different people; that it has the capacity

---

[118] Henry Bidou, 'La Musique, Opéra. – *Daphnis et Chloé*, ballet en un acte de Michel Fokine, musique de Maurice Ravel', *Le Temps* (20 November 1937). This critique seemingly refers to another performance of the same version. In the UK, *Icare* was acclaimed as another instance of 'le miracle grec': *The Dancing Times* (August 1935), 482–3: 483.

[119] 'Le Vieil Abonne', 'La Reprise de *Daphnis* à l'Opéra', *Candide* (18 November 1937). 'La triste, l'horrible, la misérable soirée! Daphnis passé au cirage, Longus plongé dans la crasse, la musique de Ravel illustrée par des barbouillages funèbres ... Le décor de Bakst n'existe plus ... Faut-il apprendre aux responsables ... qu'il est impossible, dans *Daphnis*, d'isoler la danse du décor, parce que la fusion est trop complète, trop voulue, trop préméditée?'

[120] Graeme Murphy's 1982 *Daphnis et Chloé* is preserved on a Home Vision (PMI Company) video. There is also a VHS video (PAL, 52 minutes), produced by Philippe Charluet in 1989, of the production first given in 1980 (ScreenSound Australia, no. 257075): listing for Sydney Dance Company, www.australiadancing.org (accessed 6 June 2004).

to accommodate a broader range of artistic meanings than might at first be apparent. Inherent in this music are the elemental, the fantastical and the classical. These qualities provide some explanation as to why *Daphnis* has long been regarded as a musical masterpiece.

Chagall's connection with Ravel's music at the age of seventy was initially in conjunction with further choreography of Lifar, produced for the Paris Opéra-Ballet on 8 July 1958, at La Monnaie in Brussels. This production marked the end of Lifar's thirty-year involvement with the Opéra, although he later choreographed another version, with Nicolas Zverev, 'after Fokine' at La Scala, Milan on 21 December 1962.[121] After Lifar's departure, Chagall's emblematic designs (Figure 3.5) accompanied the choreography of George Skibine (1920–81) 'at home' at the Opéra, on 4 June 1959.[122]

Figure 3.5   Marc Chagall's set design for *Daphnis*: finale (1958/59). By permission of the Bibliothèque Nationale de France. © ADAGP, Paris and DACS, London 2004.

---

[121] Interestingly, Lesure and Nectoux (eds), *Maurice Ravel*, 36, refers to three costumes after Bakst's sketches, with hand-painted Greek tunics of wool and cotton (dating from 1912), stored in the TML. One is a shepherd's costume worn by Zverev, who was a member of the Ballets Russes from 1915 to early 1926: information from Garafola. Thus both Lifar and Zverev could claim a production that bore resemblance, via an extended lineage, to Fokine's original.

[122] Figure 3.5 is catalogued as an Opéra rehearsal of 1958 (implying Lifar's work), but is credited as Skibine's choreography of 1959 in a programme for *Daphnis* produced by the Opéra de Paris, Bastille (23 June 1990). For other images, see Mary Clarke and Clement Crisp, *Design for Ballet* (London: Studio Vista, 1978), 239, plus two stage photographs (clichés Michel Petit) and a colour reproduction of the décor, B-MO.

These designs – inspired by first-hand experience of Greece – represented an offshoot of Chagall's epic project, running through the 1950s, of forty-two lithographs to accompany Longus's recounting of the *Daphnis* myth.[123] Performance of Chagall's *Daphnis* at the Opéra acquires a particular inter-textual dimension across time, since the domed theatre ceiling is adorned by his painting of 1964, a venture that led to the foyer design of the New York Metropolitan Opera House in 1966. The ceiling is typical Chagall, exhibiting apt circularity which keeps the eye moving, distinct portions divided by colour-palette and image, his signature angels playing instruments, plus birds and the requisite dancers amidst Parisian architectural landmarks.

Some of Chagall's designs for *Daphnis* may be seen in a later ballet programme;[124] a painted canvas backdrop for the final tableau anticipates, vertically, the circularity of the ceiling: a large central floral sun is surrounded by images of nature (tree, bird) and the divine (flying angelic presence) and further enveloped by dramatic swirls. Such images, if not especially Greek, celebrate luxuriously the mixture of pastoral, fantasy and Russian-inflected drama in Ravel's music, which in turn René Dumesnil thought to be 'translated ... with respect and clarity, one could even add with a piety which gave it its full meaning'.[125] Chagall's spirituality with embedded poetic allegory – Biblical allusions to the Jesse Tree and Garden of Eden – highlighted this dimension of Ravel's music (although Ravel might have found the overt religiosity problematic). For Olivier Merlin, despite Chagall's 'mouth-watering' feast of porphyry, jade, lapis, ruby and ochre, the backdrops behind the dancers distracted the spectator: 'Here, pictorially speaking, the bride is too beautiful. It is a rich reproach.'[126] This was doubtless partly a consequence of Chagall's focus upon visually autonomous lithographs. The title role was assumed by Skibine with Claude Bessy, who then partnered Cyril Atanassof in a later Opéra performance at the Palais de Versailles in May 1966. Merlin's review talks of a consistent 'light', 'agile' bucolic style, featuring ensembles from six to more than 20 dancers, and of spirituality. Once more, opposites articulated the most memorable portions: 'The gracious *farandole* dances of the shepherdesses in the first scene, [and] the brutal action steps of the pirates before the "panic" terror of the second tableau.'[127] For all its pleasantness, the choreog-

[123] Marc Chagall, *Daphnis and Chloe* (Munich, London and New York: Prestel Publishing Ltd, 1994).

[124] Programme, Opéra de Paris, Bastille (23 June 1990), 24–6.

[125] René Dumesnil, 'La Partition', *Le Monde* (5 June 1959): '[elle] a été traduite ... avec respect et avec clarté, on pourrait même ajouter avec un piété qui lui donna son plein sens'.

[126] Olivier Merlin, 'A l'Opéra, reprise de *Daphnis et Chloé*', *Le Monde* (5 June 1959): 'Ici, picturalement parlant, la mariée est trop belle. C'est un grief riche.'

[127] Merlin, 'A l'Opéra': 'Les gracieuses farandoles des bergères au premier tableau, le brutal pas d'action des pirates avant la terreur "panique" du deuxième tableau'. See too Dinah Maggie's review, '*Daphnis et Chloé* à l'Opéra', *Le Combat* (8 June 1959), which also commented on a 'unity of expression' in the 1912 *Daphnis*.

raphy and costumes were less compelling than Chagall's vigorous designs, employed again at the Opéra in March 1962.[128]

More experimental choreographic approaches have been tested on French soil and abroad. Jean-Claude Gallotta's production at the Théâtre de la Ville in January 1984 was one, not wholly successful, example likened intriguingly to Morse code: 'Some shorts and some longs. Fast and nervous little gestures, like uncontrolled modern tics, alternate with broad classical movements that constitute the strong beats of his choreography.'[129] This was a case of opposites that did not quite work. Between these punctuations were gaps: firstly, effective silences for appreciating complex images fixed as photographic stills; secondly, more problematic 'dead time' when performers were detached and distanced. While distancing is not inappropriate to the subject-matter or to Ravel's aesthetic, such rather precious intellectualism apparently distanced the audience towards indifference. In his modernist agenda, Gallotta emphasized eroticism over tender sensibilities in the relations between Daphnis (Pascal Gravat) and Chloé (Mathilde Altaraz), enjoying for himself the machinating role of Pan.

Meanwhile Graeme Murphy's truly eclectic production embeds modernity into his portrayal of the ancient, making his starting-point the Longus novel since, according to the designer Kristian Fredrikson, 'the problem with the Ravel libretto is that it has softened everything, poeticised everything and lost its spirit'.[130] But in the same way that the original *Daphnis* owed much to the *fin-de-siècle* and the Belle Epoque, so Murphy's interpretation celebrates an urban New York 1980s present, with the dance competition set in a disco. A la Gallotta, a 1980s viewpoint means direct, explicit sexual choreography, which moves beyond Skibine's and Bessy's stylized, amorous embrace on knees with entwined arms (presented in a preview photograph in *Le Figaro* (31 May 1959)). Equally, it means technological speeding gimmicks: roller blades and skateboards. Murphy also plays with internal temporal relations between dance and music, which do not map in a simple 1:1 ratio. Conversely, from a classical stance – ironically radical in context – he introduces some work *sur les pointes* plus *fouetté* turns, thought by Levinson to be features of Greek dance disregarded by Fokine. Finally, Murphy indulges in fantasy, as with Pan's mechanized vertical entrances

---

[128] See *Le Figaro* (26 March 1962).

[129] René Sirvin, 'Jeux d'esprit', *Le Figaro* (12 January 1984). 'Des brèves et des longues. De petits gestes vifs et nerveux, comme des tics incontrôlés, modernes, alternant avec de larges mouvements classiques qui constituent les temps forts de sa chorégraphie'.

[130] Michael Cathcart [interview for Radio National, Australia], 'Graeme Murphy and Kristian Fredrikson', *Arts Today* (11 May 2000): www.abc.net.au/arts/headspace/rn/artstoday/murphy (accessed 24 November 2003).

and exits – a literal *deus ex machina*, and this is where the greatest congru-ence with Ravel's aesthetic might be found.

Contemporary Greekness: Ashton, Fonteyn and more myth

The English interpretation and reception of French music constitutes a dis-crete topic, and Ashton's work with Ravel's ballets has proved especially influential. On 5 April 1951, Ashton brought Englishness with a modern twist[131] into the international *Daphnis* equation with a premiere at Covent Garden by Sadler's Wells Ballet, which in turn prepared the way for his overtly classical *La Valse* (1958). Despite the innate challenges of the *Daphnis* myth and some charges of blandness, the production's essential success, marking Ashton's full maturity, has been attested to by revivals in 1964, 1972–3, 1980–81, 1994 and in Ashton's centenary year, 2004.

While respecting Fokine's conception through attention to scenario and score and making some reference to Longus, but '[d]eclaring himself bored with barefoot pseudo-Hellenic ballets involving "tunics and veils and scarves" ... Ashton wanted a ballet that was believable in a modern context.'[132] He looked to create elegant, simple and varied solos and groupings, though some criticized his patterns as insufficiently characterized. Strictly speak-ing, the impetus for a contemporary (1950s) Greek setting may have been that of the designer, John Craxton (b. 1922).[133] Either way, this production, anticipating other postwar interpretations, played with time: although the cast wore simple trousers and skirts and alluded to handkerchief dances, they also donned ballet shoes to enable female work *sur les pointes*, while the men sported laurel wreaths and feigned playing wooden pipes.

Visually, this *Daphnis* closely approached an accurate depiction of Greece, since Craxton had substantial first-hand experience of the country. In his rough design for the first scene, with azure sky, burnt earthy colours and Mediterranean vines, fig tree, goats and hooded figure, Craxton explained that he had incorporated 'the forms of a mountain opposite Poros

---

[131] See A. L., 'A new ballet triumphs', *Daily Mirror* (6 April 1951), or M. C., 'Clever *Daphnis et Chloé* ballet', *Daily Telegraph* (6 April 1951).

[132] Christian, '*Daphnis et Chloé*', 341. Ashton's choreography has been recorded in Benesh notation by Faith Worth and others, with various layerings and endings informed by Ashton's annotated vocal score ('with production notes'), early rehearsal film footage (sadly lacking sound) and films of 1972 and 1994; see Ashton Collection, ROHA.

[133] Jill Anne Bowden, 'John Craxton, *Daphnis and Chloé*, and Greece', *The Dancing Times*, 981 (June 1992), 851–3: 852. Craxton was heavily involved in the 2004 revival that saw his sets recreated. I am most grateful to Craxton for detailed personal correspondence (5 July 2004) and lively conversation.

... called the "Kimomeni" or sleeping woman'.[134] The allusion is apt and immediately evident: female nudity concealed on set (Figure 3.6), balanced by a colossal Pan depicted on the transparent front-gauze as Greek fertility symbol. Meanwhile, Cretan designs inspired the pirates' costumes.[135] Unprepared for a literal portrayal that was far removed from lush meadows, some were taken aback by how stark and angular Craxton's contemporary images were, although years earlier Levinson had declared Bakst's second scene 'grim and desolate'. It is particularly illuminating to see what Parisians made of this English 'take' on a Russo-French artwork. In short, they were curious and astounded both by costumes ('One just has to see these shepherds of Longus, who appear to have escaped from the last Wimbledon tournament') and by sets ('the temple of Delphi transformed by Le Corbusier into a "standard living unit"').[136]

Figure 3.6   John Craxton, *Daphnis et Chloé*: Scene I (1951). By permission of the Royal Opera House, Covent Garden. © John Craxton.

---

[134] Bowden, 'John Craxton', 852; for the second scene, see 853. The original designs are held in the TML.

[135] See Bryaxis with cummerbund and knee-length breeches, in [Margot Fonteyn,] *The Art of Margot Fonteyn*, photographed by Keith Money (London: Michael Joseph, 1965), n.p.

[136] Claude Baignères, 'A l'Opéra, *Daphnis et Chloé* par la compagnie de Sadler's Wells', *Le Figaro* (4 October 1954). 'Il faut voir ces bergers de Longus, qui semblent échappés du dernier tournoi de Wimbledon ... le temple de Delphe transformé par Le Corbusier en un "bloc d'habitat conforme".' For a shepherd's costume, see Alexander Bland, *The Royal Ballet: The First Fifty Years* (London: Threshold Books, 1981).

Whatever people made of its time travel, the ballet still enjoyed a good measure of cohesion: Jill Anne Bowden talks of 'the resonance of the ballet's austere steps and climate of scorched air', and 'remember[s] it as marvellously endowed with that most elusive of all stage qualities – a sense of place'.[137] (The Royal Ballet production of May 2004 maintained this colourful and poetic stage presence, fitting for Ravel's music.) And while Ashton wisely did not try to replicate the impressionistic surface of Ravel's score, he was sensitive to the overall classical simplicity that underpinned the musical architecture. His dance patterns included initial strings of six male and six female dancers, circular formations and (in the all-action finale, matching the extended tutti) a large-scale spiral – the 'Snake', with dancers linked together via their hand-held scarves, embellished by 'step-hop-step', turning, canonic effects, *sissonnes*, 'foot slapping' and the signature 'Fred step'.[138] Ashton talked about how 'overwhelming' he found the musical waves of *Daphnis*, especially those of its final scene, and how simplicity – even complete stillness – could be the fitting choreographic answer.[139] Craxton, being a musician's son and part of the so-called neoromantic movement, was unusually attuned to parallels, or working 'à côté', between design and music. He identified each principal dancer with a colour, which 'at the same time when they were moving together ... formed changing chords *not of music* but of colour';[140] again one perceives a rethinking of verticals à la Albright.

This *Daphnis* also connects with myth – the Fonteyn legend. Margot Fonteyn (1919–91), who starred as Chloé, became arguably the best-known name in postwar English ballet, indeed almost synonymous with it – a status absolutely clinched when she later partnered Rudolph Nureyev. Even if Fonteyn's innate technique was not exceptional, she played to her strengths: artistic expressivity including arm gestures, musical sensitivity, acting skills, stage presence and ability to communicate with her audience. Comparisons have been made with Karsavina, who fully approved Fonteyn's joyous dance to flute accompaniment in the final scene (Example 3.10; Fig. 176ff.), declaring it 'one of the most felicitous imaginings of Ashton'.[141] Ashton's musicality is revealed in his response to the flute phrasing, which both marks it and visualizes a comparable, intricate filigree. One notable Ravelian literalism

---

[137] Bowden, 'John Craxton', 851.

[138] Benesh score, Fig. 196ff. Other ROHA materials include programmes, press reviews and photographs. See too Geraldine Morris, 'Dance partnerships: Ashton and his dancers', *Dance Research*, 19/1 (Summer 2001), 11–59: 15–16.

[139] See Jordan, *Moving Music*, 224.

[140] Personal correspondence (5 July 2004); see too Bowden, 'John Craxton', 852.

[141] Tamara Karsavina, review in Richard Buckle's journal *Ballet*, quoted in Bowden, 'John Craxton', 852.

Example 3.10 *Daphnis et Chloé* (piano version, 1912): Scene III (Fig. 176)

concerns the on-looking shepherdesses oscillating their raised hands to musical tremolos, around Fig. 180. In the French press, too, Fonteyn was praised. In her homage-giving 'adage', the opening of the *pas de deux* followed by solo 'variations', she revealed 'grace, surety, suppleness, poetry; this is a bravura piece doubtless conceived for her in which her talent shines in all its glory'.[142] Once again, Chloé's exquisite persona, with Fonteyn articulating spatial 'dynamic' contrasts, was set against 'the prodigious effervescence of the abduction scene'.[143] Maximizing this difference in the second scene was crucial to Craxton, who utilized a 'hottish light … to give it a more intimidating look, more snarling, to contrast with Chloé's incredibly touching choreography, her fear and vulnerability'.[144] (Such antithesis was reasonably maintained in 2004 even if Jaimie Tapper's muscular physique and

---

[142] Baignères, 'A l'Opéra': 'grâce, sûreté, souplesse, poésie, c'est là un morceau de bravoure conçu pour elle sans doute et où son talent brille de tous ses feux'. Jordan used Fonteyn's dance to illustrate how much interpretative power a dancer can bring (*Moving Music*, 264).

[143] Morris, 'Dance partnerships', 21–4; Baignères, 'A l'Opéra': 'la prodigieuse effervescence de la scène du rapt'.

[144] Personal correspondence (5 July 2004).

manner compromised Chloé's alluring fragility, a point corroborated by Debra Craine and Clement Crisp.)[145]

The Fonteyn legend is explored in an extravagant volume by Keith Money, who believed, as did Fonteyn herself, that dancing *Daphnis* was of the deepest emotional significance to her.[146] Certainly, it was the ballet in which Ashton most missed her after she retired, although the mantle was assumed admirably by Antoinette Sibley. For Fonteyn, Ravel's score had succeeded in representing its subject-matter, and Ashton's choreography inspired a similar conviction: 'Each of my variations seemed to be worked out with a brilliant off-hand casualness on Fred's part, in less than half an hour.' In Ashton's account, the enjoyment was equal, although he found *Daphnis* among his most challenging projects.[147] A strong image of the production – bringing out the antitheses referred to earlier – was created a few years later by the photographer Reg Wilson. Chloé (Fonteyn), adopting an *arabesque*, marks a line of symmetry between Dorcon (repulsion; Ronald Hynd) kneeling on the right and Daphnis (attraction; Christopher Gable) on the left, who is in turn compromised by a fondling Lyceion (Georgina Parkinson) with her more impressive *arabesque*.[148] Chloé's uncomfortable, confused demeanour is conveyed by her crossed arms, pulled in opposite directions by her competing suitors (Figure 3.7). In turn, this image acts as an apt metaphor for the anguished collaborative processes involved in the original creation of *Daphnis*.

Despite initial reservations about the time travel, Peter Brinson and Crisp were confident that, in eschewing false antiquity and folk imitation, Ashton did not sacrifice ceremony or respect. His opening group dances managed to 'recapture the feeling of ritual and homage to the god … in beautifully simple and convincing terms' (Figure 3.8). (In the 2004 revival, such simplicity was achieved again in the unanimous turning to worship and offer bread and fruit before Pan's altar, to audience left.) Equally, Ashton still managed to convey the playful frolicking of summer-loving youth. For some, Ravel's music was again perceived as complete without dance. Others, however, regarding the visual dimension as essential, applauded the combination of old and new: 'continued acquaintance soon revealed that it is one

---

[145] Debra Craine, 'Diaghilev bill', *The Times* (10 May 2004); Clement Crisp, 'Diaghilev ballets', *The Financial Times* (11 May 2004).

[146] [Fonteyn,] 'Introduction' by Keith Money, *The Art of Margot Fonteyn*, n.p. For more objective coverage, see again Morris, 'Dance partnerships', 13, 17–26. A film of Fonteyn dancing part of *Daphnis* is also preserved in The New York Public Library for the Performing Arts.

[147] Christian, '*Daphnis et Chloé*', 341. Ashton's skill in echoing reality was later confirmed on a visit he and Fonteyn made to Greece.

[148] The characters Dorcon and Lyceion are spelled respectively Dorkon and Lykanion in this production.

Figure 3.7   Frederick Ashton, *Daphnis et Chloé* (Royal Ballet, November 1964): Chloé (Margot Fonteyn), Daphnis (Christopher Gable), Lyceion (Georgina Parkinson) and Dorcon (Ronald Hynd). © Reg Wilson; reproduced by permission.

Figure 3.8   Frederick Ashton, *Daphnis et Chloé*: 'Danse religieuse' (Royal
              Ballet, November 1964; Anthony Dowell [centre]). By permission
              of the Royal Opera House, Covent Garden. © Donald Southern.

of Ashton's most moving and rewarding short ballets';[149] Money concluded
that 'Ashton was inspired to match the luminous Ravel score with one of his
most exquisite ballets, and the breathtaking perfection of Fonteyn's Chloé
… remains one of the unforgettable art images of a generation.'

Tribulations apart, *Daphnis* was a triumph for Ravel and generally well synthesized as a ballet. Its continuing evolution creates a truly multi-faceted
work, with varied responses to issues of time and place. Yet, while one
would never want to forgo Chagall's sumptuous art or Ashton's elegant choreography, it is hard to stage *Daphnis* wholly successfully; for Grigoriev,

---

[149] J. H. M., '*Daphnis et Chloé* at Covent Garden', *Manchester Guardian* (7 April 1951);
Peter Brinson and Clement Crisp, *Ballet and Dance: A Guide to the Repertory* (London:
David and Charles, 1980), 109–10.

Daphnis always remained 'an unlucky ballet'.[150] Although the musical *chef-d'œuvre* label is assured, a good case can be made for a more dramatic, less narratively dependent scenario, which in turn might have musical implications. Moreover, questions remain about Daphnis's suitability as a mythical hero, an issue recognized early on.[151] The Daphnis story has only been set to music infrequently, one example being the enacted intermezzo from Tchaikovsky's opera *The Queen of Spades*, produced effectively by the Royal Northern College of Music, Manchester, in March 2002. For Murphy's *Daphnis*, founded on Longus, the intriguing question emerges as to how far one can travel from the 1912 production before the product becomes not merely a new interpretation, but a new work, albeit with a close connection. (Certainly, a lesser new work emerged when Bakst's first backcloth was recycled for *Les Dieux Mendiants* (The Gods go a-begging, 1928); commissioned by Diaghilev, this pastorale used arrangements of Handel's music by Sir Thomas Beecham and Balanchine's choreography.)[152] Similar questions could be asked of Hans van Manen's abstract interpretation of the Second Suite. Ultimately, part of the appeal of *Daphnis* is as an elusive period piece, reflecting an attractive pre-1914 *Zeitgeist* and cultural milieu that defies recapture.

---

[150] Grigoriev, *The Diaghilev Ballet*, 196.

[151] Sokolova, *Dancing for Diaghilev*, 53. See Segal, 'In quest of the hero', in *Theorizing about Myth*, 117–34.

[152] [Balanchine,] *Choreography by George Balanchine*, 88.

Chapter 4

Essays on the waltz I: *Adélaïde ou le langage des fleurs (Valses nobles)*

Dance occupied a privileged place in Ravel's musical output, and his revisiting of its iconic form as the waltz, which superseded his earlier infatuation with the minuet, is of particular significance. Ravel's long-lived love for the waltz enables pre- and postwar comparison and relates to questions of neoromanticism and neoclassicism. This double chapter (Chapters 4–5) maintains the basic formula of exploring the genesis, scenario, collaborative processes and readings of the music in association with design and choreography. Here, however, rhythm is especially highlighted. Following on from *Daphnis* and the Ballets Russes, this treatment of waltzes enables comparison between two other predominantly Russian dance forces: the prewar troupe of Trouhanova and the postwar Ballets Ida Rubinstein, following the Ravel–Diaghilev rupture. Chapters 4–5 discuss one work that, in the spirit of *Ma Mère l'Oye* or *Le Tombeau*, evolved to become a ballet – *Adélaïde* – and one that was originally conceived choreographically – *La Valse*.[1] Although the main discussion of these waltz loci is divided to avoid overcomplication, there is prominent common ground which suggests that Ravel developed a certain sonic image of the waltz. This is the reason for housing these essays in contiguous chapters supported by comparative music examples. The idea of juxtaposing the works was rehearsed briefly by Roland-Manuel in 1939[2] and was exploited fully in Balanchine's highly successful joint production, first realized in 1951, and visited as the final port of call (Chapter 5, 'Epilogue'; see pp. 172ff. below).

Genesis, orchestration and further evolution

This balletic exploration of the waltz began life as a classical Schubertian set of waltzes for piano entitled *Valses nobles et sentimentales*; Schubert himself had produced an extensive set of lyrical *Valses sentimentales*, Op.

---

[1] Additionally, there is a single waltz for 'Beauty and the Beast' in *Ma Mère l'Oye* and a late essay in *L'Enfant* (see pp. 43 and 68–9 above).

[2] Roland-Manuel, 'Des valses à *La Valse*'.

50 (D.779, 1823) and a smaller collection of *Valses nobles*, Op. 77 (D.969, 1827). Ravel's work comprised seven waltzes concluded by a slow epilogue, and was one of several pieces premiered anonymously at a concert of the Société Musicale Indépendante in the Salle Gaveau on 9 May 1911. Listeners had to guess the respective composers, with some predictably embarrassing results. Milhaud, an astute contemporary observer, was well aware of the risks involved: 'What a dangerous game that was. The results were wildly out. Some of Ravel's friends and admirers, who were really very familiar with his music, did not recognize his style, and mercilessly ridiculed *Valses nobles et sentimentales*.'[3]

On the work's musical attributes, Ravel's own account asserts that

> The title of *Valses nobles et sentimentales* indicates sufficiently my intention of composing a chain of waltzes after the example of Schubert. The virtuosity that formed the basis of *Gaspard de la nuit* is followed by a cleaner, more clarified writing, which points up the harmony and sharpens the contours of the music ... The seventh [waltz] seems to me the most characteristic.[4]

It is worth bearing in mind from the outset Ravel's emphasis upon clarity and harmonic angularity, including the punctuating effect of modulation, as well as his singling out of waltz VII. Other qualities include the small scale of the pieces (mostly in ternary form), the sheer variety of triple metre, tempos and textures, and a generally wistful, yearning mood. These waltzes are wonderfully fluid and flexible, thus conducive to translation into the physical movements of dance,[5] with expressive dynamic 'hairpins',[6] ritardandos and, rarely for Ravel, tempo rubato. Some are end-stopped; others enjoy elision through to the next dance.

The collection begins with a declamatory, fanfare-like noble waltz which logically became a curtain-raiser, or overture in some later balletic interpretations, whilst waltz II is poignant and full of sentiment, with its opening anguished augmented harmonies within a modal G minor: Bb, D, F#; Ab, C, E (Example 4.1; bars 1–4). Other slower movements that thrive on

---

[3] Darius Milhaud, *My Happy Life: An Autobiography*, trans. Donald Evans, George Hall and Christopher Palmer (London and New York: Marion Boyars, 1995), 53.

[4] [Roland-Manuel,] 'Une esquisse autobiographique', 21. 'Le titre de *Valses nobles et sentimentales* indique assez mon intention de composer une chaîne de valses à l'exemple de Schubert. A la virtuosité qui faisait le fond de *Gaspard de la nuit* succède une écriture nettement plus clarifiée, qui durcit l'harmonie et accuse les reliefs de la musique ... La septième me paraît la plus caractéristique.'

[5] Noël Goodwin identifies particularly 'flexibility in metre and displaced accents which challenge a choreographer's invention'. Noël Goodwin, 'Ravel', in Bremser (ed.), *International Dictionary of Ballet*, vol. II, 1180–82: 1182.

[6] For definition, see Chapter 3, n. 41.

Example 4.1 *Valses nobles et sentimentales* (piano, 1911): II (bars 1–4)

expressivity include the intimate waltz V, with a kind of vocalise ('le chant très en dehors'), and, most notably, the elusive 'Epilogue' (VIII). Here harmonies are aptly suspended in air, held across the rests, for example in bars 1–4; the chords are spaciously placed, and adorned sparingly with delicate grace-notes. Although this final movement returns to the work's tonic of G major, it does so through mysterious, secretive routes that explore remote flat-key regions. The third, fourth and sixth dances offer greater forward propulsion, with the fourth interpolating delightfully fleeting gestures of arpeggiated triplets while maintaining the formal trappings of a Schubertian waltz with notated repeat marks and first- and second-time bars.

Ravel's favoured seventh waltz is a supple and subtle entity, somehow complete in itself. It embodies in a single, more extended unit many of the qualities already identified. An expressive introduction, not bluntly 'slow', but subtly 'moins vif', charts sound and silence, with three brief arching contours that are ripe for choreographic representation. A more formalized second section (bars 19–66) sharpens the melodic/rhythmic outline, with the characteristic dotted rhythms and emphasis upon the second beat of the bar (see Example 5.6, p. 177); a third section (bars 67ff.) then explores in fluid detail the potential of the fleeting triplet writing introduced earlier in the set (Example 5.7, p. 177).

Ravel was clearly particularly taken by this section and used it in analysis of his practice in a harmonic textbook published by René Lenormand in 1913. The composer explains how bars 66–78, despite looking quite complex, are based upon a single chord: F, A, C, D. This chord contains a mild dissonance, with pitch D heard against C within the localized F major tonality, which Ravel regards as an 'appoggiatura without resolution'. Interestingly, Ravel offers a Beethoven rather than a Schubert model for this neoclassical practice: the exquisite yet bold opening of the Sonata Op. 31/3 with its unprepared dissonance.[7]

---

[7] 'Ravel analyse sa propre musique', in Orenstein (ed.), *Maurice Ravel: lettres*, 391–7: 393–4. The early, published source is René Lenormand, *Etude sur l'harmonie moderne* (Paris: Le Monde Musical/Eschig, 1913) and the Ravel MS is Rés. 1093 (2) (B-MO). This material is

The second stage of genesis involved the work's swift orchestration across fifteen days in March 1912[8] and its subsequent balletic evolution; significantly, no one had heard the orchestral version of *Valses nobles*, which owes as much to Emmanuel Chabrier as to Schubert,[9] before it was premiered in its identity as *Adélaïde* the following month. The restrained instrumentation calls for double woodwind supplemented by Ravel's favoured cor anglais, whilst the brass comprises four horns, three trombones, two trumpets and tuba. This use of just two trumpets contributes to a darker sonority. It is especially through the more extensive percussion section that rich Chabrier-like sonorities are obtained. Ravel includes various drums – a small drum ('tambour'), tambourine, timpani and bass drum – together with triangle and cymbals; he also indulges himself with celesta, glockenspiel and two harps. These timbres, in conjunction with Ravel's sensuous string writing – harmonics, portamentos and muted tones (II), pizzicato (III), six-part violin scoring (IV), eighteen-part strings (VIII) and veiled fingerboard sonorities (V) – contribute to the sonic affinity with his French predecessor, as does the sheer rhythmic vivacity of the dances. Meanwhile, other moments, such as the powerful tutti in waltz VII (Fig. 52^{-2}), anticipate the sound-world of *La Valse* (Example 5.6 again).

Extra-musical themes of *Valses nobles–Adélaïde*

Ahead of discussion of the plot and ideas underpinning Ravel's scenario, two extra-musical details of the work, even in its supposedly abstract form, should be mentioned. Firstly, Ravel's score, even in its initial piano version, is prefaced by a quotation from his friend the French Symbolist poet and novelist Henri de Régnier (1894–1936) of 1904: 'le plaisir délicieux et toujours nouveau d'une occupation inutile' ('the delicious and forever novel pleasure of a useless occupation'). This quotation conveys an appropriately decadent image of the waltz, as a societal vehicle, and one which is most fitting in relation to the subsequent scenario. It may also imply a wry self-ironizing on Ravel's part regarding his act of remodelling Schubert's waltzes. Secondly, the explicit labelling of the final movement as 'Epilogue' sets up a further literary association. An epilogue may denote a speech addressed directly to the audience at the end of a play, or a postscript that provides an

---

quoted and summarized in Kelly, 'Maurice Ravel', 872, with part of the MS reproduced in Orenstein (ed.), *A Ravel Reader*, plate 16.

[8] Roland-Manuel, *Maurice Ravel*, 66. The orchestration MS (58 pp.), signed by Ravel, is held in the Carlton Lake Collection, HRC. Additional crayon markings, not in Ravel's hand, most likely originate from its use as a conducting score.

[9] This point is also noted by Goodwin, 'Ravel', 1182.

update on the fates of the work's characters. On two counts, therefore, the listener may wonder whether Ravel had at least an embryonic sense of programme for this music before its balletic evolution.

The story of *Adélaïde* presents a classic romance with a clichéd love triangle. Adélaïde is a flirtatious, fickle courtesan (to be danced by Trouhanova), who hosts an early nineteenth-century Parisian, rather than Viennese, salon. Lorédan is an archetypal tragic poet – originally to be danced by M. Robert Quinault of the Opéra-Comique[10] although the 1912 programme credits M. Bekefi of the Imperial Opera of St Petersburg – who has a deep, initially unrequited love for Adélaïde. By contrast, the aristocratic Duke, to be danced by M. Vandeleer, Maître de Ballet of the Théâtre du Châtelet, is haughty, shallow, but rich, and initially at least much more successful in his courtship.

Ravel's alternative name for the ballet is *Le Langage des fleurs*, which brings into play the well-used floral love topos 'she loves me, she loves me not'. Plant symbolism in literature, with varying signification, can be traced from its origins in Greek myth through Roman laurel wreaths to Shakespeare, with Ophelia's recitations in *Hamlet*.[11] But it was particularly in nineteenth-century France and the Victorian England of Elizabeth Barrett Browning (1806–61) that writers capitalized on this theme: more Baudelairean perfumes. Although there is no concrete evidence to support the claim, it is hard to imagine that Ravel's scenario is not at some level derived from the highly influential book of the same name, *Le Langage des fleurs*, published in 1819 by Charlotte de Latour and itself much indebted to *Emblèmes de flore* by Alexis Lucot, which had appeared earlier in the year.[12]

Ravel's scenario is set around 1820: contemporary with both Latour's book and the work's original inspiration, Franz Schubert (1797–1828). So ideas important to *Adélaïde* include nostalgia as the constructing of an idealized image rather than historical reality, transition between classicism and romanticism, a revisiting of clichés – even, Ravel's favourite, the last waltz before the 'Epilogue'. *Adélaïde* invokes opposites in respect of the courtesan (mistress or prostitute?) and her suitors. Returning to Shakespearian allusion, one perceives echoes of *Romeo and Juliet*, not least the balcony

---

[10] See the advance notice in *Le Courrier musical* (1 April 1912), 211.

[11] Sheila Pickles (ed.), *The Language of Flowers* (London: Pavilion Books Limited, 1990), 5.

[12] Susan Loy, *Flowers, The Angel's Alphabet: The Language and Poetry of Flowers* (Moneta, VA: CSL Press, 2002). Larner (*Maurice Ravel*, 127) also suggests *La Traviata* Act I and the ballet *Le Spectre de la rose* – a series of waltzes with floral connections danced by Nijinsky with the Ballets Russes in 1911 – as possible sources of inspiration.

scene, but Ravel's ending is more ambiguous: is the couple ultimately united in life or death?[13]

Ravel's scenario for *Adélaïde*

At this juncture, it is appropriate to present Ravel's scenario in its most succinct form, from the French catalogue of his works produced in 1954:

> Paris, around 1820, at the house of the courtesan Adélaïde. A salon [decorated] in the style of the day. At the back [of the stage], a window looking out over a garden. On each side, vases filled with flowers are placed on pedestal tables.

> I. A party at the home of Adélaïde. Couples are dancing. Others, seated or walking about, are talking tenderly. Adélaïde mingles with her guests; she breathes in the perfume of a tuberose (voluptuousness).
> II. Lorédan enters, sombre and melancholic. He offers Adélaïde a buttercup. An exchange of flowers expressing Adélaïde's coquettishness and Lorédan's love.
> III. She picks the petals off the first flower and sees that Lorédan's love is sincere. The daisy reveals to Lorédan that he is not loved. Adélaïde is keen to try the test again. This time the response is favourable.
> IV. The two lovers dance, expressing their affections. But Adélaïde sees the Duke enter and stops, taken aback.
> V. The Duke presents her with a bouquet of sunflowers (empty riches), then a jewel case containing a diamond necklace, with which she adorns herself.
> VI. Lorédan's despair. Passionate pursuit. Adélaïde pushes him away coquettishly.
> VII. The Duke entreats Adélaïde to grant him this last waltz. She declines, and goes to seek out Lorédan, languishing at a distance in a tragic pose. He hesitates at first, then lets himself be won over by the gentle insistence of the courtesan.
> VIII. The guests retire. The Duke hopes that he will be detained. Adélaïde offers him an acacia branch (platonic love). The Duke leaves, making clear his displeasure.

> Lorédan comes forward, desperately sad. Adélaïde offers him a poppy (oblivion). He declines it and runs off, making gestures of eternal farewell.

> Adélaïde goes to the window at the back and opens it wide. Voluptuously she breathes in the scents of the tuberose.

> Scaling the balcony, Lorédan appears, destiny written in his eyes, his hair in disarray. He dashes towards Adélaïde, falls to his knees, and takes out a pistol which he brings to his temple.

---

[13] In a Lancaster University course on Ravel's ballets given by the present author in 2002, students were struck by similarities of plot between *Adélaïde* and the film *Moulin rouge* (2001), starring Nicole Kidman as a *fin de siècle* courtesan and Ewan McGregor as the sensitive poet. (The original film of 1952 featured George Auric's score, the theme tune of which reached the top of the 'hit parade' in May 1953.)

Smiling, she pulls a red rose from her bodice and sinks into Lorédan's arms.[14]

The catalogue offers a good working synopsis of the *Carmen*-like plot, but it is fascinating to realize that, as with *Ma Mère l'Oye*, even for a small-scale work there are several variant versions. The primary source of the scenario is Ravel's manuscript, written in black ink on four sides of old lined paper from a notebook (A); this corresponds quite closely with his annotated copy of the piano score of *Valses nobles* (B), where the scenario is carefully overlaid on the music, bar by bar, again in black ink. There is the scenario as printed in the programme of the *Concerts de danse, N. Trouhanowa* [*sic*] of 1912, headed by Drésa's sketch of the set and including a signed manuscript fragment of the opening of waltz II (C). A similar document, a handwritten facsimile published by Durand (D), shows a layer

---

[14] *Catalogue de l'œuvre de Maurice Ravel*:

'A Paris, vers 1820, chez la courtisane Adélaïde.

Un salon dans le goût du jour. Au fond, une fenêtre donnant sur un jardin. De chaque côté, des vases remplis de fleurs sont posés sur des guéridons.

I. – Une fête chez Adélaïde. Des couples dansent. D'autres, assis ou se promenant, conversent tendrement. Adélaïde va et vient parmi ses invités; elle respire le parfum d'une tubéreuse (volupté).

II. – Entre Lorédan, sombre et mélancolique. Il lui offre une renoncule. Echange de fleurs exprimant la coquetterie d'Adélaïde et l'amour de Lorédan.

III. – Elle effeuille la fleur du début et voit que l'amour de Lorédan est sincère. La marguerite révèle à Lorédan qu'il n'est pas aimé. Adélaïde veut bien renouveler l'épreuve. Cette fois la réponse est favorable.

IV. – Les deux amoureux dansent en marquant leurs sentiments. Mais Adélaïde voit entrer le Duc et s'arrête, interdite.

V. – Le Duc lui présente un bouquet de soleils (vaines richesses), puis un écrin contenant un collier de diamants dont elle se pare.

VI. – Désespoir de Lorédan. Poursuite ardente. Adélaïde le repousse avec coquetterie.

VII. – Le Duc supplie Adélaïde de lui accorder cette dernière valse. Elle refuse et s'en vient quérir Lorédan, resté à l'écart dans une attitude tragique. Il hésite d'abord, puis se laisse entraîner par la tendre insistance de la courtisane.

VIII. – Les invités se retirent. Le Duc espère qu'on retiendra. Adélaïde lui fait présent d'une branche d'acacia (amour platonique). Le Duc sort en marquant son dépit.

Lorédan s'avance, triste à mourir. Adélaïde lui offre un coquelicot (oubli). Il refuse et s'enfuit en faisant des gestes d'adieux éternels.

Adélaïde va à la fenêtre du fond et l'ouvre toute grande. Elle aspire voluptueusement les senteurs de la tubéreuse.

Escaladant le balcon, Lorédan paraît, l'œil fatal, la chevelure en désordre. Il se précipite vers Adélaïde, tombe à ses genoux et sort un pistolet qu'il approche de sa tempe.

Souriante, elle tire de sa poitrine une rose rouge et s'abandonne dans les bras de Lorédan.'

of textual corrections that link it to source B.[15] The catalogue will be referred to as source E.

Exhaustive comparisons would not be engrossing or purposeful since the modifications are relatively minor and since the language of these documents is intentionally pragmatic rather than poetic. It is still pertinent however to offer selected observations. Ravel's manuscript (source A) describes *Adélaïde* as a 'ballet-pantomime en 1 acte', and the allusion to French 'pantomime' indicates contemporary common ground with *Ma Mère l'Oye* and part of *Daphnis*. It also conveys the possibility of light-hearted interpretation: is the spectator supposed to take everything at face value, or might a subtle humour underpin this heart-on-sleeve, gestural miniature? Source A has initial stage directions that were later superseded: 'On the right, a door. To the left, a half-opened window looks out on the gardens. In the foreground, on each side of the scene, vases filled with flowers are placed on pedestal tables.'[16] In VIII of this version, Ravel is in fact inconsistent in referring to 'The window at the back.'

This text, like those of sources B, C and D, is more detailed than the version from source E given above. The rising of the curtain, for instance, is noted in Ravel's manuscript at the start of waltz I. In waltz II, Lorédan is described as 'elegant' rather than 'sombre', and the symbolic meaning of the buttercup is included: 'your beauty is full of attractions'. In the text for this expressive anxious waltz, several other floral symbolisms – probably too many to fit comfortably in the musical space available – are invoked: hawthorn (hope), lilac (fraternal love), flame-coloured and black irises, heliotrope ('I love you') and daisies ('I will dream on it').[17] Waltz IV is originally

---

[15] (A): LAS Ravel, 14 [autograph letter, n.d.] (B-MO); (B) Rés. 2249, Maurice Ravel, *Valses nobles et sentimentales* [autograph annotations on piano score, n.d.] (Paris: Durand, 1911; B-MO); (C) *Concerts de danse, N. Trouhanowa* [original programme] (Paris, April 1912); (D) *Adélaïde ou le langage des fleurs, d'après 'Valses nobles et sentimentales' de Maurice Ravel* [facsimile of scenario, illustrated by Drésa] (Paris: Durand, n.d.). I am most grateful to Nigel Simeone for access to these latter two documents and for permission from Durand regarding references to source D; copies may be viewed in the B-MO.

[16] Source A, reproduced in Lesure and Nectoux (eds), *Maurice Ravel*, 34. 'A droite, une porte. A gauche, une fenêtre entr'ouverte donnant sur les jardins. Au 1er plan, des 2 côtés de la scène, des vases remplis de fleurs sont posés sur des guéridons.'

[17] Sources A, B, C and D: 'Entre Lorédan, élégant et mélancolique. Il se dirige vers Adélaïde et lui offre une renoncule ("votre beauté est pleine d'attraits"). Elle accepte l'hommage en minaudant et attache la fleur à son corsage.

Il l'interroge anxieusement du regard en lui désignant l'aubépine (espérance) qui garnit le vase de droite. Elle cueille au vase de gauche une tige de syringa (amour fraternel) et la lui tend. Il refuse vivement et va prendre un Iris flamme qui peint l'état incandescent de son cœur. A son tour, elle prend un Iris noir et pose mystérieusement un doigt sur sa bouche. Enivré, il se précipite à ses pieds en brandissant une branche d'héliotrope ("Je vous aime"). Elle détache deux marguerites ("J'y songerai") et en présente une à Lorédan.'

described as a 'Pas de deux' between Adélaïde and Lorédan, and waltz VII concludes with the direction 'Danse générale' that occurs in *Daphnis*. In the 'Epilogue' (VIII), Adelaïde dreams briefly before the reappearance of Lorédan 'wrapped in a cloak', who throws at Adélaïde's feet a branch of cypress and marigolds, as symbols of his despair. Again, the actions were presumably too numerous to be executed with suitable decorum, let alone decadence. Adélaïde, meanwhile, having revealed her red rose, lets it fall carelessly to the ground. Additional meaning could easily be ascribed to this gesture: is she still only playing her teasing games?[18]

Most details are preserved in sources B, C and D; discrepancies arise, however, over the date of the setting – 1825 (C) versus 1820 (A, B, D) – and over the acute accent on Lorédan's name. The most striking correction marked in source D, which causes it to match up broadly with source B, concerns the incorporation of two additional characters. In waltz VII, a final sentence which originally read 'All the other guests follow their example' is replaced by a parenthetical text: 'The Duke, Hortense and Paméla – Lorédan and Adélaïde – General dancing'. Source B contains another reference to this couple in the 'Epilogue' across bars 18–20: 'The duke leaves, showing his displeasure somewhat. Hortense and Paméla accompany him.' The inclusion of Paméla and Hortense appears to relate to Trouhanova's requirements, but on the evidence of the 1912 programme these characters have already been dispensed with by the time of the premiere.[19]

Ravel's scenario annotations and the score of *Valses nobles*

Ravel's customary precision is well illustrated in source B by annotations to the piano score of waltz III (compare Example 4.2 and Table 4.1). The placing of these annotations reveals how clearly Ravel's programmatic conception of the work respects his existing musical phrase structures. Actions generally begin at the start of a four-bar phrase, with occasional elision across phrases for an extended span of activity. Ringing of the *Cédez* markings, which may

---

[18] Source A, identical beyond its first sentence with source C and the original version of D (before minor alterations were superimposed within D): 'Restée seule, Adélaïde songe, les yeux fermés, aspirant fortement la tubéreuse qu'elle a reprise sur un guéridon ... Apparaît Loredan, enveloppée dans une cape, l'œil fatal, la chevelure en désordre. Il s'avance vers Adélaïde, qui semble ne pas se douter de sa présence, tombe à ses genoux, jette à ses pieds une branche de cyprès et des soucis, symboles du désespoir, et sort de dessous sa cape un pistolet qu'il approche de sa tempe. Souriante, elle tire de sa poitrine une rose rouge, la laisse tomber négligemment et s'abandonne dans les bras de Lorédan.'

[19] Source B: 'Le duc sort en marquant quelque peu son dépit. Hortense et Paméla l'accompagnent.' A letter from Trouhanova to Rouché also mentions 'Paméla', not only as a character but also as the ballet's working title: see n. 27.

Example 4.2 *Valses nobles et sentimentales*: III (bars 33–40)

or may not be in Ravel's own hand, suggests that performance time needs to be maximized in order to complete these actions within the allotted space. Ravel's fastidiousness is indicated by his use of a numerical code system and an asterisk, both notated at the bottom of this page of his score.

Clearly in this instance the music came first, but it matches the fine detail of Ravel's scenario so well that one might almost imagine it to be word-painting, even though the process has been worked in reverse. In waltz II, the slower tempo ('avec une expression intense') and the sustained seventh chords, with uncomfortable augmented triads, are well suited to the entrance and character of Lorédan. Melodically, the sigh-like descending thirds F♯–D♯ and E–C♯ (bars 1–2; text: 'Entre Lorédan ...'), coupled with diminuendos that portray his waning confidence, are especially effective (Example 4.1). By contrast, Adélaïde's lighter music, marked 'doux et expressif' (bars 9ff.; text: 'Elle accepte l'hommage ...'), has greater momentum and a melodic shape embellished by grace-notes across bars 13–15. Plaintive oboes play Lorédan's material in the orchestrated version (Fig. 11; bars 1ff.), while Adélaïde's line is taken by flute (Fig. 12; bars 9ff.). The dialogue structure is inherent in the music, which again raises the unanswerable question as to whether Ravel had some extra-musical image in mind during the original compositional process.

Another interesting music–text relationship occurs in waltz V when, following the Duke's entry, Adélaïde dances with added affectation. Across bars 17–20, at a quiet dynamic in sharpened tonality, the Duke presents Adélaïde with the sunflowers; then at an extremely quiet dynamic (bars 21–4), articulated by an enharmonic change into flattened tonality, Adélaïde

Table 4.1 *Valses nobles*: Ravel's scenario annotations in waltz III (bars 33–47)

Bars	Ravel's notes	Text of scenario (and translation)
33–6	1. demande	Il renouvelle sa déclaration. (He renews his declaration.)
37–40	2. réponse	Elle lui oppose la réponse de la fleur. (It contradicts the response of the flower.) [*Cédez très peu*, ringed in blue crayon.]
41–4	1. demande	[*au Mouvt.*] Peu à peu, ce jeu gagne tous les couples et les réponses causent [line elided] (Gradually, this game overtakes all the couples and the responses cause [line elided])
45–7	2. réponse	des brouilles, suivies de promptes réconciliations.* (quarrels followed by prompt reconciliations.) [*Cédez*, ringed in blue crayon.]

* Ce jeu de scène générale doit commencer au 1er 1.
(This general stage activity should begin at the first no. 1.)

dons the diamond necklace. In this context, musical whispering suggests subterfuge, with Lorédan excluded, while the switch from sharps to flats (bar 21) symbolizes nicely the fickle nature of Adélaïde and perhaps the untrustworthy character of the Duke.

Conversely, Ravel dispenses with scenario for the greater part of waltz VII, which is to be enjoyed as pure, abstract dance (Examples 5.6 and 5.7 below) – as Ravel claimed he wanted for *La Valse* (see p. 155 below). Finally, the 'Epilogue', with its dramatic dénouement, conforms to the character-update formula identified earlier (see p. 129 above): its melodic material resembles strongly that used in waltz II for Lorédan's entrance, and at its more intense presentation (Fig. 67; bars 21ff.), Lorédan comes forward 'desperately sad'. Other earlier numbers are also embedded in this finale. As already mentioned, Ravel tried sometimes to pack too much action into a short musical time-span. This tendency is apparent in source B across bars 21–40 where he has rethought the textual overlay of the scenario upon the music; reconstruction of the history is possible because the initial placement is legible beneath the crossings-out. Originally, Ravel gave only two bars for Lorédan's approach, with Adélaïde offering him the humiliating poppy at the end of bar 23. This schedule was clearly too rushed for melodramatic impact, so that the revision postpones Adélaïde's action until a whole phrase later at bar 29.

At the 'Plus lent' (Fig. 72[-2]; bar 46), Ravel marks the reappearance of the maddened Lorédan 'scaling the balcony'[20] with the distinctive augmented triad from waltz II (here F, A, C♯), which fittingly had been held in reserve. Lorédan's chaotic demeanour and frantic actions then receive literal depiction in the rising and intensifying off-beat three-semiquaver groupings of bar 50 through to the 'Sans ralentir' (Fig. 73[-4]; bar 51). Adélaïde falls into Lorédan's arms at the descending figuration of the 'Au mouvt.'(Fig. 74; bar 59), pointed by the dynamic hairpin. The scenario is then complete and all movement spent. At the 'Même mouvt. un peu las' (Fig. 75; bar 62), the music has a chorale-like quality, whence melodic definition and dynamic are reduced to nothingness.

Balletic collaboration (Drésa and Trouhanova)

Beyond Ravel's double contribution as composer and scenario-writer, collaboration for *Adélaïde* involved a mixture of Russian and French personnel. In contrast with *Daphnis* in the summer of 1912, but in common with *Ma Mère l'Oye* early in the year, this enterprise of spring 1912 was not a fiery meeting of superstars and is consequently much less well documented. Nonetheless, various letters survive that were exchanged between the principal protagonists: Ravel, the lead-dancer and director Natalia Trouhanova,[21] the choreogapher Clustine, the designer Drésa and Rouché (then Director of the Théâtre des Arts, and so often a supporting background force for innovative Parisian ballet projects).

Correspondence between Ravel and Rouché on 9 February 1912 secured Ravel's choice of designer, Drésa, with whom he had just finished working amicably on *Ma Mère l'Oye*:

> Mlle Trouhanova has written to me that she has made you privy to my wishes on the subject of the costumes and décor of the little ballet that she is committed to dancing at the [Théâtre du] Châtelet.
> I would be, in fact, very happy to see Drésa entrusted with the decoration of this work.[22]

---

[20] Compare with Trouhanova's letter, n. 27.

[21] Trouhanova's first name appears in some sources (Garafola, Ivor Guest) as 'Natalia', while others (Gabriel Astruc, Larner and Orenstein) favour the diminutive form Natacha. Discrepancies exist even between two BNF sources, the FR (with the signature 'Natacha' found in some items of Pièce 99 and Pièce 100) and the BNF catalogue (which refers consistently to 'Natalia Vladimirovna Trouhanowa (1885–1956)'). Surname transliterations include Trukhanova.

[22] Autograph letter from Ravel to Rouché (9 February 1912): LAS Ravel, 2 (B-MO), reproduced in Lesure and Nectoux (eds), *Maurice Ravel*, 34. 'Mlle Trouhanova m'écrit qu'elle vous a fait part de mon désir au sujet des costumes et des décors du petit ballet qu'elle doit danser au Châtelet. Je serais en effet très heureux de voir confier à Drésa la décoration de cet ouvrage.'

Drésa responded the same day in very positive terms, thanking Rouché for having offered him *Paméla*, as the work was still known at this point (see p. 139), and adding that he thought this commission would suit him better than d'Indy's *Istar*, with its archaeological and symbolic problems.[23] He continued that all was now understood and that he would chat with Rouché and Ravel whenever convenient. In the same letter, he expressed the pleasure he had experienced with 'our little fairytale': *Ma Mère l'Oye*. Drésa's views, in aesthetic sympathy with Ravel, on avoiding illusion or simulated reality in favour of imagination and fantasy were covered earlier (pp. 57–8 above). So it suffices to discuss briefly his practice as presented primarily in the 1912 programme (source C).

A line drawing of the set, signed by Drésa, is reproduced above the scenario in the programme (Figure 4.1; a rather crude reprint of this sketch appears in source D). Adélaïde and the Duke dance in front of a plush nineteenth-century-style couch placed at the left side of the stage, with tied-back drapes framing the set. The mode is cartoon-like: simple, slightly comical, yet with an erotic hint of Beardsley; both figures perform stylized

Figure 4.1   Jacques Drésa's set design sketch for *Adélaïde* (programme, 1912). Private collection.

---

[23] Letter from André Saglio [Drésa] to Rouché (9 February 1912). FR, Th. des Arts, Arch. R8 (4), Pièce 19 (4). Vincent d'Indy's *Istar*, also part of the programme, was taken on by the little-known George Desvallières.

movements on their toes, evoking their airs and graces. Adélaïde appears slightly off-balance, falling – doubtless with intended innuendo – in the direction of the settee. Paradoxically, she appears coquettish yet is depicted rather stiffly, facing front stage with arms outstretched as befits a courtesan, her decorated party bag hanging on her right arm. Meanwhile, the Duke in left profile advances towards her, one arm in front, the other wafting a hand-kerchief behind, with hands tilted downwards in an affected, mincing pose. His coat tails flow behind him like the forked tail of a demon.

Adélaïde wears an elegant high-waisted evening dress, typical of the early nineteenth century, with a tightly fitted bodice, puffed sleeves and a long skirt adorned at the hemline by roses and flounces. An ostentatious feathered hat, a diamond necklace, long gloves and slippers complete the outfit. A coloured lithograph reproduced in the programme reveals that her ensemble is pale pink, accented by soft green at the neckline, waist-band and striped sleeves.[24] Her face is pretty, yet nonchalant and lacking in expression, though in source D she appears threatened. The Duke wears a buttoned evening coat-and-tails with a frilled dress-shirt. His hair is especially foppish; his facial expression exudes charm in his approach of Adélaïde.

Also contained in the programme is a small sketch of Lorédan sporting a dark jacket with tails, a shirt with ornate collar and cuffs, and dress-trousers. His youthful hair is full on his head, especially at the front, his right arm outstretched in a welcoming gesture towards Adélaïde. Lorédan's demean-our, with weight on his leading right foot, suggests one half of a waltzing couple, as yet lacking a partner. The head of the final page of scenario is decorated with a flouncy ribbon, tied into a central bow, and entwined with a floral garland and leafy stems. Below is featured a highly ornate vase, amply filled with flowers, their leaves trailing down either side.

As a further insight into this visual dimension and Ravel's singular delight in miniatures, one needs only to visit Ravel's small and exquisite house, Le Belvédère, now the Maison-Musée Maurice Ravel, at Montfort-L'Amaury:

> There was the wonderful sailing boat which, at the turn of a hidden handle, used to rock to and fro among waves of wallpaper … and Adélaïde, the doll in a globe, made by Suzanne Roland-Manuel in honour of the ballet *Adélaïde, ou le langage des fleurs*.[25]

---

[24] For a similar coloured image, see Jankélévitch, *Ravel*, 151. For Trouhanova wearing the costume, see the plate in Robert Brussel, 'De la musique et de la danse, les concerts de Mlle Trouhanowa', *Revue musicale de la S.I.M.* (15 May 1912), 55–60.

[25] Hélène Jourdan-Morhange, *Ravel et nous: l'homme, l'ami, le musicien* (Geneva: Editions du Milieu du Monde, 1945), 24; quoted in Nichols (ed.), *Ravel Remembered*, 121. Suzanne was Roland-Manuel's wife.

As with so many ballet projects, it is the choreographic dimension that remains most elusive. Thus, although it is known that Clustine – noted for suppressing the tutu(!) – provided the choreography for *Adélaïde*, having danced with Trouhanova and Carlotta Zambelli at the Opéra de Monte Carlo, there is (fairly typically) little detailed information. A letter to Rouché of early January 1912 apologizes for a tardy response to Rouché's own correspondence: Clustine explains that so much of his time is currently occupied by his work as Maître de Ballet at the Opéra that it seems almost impossible for him to take on the choreography that Rouché is requesting.[26] Despite these difficulties, Clustine did fulfil his brief, but this letter may explain why the choreography seems to have been one of the weaker aspects of the collaboration, as with *Ma Mère l'Oye*.

Correspondence from Trouhanova to Rouché provides a new perspective on Ravel's scenario. It makes clear Trouhanova's central role in pulling together the ballet of *Adélaïde*, including her commissioning the music from Ravel, and confirms Rouché's organizational and financial support behind the scenes:

> I've just written to MM. Drésa and Ravel so that they understand you! M. Ravel's idea would be a romantic pastiche, possibly entitled *Paméla or the two roses*. It would be his *Valses nobles et sentimentales* recently orchestrated and with a change of title! Thus: ball at the home of a courtesan, Paméla, 8 couples dancing. Herself. The Poet. The Old Beau. A pale rose, a red rose. A window or balcony for scaling …[27]

As late as March 1912, Trouhanova appears to have regarded Paméla as a possible name for the central character, yet Ravel's documents all refer to Adélaïde as the main figure, with sources B and D mentioning Paméla only *en passant*.[28] The idea of keeping an either/or title is equally apparent. While light-heartedness has a place in Ravel's scenario, Trouhanova's use of note form and exclamation marks hints at a somewhat flippant attitude to Ravel's scenario, and perhaps at a collaborative tension beneath the surface.

---

[26] Autograph letter from Clustine to Rouché (1 January 1912). FR, Th. des Arts, Pièce 268. Other limited information is found in a separate slim folder: Dossier d'artiste, Ivan Clustine (B-MO).

[27] Letter to Rouché (March 1912). FR, Th. des Arts, Pièce 74 (5); reproduced in Lesure and Nectoux (eds), *Maurice Ravel*, 34. 'Je viens d'écrire à MM. Drésa et Ravel afin qu'ils s'entendent avec vous! L'idée de M. Ravel serait un pastiche romantique sous, peut-être, le titre de "Paméla ou les deux roses". Ce serait ses *Valses nobles et sentimentales* récemment orchestrées et changeant de titre! Donc: bal chez une courtisane, Paméla, 8 couples dansant. Elle. Le Poète. Le Vieux beau. Une rose claire, une rose rouge. Une fenêtre ou balcon à escalade'.

[28] An earlier letter from Trouhanova to Rouché (11 February 1912) also refers to Ravel's ballet as *Paméla*. FR, Th. des Arts, Pièce 100 (4).

Whether or not Trouhanova was overly frivolous in that particular letter, she was undoubtedly serious when it came to acknowledging the many tasks she faced in staging the *Concerts de danse*, an exotic extravaganza designed to showcase her own talents. A contemporary, handwritten *aide-mémoire* document for the various ballets to be prepared – Paul Dukas's *La Péri, poème dansé* (1911), Florent Schmitt's *La Tragédie de Salomé* (Op. 50, 1907), Vincent d'Indy's *Istar*, Mily Balakirev's *Thamar* (later dropped), and implicitly *Adélaïde* – shows the numerous concerns to be dealt with by the director of a production.[29] On a large piece of paper, Trouhanova presents headings and listings for all the elements involved: budget, composers, sets/ scenery, costumes, issues of organization and secretarial support.

Trouhanova questions which musicians might be brought into the project to ensure originality, and jots down the names of the well-known Ravel and little-known Déodat de Séverac (1873–1921) from southern France. Similarly, she wonders which painters to use, and favours Dethomas, Bakst, Piot and Drésa. Beyond the collaborators themselves, she questions which costume makers to employ (Muelle, Poiret, Souplet or Pascard); which theatre (Sarah-Bernhardt, Gaîté, Châtelet, or Opéra-Comique); which orchestra (Orchestre Colonne); which conductor (Pierné, d'Indy, Dukas); and what dates and time (second half of January 1912, afternoon or evening?). In the end, she selected the costumier Marie Muelle, the Théâtre du Châtelet and the Orchestre Lamoureux, conducted by the composers, but it is fascinating to speculate how the ensuing productions might have differed had she opted otherwise. As for the time-scale, January was clearly unrealistic. For one thing, Ravel was fully preoccupied with *Ma Mère l'Oye*; only by the March was he in a position to orchestrate *Valses nobles* (albeit with uncharacteristic speed, since Trouhanova's commission was by then an urgent one).[30]

Other issues include securing dance and 'pantomime' artists, organizing electricians and projector-operators for the theatre, as well as scheduling orchestral and dance rehearsals. Another sheet provides a detailed 'Order of Rehearsals', including those for *Adélaïde*: 16 April in the theatre at 3 o'clock, 18 April in the foyer, followed by full rehearsals on 19 and 20 April. An extra orchestral rehearsal at the Schola Cantorum was even pencilled in for

---

[29] FR, Th. des Arts, Pièce 75 (5). Although this document is undated, it may be contemporaneous with a letter from Trouhanova to Rouché (11 December 1911; FR, Th. des Arts, Pièce 99 (7)) in which she lists the works that she was interested in performing, including a possible Debussy item. Interestingly, Trouhanova was probably Dukas's mistress at this time, hence her role-play as Adélaïde held another layer of significance. See n. 39.

[30] See Larner, *Maurice Ravel*, 126–7. Ravel was audacious in agreeing to deliver the fourth, missing work for Trouhanova's programme. Politically, his acceptance was sensitive since the other premiere was *La Péri*, which Diaghilev had dropped from the 1911 Ballets Russes season. Ravel's *Daphnis* was due to be staged by Diaghilev in the same Théâtre du Châtelet six or so weeks later.

the afternoon of the premiere.[31] Trouhanova recognizes the need for publicity: she considers programmes, posters, newspaper coverage and whether she should contact the magazine *Comœdia*. She also advocates an album consisting of drawings of the sets and costumes.

Confirmation of Trouhanova's choice of main costumier and the fact that Rouché was underwriting the venture are provided by a further document: an initial bill from the firm of Muelle, resident at '12, rue de la Victoire', for the attention of Rouché, in respect of costumes for *Adélaïde*.[32] Even for a modest production, costs were substantial: some thirteen costumes were required for the main dancers, making a subtotal of 2,600 French francs, to which was to be added a further 300 francs for Trouhanova's outfit as Adélaïde, excluding her headdress and shoes. Further requirements were invoiced in a second bill of 19 April 1912.[33]

Premiere, contemporary criticism and interpretation

Adélaïde was premiered on 22 April 1912, also providing the first opportunity to hear *Valses nobles* in its scintillating orchestration. Ravel conducted the Orchestre de l'Association des Concerts Lamoureux in his own work at the Théâtre du Châtelet, as part of the *Concerts de danse, N. Trouhanowa* (the premiere of *La Péri*, conducted by Dukas, together with productions of *La Tragédie de Salomé* and *Istar*, made up the rest of the programme). The performance commenced at 9.15, with seat prices ranging from the exclusive stalls at 20 francs each, to the third amphitheatre, up in the 'gods', at an affordable 1.5 francs. Fittingly, given *Adélaïde*'s preoccupation with social graces, there remains in the Bibliothèque Nationale an invitation ticket, which points out politely that ladies will not be received without a hat.[34] Ravel's pupil and friend, Roland-Manuel, offers a sympathetic critique of his teacher's appearance as conductor:

Ravel had not held a baton since the isolated performance of the Ouverture to *Shéhérazade*. His performance of *Adélaïde* was correct, if not masterly: 'It isn't difficult,' he admitted the first evening, 'It's always in three-time ...' And when we objected that the seventh waltz contained superimposed binary and ternary

---

[31] Dossier d'artiste, 'Trouhanowa' (B-MO). According to this list, *La Péri* received most rehearsal time.

[32] FR, Th. des Arts, Pièce 74 (13).

[33] FR, Th. des Arts, Pièce 74 (15). Other documentation relevant to *Adélaïde* includes: Pièce 75 (7) (accounts); Pièce 98 (7) (correspondence on décors and costumes) and Pièce 113 (scenarios and organization).

[34] Dossier d'artiste, 'Trouhanowa'.

rhythms, he agreed that made it difficult; 'but when I get to that point, I just go round and round'.[35]

Tantalizingly, the programme informs the listener that there were fanfares composed especially for the occasion by d'Indy, Dukas, Ravel and Schmitt to announce the start of each part of the programme. But whereas Dukas's fanfare is reasonably well known to brass players and concert-goers, there is no evidence that Ravel's fanfare is still extant. The role of Rouché is properly credited here, and all personnel who have collaborated in the four-work programme are recognized: other designers such as MM. Piot and Dethomas, the various dancers of the *corps de ballet*, the rehearsal pianist, M. Marseillac, through to the other costumiers (M. Monnot and Mlle Hortense) and the set painters (the respected MM. Mouveau and Cillard). 'Mlle N. Trouhanowa', rather fulsome of build, is photographed with her veils for *La Tragédie de Salomé* (see Figure 4.2). In this way, the sheer complexity of balletic collaboration and organization is emphasized, and Trouhanova's coup, as self-appointed, controlling star of the show – à la Ida Rubinstein – reinforced.

Although critical response to the premiere of *Adélaïde* was limited, Trouhanova did secure at least a modest proportion of the journal coverage she had sought, notably from Jacques Pillois in *Le Courrier musical* and the respected Robert Brussel in the *Revue musicale de la S.I.M.* These two critics offer complementary views of the dance event, thereby contributing to an argument for interpretative plurality; both have positive points to make, but whilst the second assessment is generally much more supportive than the first, it is still unsure about the choreography of *Adélaïde*.

Pillois opens by confronting his equivocation:

> It is a little bit troubling, in a review which prides itself on upholding the best studies on the 'renewal and development of musical dance', to have to express the strangely contradictory impressions left to us by the spectacle of complex art, mixing puerile realization with noble idealism, of Mlle Trouhanowa's dance concert.[36]

Essentially, Pillois identifies a mismatch between theories of poetic symbolism, tragic action or subtle emotion and the actual execution of such

---

[35] Roland-Manuel, *Maurice Ravel*, 66.

[36] Jacques Pillois, 'A propos d'un *Concert de danse*: Mlle Trouhanowa dans des œuvres de Vincent d'Indy, Paul Dukas, M. Ravel et F. Schmitt', *Le Courrier musical* (1 May 1912), 266–8: 266. 'Il est quelque peu troublant, dans une Revue qui s'honore d'abriter les meilleures études sur la "rénouvation et le développement de la Danse musicale", d'avoir à formuler les impressions étrangement contradictoires que nous a laissées le spectacle d'art complexe, mêlé de réalisation puérile et de noble idéalisme, du concert de danse de Mlle Trouhanowa.'

Figure 4.2   'Mlle N. Trouhanowa' in *La Tragédie de Salomé* (programme, 1912). Private collection.

signifying gestures in space. He perceives a lack of clarity between structural dance movement and its small-scale decoration: 'In each of these
works – so varied in their poetic meaning, their musical qualities, their
rhythm – the elements of movement, line and plastic ornamentation could
not be so easily disentangled.'[37] He recognizes that this was a demanding
high-risk task, not least because it could compromise the high stature of
the music, and that it was to Trouhanova's credit to have attempted the
feat with some 'glory'.

As for Ravel, Drésa and their aesthetic congruence, Pillois has only
praise:

> The fantasy that M. Maurice Ravel imagined … renews the amusing and roman-
> tic French game of the *Langage des fleurs*. Around a score orchestrated with ele-
> gance, he entwines an amorous plot between Lorédan and Adélaïde. It is the
> pretext for graceful effects that M. Drésa emphasizes with picturesque costumes
> and décor.[38]

For Brussel, in his extensive review, one distinguishing feature of the production, notwithstanding the central role of Trouhanova, is its essential
Frenchness. Like Pillois, he recognizes first-rate music, but unlike him, he
appreciates the novel interpretative quality of the dancing.[39] Indeed, what
seems to him so original is Trouhanova's highlighting of French symphonic
music in a choreographic spectacle, without any compromising arrangement or adaptation; witness the term 'dance concerts' (including Dukas's
poème dansé). Brussel regards Trouhanova as exceptional and distinctive in
her intellect and 'artistic physique', and his distance from Pillois becomes
increasingly apparent: 'She has above all what matters to art: very striking
views and judgement which are her own. She excels in composing … syn-
theses remarkable as much for their clarity and accuracy as for the picturesque turn that she gives them.'[40] Crucially, Brussel puts forward in

---

[37] Ibid. 'Dans chacune de ces œuvres – si diverses par leur signification poétique, leur
musicalité, leur rythmique – les éléments de mouvement de ligne et de décoration plastique
ne se démêlent pas tous aussi aisément.'

[38] Ibid., 267–8. 'La fantaisie qu'imagina M. Maurice Ravel … renouvelle l'amusant et
romantique jeu français du *Langage des fleurs*. Autour d'une partition instrumentée avec
élégance, il noue une intrigue amoureuse entre Lorédan et Adélaïde. C'est prétexte à de
gracieux ensembles que M. Drésa souligne de costumes et de décors de style pittoresque.'

[39] Brussel, 'De la musique et de la danse', 58. As a friend and recipient of joint postcards
from Trouhanova and Dukas before and after the event (Trouhanova correspondence: BN
Mus. N.L.a. 26: 082, 599), Brussel must however be regarded as a more partial witness.

[40] Ibid., 59. 'Elle a sur tout ce qui concerne l'art, des vues et un jugement très frappants
qui lui appartiennent en propre. Elle excelle à composer … des synthèses remarquables aussi
bien par leur netteté et leur justesse, que par le tour pittoresque qu'elle leur donne.'

hyperbolic language an idea that may be developed into a paradox. Contrary to any superficial impression of Trouhanova's egotism,

> the ordinary egotist personality of any interpreter seems to be absorbed here within the working of the creative mind: zeal and respect so absolute that not only does the interpreter identify with the work, she ends up by effacing herself … so as to leave her designs, her light and shade to the music and to the poetic thought that has engendered it.[41]

But, while Brussel applauds 'the spiritual and piquant elegance of *Adélaïde*', he is forced to acknowledge that Trouhanova's conception in this final work conformed to a more conventional 'ballet silhouette'.

Many years later in Lyon, fond memories persisted of Trouhanova's dance concerts: where *Adélaïde* was concerned, one layer of nostalgia placed upon another. 'Mme Trouhanowa-Ignatieff', as she was later known, was still being credited with her prewar achievement as late as 1935. An unnamed reporter quotes from a remarkably superlative, if repetitious, earlier review by the normally vitriolic Pierre Lalo, who had lauded 'the most choice and beautiful, harmonious and complete spectacle that had been offered to us. A spectacle where music, pantomime, dance and décor combine and are united. Mlle Trouhanowa offered us [this] as a synthesis of the art of our times.'[42]

Later productions and interpretations

The purely orchestral premiere took place on 15 February 1914, conducted by the inimitable Monteux, as part of the Concerts Pierre Monteux for the Société des Concerts Populaires (Figure 4.3).[43] By this point, Trouhanova had already left professional dance because she felt there was no place for classically trained Russians, as reported by René Bizet in 'Les Adieux à la

---

[41] Ibid.: 'la personnalité d'ordinaire égoïste de toute interprète semble y absorber dans la production de l'esprit créateur: Zèle et respect si absolus, que non seulement l'interprète s'identifie à l'œuvre, mais qu'elle finit par s'effacer elle-même … afin de laisser à la musique et à la pensée poétique qui l'a engendrée ses plans, ses reliefs et ses ombres.'

[42] Uncredited article, 'Mme Trouhanowa-Ignatieff à Lyon', *Lyon-Républicain* (17 March 1935), in Dossier d'artiste, 'Trouhanowa': 'le spectacle le plus choisi et le plus beau, le plus harmonieux et le plus complet qui nous ait été offert. Spectacle où la musique, la pantomime, la danse et la décoration se combinent et s'unissent. Mlle Trouhanowa nous a offert comme une synthèse de l'art de notre temps.'

[43] This programme is preserved in the Fonds Rondel (B de l'A, BNF): Cliché 81 C 70892, Arsenal Rondel 4179.

SALLE DU CASINO DE PARIS
16, Rue de Clichy, 16

Société des Concerts Populaires
CONCERTS PIERRE MONTEUX
Sous le patronage de la Société Française des Amis de la Musique

DIMANCHE 15 FÉVRIER 1914, à 2 heures 1/2
DEUXIÈME CONCERT
Avec le concours de

Mlle SUZANNE VORSKA
M. ARTHUR DE GREEF

PROGRAMME

1. Ouverture de Gwendoline..   Chabrier

2. 5me Concerto en fa (p. piano)..   Saint-Saëns
    1) Allegro animato
    2) Andante allegretto
    3) Molto allegro
         M. ARTHUR DE GREEF

3. Valses nobles et sentimen-
    tales .. .. Maurice Ravel
       PREMIÈRE AUDITION
    1) Modéré. 2) Assez lent. 3) Modéré
      4) Assez animé. 5) Presque lent
        6) Assez vif. 7) Moins vif
           8) (Epilogue) lent.

4 a) Chanson triste .. .. H. Duparc

   b) L'invitation au voyage .. ..   —
        Mlle SUZANNE VORSKA

5. La tragédie de Salomé.. .. Fl. Schmitt
    1) Prélude. Danses des Perles
    2) Les enchantements de la mer
       Danse des éclairs, danse de l'effroi
    Une voix : Mlle Magda Leymo

     Chef d'orchestre : Pierre MONTEUX
       Piano Pleyel : Celesta Mustel

Figure 4.3   Programme for the orchestral premiere of *Valses nobles et sentimentales* (1914). By permission of the Bibliothèque Nationale de France.

danse de Mlle Trouhanowa'.[44] There is also a superb early orchestral recording conducted by Piero Coppola with the Orchestre de la Société des Concerts du Conservatoire, performed in the Salle de Conservatoire on 5 February 1934.[45]

A limited number of staged productions ensued, two at the Opéra – one on 9 February 1916[46] and another in 1917 staged by François Ambroisini – being further Rouché initiatives early in his directorship (1915 onwards). The next significant outing for *Adélaïde* was on 28 December 1938, also at the Opéra, to commemorate the first anniversary of Ravel's death. Costumes and sets were designed by Maurice Brianchon, with choreography by Lifar, who also choreographed *Daphnis* and *Boléro*.[47] According to the *Maurice Ravel* exhibition catalogue, this was the eighth production of *Adélaïde*.[48]

Louis Laloy explains that it was because *Adélaïde* had officially just entered the Opéra repertory that its choreography fell to the then Maître de Ballet, Lifar, who in seeking something new could not resist making alterations to the plot. According to Laloy, Lifar did away with the Duke's noble status, making him simply another dancer, and introduced a few new characters:

> I confess to having understood nothing of the plot; but no matter, since the dances retain their characteristic alternation between playfulness, languor, anxiety, hope and joy. M. Serge Lifar, who is the poet, achieved his customary success…[49]

Of course, since the aim was presumably for a coherent, composite work, this shortcoming was probably more consequential than Laloy admits.

---

[44] René Bizet, 'Les Adieux à la danse de Mlle Trouhanowa, une comédienne de demain' (2 February 1913). Dossier d'artiste, 'Trouhanowa'. Although Trouhanova was ribbed for some unfortunate comments about comedy, her real future was in fact to lie in the much more serious business of translating Soviet literature.

[45] CD recording *Maurice Ravel et son temps* (vol. II: 1910–1925): *Valses nobles et sentimentales*, conducted by Piero Coppola (15′02″), Gramophone DB 4935/4936 (2 PG 1294-1, 1295-1, 1304-2, 1305-1).

[46] This 1916 production is confirmed by Louis Laloy, 'Revue musicale', *Revue des deux mondes* (August 1939), 699–711: 700, and by Léandre Vaillat, *Ballets de l'Opéra de Paris* (Paris: Compagnie Française des Arts Graphiques, 1943), 62.

[47] Brianchon's costume designs are preserved, together with those for staging Dukas's *La Péri* in 1937, within a large scrapbook: D. 216, 93 (B-MO). Some characters, including a new one, Le Grand Botzzani [*sic*], sport military-style jackets with epaulettes.

[48] Lesure and Nectoux (eds), *Maurice Ravel*, 34.

[49] Laloy, 'Revue musicale', 700. 'J'avoue n'avoir rien compris à l'intrigue; mais peu importe, puisque les danses gardent leur caractère alterné d'enjouement, de langueur, d'inquiètude, d'espérance et de joie. M. Serge Lifar, qui est le poète, obtient son succès coutumier…' For another review, see Dominique Sordet, '*Adélaïde* de Maurice Ravel', *Action française* (27 January 1939).

Despite the confused scenario on stage, Laloy is struck by how well the music transmits 'the coded message of gestures or flowers': further corroboration of the earlier point that the music sounds as if it were composed to illustrate the extra-musical. Laloy also confirms its highly varied rhythmic personality, whereby 'each one sets off with a different step'.

As for later productions, whilst there was Balanchine's extended waltz interpretation joining *Valses nobles* to *La Valse*, there was at least one shortened version that related to an unidentified production score preserved in the Archives Internationales de Danse.[50] This score, with annotations in English, details lighting requirements (spots, red, white and blue lights, footlights and floodlights) for a mysteriously curtailed production in which the curtain was to rise at the close of waltz I and descend part-way through waltz V. Other interpretations have included Ashton's choreography of 1947 for the junior company of Sadler's Wells with scenery by Sophie Fedorovitch, previously worked in the mid-1930s as *Valentine's Eve*;[51] that from 1966 by Kenneth MacMillan, who had danced in Ashton's production; and Ravel centenary presentations by van Manen and Hynd in 1975.

In the premiere of *Adélaïde*, music, scenario and art enjoyed a successful, close correspondence, catalysed by Trouhanova, but the choreography remained more questionable. On the evidence that he was not involved in additional music – apart from the lost fanfare – or staging detail, it might be argued that the composer was less engaged with this ballet than with *Ma Mère l'Oye*. On the other hand, time was in short supply, both in general terms and in particular because Ravel was committed simultaneously to *Daphnis*. Certainly, Ravel's affection towards *Adélaïde* was evidenced physically by his treasuring of Suzanne Roland-Manuel's model on his piano throughout his life. During World War I, having found a way to contribute to the war effort as a driver, he also named his truck Adélaïde,[52] so revealing his attraction to things mechanical that were perhaps generally more reliable than people. And while *Adélaïde* would not attain the colossal stature of *Daphnis*, it was nevertheless moderately successful, later being taken into the repertory of the Opéra.

    [50] Archives Internationales de Danse (AID), Mus. 646 (B-MO). There are also annotated piano scores of *Valses nobles*, notably those of Robert Casadesus (BN Mus. Vm. Casadesus 000489 (7)) and Yvonne Loriod (BN Mus. Vmg. 039507).

    [51] See Marie Rambert, *Quicksilver: An Autobiography* (London: Macmillan, 1972; repr. 1983), 156. 'He [Ashton] invented a charming sentimental synopsis. At a ball a young man gives his heart to a girl – symbolized by a heart-shaped ornament on a ribbon. In the next dance she passes it on to her partner who passes it to a girl and so on, till it returns, to his dismay, to the true lover and breaks his heart.' For design, see Beaumont, *Ballet Design*, 171.

    [52] Letter to Major A. Blondel (27 May 1916; BNF Mus).

Chapter 5

Essays on the waltz II:
La Valse and epilogue

Prewar genesis of *La Valse*

In terms of its Parisian premiere (1929), *La Valse* represents Ravel's final completed ballet; in its origins, however, it actually predates *Valses nobles*. As far back as 1906, Ravel had in mind a celebration of the waltz, to be entitled simply *Vienne* (Vienna). Just as *Valses nobles* was to take Schubert as its model, so *Vienne* would pay tribute to another eminent Viennese composer;[1] in a letter to Jean Marnold of February 1906, Ravel explains:

> It's not subtle what I'm undertaking at present: a grand waltz, a kind of homage to the memory of the great Strauss, not Richard, the other one, Johann. You know of my profound empathy with these admirable rhythms, and that I rate the *joie de vivre* expressed by the dance much more deeply than Franckist puritanism.[2]

In July of the same year, however, when he contacted his friend and would-be dedicatee Misia Edwards (later Sert), the composition sounded more theoretical: 'I will perhaps decide to undertake *Vienne*, which is destined for you, as you know.'[3] Some eight years on, following the outbreak of the First World War, Ravel was still writing enthusiastically, this time to Roland-Manuel, about plans that included his 'symphonic poem', *Wien*.[4] The term implies, even at this stage, an extra-musical programme, but Ravel was, wisely, reluctant to be drawn too far on this; also notable is that the original title – albeit now in its German spelling – was still being employed.

---

[1] For an analytical reading, see Mawer, 'Ballet and the apotheosis of the dance', 150–55. Ravel's successful capturing of Viennese spirit is noted among foreign tributes following his death: Andreas Liess, 'Ravel et l'esprit viennoise', *La Revue musicale*, 19 (December 1938), 233–5.

[2] Letter to Jean Marnold (7 February 1906), in Orenstein (ed.), *Maurice Ravel: lettres*, 83. 'Ça n'est pas subtil, ce que j'entreprends pour le moment: une grande valse, une manière d'hommage à la mémoire du grand Strauss, pas Richard, l'autre, Johann. V[ou]s savez mon intense sympathie pour ces rythmes admirables, et que j'estime la joie de vivre exprimée par la danse bien plus profonde que le puritanisme franckiste.'

[3] Letter to Misia Edwards (19 July 1906), in ibid., 85–6. 'Je vais peut-être me décider à entreprendre *Vienne* qui v[ou]s est destiné, comme v[ou]s le savez.'

[4] Letters to Roland-Manuel (26 September and 1 October 1914), in ibid., 144.

Although Ravel had been hoping to finish *La Valse* in 1914, the trauma of the war and huge impact of his mother's death exacerbated his habitual compositional struggle. As late as February 1919, in communication with Rouché, he was only 'thinking' about his second essay on the waltz, yet significantly the work was by then referred to as a 'choreographic' poem entitled *La Valse*: a French perspective on the Viennese waltz.[5] Despite the challenges, between December 1919 and February 1920 in the secluded village of Lapras in the Ardèche, Ravel did complete the original solo piano version, the manuscript of which concludes with fascinating ink doodles of spiralling whirls that suggest both a visual and physical dimension to *La Valse* in Ravel's mind;[6] see also Figure 5.1, a later painting which pursues

Figure 5.1   Uncredited painting entitled *'La Valse* de Ravel' (from *Le Courrier musical*, December 1932). By permission of the Bibliothèque Nationale de France.

---

[5] Letter to Rouché (20 February 1919), in ibid., 171.

[6] This MS (15 pp.), signed and dated, is housed in the Mary Flagler Cary Music Collection, The Morgan Library. I am grateful to Roy Howat for first bringing these curious markings to my attention.

this dramatic image. There exists also a two-piano version from the same period.[7]

Orchestration, balletic status and the Diaghilev fiasco

By January 1920, *La Valse* was evolving further as orchestral sonority, a development which Ravel mentions in a letter to his good friend Ida Godebska:

> And I am working: on 31 December I began the orchestration of *Wien* [*sic*]. I hope to finish towards the end of this month. I wrote to Misia that I could let Diaghilev hear it from this time onwards, but that I would prefer to rearrange this hearing for the middle of February.[8]

Misia Sert, half-sister of Ravel's friend Cipa Godebski and then wife of the Spanish painter José-Maria Sert, was still to be the dedicatee. Diaghilev now enters the story because the work was intended for the Ballets Russes, with Sert as designer and Massine as choreographer, though how definite a commitment this was on Diaghilev's part remains open to question. Typically, Ravel's initial schedule turned out to have been optimistic: the final orchestral manuscript was finished, in Lapras, later in spring 1920. During the orchestration process, he had also had to deal with the unfortunate business of the Légion d'honneur, sprung upon him publicly without prior consultation. Ravel dated the final manuscript March 1920; however, in a letter to Georgette Marnold of mid-April 1920 he admits that he has completed the work just the previous night: 'Ouf! I finished yesterday evening – 76 pages – accompanied by the most dreadful God-sent flood and thunder.'[9] The occurrence of this wild weather seems highly apt in view of the destructive force of the music itself. In a letter to an unknown recipient the following month – in the spirit of fishermen's stories – the length of the score has increased to 100 pages, half-killing him in the process; another

---

[7] This MS (22 pp.), with many pencilled corrections, is held in the ROLC. A second, signed MS (25 pp.) is held privately.

[8] Letter to Ida Godebska (15 January 1920), in Orenstein (ed.), *Maurice Ravel: lettres*, 178. 'Et je travaille: le 31 décembre, j'ai commencé l'orchestre de *Wien*. J'espère terminer vers la fin de ce mois. J'ai écrit à Misia que je pourrais dès cette époque, faire entendre ça à Diaghilew, mais que je préférais remettre cette audition au milieu de février.'

[9] Letter to Georgette Marnold (13 April 1920), in Marnat, *Maurice Ravel*, 474. 'Ouf! J'ai terminé hier soir, soixante-seize pages, accompagné d'une flotte et d'un tonnerre de Dieu épouvantables.' The final MS (75 pp., not 76), signed and dated Lapras, December 1919–March 1920, is again part of the ROLC, whilst a MS (70 pp.) notated in pencil is held in the BNF Mus (MS. 17140).

communication of early July 1920 is more pragmatic, detailing the time-consuming corrections for the two-piano transcription in advance of its being lodged with Durand on the following Monday.[10]

Relations between Ravel and Diaghilev had already been severely strained by the traumatic experience of *Daphnis*; they were about to deteriorate to a state of permanent rift.[11] In the company of Stravinsky, Massine and others, Diaghilev finally heard *La Valse* in its two-piano version played by Marcelle Meyer and Ravel at Misia Sert's house. His immediate response was the infamous remark, significantly not granted house-space in Ravel's own cor-respondence: 'Ravel, it's a masterpiece ... but it's not a ballet ... It's the portrait of a ballet ... It's the painting of a ballet.'[12] (A late Edgar Degas painting, perhaps, of a decade earlier?) The commentator on this occasion, Francis Poulenc, continues that Ravel 'picked up his music quite quietly and, without worrying about what we all thought of it, calmly left the room'. Any calmness must surely have been in appearance only: Ravel was furious and never forgave Diaghilev. Garafola comments: 'one ... detects that streak of cruelty that tinged so many of Diaghilev's relationships with "disloyal" or discarded artists. For *La Valse* was very much a ballet.'[13] She adds that Diaghilev may have seen *La Valse* as a mere re-make of its cousin *Valses nobles* (which had flourished despite Diaghilev's rejection of Trouhanova, and which had temporarily distracted Ravel from *Daphnis*).

As for the status of *La Valse*, Diaghilev's outburst raises fascinating ques-tions about the nature of ballet. His argument was that the music was self-sufficient and therefore could not work with dance: there was no space or need for dance. The irony of this perception – with which Poulenc con-curred – was that it did relate to Ravel's successful realization of his 'poème chorégraphique': a symphonic poem totally absorbed by the rhythmic movements of the waltz. Given Ravel's profound interest in Symbolism, from *Sites auriculaires* of 1897 onwards, one might suggest within this music a synaesthetic dimension – the experiencing of one sense (and associ-ated discipline?) via another. Certainly, up to a point *La Valse* does explore the sheer physicality of dance through the aural domain of music.

---

[10] Letter (21 May 1920) and letter to Lucien Garban (3 July 1920), in Orenstein (ed.), *Maurice Ravel: lettres*, 183–4.

[11] The situation was further exacerbated in March 1925 regarding *L'Enfant*, with its cho-reography by Balanchine in his first Ballets Russes engagement. Just a week before the pre-miere, Diaghilev again sought to sabotage a Ravel event by attempting to withdraw his dancers. See Garafola, *Diaghilev's Ballets Russes*, 240.

[12] Francis Poulenc, *Moi et mes amis* (Paris: Editions la Palatine, 1963), 179, quoted in Nichols (ed.), *Ravel Remembered*, 118.

[13] Garafola, *Diaghilev's Ballets Russes*, 239.

Ravel's musical and orchestral style

As a consequence of these aborted plans, *La Valse* was first heard as a concert work; the premiere performed by the Orchestre Lamoureux, with Camille Chevillard as conductor, took place in Paris on 12 December 1920. While *La Valse* was widely acknowledged as the masterpiece that even Diaghilev could discern, a young and, in the circumstances, distinctly tactless Milhaud reviewed the work deprecatingly as 'Saint-Saëns for the Russian ballet'.[14]

The orchestral forces are greater than those for *Adélaïde/Valses nobles*: triple rather than double woodwind, three trumpets, three timpani and additional percussion including castanets, tam-tam and crotales. Although the string section is standard, it is Ravel's extraordinary treatment, such as his opening three-part double bass scoring, that ensures originality.

As a preface to a more detailed musical reading, it is useful to present Noël Goodwin's succinct summary of *La Valse*:

> The music, basically in D major, is a kind of apotheosis of the Viennese waltz in two well-defined sequences, each growing to a climax. The first waltz-chain is exuberant and cheerful in the Viennese manner, but the second is harsher and more turbulent, ending in discord, the brilliance of instrumental effect overshadowing subtleties of rhythm and harmony.[15]

La Valse adopts a conventional ternary form, *ABA'* (opening; Fig.18ff.; Fig. 54ff.), but ultimately for unconventional ends. Out of an unformed, primordial beginning with pulse alone, melody is gradually created to establish a rich, romantic sonic image of the mid-nineteenth-century waltz: specifically a 'Mouvement de Valse viennoise', as stated in the score. Warm string writing on violas (Fig. 9^{+3}; letter A of Ravel's scenario below) denotes the arrival of the first significant thematic material, still questioning and uncertain (Example 5.1, p. 168); true aural intensity is achieved simultaneously with Ravel's direction for full lighting intensity (Fig. 17; Ravel's letter B). Portamentos and intervallic leaps (Figs. 13–17) are wonderfully evocative of romantic sweeps and swoons, yet this powerful emotional content is restrained by appropriate decorum and control. With its leapings, swayings, fancy footwork and rhythmic drive through to cadential points, the music of *La Valse* offers a kind of commentary on, or critique of, physical movement. In this way, formal block *A* establishes Ravel's full orchestral palette, which

---

[14] Darius Milhaud, BBC interview (24 October 1957): 'When the first performance of *La Valse* was given, I was a critic for one of the newspapers and I remember I wrote a very impertinent review.' Quoted in Nichols (ed.), *Ravel Remembered*, 114.

[15] Goodwin, 'Ravel', 1182.

is then contrasted by much more intimate chamber writing in section *B* (Fig. 18ff.) and usually matched balletically by smaller forces. Effectively, section *B* constitutes a suite of closely related dances, although it is interrupted by an episode of boisterous octave leaps, characterized by dotted rhythms (Figs. 36–9) rather reminiscent of section *A*.

Following the appearance of *B* (essentially different), the listener is conditioned to expect some sort of return to *A* (essentially similar). This similarity and familiarity is initially granted (Fig. 54), but all is not as it might first seem on the surface, and indeed right from the start Ravel has brought ambiguity and uncertainty into play. There is a process of dramatic complementation between sections *A* and *A'* – intricately connected and matching opposites, Jungian 'othernesses', or ego and alter ego. These opposites, or dualities, might be read as order/chaos; the civilized/the barbaric. Section *A'* cannot quite be relied upon. The first sign that connotes a possible loss of classical control is a semitonal slippage of the original viola pitches from section *A* (cf. Figs. 57 and 5), but on first hearing the listener might consider this an isolated, minor aberration. For section *A'* to represent the complement of section *A*, it needs to achieve a delicate balance between sameness and fundamental difference. This is exactly what Ravel succeeds in doing: whilst section *A'* assumes the same initial direction as section A, its path gradually deviates and goes more and more horribly awry (especially Fig. 93ff. within the coda). This is a road of no return. Civilized control becomes lost in a hallucinatory, disorientated whirling which approaches the barbaric, and the orchestral waltz is robbed of its very identity: in the penultimate bar, its triple metre mutates into four, heavily accented beats. Cleverly, Ravel has removed the expectation that section *A* must lead into *B*, partly by subsuming the dotted, octave interjections from section *B* within *A'*. Cataclysmic finality has been achieved through section *A* material that had first denoted a beginning.[16]

Ravel's scenario for *La Valse*

Although the early acclaimed existence of *La Valse* was as music alone, Ravel was never in any doubt that 'This "choreographic poem" is written for the stage.'[17] As before, he produced a scenario in relation to his score.

---

[16] For another reading, see George Benjamin, 'Last dance', *The Musical Times*, 135 (July 1994), 432–5. The musical stature of *La Valse* is indicated by dedicated articles as early as 1921: Robert Bernard, '*La Valse* de Maurice Ravel', *La Revue mensuelle, variétés littéraires art, science, philosophie*, 239 (July 1921), 14–21 (FM).

[17] Letter to Maurice Emmanuel (14 October 1922), in Lesure and Nectoux (eds), *Maurice Ravel*, 68. 'Ce "poème chorégraphique" est écrit pour la scène.'

Sadly, the manuscript that provided the detailed version of this scenario has long been lost (although this lack has afforded greater scope for subsequent reinterpretation), but the short version by the composer, first published by Durand in 1921, prefaces the orchestral score:

> Through breaks in the swirling clouds, waltzing couples may be glimpsed. Little by little they disperse: an immense hall filled with a whirling crowd can be made out (A [Fig. 9]).
> The stage is illuminated gradually. The light of the chandeliers peaks at the *fortissimo* (B [Fig. 17]).
> An Imperial Court, about 1855.[18]

Significant features include the lack of initial visual definition, fully embedded in the musical structure; the allusions to whirling and swirling; the specific pinpointing of scenario against music (letters A and B); the grandeur of scale, of both the building and the people; a correlation between increased visual intensity and musical dynamic; and the aristocratic mid-nineteenth-century setting.

From the beginning, many commentators have sought to interpret *La Valse* variously as some sort of allegory for Franco-German revolutionary unrest of 1848, the Franco-Prussian War of 1870, the fall of the Habsburg Empire or the atrocious destruction of the First World War.[19] Ravel felt obliged, even early on, to defend his artistic aesthetic:

> One is forced to believe that this work needs to be illuminated by footlights, so much has it provoked strange comments. While some people detect an intended parody – or even caricature – others definitely see a tragic allusion – the end of the Second Empire, the state of Vienna after the war …
> Tragic this dance may seem, as with all feeling – desire, joy – pushed to the extreme. One should see in it only what the music expresses: an ascending progression of sonority, to which the stage will add those of light and movement.[20]

---

[18] Maurice Ravel, *La Valse* (Paris: Durand, 1921). 'Des nuées tourbillonnantes laissent entrevoir, par éclaircies, des couples de valseurs. Elles se dissipent peu à peu: on distingue (A) une immense salle peuplée d'une foule tournoyante.

La scène s'éclaire progressivement. La lumière des lustres éclate au *ff* (B).

Une Cour impériale, vers 1855.'

This scenario appears identically in the *Catalogue de l'œuvre de Maurice Ravel*, 19.

[19] See Anatole Chujoy, quoted in Nancy Reynolds, *Repertory in Review: Forty Years of the New York City Ballet* (New York: Dial, 1977), 118, or Jacques Bonnaure in *Ravel par lui-même et ses amis* (Paris: Editions Michel de Maule, 1987), 25.

[20] Letter to Maurice Emmanuel (14 October 1922), in Lesure and Nectoux (eds), *Maurice Ravel*, 68. 'Il faut croire que cette œuvre a besoin d'être éclairée par les feux de la rampe, tant elle a provoqué de commentaires étranges. Tandis que les uns y découvraient un dessein

Ravel's desire for a crescendo of 'light and movement' to parallel a crescendo of 'sonority' is very much in keeping with his aesthetic view of close artistic interplay (see pp. 20–22 above). A little later, in 1928, Ravel elaborated on the musical sensations of his waltz: 'I conceived this work as a kind of apotheosis of the Viennese waltz, mixed, in my mind, with the impression of a fantastic and fatal whirling.'[21] In so doing, he may well have encouraged those who sought extra-musical meaning, especially in his recourse to the 'fantastic' and 'fatal'. Ravel was deeply influenced by the short-lived Edgar Allan Poe (1809–49), as he admitted openly in his lecture to the Rice Institute in Houston, Texas, of 7 April 1928, and one may speculate on a possible linkage with Poe's grisly *Masque of the Red Death* of 1842. Certainly, Massine in his later production of 1950 (see p. 172 below) would seek connection with the moving and murderous play *Maskarad* (Masquerade) by the even more short-lived Mikhail Lermontov (1814–41), and others have noted Ravel's increasing obsession with a dramatic death, possibly his own.[22] Given the synaesthetic tendencies, one could also venture a more specific Symbolist affinity with Baudelaire's *Harmonie du soir*, published in 1857, contemporary with Ravel's scenario date. Apart from the title, musical imagery includes a reference to a trembling heart-like violin, but the crucial lines would surely be those on disorientating waltzing: 'Les sons et les parfums tournent dans l'air du soir; / Valse mélancolique et langoureux vertige!' As with Ravel's waltz, time flows inexorably on and the sun meets a bloody 'death', living on only in memory: 'Le soleil s'est noyé dans son sang qui se fige.'[23] One way or another, *La Valse* emerges as a second, rather complex representation of a *Zeitgeist* (see Chapters 3 and 8, pp. 123 and 254).

---

parodique, voire caricatural, d'autres y voyaient carrément une allusion tragique – fin du second Empire, état de Wien après la guerre …

Tragique, cette œuvre peut l'être comme toute expression – volupté, joie – poussée à l'extrême. Il ne faut y voir que ce que la musique y exprime: une progression ascendante de sonorité, à laquelle la scène viendra ajouter celle de la lumière et du mouvement.' See too Ravel's account in C.v.W, 'Het Fransche Muziekfeest', *De Telegraaf* (30 September 1922) and his appreciative letter to the conductor Ernest Ansermet (20 October 1921) on similar lines, in Orenstein (ed.), *Maurice Ravel: lettres*, 345–6, 190–91.

[21] [Roland-Manuel,] 'Une esquisse autobiographique', 22. 'J'ai conçu cette œuvre comme une espèce d'apothéose de la valse viennoise à laquelle se mêle, dans mon esprit, l'impression d'un tournoiement fantastique et fatal.'

[22] See Manuel Rosenthal, quoted in Nichols (ed.), *Ravel Remembered*, 62.

[23] Baudelaire, *Selected Verse*, trans. Scarfe, 143: 'the sounds and perfumes spiral in the evening air, in a melancholy waltz, a slow, sensual gyre … the sun has drowned in its congealing blood'.

Choreographic developments and the Ballets Ida Rubinstein

After the distressing Diaghilev episode, the next plans were for a production with the Vienna Opera, as evidenced by Ravel's letters of 1922.[24] Nothing appears to have come of this, although there was a staging in Vienna in the late 1920s, courtesy of Rubinstein's troupe. In fact, the balletic premiere was given in Antwerp by the Royal Flemish Opera Ballet in October 1926. Choreography was by Sonia Korty, who also danced in the production, and costumes were created by Jean Vanderborght;[25] Korty's dress as revealed in a contemporary newspaper cutting comprised a full-skirted, layered petticoat, with fitted, off-the-shoulder bodice. The company was justly proud of its coup in staging the work before it had been seen in Paris or Vienna: *Le Courrier d'Anvers* declared that 'With the creation of *La Valse*, the Flemish Opera adds a sparkling finial to its artistic crown.' The reviewer detailed the seemingly sensitive and dramatic character of the production built upon Ravel's rhythms:

> These couples turning without respite, conjured up from the night, and swept along within a sort of continuous and tragic rotation, truly create the hallucination of vertigo intended by Ravel. It is the rhythm of life itself, implacable in its eternal force, which precipitates humanity to the disturbing chasm of Chaos.[26]

Nonetheless, *La Valse* was really put on the map via productions of the Ballets Ida Rubinstein,[27] with choreography by Nijinska and set designs by Benois, and it is pertinent at this point to compare Nijinska's choreographic approach with Ravel's musical and literary stance. While varied documentation may be used to establish Nijinska's position, a retrospective article in

---

[24] Letters to Calvocoressi (3 February 1922) and Emmanuel (14 October 1922), in Orenstein (ed.), *Maurice Ravel: lettres*, 193–4: 194; 205–6: 205.

[25] Although an earlier English ballet used Ravel's *La Valse*, this was in a retitled form, seemingly without the composer's involvement: *The Art of the Theatre* (1925), choreographed by de Valois; see Kathrine Sorley Walker, *Ninette de Valois: Idealist without Illusions* (London: Hamish Hamilton, 1987), 61 and Appendix. Further research is needed to establish the precise status of this production.

[26] Alceste, 'Création de la *Valse* de Ravel', *Le Courrier d'Anvers* (8 October 1926; FM). 'Avec la création de la *Valse* de Ravel, l'Opéra flamand ajoute un étincelant fleuron à sa couronne artistique … Ces couples tournant sans relâche, surgis de la nuit, et entraînés dans une sorte de rotation continue et tragique, créent véritablement l'hallucination du vertige qu'a voulue Ravel. C'est le rythme de la vie même, implacable en sa force d'éternité, qui précipite les humanités au gouffre inquiétant du Chaos'. Review dates (unless of a preview) conflict with the commonly given premiere of 20 October 1926.

[27] For a pertinent introduction to the Ballets Ida Rubinstein, see Roger Nichols, *The Harlequin Years: Music in Paris, 1917–1929* (London: Thames & Hudson, 2002), 166–72.

The Dancing Times offers a good introduction (it is also relevant to *Boléro*: see pp. 227–8 below.)[28]

Nijinska begins by clarifying that she does not want to pin herself down 'with lawyer-like precision' but, like Ravel, retains her right to artistic independence and spontaneity. She seeks to uphold the most innovative early principles of Diaghilev's Ballets Russes, yet explicitly respects a classical basis, 'so as to realise new life, new paths and a new technique in ballet composition'.

Around 1920, in Diaghilev's pioneering spirit, Nijinska presented abstract ballets conceived without librettos or scenarios. Ironically, Diaghilev was as hostile to this idea as he had been to Ravel's 'poème chorégraphique'. Using almost identical language and arguments, he complained, seemingly with reference to *Les Biches*, that 'it is not a ballet ... it is some abstract idea, a symphony. It is foreign to me.'[29] (With the benefit of hindsight, his response becomes doubly ironic because the supposedly forward-thinking Diaghilev failed to see that this was where dance's future lay.) Nijinska looked to a pure dance foundation upon which to build her new compositions, yet paradoxically she employed musical imagery to convey such forms in words, thereby creating, at least superficially, a balanced complement in relation to Ravel's terminology in *La Valse*: Nijinska's symphony and Ravel's 'poème choréographique'. She explains how '*Noces* [*sic*] was the first work where the libretto was a hidden theme for a pure choreography; it was a choreographic concerto' which heralded 'a long series of ballets in the form of a choreographic symphony, sonata, etude, or concerto ... *Bolero* (1928), *Nocturne* (1928), *La Valse* (1929)'.[30]

Beyond surface-level linguistic similarities, however, Nijinska's symphony and Ravel's 'poème' are quite different, even opposed, in their meanings. In *La Valse*, Ravel does reach out toward dance via the medium of music;[31] Nijinska, on the hand, uses music as a model of autonomy at the

---

[28] Bronislava Nijinska, 'Reflections about the production of *Les Biches* and *Hamlet* in Markova–Dolin ballets', trans. Lydia Lopokova, *The Dancing Times*, 317 (February 1937), 617–20. For another critique, see Jordan, *Moving Music*, 44–5. Other important documentation includes autograph letters (LAS Nijinska, 1–15 (B-MO)); the colossal Nijinska Collection Scrapbooks (60 volumes of newspaper clippings, photographs, playbills and so on, dated 1920–96, on 9 microfilms) in the Music Division, Library of Congress, Washington DC; and Bronislava Nijinska, *Early Memoirs*, trans. Irina Nijinska and Jean Rawlinson (New York: Holt, Rinehart & Winston, 1981; Duke University Press, 2/1992).

[29] Nijinska, 'Reflections', 617. It is not wholly clear from Nijinska's text to which work Diaghilev's comments applied.

[30] Ibid., 618.

[31] Even in concert performance, the listener is unusually aware of the energetic and dramatic physical existence of this piece, directed through its performers, in time and space. As Jordan has noted, 'music can contain or express motion' (*Moving Music*, 68–9) as a manifestation of dance. There is an orchestral choreography of bowing patterns that works with frightening unanimity as the music starts to stutter.

same time as looking to distance herself from it. Nijinska maintains that on 'the matter of literature, of painting, of music, each has its own separate nature'.[32] She is concerned to make distinctions between music and choreography, arguing in favour of the 'independent formation' of their ideas, and wants, quite understandably, to raise the status of dance as a more self-sufficient discipline. She claims, for instance, that she has avoided working with symphonies because she has not wanted to be constrained by the 'already fixed ideas and forms of the musician'. (It is a moot point, however, whether a symphony is more prescriptive than any other musical genre; besides, almost all music that predates its choreography is necessarily fixed to a degree, if one is to pay some attention to the composer's wishes.) Nijinska draws parallels between absolute music – without visual imagery or, by extension, literary programme – and her ballet without literature.

The contrast with Ravel's general pro-synthesis stance, seeking to break down disciplinary boundaries, whereby there are not different artists but simply different specialists, could not be clearer.[33] This in turn raises questions about how sympathetic Nijinska's choreography might be in relation to Ravel's existing score and scenario.

Rubinstein was the other strong, uncompromising woman in this collaborative team.[34] She too had a Ballets Russes background, having danced in its prewar productions, and also had to endure her share of harsh treatment from Diaghilev. While not a great dancer, she had real presence, a sense of the dramatic and compelling ambition.[35] Despite the destruction of many of Rubinstein's papers in the Second World War, or in her later years, various records such as accounts, listings and letters remain to demonstrate the organizational complexity required for *La Valse* and other contemporary ballets.[36]

---

[32] Nijinska, 'Reflections', 619.

[33] One may relate back to Albright's setting out of opposed stances represented by the eighteenth-century separatist Lessing and Roman synthesizer Horace (Chapter 1): Albright, *Untwisting the Serpent*, 8–10.

[34] For recent biographies, see Jacques Depaulis, *Ida Rubinstein, une inconnue jadis célèbre* (Paris: Honoré Champion Editeur, 1995) and Vicky Woolf, *Dancing in the Vortex: The Story of Ida Rubinstein* (Amsterdam: Harwood Academic Publishers, 2000). Unfortunately, this latter text is seriously compromised by a lack of proper sources for quotations and full publication citations.

[35] A photograph in the *Galas Ida Rubinstein* programme for 23, 25 June 1931 presents her as the centre of attention: worldly-wise yet feigning coyness (Carton 2238 (B-MO)).

[36] See especially Rés. Pièce 78 (Rubinstein, I), fols 1–92 (B-MO). Unfortunately, most surviving letters date from the mid-1920s or mid-1930s (LAS Rubinstein, 1–27), so missing the creation of *La Valse* (and *Boléro*). Letters to Rouché reveal Rubinstein as a confident, colourful figure – her large French handwriting in deep purple or turquoise ink sometimes flamboyantly covers the paper horizontally and then vertically – LAS Rubinstein, 9 (17 June 1928), 13 (6 March 1933), 16 (27 July 1934).

A telegram from Rubinstein in Rome of 25 November (1926?) to M. Blondot at the Opéra expresses her anxiety to know whether Benois has accepted a design brief. Rubinstein's faith in Benois is apparent since she comments that he alone would be able to produce designs for costumes to accompany this particular décor.[37] Another document, headed 'Théâtre National de l'Opéra', comprises a handwritten list of dates and requirements for booking purposes, including an entry for 23 May 1929 at 2.00 p.m. for the 'Ballets Rubinstein', almost certainly the final dress rehearsal for the long-awaited French premiere of *La Valse*. An evening slot at 9.00, requiring light-ing, is also listed alongside three works: Milhaud's *La Bien-aimée* Op. 101 after Schubert–Liszt; *La Princesse* [*Cygne*] after Rimsky-Korsakov's *Tsar Saltan*; and *La Valse*.[38] Accounts for May 1929 enumerate the personnel and equipment for this venture, including 'authors', orchestral musicians, electri-cians, machinists, dressers, as well as theatre hire charges, the cost of props and the need for additional payments. The special linen cloth required for *La Valse* and some other furnishings appear to have cost 5,568.95 francs. These accounts reveal a total expenditure of 325,202.30 francs against receipts of 298,062.95, resulting in a smallish loss.[39]

The Parisian premiere and its critical interpretation

Although the production of *La Valse* was tested out in Monte Carlo on 12 January 1929, the main event was doubtless the Parisian outing at the Opéra on 23 May of the same year, again supported behind the scenes by Rouché. The programme, sold for a cover price of 10 francs, credits Ravel as conductor of his own work, in the company of the other main stars, Nijinska and Rubinstein. Below are listed fourteen men, including Ashton, and twenty-two women, including Mlle 'Tikhonova' [Tikanova], of the *corps de ballet*. Benois produced the décor and costumes, with scenery painted by Monsieur O. Alleri and Rubinstein's costume specially supplied by the Maison Mirande.[40]

Unfortunately, the critical response was generally negative, and for good reason: Rubinstein and especially Nijinska disregarded Ravel's artistic inten-tions in the music and scenario in favour of a frivolous *divertissement*. The choreographic approach was also at odds with Benois's grand, romantic hall

---

[37] Rés. Pièce 78, fol. 10.

[38] Rés. Pièce 78, fols 16–18. Fol. 15 is a letter confirming Opéra bookings for 16, 21, 23 and 30 May 1929.

[39] Rés. Pièce 78, fol. 14.

[40] *Mme Ida Rubinstein* programme (May 1929), Carton 2238 (B-MO). Rubinstein's exotic cover portrait mimics a fairground fortune-teller.

of marble with short flights of steps, crystal chandeliers and voluminous drapes of blue velvet.[41] According to Henry Malherbe, 'We are, on the bank of the Danube, in a marble swimming pool surrounded by high, massive columns … Mme Ida Rubinstein, in a silver corset and a cap with flaxen plumes, appears as a kind of water goddess of the Waltz.' [42] Another commentator meanwhile was not convinced of any Austro-Hungarian allusion: 'It [*La Valse*] was realized by Mme [*sic*] Nijinska's rather unexpected choreography, in which stylized figures were made to revolve in an Italianate setting, evoking the age of the crinoline only from a considerable distance.'[43]

Nijinska's abstract approach – so well suited to *Les Noces* (see p. 158 above) – represented the crux of the problem. Nina Tikanova, who had danced in the premiere, recalled in her memoirs that 'Even the most impassioned admirers of Nijinska could not accept her choreography of Ravel's *La Valse* … it was counted a "very grave error"', while André Levinson described it as 'geometric', 'accented', 'brutal' and 'garish'.[44] Gustave Bret went so far as to claim that the fault with this choreographic interpretation was that it lacked the very waltz itself.[45] Through all this criticism, the musical calibre was never in doubt: 'Let us just savour M. Maurice Ravel's masterly symphonic score, its meticulously thought-out plan, its delicate nuancing, its fastidious working amid its detours and scintillating effects.'[46] It is only fair to conclude that this production constituted a prime case of mismatch between the composite elements: a collage of the unrelated, to the

---

[41] Jane Pritchard, '*La Valse*', in Bremser (ed.), *International Dictionary of Ballet*, vol. II, 1454–6: 1455. See illustration in Jankélévitch, *Ravel*, 111.

[42] Henry Malherbe, 'Chronique musicale', *Le Temps* (29 May 1929). 'Nous sommes, au bord de la Danube, dans une piscine de marbre entourée de hautes colonnes massives … Mme Ida Rubinstein, en corset d'argent et en toque aux aigrettes blondes, figure une sorte de divinité aquatique de la valse.'

[43] Paul Bertrand, 'La Semaine musicale, Opéra – Les Ballets de Mme Ida Rubinstein', *Le Ménestrel*, 22 (31 May 1929), 248. 'Elle se trouva réalisée par une chorégraphie un peu inattendu de Mme Nijinska faisant évoluer, dans un cadre italien, des personnages stylisés n'évoquant que de fort loin l'époque de la crinoline.'

[44] Nina Tikanova, *La Jeune Fille en bleu, Pétersbourg–Berlin–Paris* (Lausanne: L'Age d'homme, 1991), 103. 'Mais même les admirateurs les plus passionnés de Nijinska ne purent accepter sa chorégraphie de la *Valse* de Ravel … elle fut qualifiée de "très grande erreur".' See too André Levinson, 'Les Ballets de Mme Ida Rubinstein: *La Valse*', *Comœdia* (25 May 1929), 1.

[45] Gustave Bret, 'Théâtre de l'Opéra – Ballets de Mme Ida Rubinstein' (25 May 1929), 8: Dossier d'œuvre, *La Valse* (B-MO).

[46] Malherbe, 'Chronique musicale'. ' Ne pensons qu'à goûter la magistrale page symphonique de M. Maurice Ravel, d'un plan minutieusement étudié, d'une gradation délicate, d'un mécanisme précieux parmi ses detours et ses scintillements.' For more detail, see Levinson, 'Les Ballets de Mme Ida Rubinstein'.

detriment of Ravel's music; or, to reuse Albright's terms, an unworkable rather than piquant 'dissonance' – 'a state of utter contradiction'.[47]

Revised Rubinstein productions

Much more auspicious was the second production of 25 June 1931,[48] presented at the Opéra and also in the London season across 6–17 July 1931 at the Covent Garden Theatre, with revised choreography by Nijinska and costumes that respected the intentions of Ravel and the now middle-aged Benois. Finally, after a most extended gestation, *La Valse* was properly realized as a three-dimensional moving image. Even the usually implacable Levinson was forced to concede that, on this occasion, the public had been given the '*Valse chorégraphique* according to Ravel'.[49]

One of the fullest descriptions is that offered by Cyril Beaumont, which although undated clearly tallies with the 1931 production. In a style redolent of the nineteenth-century (military) painter Eugène Lami, the curtain rose to reveal 'a crimson and gold ballroom lined with enormous mirrors and lit with groups of candelabra. At the far end folding doors give onto a second ballroom.' Choreographic focus was provided by a central waltzing couple, referred to in anonymous terms as Elle ('She': Ida Rubinstein) and Lui ('He': Anatole Vilzak) and thus conveying well the impersonal, massed nature of the gathering. The costumes of the *corps de ballet* met expectations with crinoline dresses for ladies and formal military attire for gentlemen, who included officers, hussars and dragoons; the full personnel is listed in the *Galas Ida Rubinstein* programme.

---

[47] Albright, *Untwisting the Serpent*, 29, 7.

[48] Sources conflict as to whether this production was first given on 23, 25, or possibly 22 June 1931. Documentary evidence favours 25 June: Rés. Pièce 78, fols 59–60 (letter of 1 May 1931; B-MO), confirms 23 and 25 June for Ida Rubinstein ballets. Rés. Pièce 78, fol. 18 presents a list of rehearsal and performance times, with *Boléro* noted for 23 June and *La Valse* to be rehearsed on 24 June and performed, with Honegger's *Amphion*, at 9.00 p.m. on 25 June. A letter to Rouché of 24 June (LAS Rubinstein, 10) confirms a performance on the previous evening, but does not specify works. This argument is consistent with the general programme and at least one review, by Guy de Teramond, which explains that *La Valse* replaced *Boléro* in the second performance. On the evidence of reviews, the London premiere was on 8 July 1931, conducted by Ravel. Contrary to Depaulis's account (*Ida Rubinstein*, 388, 391, 396), Ravel conducted on the 1931 London trip (including *Boléro*), but not in Paris.

[49] André Levinson, 'Les Ballets de Mme Ida Rubinstein: *La Valse* de Maurice Ravel (Nouvelle version chorégraphique)', *Comœdia* (27 June 1931). Ravel's views were quite conservative and he would not live to see the more radical (often abstract) approaches that would gain prominence in ballet after the Second World War.

Regarding movement, Beaumont commented that 'a very interesting form of choreographic counterpoint is provided by the dancers in the second room moving quickly in a chain, while those in the foreground slowly revolve to the languorous strains of the waltz; later the rhythms are reversed'.[50] Such intricate, invertible dance counterpoint suggests a much more effective realization of Ravel's balanced musical phrases, but the choreographic treatment of the cataclysmic ending remained more elusive. Raymond Balliman claimed that the languorous choreographic interpretation was at odds with the music at the climactic point; but despite his ostensibly representing the popular view, his stance does not seem to have been widely shared.[51]

Benois's set design for this second production is typical of his bold, romantic yet cartoon-like style (Figure 5.2),[52] the use of sumptuous framing

Figure 5.2   Alexandre Benois's set design model for *La Valse* (1931). By permission of the Bibliothèque Nationale de France. © ADAGP, Paris and DACS, London 2004.

[50] Cyril Beaumont, *The Complete Book of Ballets* (London: Putnam, 1937, rev. edn 1949), 812–13. See also Pritchard, '*La Valse*', 1455, and André Levinson, *Les Visages de la danse* (Paris: Editions Bernard Grasset, 1933), 112–14.

[51] Raymond Balliman, 'Spectacles de Mme Ida Rubinstein: *La Valse* de M.M. Ravel', *L'Ami du peuple du soir* (27 June 1931).

[52] This photograph of Benois's 1931 design is taken from the *Ballets Ida Rubinstein* programme of 1934: B de l'A, Fonds Rondel, Ro 12744.

drapes and high symmetrical arches towards the back of the stage being broadly similar to that for *La Dame aux camélias* of 1923. In his astute review, Levinson suggested that Benois drew inspiration partly from the flamboyant ornamentation of eighteenth-century Louis XV style, which in turn suited the interior of the Opéra. (Brief association may be made with his best-known prewar theatrical art: for instance, his dramatic and grand set for the second act of Stravinsky's *Le Rossignol* (1914), depicting 'The Emperor's Palace, The Throne Room', whose watercolour-gouache design is held in the Russian Museum, St Petersburg.) For *La Valse*, these rear arches – focused upon a higher central one – allow glimpses of the distant, adjoining ballroom that Beaumont described. The designs also made use of a scrim (gauze veil), which became traditional in later productions, to realize Ravel's required lack of initial visual definition.

An interesting aspect of the 1931 production was the export to England of a most successful Ravel stage-work that would be highly acclaimed there too. Indeed, the contemporary English love affair with the waltz is nicely demonstrated in *The Dancing Times*; for those who were truly serious in their waltzing endeavours, the first in a series of articles by Victor Sylvester appeared in July 1929, entitled 'Questions and answers for a ballroom examination', with Sylvester and his wife photographed in performance of 'A waltz hesitation'. A further article details the waltz characteristics: its tempo should allow about 38 bars per minute; its basic steps comprise 'the natural turn, the reverse turn, and the change step'; dancers should rise onto toes at the end of the first beat and fall at the third.[53] In a later issue of February 1931, which included an advance notice about Rubinstein's *La Valse*, Sylvester and partner demonstrate the delightfully entitled 'A not too difficult spin in the valse'.[54] The warmth of English reception for the Rubinstein/Ravel waltz is well illustrated by William McNaught's review in *Dancing Times*'s sister journal *The Musical Times*, which pursues further arguments in favour of an emergent artistic unity:

> There was an artistic parallel between the sumptuous treatment of the waltz on the stage and Ravel's well-known orchestral elaboration, and the result was of a unified creation, single and complete, and too strong in its impersonal quality to be affected by what any individual dancer did, or wore, as a unit in the ensemble.[55]

---

[53] Victor Sylvester, 'Questions and answers for a ballroom examination', *The Dancing Times* (July 1929), 338–9; Sylvester, 'Questions and answers' [fourth article], *The Dancing Times* (October 1929), 21.

[54] Sylvester, 'A not too difficult spin in the valse [*sic*]', *The Dancing Times* (February 1931), 588–9; advance notice of *La Valse*, 562.

[55] William G. McNaught, 'Ida Rubinstein Ballet', *The Musical Times* (1 August 1931), 745–6: 745. See too an unsigned review for *The Times* (9 July 1931).

(The slight reservation in tone relates to another of Mme Rubinstein's larger-than-life costumes: the temperament of the diva clearly found difficulty in maintaining the necessary artistic anonymity.) McNaught concluded that within the current season, 'it is the best of the ballets, although the simplest in form'.

Finally, one thoughtful reviewer, Raoul Brunel, addressed a most pertinent issue for musicians that in a sense underlies this whole book: 'the question arises again of knowing whether Ravel's score gains in being used in presentation of a ballet'. Notwithstanding the production's success, the reviewer decided: 'I really think that no simultaneous visual image can ever be worth as much as those which are born spontaneously in the listener's head.'[56]

Following Nijinska's departure for South America, Fokine choreographed a further Rubinstein production of *La Valse* at the Opéra in the April–May season of 1934, advertised as appearing on 30 April, 4 and 9 May, in tandem with the premieres of Stravinsky's *Perséphone* and Jacques Ibert's *Diane de Poitiers*.[57]

The classical choreographic reading of Ashton

Ravel's composition within the milieu of 1920s Paris of a work that revisited and reinterpreted a dance form, in the common-practice tonality of D major with balanced phrases, was essentially a neoclassical act.[58] Such classicism was picked up on choreographically, notably in Ashton's productions for La Scala Milan (1958) and the Royal Ballet, Covent Garden (1959).[59] As

---

[56] Raoul Brunel, 'Les Ballets de Mme Rubinstein: *La Valse* de M. Maurice Ravel', *L'Œuvre* (28 June 1931): 'la question se pose encore de savoir si la partition de Ravel gagne à servir de présentation à un ballet ... Je crois bien d'aucune image visuelle simultanée ne vaudra jamais celles qui naissent spontanément dans le cerveau de l'auditeur.'

[57] The poster for this production is found in Dossier d'artiste, Ida Rubinstein (B-MO). For reviews, see Jean Chantavoine, 'Ballets d'Ida Rubinstein, *La Valse* de M Maurice Ravel', *Le Ménestrel* (11 May 1934), 178–9: 179, and for brief English coverage: G. C., 'Paris', *The Musical Times* (June 1934), 557–8: 557.

[58] See Joseph N. Straus, *Remaking the Past: Musical Modernism and the Influence of the Tonal Tradition* (Cambridge, MA: Harvard University Press, 1990).

[59] Ashton's Royal Ballet production is available commercially: Margot Fonteyn, Rudolf Nureyev, *An Evening with the Royal Ballet* (London: British Home Entertainment, film c. 1963), VHS video and DVD. (A revival was presented, not wholly successfully, in a Ravel evening in October 1996.) Harald Lander's Opéra production appeared contemporaneously on 24 January 1958, following the twentieth anniversary of Ravel's death. Although Claire Motte's dancing was praised, Lander's version, with a young girl (Motte), Prince Charming (Alexandre Kalioujny) and a chateau, but little musical understanding, by most accounts did a disservice to Ravel's score. For typical reviews, see Catherine Clairval, 'Hommage à Maurice Ravel', *Danse et rythmes* (March 1958), 6–7, and Antoine Goléa, '... mais où est la Valse de Massine?', *Carrefour* (29 January 1958).

a former member of Rubinstein's *corps de ballet* in 1929, Ashton had a direct link to the Opéra premiere, choreographed by Nijinska, although 'His [Ashton's] arrangement was very different – an ultra-chic swirl of waltzing couples in elegant costumes designed by André Levasseur.'[60] Ashton's oft-quoted phrase, almost a motto, was 'You see, like Balanchine, I'm a classical choreographer': Andrew Porter maintained that in each ballet 'Classical choreography was used in new patterns, and subtly enriched', while for Alastair Macaulay the 1950s was the period of Ashton's career during which he realized 'his most audacious extensions of dance classicism.'[61]

Levasseur's set design is symmetrical in form, with four large chandeliers on each side and substantial drapes. At the back of the stage is a shallow flight of steps, the central portion of which is adorned with a red carpet. Four male figures stand motionless atop the steps, holding candelabras. Costumes too are conservative but of their period: the ladies have full-skirted dresses, with black detail at the base of the bodice as a visual hint of impending fate, and tiaras; gentlemen don delightfully impractical coats with flailing full-length tails over black tights (Figure 5.3).

To impart a flavour of Ashton's choreography and its counterpoint with the music, moments from the recording of 1963 are selected for discussion.[62] This is an individual interpretation of one performance – a fluid concept rather than some fixed object – and, at least in theory, there is limitless scope for variation in performance and perception. To use Jordan's expression, this is but 'a [single] translation of the ballet'.[63] The commentary (and that for Balanchine's version) respects the internal chronology of the score/film so that the reader may follow the work's journey in 'real' time.

Corresponding with an eerie chromatic flute ascent–descent figure (Figure 7-5; bars 46–9) a solo female dancer is carried, with arched back, in a travelling half-shoulder lift, moving in a semicircle from front to rear of the stage (audience left); this is the 'wonderful moment near the start when a woman in a red dress is swung into the air. Her flaring skirt is a distress beacon, doomed to go unanswered.'[64] From an aerial perspective, the dancer traces

---

[60] Bland, *The Royal Ballet*, 123.

[61] Andrew Porter, 'Frederick Ashton, 1960–1970', *About the House*, 8 (Summer 1970), 65–70: 66; Alastair Macaulay, 'Hidden steps in the choreography' [review of Kavanagh, *Secret Muses*], *Financial Times* (16 August 1996). For a detailed account of Ashton's approach, see Jordan, *Moving Music*, 187–266.

[62] I am appreciative of Stephanie Jordan's feedback on an early version of this reading. A Benesh score of Ashton's choreography, created in 1994 by the Royal Ballet's principal notator Grant Coyle from the film footage and notes, may also be studied at the ROHA.

[63] Jordan, *Moving Music*, 101.

[64] Jann Parry, 'Waltzing off to war', *The Observer* (10 December 2000). I am grateful to my research student, Laura Halsey, for some of these dance observations. See Ashton/Coyle score, 7.

Figure 5.3   *Corps de ballet* in Frederick Ashton, *La Valse* (Royal Ballet, 1958). Photograph by Houston Rogers. By permission of the Theatre Museum, London; © V & A Images.

physically on stage a curved, symmetrical trajectory very similar to that of Ravel's flute phrase.

Once the mists have subsided (Fig. 9; Ravel's letter A), a most effective music–dance counterpoint is created across bars 70–73 (Example 5.1). Expressive violas present their searching theme in warm thirds, with a hairpin, followed by a *portamento* rise to the melodic peak coupled by a second hairpin, and then silence. The phrasing works as 2 + 1 + bar's rest. Two rows of dancers face each other across the stage: men on the audience left, women on the right. Their movements also work in conjoined two-bar phrases; the main movement is a lunge/*grand plié* forward with one foot, with the musical *portamento* anticipated by the women in an unusual, spatially equivalent, 'fluttering' gesture as they edge questioningly towards centre stage on point (bars 70–71).[65] Like the *portamento*, this step constitutes an ornamentation of the basic movement. As the music peaks and extends into silence, so Ashton's dancers extend their arms towards centre stage (bar 72), with feet now still. For all that, one should clarify that Ashton responds primarily to the melodic sweep rather than to precise rhythmic details: 'Fred never worked on the beat of the music. He always worked on the melody.'[66]

This close music–dance relationship involves correspondence or mirroring (simultaneity) and possible imitation (succession) – a kind of inter-arts invertible counterpoint, finished by relative stillness in both domains. Rather as Jordan has said of the influential dance critic Edwin Denby, this is strong evidence of 'a listening eye',[67] enabling one to 'see the music'. Aptly, the classical sequential nature of the music is reflected in choreographic repetition (cf. Fig. 10; bars 80–83 and 70–73). But while such 'consonance' is initially attractive, some critics, including Ashton's biographer David Vaughan, have regarded it as excessive: 'certain steps are introduced each

Example 5.1 *La Valse* (orchestral score, 1921): Ravel's letter A (Fig. 9[+3]; bars 70–77)

---

[65] Ashton/Coyle score, 8, confirms these two-bar groupings and the spirit of 'yearning', or 'feeling your way'.

[66] Alexandra Tomalonis and Henning Kronstram, 'Dancing for Ashton, *Dance Now*, 3/3 (Autumn 1994), 34–44: 40.

[67] Jordan, *Moving Music*, xiii.

time the musical phrase they originally accompany recurs, with very little variation'.[68]

Later on, Ravel's stipulation that 'The light of the chandeliers peaks at the *fortissimo* (B)' is highlighted in the recording by the first close-up camera angle, to audience left, followed by a swift switch to audience right (Fig. 17), with the closing tutti of the first section balanced by the presence of the full *corps de ballet*: some twenty-one waltzing couples. By contrast, and in keeping with the ensuing chamber textures featuring oboe, flute and cor anglais (Fig. 18), choreographic forces reduce to a female trio, in pink, white and yellow skirts, who position themselves across centre stage with arms outstretched, so drawing attention to their elegant long white gloves. Ashton's use of the male partners also conforms to classical convention with an elaborate set of choreographic moves as they introduce themselves chivalrously, in turn (Figs. 22–4; bars 180–95), on the right and then the left bended knee (see Table 5.1).[69] In the fourth phrase (bars 192–5), the dancers unite as three couples in decorous rotation. Ashton also subscribes to traditional gender roles when the forceful, rhythmic brass herald on B♭ (Fig. 26) cues his effective, if clichéd, 'macho' moment: men alone take centre stage, enjoying powerful leaps – *sissonnes ouvertes* – which are impossibly hard to synchronize in full tails. (Challenges of synchronization are evident in Figure 5.3.)

Ashton's visualization results in expressive classical gesturing – bowing, sighing, swooning and supported lifts, involving arms and head, as well as feet – which respects phrasing and punctuation, revealing his instinctive musicality and sensitivity. In one phrase of the reprise, outstretched arm gestures enhance a hemiola in the melodic line played by bass clarinet and cello (Fig. 56), where stressed dotted-crotchet values occur at two beats' distance within triple metre: still essentially a melodic underlining. Through differing means, melody and dance conspire to create an inherent two-versus-three metric tension (Example 5.2), and thus an instance perhaps of

Bars/beats

454			455			456			457		
1	2	3	1	2	3	1	2	3	1	2	3
	X		X		X		X		X		X

Melodic/choreographic emphases

Example 5.2 *La Valse*: hemiola in melody and dance (Fig. 56; bars 454–7)

---

[68] Vaughan, *Frederick Ashton and His Ballets*, quoted in Kathrine Sorley Walker, 'Ashton ballets: post-mortem performance', *Dance Now*, 3/3 (Autumn 1994), 45–51: 50.

[69] See Ashton/Coyle score, 15–16.

Gorbman's 'mutual implication' of meaning, connoting a complicit instability that challenges, locally, the identity of the waltz.[70]

But despite these strengths in Ashton's interpretation, questions remain about the larger-scale choreographic treatment as the music deteriorates and ultimately destroys itself. In Ann Nugent's view, 'It is disappointing ... that Ashton waits until the end to make use of the dark undertones that Ravel impresses on us from the start.'[71] Certainly in the recorded performance, some unease is usefully conveyed by other means: clever camera work (fast left–right angle changes; close-up versus panoramic views) and lighting filters (darker shades to connote ominous overtones, such as the deep green for the flattened key change – Fig. 68). Levasseur's costumes too play a role.

But Nugent's assertion that Ashton waits until the end is not strictly accurate; it is more a case of too little than too late. At the restoration of the D major tonic (Fig. 76) signifying the final fateful chapter, the *corps de ballet* is assembled on stage in an atmosphere of quiet anguish and expectation. Three solo ballerinas perform flexing gestures up onto wide-spaced points in second position, supported by wide-stretched arms, in an intricate sequence of steps which subversively stresses, with bassoons and cymbal, the second beat of the triple metre. This, together with chromatic scales accented on the first beat, creates a feeling of instability.

After Fig. 83, the choreography does at least partially realize Ravel's 'hallucinatory whirling': initially, the turning is measured at one revolution per bar, but rotation then becomes continuous and the dance movement more 'modernist'. Bodies are arched and straightened (Fig. 85); supported lifts parallel the arching ascent–descent of Ravel's glissandos. Movements become enlarged, more angular and less finely controlled; but the issue

Table 5.1 *La Valse*: stage layout and choreographic moves (bars 184–91)

Stage layout (viewed from audience left–right)		
Pink ballerina 2 (rises to arabesque)	White ballerina 1 'Elle' (rises to arabesque)	Yellow ballerina 3 (rises to arabesque)
Male dancer 2 (runs diagonally from front stage [left] to centre, leaps, lands, turns right/left knee)	Male dancer 1 'Lui' (runs diagonally from front stage [left] to centre, leaps, lands, turns right/left knee)	Male dancer 3 (runs diagonally from front stage [right] to centre, leaps, lands, turns right/left knee)
Phrase 2: bars 184–7	**Phrase 1: bars 180–83**	**Phrase 3: bars 188–91**

---

[70] See Jordan, *Moving Music*, 64 and Ashton/Coyle score, 34. Jordan has commented on such syncopations in *La Valse* as a device to escape predictability (*Moving Music*, 228).

[71] Ann Nugent, 'Valedictory fare well', *Dance Theatre Journal*, 17/1 (2001), 34–8: 37.

remains as to whether there is sufficient scope within the aesthetic limits of neoclassical ballet for the dance steps to reach a state of breakdown similar to that of the musical 'danse macabre'. Heralded by orchestral stutterings (Fig. 94^{-6}), the dance gestures move up a gear into exaggerated, sweeping circular arm movements, which match quite well the circularity and increasing musical impotence. After four repetitions, a *pirouette* in fifth position is added to increase the visual blur and replicate the harp glissando (Figs. 95–6; 'Turning' in Ashton/Coyle score, 48). This portion corresponds with Nugent's comment that 'Only in the panic of the closing moments does Ashton begin to develop the movement as a drama and show that his physical and metaphorical structures … are falling apart.' But even here, the dancers' broad smiles, as if enjoying a good-humoured, invigorating exercise routine, rather undermine the unfolding musical tragedy.

The section across Figs. 98–100 (bars 723–39) is notable for its intensifying techniques, preceded in the choreographic score by the marking 'renversé' ('topsy-turvy', 'bowled over'); the spectator experiences a complex of competing phrase structures, which move in and out of synchronization, articulated at bars 723, 726, 731 and 734. Most apparent are percussive crashes of cymbals, bass drum, tambourine and then timpani (beat 1), opposed noisily by tam-tam (beat 2), amid which the dancers make their highest lifts, with the supported female soloists in fifth position, for both arms and legs. Beyond, dancing deteriorates to mechanical repetitions, so recalling the musical stutterings yet still within extended bounds of classical decorum. All too swiftly (Fig. 101), the whirling vision is obscured by the returning mist; the Ashton/Coyle score is empty for the last 12 bars. 'Classical' melody was subjugated and destroyed some time earlier, but at the penultimate bar where the waltz itself fails (Example 5.3), mutated into four artless accented crotchets, nothing supports but 'smoke'.

Notwithstanding Ashton's impressive musical empathy, given the unequivocal musical collapse, the choreographic/visual ending is at least underplayed. Should Ashton's dancers have collapsed to the floor, or would this have appeared clichéd, crude or – even worse – humorous? Presumably Ashton would have argued that such a gesture would have inappropriately

Example 5.3 *La Valse*: ending (Fig. 101^{+4}, reduction)

exceeded the beautiful, classical aesthetic within which he worked so successfully. Despite the earlier fitting 'consonances' and elegant, period
images that linger powerfully in the mind, the ending does leave the spectator with an unexplained divergence and unsatisfactory 'dissonance' – a
feeling that the music has, somehow, been let down.

Epilogue: the romantic reading of Balanchine, via Massine

Although any act of rewriting the past constitutes a neoclassical undertaking, the specific locus of Ravel's enquiries was unashamedly neoromantic:
aristocratic waltzes of the mid-nineteenth century, viewed first with affec-
tionate nostalgia, but then curtailed by violent destruction. Various choreographers have taken their cue from Ravel to point up the romantic, dramatic
dimension of his work-concept. In turn, they have realized, and further
developed, macabre aspects that were previously only imagined.

It was the devilish maverick Massine who first seized on this dimension
of *La Valse* – a work that had haunted him since as the intended choreographer he had first heard it with Diaghilev in 1920. Despite having taught the
young Ashton, Massine's outlook could not have been more different, his
motto being'Moi classique? Mon œil! (Me classical? My foot!)'[72] Massine
sought to redevelop Ravel's scenario along the lines of Lermontov's
Maskarad, with its explosive mix of a love triangle, jealousy and death set
at a masked ball, and collaborated for a final time with the ageing painter
and sculptor André Derain (1880–1954), whose Fauvism had been so influential in the prewar years. Derain's watercolour costume drawings are
attractive if fairly conventional, as illustrated by Lermontov's aristocratic
Prince Zwedzich (M. Paul 'Goubé') in military attire (Figure 5.4). Although
Massine danced the leading role in his own production at the Opéra-Comique
on 17 May 1950[73] and judged the ballet to be effective in places, he concluded that his realization did not work. Most uncharitably, he then offloaded
the blame for this failure onto Ravel: 'the music was too repetitive. I had
hoped to overcome this problem through the dramatic elements in the
libretto, but my choreography was defeated by the monotony of the music.'[74]
In fact, Massine had made the initial mistake of devising an overly involved
plot to a short piece of music; in addition, by blacking out the stage as the

---

[72] Quoted in *Libération* (6 March 1989): Dossier d'artiste, Léonide Massine.

[73] The *Festival Ravel* programme for Ravel's 75th anniversary, also including *L'Enfant*
and *L'Heure espagnole*, details the new scenario: Carton 2239 (B-MO). For photographs of
Derain's designs, see D. 216, O.C.13, fols 2 and 3 (B-MO).

[74] Massine, *My Life in Ballet*, 237. Mary Clarke, à la Diaghilev, also charges Ravel with
'defeating' Ashton: '*La Valse*', *The Dancing Times* (May 1959), 405.

Figure 5.4   Costume design by André Derain for Léonide Massine, *La Valse* (1950). By permission of the Bibliothèque Nationale de France. © ADAGP, Paris and DACS, London 2004.

scenario drew towards its climax, he had contravened   Ravel's original intentions.

Fortunately for posterity, Balanchine's romantic interpretation of *La Valse* was first produced the following year on 20 February 1951, for the New York City Ballet (a slightly revised version dates from around 1974). Distinctively, it utilizes the music of both *Valses nobles* (with waltz I as an overture) and *La Valse* to confect a single extended essay on the waltz.[75] While still classically founded and as musically sensitive as Ashton – 'Balanchine est musicien'[76] – Balanchine comes closer to the sinister, destructive potency of *La Valse*. Even at the start, to the music of *Valses nobles*, II, Balanchine's setting is notably sombre and menacing, as if the sinister elements of *La Valse* have been projected back in time. Stage detail is deliberately and effectively limited to a central, seven-branched candelabra design which is projected from the backdrop of the stage onto the floor, creating ominous, shadowy lighting. A trio of ballerinas adopt the stage, as in Ashton's *La Valse*, with glamorous dark purple, full-skirted gowns designed by Balanchine's close associate Barbara Karinska. The dancers' mannered gestures, 'oddly "Chinese"' as Lincoln Kirstein considered them,[77] are artificial and untrustworthy. Long white gloves play a role here, as in Ashton's later setting.

Waltzes III to V present the equivalent of 'Elle' and 'Lui' from Rubinstein's *La Valse*, as three sets of lovers come and go with similarly affected gestures. Musically, the main effect of this production is to encourage one to connect Ravel's essays on the waltz; one is also aware of anticipation in waltz III of the 'Menuet' from *Le Tombeau* (Example 5.4). As well as triple metre, the two dances share a one-sharp key signature – initially E minor for the waltz and G major for the 'Menuet' – and a descent–ascent melodic contour in bars 1–2. Both enjoy a lightness of touch, with a combination of slurs and 'léger' staccato markings at *pp* dynamic. The two-beat hemiola groupings are particularly effective. Both feature oboe melodies supported by pizzicato string accompaniment. Parallels exist too between the rhythmic punctuation of waltz I and the 'Rigaudon' of *Le Tombeau*, in the

[75] Various film/video recordings of Balanchine's production may be found in The New York Public Library for the Performing Arts, Jerome Robbins Dance Division. For another reading, albeit marred by infelicities regarding Ravel, see Hubert Doris, 'Some thoughts on Balanchine and the waltz', *Choreography and Dance*, 3/3 (1993), 49–57: 49–52. Balanchine had first choreographed one of the *Valses nobles* as early as 1923: *Choreography by George Balanchine*, 61.

[76] Jacques Bourgeois, 'Le New York City Ballet à l'Opéra – Balanchine' (24–30 October 1956): Dossier d'artiste, George Balanchine (B-MO). Unlike Ashton, Balanchine was a fluent score reader who had studied music alongside ballet at the Conservatoire in St Petersburg. See Jordan's extensive discussion: *Moving Music*, 105–85.

[77] Kirstein, *Thirty Years*, 120.

Example 5.4 Comparison of *Valses nobles* et *Le Tombeau de Couperin*
    (a) *Valses nobles*: III (bars 1–4)
    (b) *Le Tombeau* (piano suite, 1918): 'Menuet' (bars 1–4)

emphatic cadential gesture of the first (bars 19–20; 79–80) and recurrent accentuated fragment of the second (e.g. bars 1–2 and 127–8). This common ground, also closely replicated in the solo piano ending of *La Valse*, comprises an accented note followed by four (semi-)quavers and another single accentuation.[78]

Balanchine's juxtaposition of the waltzes causes similarities to be set in relief, with the prewar, pre-*Valses nobles* origin of *La Valse* becoming more evident. Conversely, it is apparent how small distortions of the 'straight' waltzing in *Valses nobles* can cue the destructive forces of *La Valse*. In this context, waltz IV of *Valses nobles* looks ahead to the melodic–rhythmic hallmarks of *La Valse*, especially dotted rhythms and tied notes that work in hemiola units – that is, grouped in threes, as 3/2 metre set against 3/4. Compare the opening of IV, marked *pp*, with the start of the quiet central section (Fig. 18) of *La Valse* (Example 5.5), itself reappearing in the slow-motion 'flashback' moment near the close (Fig. 97^{-2}). Apart from rhythmic similarities, both waltzes share melodic contour, with uppermost pitches emphasized; they also utilize dynamic hairpins: waltz IV across two-bar groupings and *La Valse* inside single bars of the string accompaniment

[78] Emile Vuillermoz, '*La Valse*: *Valses nobles et sentimentales* et *La Valse*' (n.d.), Dossier d'œuvre, *La Valse*.

Example 5.5 Comparison I of *Valses nobles* and *La Valse*
          (a) *Valses nobles*: IV (bars 1–4)
          (b) *La Valse* (Fig. 18; bars 148–51)

figure. The wistfully meandering waltz V also explores ties over the bar-line, nicely accentuated by extended balletic poses of the two lovers.

In his special waltz VII, Ravel's three initial phrases articulated by rests (bars 1, 5 and 9) are fittingly transferred to the stage by being identified with each ballerina in turn, as the sinister trio surrounds the leading male dancer. This movement builds in excitement as a small-scale anticipation of the climax of *La Valse*. Especially notable are repeated two-bar tutti phrases of articulated dotted rhythm that commence via a flourish on the second beat: one may compare the end of the first section of VII (Fig. 52[-2]) with Ravel's letter B (Fig. 17) of *La Valse* (Example 5.6). The two waltzes also share a melodic contour – a combination of repeated upper pitches and strong descents – and an emphatic three-quaver concluding figure. A further similarity concerns the use of half-bar dotted-crotchet divisions for more fluid, unstable transitional material, at a subdued dynamic level. Compare the middle portion of VII (*Un peu plus animé*; Fig. 53), pitting dotted crotchets against crotchets, with the similar, yet more developed sonic image of instability in the reprise of *La Valse* (Fig. 58[-1]), where crotchets, dotted crotchets and quadruple quaver figures become entangled (Example 5.7). Harmonically, these prominent augmented chords of *La Valse* (Example 5.7b) are reminiscent of those that govern the opening of *Valses nobles*, II; conversely, the pitting of E against F (Example 5.7a) foreshadows the start of *La Valse*.

Balanchine's 'Epilogue' (VIII) sees the emergence of a pure, white balle-rina, slightly haughty as Adélaïde, then courted by the imploring male

Example 5.6 Comparison II of *Valses nobles* and *La Valse*
  (a) *Valses nobles*: VII (Fig. 52^{-2}; bars 59–66)
  (b) *La Valse* (solo piano version, 1920): Ravel's letter B
      (Fig. 17; bars 139–47)

Example 5.7 Comparison III of *Valses nobles* and *La Valse*
  (a) *Valses nobles*: VII (bars 67–70)
  (b) *La Valse* (Fig. 58^{-1}; bars 467–70)

dancer, Lorédan perhaps. The white ballerina was originally portrayed in 1951 to stunning effect by Tanaquil LeClercq (Figure 5.5),[79] who married Balanchine the following year and whose own career was to be cut tragically short in 1956. 'Fleet, fragile, touchingly young, incredibly lovely, she brought it [*La Valse*] a haunting quality which lifted it into the realm of poetry.'[80] At the final reprise of the 1974 revision, a devil-like face, Death – a much more sinister, if slightly clichéd, reincarnation of Ravel's Duke – appears half-obscured behind the curtain. This modification of the 1951 version, where Death had not been sighted before the start of *La Valse* proper, further dovetails the musical loci. The apparition of Death is one of the 'surrealist trappings of *La Valse*', as Garafola expresses it in her celebration of the New York City Ballet – a thread in Balanchine's work that may be traced back as far as *Le Bal* (1929) and especially *Cotillon* (1932).[81]

Seamlessly, the dark setting and deep red-purple costumes continue in *La Valse* itself after the girl in white has disappeared and is searched for by her partner. Ravel's letter A, where structure becomes formed, sees the trio of ballerinas and male dancers waving eerily, with groups from the *corps de ballet* then creating horizontal lines and performing controlled waltzing revolutions (letter B). Balanchine visualizes Ravel's central 'chamber music' section as a delicate female interlude, with the full *corps de ballet* active at the dotted, octave descents (Ashton's 'macho' moment). A particularly strong image of Ravel's 'whirling' is produced by a large-scale, eight-point, rotating human star. 'Elle' in white and 'Lui' appear together again, still maintaining 'classical' control.

But just before section *A'* (Fig. 54), the light turns deep green, and Death, clad entirely in black, reappears at the back of the stage with his accomplice. The other dancers are now spellbound in a trance upon the floor, as the white ballerina, vulnerably alone, is seduced by Death. Buckle aptly proposes the triangular association with Poe's fantastically grotesque *The Masque of the Red Death*,[82] where the Red Death strikes off unsuspecting revellers at a masquerade. In a gothic scene (Figure 5.5), Death proffers a necklace of jagged black teeth, and shows the girl her reflection in a broken mirror – those beautiful mirrors of the 1931 production, now distorted and spoilt. Once under his spell, she accepts and dons the black gloves and black veiled cape. 'Elle' is taken over; she smells voluptuously a black floral bouquet and dances with Death/the devil, entrapped in an increasingly

---

[79] For other photographs of Le Clercq, Francisco Monción and Diana Adams, see Garafola with Foner (eds), *Dance for a City*, 17, 139, and Buckle, *George Balanchine*, plate 23.

[80] Lilian Moore quoted in Bernard Taper, *Balanchine* (London: Collins, 1964), 209.

[81] Lynn Garafola, 'Dance for a city: fifty years of the New York City Ballet', in Garafola with Foner (eds), *Dance for a City*, 1–52: 16.

[82] Buckle, *George Balanchine*, 186–8: 86.

Figure 5.5   Tanaquil LeClercq, Francisco Monción and Edward Bigelow
in George Balanchine, *La Valse* (New York City Ballet, 1951).
Photograph by George Platt Lynes; reproduced by generous
permission of George P. Lynes, II. Jerome Robbins Dance
Division, The New York Public Library for the Performing
Arts, Astor, Lenox and Tilden Foundations.

frantic whirling. At the point of the musical stutterings, Death discards her body and the others awaken from their trance. The dead girl is carried in the arms of 'Lui' into centre stage, surrounded by the other couples. Finally 'Elle', with arched (broken?) back, is lifted high on massed up-stretched arms, sacrificially, anticipating the conclusion of the Stravinsky/Béjart *Le Sacre du printemps* (1959) or the Stravinsky/MacMillan *Rite of Spring* (1962) – a gesture that while originally very powerful ultimately became a cliché.

Balanchine's extended version of *La Valse* received wide critical acclaim; as Jacques Bourgeois notes, despite some spectators' snobbishness over the musical splicing of two works, 'In fact the choreographer knew perfectly how to recreate visually the fantastical climate of this music.'[83] Merlin returned to the topic of seeing/hearing with these quasi-synaesthetic words: 'Balanchine [is] this man who hears the dance while seeing the music.'[84] One might also sum up Balanchine's reading of destructive passion in terms of the title of a recent book that includes coverage of *La Valse*: 'Sex, steps, and sound'.[85]

One may speculate what Ravel might have made of the Ashton and Balanchine readings. Undoubtedly, Ashton's reading respects the classical aesthetic beauty and control that was so important to Ravel, although there is too much direct imitation and repetition; equally, it maintains Ravel's idea of an initial vision obscured by mists, or veils. What it also does, however, is to underplay – even emasculate – the power of the destructive musical ending. Ashton's dance, whilst stretched and distorted towards the end of section *A'*, is not destroyed; the final descending mist suggests that a return to the beginning, a circularity, might be possible. For Ravel's music, however, this is out of the question. By contrast, Balanchine's reading is more dramatic. He shares (perhaps exceeds) Ashton's musical intuition and understanding, as well as Ravel's neoromanticism, but he is prepared to take greater risks. Ravel might well have taken exception to Balanchine's running roughshod over his scenario for *Adélaïde* (*Valses nobles*), compromising the autonomy of two separate waltz works and thereby subsuming the identity of *Valses nobles* within *La Valse*. On the other hand, Ravel's scenarios were not always terribly sophisticated – a limitation that the composer admitted – and *Adélaïde* has not enjoyed huge popularity as a production ballet. Ravel himself had fashioned the work from its earlier existence as a

---

[83] Bourgeois, 'Le New York City Ballet à l'Opéra'. 'En fait le chorégraphe a parfaitement su recréer visuellement le climat fantastique de cette musique.'

[84] Olivier Merlin, 'Balanchine, cet homme qui écoute la danse en voyant la musique', *Le Figaro littéraire* (26 December 1963–1 January 1964).

[85] Sevin Yaraman, *Revolving Embrace: The Waltz as Sex, Steps, and Sound*, Monographs in Musicology No. 12 (Hillsdale, NY: Pendragon Press, 2002). See too Chapter 7.

piano piece in homage to Schubert, so why should not others exercise interpretation in establishing another new identity for it? Moreover, *Valses nobles*
and *La Valse* were quite short as stand-alone ballets, and a longer run of
music could create more choreographic scope. Balanchine's fashioning of a
larger-scale, freer scenario allows *Valses nobles* particularly to enjoy a place
in more 'modern' ballet, whereas its original narrative plan would have been
too restrictive.

In summary, Balanchine's practice has two main strengths in relation to
enhancing the listener's musical insights. Firstly, joining essays on the waltz
as a single trajectory points up striking compositional similarities that justify
the choreographer's musical decision. Balanchine has helped the listener to
recognize Ravel's well-developed and distinctive sonic image of the waltz:
dotted rhythms, use of hemiola, emphasis on the second beat, half-bar divisions and hairpin dynamics. Secondly, Balanchine's version offers an exceptionally strong vision of the unease-through-to-destruction that is the essence
of Ravel's score. Even if this composite product ('one of the most enchanting and mysterious of Balanchine's ballets')[86] is like eating a rich, layered
cake, one would be hard pressed to decline the feast on the grounds that all
is not left to the imagination, as did Brunel in discussing Rubinstein's 1931
realization. In short, it works. The main elements of music and dance are so
well matched that Balanchine's interpretation can be claimed as one where
the synthesized whole is indeed greater than the sum of its components.

---

[86] Garafola, 'Dance for a city', 15.

Chapter 6

Neoclassical *divertissements*: *Le Tombeau de Couperin* and 'Fanfare' from *L'Eventail de Jeanne*

Neoclassicism has already been a background theme in consideration of the postwar *La Valse*, *L'Enfant* and implicitly *Boléro*; in a looser stylistic sense, the idea was germane to treatment of the past in the prewar *Daphnis* and *Valses nobles*. But it is the wartime *Le Tombeau de Couperin* (1914–17; orchestrated 1919) that acted as a distinctive neoclassical prototype, not only for later works of Ravel but for those of the next French generation, especially Les Six, with their more popular customizations. More broadly, *Le Tombeau* symbolized 'le nouveau classicisme',[1] predating and then rivalling Stravinsky's *L'Histoire du soldat* (1918) and *Pulcinella* (1919–20). This chapter examines the genesis of *Le Tombeau* as a piano work, its partial orchestration and its subsequent reconception as a ballet for the Ballets Suédois.[2] Ravel's music is viewed in association with the classically inspired, if idiosyncratic, designs of Pierre Laprade (1875–1931) and Jean Börlin's choreography.

Before examining the work in detail, it is useful to open up a few lines of enquiry on neoclassicism. In a postwar world reacting against Impressionism (itself a reaction against the past), Ravel's own thoughts provide a logical starting-point. 'We are perhaps today in the process of another reaction', he mused, 'but this reaction, which will balance itself, is in the direction of our oldest traditions, from which we will never turn.'[3] Even if slightly contradictory, the idea of being consumed by the past as a result of a journey from the present is noteworthy. Distance, interplay and balancing between new/now and old are picked up by Pieter van den Toorn: 'the immediacy of aesthetic

---

[1] Scott Messing, 'Polemic as history: the case of neoclassicism', *Journal of Musicology*, 9/4 (Fall 1991), 481–97: 491–2.

[2] For background beyond Häger, *Ballets Suédois*, see *La Danse, numéro consacré aux Ballets Suédois de Rolf de Maré* (November–December 1924): PRO.F.94 (B-MO); Sally Banes, 'An introduction to the Ballets Suédois', *Ballet Review*, 7/2–3 (1978–9); Erik Näslund, *Les Ballets Suédois 1920–1925* [exhibition catalogue] (Paris: Bibliothèque Nationale de France/Louis Vuitton, 1994).

[3] Olin Downes, 'Maurice Ravel: man and musician', *New York Times* (7 August 1927).

contemplation, that which is sensed and felt' – apt terminology for Ravel – in relation to 'the musical traditions (or social conditions, possibly) that are alleged to enter into that immediacy'.[4] The mention of 'social conditions' is again fitting when considering the mores of aristocratic, courtly dance. Distinctions exist between an artefact and its cultural baggage, almost a sense of 'signifier' and 'signified(s)' as understood by creator/receiver.

On the subtle complexities of genre and meaning pertaining to *tombeaux*, Carolyn Abbate provides a wealth of information and insight.[5] From sixteenth-century literary practice, the notion was taken up by French composers of the seventeenth century and fell into obscurity in the eighteenth. At the risk of oversimplification, the metaphor from funerary architecture as invoked in music commonly denotes 'a work written in memory of someone who has died'.[6] Where his *Le Tombeau* was concerned, Ravel claimed (not wholly convincingly, given his close reworking of Couperin) that 'The homage is directed less in reality to the unique Couperin himself than to French music of the eighteenth century.'[7] Certainly, Ravel's work is an act of reverent homage that takes a generously inclusive view of its past, along the contemporary lines of T.S. Eliot, rather than subscribing to a Bloomian theory of anxiety through needing to rewrite history,[8] although Ravel's view still allows for recomposition from past 'models'. Moreover, Ravel was extremely fond of the eighteenth-century epoch, the period for *Ma Mère l'Oye*, with its refined formality, symmetry and craftsmanship – in short, its civilized order. The mechanical dimension of *Fortspinnung* ('spinning out') was also an integral part of this appeal and by the mid-1920s Ravel was already acknowledged as 'The mechanic of *Le Tombeau de Couperin*'.[9] In 1928, he declared publicly his attraction to 'the objectivity and clarity of design exhibited by our earliest composers'.[10] He also liked the fact that invoking the past could act as another mask, and while he was not politically nationalistic, the French past was artistically most

---

[4] Pieter C. van den Toorn, 'Neoclassicism revisited', *Music, Politics and the Academy* (Berkeley: University of California Press, 1995), 143.

[5] Carolyn Abbate, 'Outside Ravel's tomb', 469–72.

[6] Ibid., 469.

[7] [Roland-Manuel,] 'Une esquisse autobiographique', 22. 'L'hommage s'adresse moins en réalité au seul Couperin lui-même qu'à la musique française du XVIIIᵉ siècle.'

[8] See Straus, *Remaking the Past*, 10–11; T. S. Eliot, 'Tradition and the individual talent' (1919), in *Selected Essays* (New York: Harcourt Brace, 1950); Harold Bloom, *The Anxiety of Influence: A Theory of Poetry* (Oxford: Oxford University Press, 1975).

[9] Alexis Roland-Manuel, '*L'Enfant et les sortilèges*', *Le Ménestrel* (5 February 1926), 60–61: 60.

[10] Maurice Ravel, 'Contemporary music', repr. in Orenstein (ed.), *A Ravel Reader*, 45. See Mawer, 'Neoclassicism and l'objet retrouvé' within 'Musical objects and machines', 53–7.

becoming. Paul Griffiths first offered the attractive image of the dances of *Le Tombeau* constituting a physical, 'disguising' receptacle for original ideas of Ravel: a locus 'where the forms of a French Baroque suite are made to hold self-contained ideas of characteristic finesse'.[11]

Ravel related closely to specific French models where at least two dances were concerned: the 'Forlane' after Couperin, which he was editing contemporaneously, and 'Rigaudon' after Rameau (see below). More generally, the art of François Couperin 'Le Grand' (1668–1733) held much to inspire a neoclassical aesthetic: humour in the instructive *L'Art de toucher le clavecin* (1716); stylistic imitation of Corelli and Lully in *Le Parnasse ou l'Apothéose de Corelli* (1724) and *L'Apothéose de Lully* (1725); through to satirical commentary on a Parisian minstrels' guild in *Les Fastes de la grande et ancienne Mxnxstrxndxsx* (*Ménestrandise*) from the second volume of *Pièces de clavecin* (1717). Thus *Le Tombeau* in turn serves as a more general icon for neoclassicism.

What is special about Ravel's *Le Tombeau* is its dual tribute: to the distant past – both collective and individual – and, throughout the course of its composition,[12] to the immediate past and the horrific, continuing present of the First World War. By 1917, it becomes a miniature musical representation of the massive stone memorials inscribed with thousands of names, or of the endless cemeteries of Northern France; thus one may relate literally to the theoretical ideal of Troussevitch whereby 'An art-work is a minuscule thing which contains a great thing.'[13] It also becomes an intensely personal memorial to seven friends killed during the War (see Table 6.1, p. 188) and surely also to Ravel's beloved mother who died in January 1917. There is irony in the use of a civilizing mask of neoclassicism, including mechanisms devoid of emotion, in the face of European civilization destroyed. Similarly, Ravel's dedications to the dead offer a most poignant rereading of the fanciful titles that headed Couperin's keyboard pieces (which the composer himself had referred to as 'musical portraits'). In this way, one finds a complex, contradictory blend of frothiness and gravity.

After *Le Tombeau*, Ravel paid compositional tribute to contemporary composers – the Sonata for Violin and Cello (1920–22) to the memory of Debussy, orchestrations of Debussy's *Sarabande* (1922) and *Danse* ([*Tarantelle styrienne*], 1922), and the *Berceuse sur le nom de Fauré* (1922) – while *Ronsard à son âme*, his contribution to the collective *Tombeau de*

---

[11] Paul Griffiths, *Modern Music: A Concise History from Debussy to Boulez* (London: Thames & Hudson, 1978), 82–3.

[12] For detail, see Roger Nichols, Preface to Maurice Ravel, *Le Tombeau de Couperin* (London: Peters, 1995), 4.

[13] Troussevitch, 'La Chorégraphie', 346 (for French, see above, p. 32).

Ronsard printed in *La Revue musicale* of May 1924, evokes the sixteenth-century French literary past.

L'Eventail de Jeanne (1927) is considered briefly as another neoclassical product. This collective *divertissement* involved ten composers headed by Ravel, plus choreographers, stage and costume designers, under Rouché's customary direction. While *Le Tombeau* appreciates its heritage respectfully, Ravel's 'Fanfare' for *L'Eventail* is distinctly parodistic and humorous (though sharing the mechanistic fascination of *Le Tombeau*), if not quite as sharp-edged as *L'Enfant*. Treatment of this piece also enables comparison with the 'Prélude' to *Ma Mère l'Oye* and offers a codicil to the topic of childhood.

Music and evolution of *Le Tombeau*

The initial genesis of *Le Tombeau* was as a six-movement piano suite – a modern-day harpsichord *ordre*, begun in July 1914 at St-Jean-de-Luz, just before the War. (See too 'Genesis and evolution' of *Boléro*, Chapter 7.) As is now well documented, the Forlane appears to be Ravel's starting-point, mentioned in a letter to Godebski during late spring 1914: 'I am transcribing a Forlane by Couperin. I will see about getting it danced at the Vatican by Mistinguett and Colette Willy in drag.'[14] Ravel's colourful image nicely conflates new and old: the topical quip about the Pope sanctioning the Forlane and the jibe about Colette's transvestism (worth bearing in mind in view of the later, half-hearted collaboration for *L'Enfant*: see Chapter 2). Furthermore, Ravel's interest was, as argued by Scott Messing,[15] most likely awakened by Albert Bertelin's transcription of the 'Forlane' from Couperin's *Quatrième concert* of the *Concerts royaux*. A little later, on 1 October 1914, Ravel wrote to Roland-Manuel mentioning a gigue in addition to his own (re)composed 'Forlane' destined for a 'French suite'.[16]

---

[14] Ravel quoted by Barbara Kelly, 'History and homage', in Mawer (ed.), *The Cambridge Companion to Ravel*, 7.

[15] See Messing, 'Polemic as history', 484–6, and Kelly, 'History and homage', 19–22, which compares part of the fourth couplet of Ravel's edition with that of Bertelin, and with Ravel's own 'Forlane'. Bertelin's harmonization appeared in Jules Ecorcheville, 'La Forlane', *Revue musicale de la S.I.M.* (April 1914), to which issue Ravel also contributed. That Bertelin was also interested in dance is evidenced by his earlier article, 'L'Art de la danse', *Le Courrier musical* (15 January 1912), 38–41, which evinced a complimentary response and a lengthy plea for the cause of eurhythmics ('la *Gymnastique rythmique*') from Jean d'Udine: 'Lettre ouverte à M. Albert Bertelin', *Le Courrier musical*, 15/3 (1 February 1912), 62–7. See above, Chapter 2, n. 81.

[16] Roland-Manuel, *Ravel*, 76.

Composition was interrupted in March 1915 by Ravel's war service and finally concluded, following a discharge for ill-health, across June–November 1917.[17] On 7 July 1917, Ravel informed Jacques Durand that a 'Menuet' and 'Rigaudon' were finished, with the remainder developing. One may thus reasonably surmise, as does Nichols, that sketches discussed by Orenstein date from around this period.[18] As with the 'Forlane', there is a possible compositional model – also proposed by Messing – for the 'Rigaudon' in Rameau's 'Premier tambourin' from his *Troisième concert*.[19] Rhythmic correspondence is undeniable, but close links exist too with the opening waltz of Ravel's earlier *Valses nobles*, as indeed is the case with the 'Menuet' and Ravel's third waltz (Chapters 4–5). (This 'Menuet' marks the end of Ravel's set of four essays on the form, the previous three of which were composed before he transferred his affections to the waltz.)

An opening 'Prélude' and three-voiced 'Fugue', with inevitable Bachian association, lead to three more overtly eighteenth-century dances ('Forlane', 'Rigaudon' and 'Menuet'), the main items later to be choreographed. And the whole is rounded off with a demanding percussive 'Toccata', in place of Ravel's originally intended gigue. Stylistically, these pieces accord with the characteristics described above. Tightly controlled small-scale forms (binary; ternary; *rondeau* with refrains and *couplets*) use traditional notational conventions such as repeat marks and first-/second-time bars. Metre is regular; incisive rhythms articulated by varied ornamentation occur within clearly identifiable phrases. The musical language is based on an overall melancholic 'minor' mode on E, with cadences favouring antique-sounding major seconds rather than semitones. But the twentieth-century imprint is nonetheless quite audible: modal ambiguities between tonic and relative major, wide pitch ranges, pentatonic and wholetone fragments,[20] mild to moderate dissonance, chromatic modulation, phrase extensions and reversals of expectation,[21] dynamic contouring, and textural treatment that blurs melodic/harmonic roles. Wonderful rhythmic games cause subtle distortions that wrong-foot the unwary, such as emphasis on the second beat or bar, rather than the first. More specifically, commentators such as Antoine

---

[17] Ravel's piano MS (18 pp.) bears the dates 'July 1914, June–November 1917' and was published by Durand in 1918.

[18] Nichols, Preface, 4; Orenstein, *Ravel: Man and Musician*, 211–12. Nichols points out that it was the 'Menuet' and 'Rigaudon' which Ravel felt comfortable performing in public, such as on his 1928 tour of the United States (Preface, 5).

[19] Messing, 'Polemic as history', 485, 487–8. For more on Ravel's remodelling in relation to an actual or imagined source, see Mawer, 'Musical objects and machines', 56.

[20] See Roy Howat, 'Modes and semitones in Debussy's *Preludes* and elsewhere', *Studies in Music*, 22 (1988), 81–91: 89.

[21] For a detailed reading of Ravel's play in *Le Tombeau*, see Roy Howat, 'Ravel and the piano', in Mawer (ed.), *The Cambridge Companion to Ravel*, 86–93: 90.

Goléa noted the influence of Albéniz's *Iberia*, amid a broad musical spectrum including Mozart and Schubert.[22] This *Iberia* reference is apt in view of Ravel's later association *en route* to *Boléro*; furthermore, the ballet version of *Le Tombeau* shared the stage with Inghelbrecht's orchestration of parts of *Iberia*. Most importantly, the whole enterprise has a bittersweet piquancy: smiling through tears.

As can be seen in Table 6.1, each movement is dedicated to one or more of Ravel's lost friends. Jacques Charlot was a fellow musician who had produced the piano reductions of *Ma Mère l'Oye*; Marliave was an amateur musician married to Marguerite Long; Jean Dreyfus was Roland-Manuel's half-brother whose well-being Ravel had enquired after in a letter of September 1914; Jean Cruppi was the son of an influential woman who had helped secure the premiere of *L'Heure espagnole*; finally, Deluc and the Gaudin twins were old friends of Ravel.[23]

Although the *tombeau* concept predated the deaths of Ravel's friends, the work certainly acquired strong funeral associations during its compositional gestation. This tomb-like aspect has typically been underplayed even if Abbate's article has helped to achieve a rethink. On this theme and the importance of the inter-arts dimension, it is worth highlighting Ravel's drawing that became the frontispiece to the first piano edition of *Le Tombeau* (Figure 6.1).[24] The attractive black-ink sketch is signed in full by the composer in the top left corner; the main depiction in classical style is of a decorative funerary urn placed upon some kind of altar covered by a drape or swag, secured at either

Table 6.1 *Le Tombeau de Couperin*: dedications and (re-)ordering of movements

Piano original (key)	Orchestration/ballet (key)	Dedication: 'à la mémoire de/du'
I. Prélude (e)	I. Prélude (e)	Lieutenant Jacques Charlot
II. Fugue (e)	—	Sub-lieutenant Jean Cruppi
III. Forlane (e)	II. Forlane (e)	Lieutenant Gabriel Deluc
IV. Rigaudon (C/c)	IV. Rigaudon (C/c)	Pierre and Pascal Gaudin
V. Menuet (G/g)	III. Menuet (G/g)	Jean Dreyfus
VI. Toccata (e/E)	—	Captain Joseph de Marliave

[22] Antoine Goléa, *Esthétique de la musique contemporaine* (Paris: Presses Universitaires de France, 1954), quoted in Marnat, *Maurice Ravel*, 436–7.

[23] Nichols, Preface, 5; Orenstein, *Ravel*, 75.

[24] After Ravel's death, the full piano MS was in the possession of Mme Alexandre Taverne.

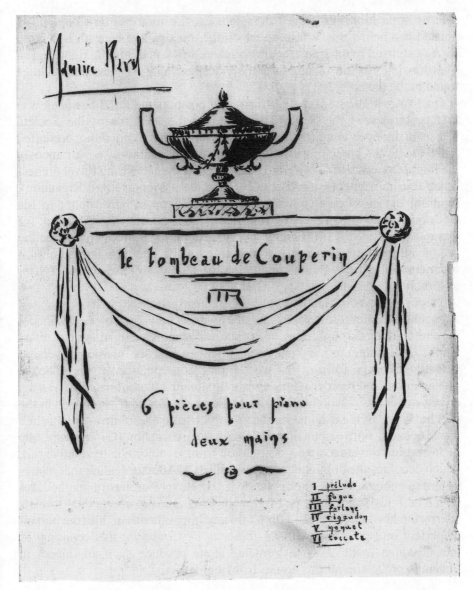

Figure 6.1   Ravel's frontispiece drawing for *Le Tombeau de Couperin*
(1918). By permission of the Bibliothèque Nationale de France.

side by what look like carved floral bosses. 'Le tombeau de Couperin' is notated just below the surface on which the urn sits, and beneath is centred Ravel's stylized monogram: the mechanized 'MR', maximizing right angles. The drawing's blend of charm and seriousness aptly reflects the qualities found in the music.

On 11 April 1919, following frustrating postponement, *Le Tombeau* was first performed at the Salle Gaveau, under the auspices of the Société Musicale Indépendante, by the pianist Marguerite Long (who presented much of Ravel's piano music to its Parisian public, including most famously the Piano Concerto in G early in 1932). Around the same time Ravel orchestrated four movements, the 'Prélude', 'Forlane', 'Menuet' and 'Rigaudon', omitting the most contrapuntal 'Fugue' and 'Toccata'. In a letter to Ida Godebska of 24 May 1919, he said that he was completing this work for Durand,[25] but he was still finding it very difficult to be productive. (See the protracted gestation of *La Valse*, described in Chapter 5.) The orchestral premiere with Rhené-Baton conducting the Orchestre Pasdeloup duly followed on 28 February 1920.

Much of Ravel's piano writing subsequently orchestrated acquires an indispensable new dimension, but this is especially true of *Le Tombeau*, despite the fact that only four of the six movements were so treated. Even Cortot, as a contemporary pianist, maintained that the orchestral version was the definitive form of the work.[26] One consequence of this selective orchestration and reordering of items to maintain a lively finale is a new set of key relations. The orchestration starts at the beginning, yet it ends in the middle. Whereas the original reinflects E minor into a resolute major through the 'Toccata', with submediant (C) and relative major (G) *en route*, the orchestration travels to a new destination from E minor, via its relative (G), which becomes the dominant of a new tonic (C). Another feature that relates in turn to choreographic interpretation is that Ravel's orchestral method, for which he finds an unlikely bed-fellow in *Tosca*(!), is to create dual soloists (mirroring his dual tribute): 'I didn't do anything other than this [the pursuit of perfect orchestration] with *Le Tombeau de Couperin*: this economy of means which makes two instruments alone produce such an impact in Puccini's orchestra: all this comes from a great artist'.[27]

---

[25] The orchestral MS (26 pp.) is dated June 1919 and is held with some sketches in the ROLC. Publication followed later in 1919.

[26] Jeanne Thieffry (ed.), *Alfred Cortot, cours d'interprétation* (Paris: Legouix, 1934), 85. This reference is identified in Howat, 'Ravel and the piano', 88.

[27] Manuel Rosenthal, 'Entretiens avec Rémy Stricker', *France Culture* (April 1985), in Marnat, *Maurice Ravel*, 145: 'je n'ai pas fait autre chose avec *Le Tombeau de Couperin*: cette économie de moyens qui fait que deux instruments seuls produisent un tel choc dans l'orchestre de Puccini: tout cela vient d'un grand artiste'.

Ravel's forces are modest: a chamber orchestra of double wind, single trumpet, harp and strings; a brief tour presents his orchestrated music in its new-found order. The fleeting 'Prélude' in 12/16 metre swirls around seeking thematic definition, pushing onto the second bar of each grouping, but the oboe – an instrument with strong eighteenth-century credentials – instantly signs up as a principal protagonist (Example 6.1), supported amongst others by clarinet, in imitative counterpoint. Chromatic meanderings create wave-like ebb and flow, with momentary sweeping climaxes (Figs. 4^{-2}, 10). Essentially, the mood is one of quiet introspection, delicately characterized by pizzicato strings, mutes (trumpet, violins) and harmonics (harp, cello). A final glissando-tremolo surge (Fig. 12) acts as a perfect herald for the rise of a ballet curtain. The harpist is instructed to 'smother' the sound, just as the life of Ravel's friend had suddenly been extinguished.

Feigned levity and eighteenth-century manners are suggested in the 'Forlane' through, in Messing's parlance, 'readily identifiable clichés': lilting dotted rhythms in compound duple metre. But the illusion is exposed by twentieth-century inflection: the angular, poignant seventh contour of the melody, with stressed off-beat (Example 6.2), combined with the cor anglais's nasal melancholy and dissonant harmonies. The effect is of a ghostly *danse macabre*. No soloists as such appear in this opening, which is concerted chamber music composed of eight active instrumental staves, well suited to chamber dancing. Although the oboe reasserts itself (Fig. 1), the melody passes through the woodwind ranks more equitably. Three episodes or *couplets* (B, C, D) separating the refrain (A) create more distant, nostalgic yet forlorn, moments. Appearance and actuality are again deceptive: an arrival on E major (Fig. 14) for the third couplet promises a sweetening, but the

Example 6.1 *Le Tombeau de Couperin* (orchestral suite, 1919) 'Prélude' (bars 1–4, reduction)

Example 6.2 *Le Tombeau de Couperin*: 'Forlane' (bars 1–5, reduction)

reality is an awesome infiltration of dissonance (Fig. 15ff.) that threatens the existence of the dance.

A stately 'Menuet' now preceding the 'Rigaudon' is led again by solo oboe, promoting Ravel's brand of lush, soft-edged neoclassicism (Example 5.4, p. 175). The cor anglais's counterpoint offers initial support, but the main instrumental partner is the flute, its tone intensified in the central 'Musette' by bassoon (Fig. 4). A spectral quality thrives in this lament in the dorian mode on G, with *pp* drone bass and ghostly harmonics. Increased 'edge' is achieved as trumpet and muted horn appropriate the melodic repeat (Fig. 5), while the accented tutti peak, at *ff*, feels like a physical body blow (Fig. 7). Back in the reprise, a new duality is achieved with Ravel's typical thematic combination, which cleverly reinflects the 'Musette' idea within an overall G major (Example 6.3; Fig. 9). The interval pattern of the central 'Musette': B♭–A–G–F, semitone–tone–tone, is reversed in the reprise: B–A–G–F♯, tone–tone–semitone. Compare too the different 'Menuet' phrasings (Examples 5.4 and 6.3). After the final climax and cued by the harp, time seems to become frozen (Fig. 15).

The newly concluding 'Rigaudon' contrasts rudely with forthright sounds, fit for the childhood fairground – perhaps that at St-Jean-de-Luz to which Ravel had returned with Benois in early summer 1914 – articulated by loudly accented trumpet and horns. In the outer sections, this forward-propelling

Example 6.3 *Le Tombeau de Couperin*: 'Menuet' (Fig. 9, reduction)

mechanism resembles a *moto perpetuo* (Example 6.4). Various instrumental pairings try their luck with the semiquavers: clarinets doubled by violins, bassoons, then horns, but it is the oboe that returns for the sombre *minore* (Fig. 5), partnered by cor anglais, and followed by a second partnership between flute and clarinet. Enforced merriment returns (Fig. 12).

Balletic design and dance

Ravel conceived the ballet version of *Le Tombeau* for the Ballets Suédois (1920–25), Swedish would-be rivals of the Ballet Russes, at the Théâtre des Champs-Elysées, under their director De Maré. By contrast with *Ma Mère l'Oye* or *Adélaïde*, the new project – proposed by Ingelbrecht[28] and championed by De Maré – did not involve further composition, orchestration or the devising of a scenario. Nonetheless, Ravel seemingly gave it his full support (see pp. 201 and 252 below).

Ravel's drawing apart, the designs for *Le Tombeau* were created by a contemporary friend of some years, Pierre Laprade: he, Ravel, and Bonnard had met back in June 1905 when they were invited on an extended yachting cruise through Belgium, the Netherlands and Germany with Misia Edwards (later Sert) and her second husband Alfred. Frustratingly, Ravel's contemporary letters say nothing about his interaction with Laprade or Bonnard, yet the trip apparently stimulated much artistic activity. Various materials for set and costume design survive, including a rough ink sketch for the main set (Figure 6.2) showing stylized leafy arbours, the trunks of which provide punctuation across the set and perspective from foreground, with two trunks/'columns', through to middle distance: two further trunks, the left one of which features a statue. A watercoloured version of this sketch exists, with a sombre blue-green wash to bring forward the near 'arch' and

Example 6.4 *Le Tombeau de Couperin*: 'Rigaudon' (bars 1–4, reduction)

---

[28] Inghelbrecht is credited with the initiative in Rolf de Maré, 'Ravel et les ballets', *La Revue musicale*, 20 (January–February 1939), 15–16: 15. Ravel had previously proposed Inghelbrecht as conductor for the Théâtre des Arts (Chapter 2, n.27).

Figure 6.2   Pierre Laprade's sketch for the garden set of *Le Tombeau de Couperin* (1920). By permission of the Bibliothèque Nationale de France.

the statue repositioned to centre right.[29] These softened images, somewhat impressionistic, accord with Ravel's particular mode of neoclassicism. This eighteenth-century garden bears some affinity with that which Ravel imagined in his early scenario (sources A/B) for *Ma Mère l'Oye* and indeed with leafy garlands associated with his scenario for *Adélaïde*.

Extant costume designs include one for a female dancer with fixed, slightly vacant expression, avoiding the viewer's gaze: her dramatic hair, or wig, features formal curls festooned by ribbons; her dress has a low-cut neckline accentuated by a lack of jewellery, short slightly puff sleeves and a narrow waistband (Figure 6.3). A related watercolour image with lemon yellow highlighting reveals a scallop-edged apron and layered skirt.[30] The costume for the leading female dancer, initially to be Jenny Hasselquist, is very similar, but includes a short string of pearls. Another sketch is of a foppish male dancer – wearing Börlin's costume – with a flouncy high-necked shirt, a double-breasted wide-collared coat with tails, a curled wig, and boots which sport a V-shape across the shin.[31] There is an analogous,

---

[29] See Häger, *Ballets Suédois*, 101.

[30] Ibid,. 103.

[31] Costume designs for the two leading dancers are reproduced in the plates of Rolf de Maré (ed.), *Les Ballets Suédois dans l'art contemporain* (Paris: Editions du Trianon, 1931). Similar designs appeared in Paul-Sentenac, 'Les Ballets Russes et les Ballet Suédois', in *Les Spectacles à travers les âges: musique, danse* (Paris: Editions du Cygne, 1932), 235–64: 240, 241.

Figure 6.3   Lady's costume design for *Le Tombeau* (1920) by Pierre Laprade
(from Roland-Manuel, *M. Ravel et son oeuvre dramatique*,
1928). By permission of the Bibliothèque Nationale de France.

broadly classical, elegance to that found in Drésa's earlier designs for
Adélaïde. In fact, Hahn criticized these costumes, especially that of Börlin,
as veering more towards the later styles of Louis XV and XVI and the
Directoire – the period prior to 1799 – than to that of the celebrated Sun
King, Louis XIV, whose reign from 1643 to 1715 spanned most of Couperin's
life.[32]

   The choreography of *Le Tombeau* was conceived by the tragically short-
lived principal dancer-cum-choreographer of the Ballets Suédois, Jean Börlin,
'whose grace and audacious youth allowed him to move from classical to
modern, from Chopin to Darius Milhaud, from Ravel to Debussy'.[33] Börlin
had been a pupil of Fokine at the Royal Opera of Stockholm from around

---

[32] Reynaldo Hahn, quoted in Häger, *Ballets Suédois*, 102.

[33] S. A., *Le Figaro* (9 December 1930): 'dont la grâce et l'audacieuse jeunesse lui per-
mirent de passer du classique au moderne, de Chopin à Darius Milhaud, de Ravel à Debussy'.
Börlin's untimely death in New York from a brain haemorrhage also received press coverage
from *Comœdia*, *Paris-midi* and *La Volonté*. A less partial obituary writer in *Comœdia*
(December 1930) felt that despite its culture and 'nobility', Börlin's art lacked the fervour
and 'acuity' of the Ballets Russes, and that his dancing was not sufficiently original. (Jean
Börlin, Dossier d'artiste, B-MO.)

1913, gaining a thorough foundation in classical dance, as well as in musical composition and harmony. Fokine evidently thought very highly of him, claiming that discovering Börlin had given him great artistic joy, and later recommending him to de Maré. Börlin's physical presence as a dancer, according to Fokine, had no hint of a cold North European attitude: 'He crossed the stage in huge leaps, fell with all his weight and glided across the parquet floor … What a temperament! What ecstasy! The fanatical sacrifice of a bruised body in order to give the maximum choreographic expression.'[34]

According to Fokine, Börlin choreographed with passion, creative élan and stylistic flexibility. He heeded Fokine's basic 'five principles', which forged close connections between the ballet's subject-matter and its various artistic components including dance itself, whose movements used the whole body expressively. Similarly, he respected the *corps de ballet* and sought to integrate its role.[35] Upon this foundation, Bengt Häger makes clear that 'as a creator he [Börlin] invented a new aesthetic of movement, freed from the old academic rules … he endeavoured to express the new age, modern man and his radically changed life-style'.[36] In *Le Tombeau*, however, heeding period style meant that Börlin necessarily returned to the separate 'numbers' that Fokine had sought to avoid.

Börlin's approach is well illustrated by an example of his choreographic notation, contrasted appropriately enough with typical eighteenth-century samples (Figure 6.4). Although notation cannot tell the full story regarding danced interpretation, the differences are striking. Whereas the earlier notations graph the requisite steps mechanically and plot them aerially, Börlin's small figure drawings emphasize poetic plasticity: expressive, flowing full-body movements (crouching forwards, extending backwards), most especially arms curved over the head. This approach, inspired by notions of aesthetic beauty with which Ravel could identify, is demonstrated by two photographs of studio rehearsals at the Théâtre des Champs-Elysées. The first depicts similar sweeping arm motions with arched backs, supporting the leg positioning, to those presented in Börlin's notation. The *corps de ballet* looks to be engaged in an exercise routine in organized formation,

---

[34] Michel Fokine, 'Börlin, mon élève', in de Maré (ed.), *Les Ballets Suédois*, 148–51: 149. 'Il parcourait la scène en sauts immenses, tombait de tout son poids et glissait sur le parquet … Une nature! Une extase! Le sacrifice fanatique d'un corps meurtri afin de donner le maximum de l'expression chorégraphique.' This volume also contains an article on Börlin's rehearsal practice by Alexis Roland-Manuel: 'En regardant travailler Jean Börlin', *Les Ballets suédois*, 151–4.

[35] Claudia B. Stone, 'Jean Börlin', in Bremser (ed.), *International Dictionary of Ballet*, vol. I, 181–2: 182. For more, see Paul-Sentenac, 'Les Ballets Russes et les Ballets Suédois', 254, 260.

[36] Häger, *Ballets Suédois*, 293.

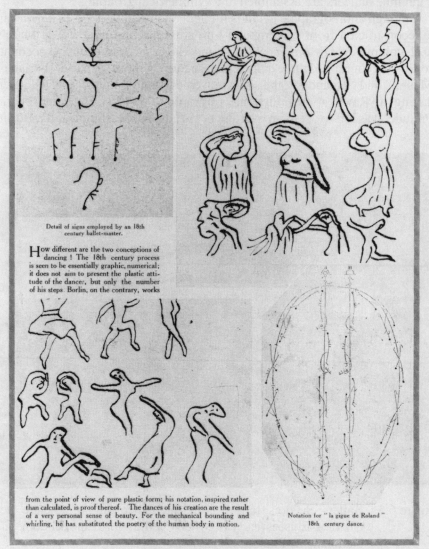

Figure 6.4   Comparison of eighteenth-century notations and those of Jean
Börlin (Ballets Suédois general programme). By permission of
the Bibliothèque Nationale de France.

with Börlin in the centre of the first row (Figure 6.5); in a second photograph nine dancers are assembled in a symmetrical grouping.

Although choreographic detail is limited,[37] something of *Le Tombeau* can be reconstructed from contemporary programmes and reviews, de Maré's 1931 volume on *Les Ballets Suédois* and Häger's comprehensive account. Börlin choreographed three dances in pure form without scenario: 'Forlane', 'Menuet' and 'Rigaudon', the same movements that Poulenc selected when playing to Ravel at their first meeting around 1917.[38] The atmospheric 'Prélude' was left to act as an overture or curtain-raiser. Significantly, Börlin

Figure 6.5   Ballets Suédois rehearsal in the dance studio, Théâtre des Champs-Elysées (early 1920s). By permission of the Bibliothèque Nationale de France.

---

[37] Erik Näslund of the DansMuseet in Stockholm has stated regretfully in personal correspondence (8 January 2003): 'Unfortunately there is very little on *Le Tombeau*, except for a few photos, published elsewhere, no choreographic notes or any similar primary source material.' The *Cinquantenaire des Ballets Suédois 1920–1925, Collections du Musée de la Danse de Stockholm* (Malmö: Skånetryck AB, 1970), 20, lists Laprade's scenic model, set sketch, and five groups of costume designs (ink and watercolour) among exhibits for a 1970 Paris exhibition, but makes no mention of any choreographic material.

[38] Poulenc, *Moi et mes amis*, repr. Nichols (ed.), *Ravel Remembered*, 116.

had a point of mediation with the past somewhat similar to Ravel's with Couperin: he had special experience of eighteenth-century French courtly dances because, paradoxically, such 'style dances' still formed part of a Swedish performing tradition. As a neat inversion of the twentieth-century Swedish Ballet in Paris, Stockholm's company had been founded in the eighteenth by French dancers.[39] And so Swedes were returning to the French part of their own heritage.

Börlin's 'Forlane' was composed for a single quadrille: a set of four female–male couples, sometimes subdivided (see Boschot's review, p. 203 below). Thus an interesting parallel emerges with Ravel's treatment, which also promotes the idea of concerted chamber music. The oboist's role, as equivalent of a principal dancer, is less apparent here. Meanwhile, the 'Menuet' and 'Rigaudon' were choreographed for two soloists, Börlin and Hasselquist, working with a *corps de ballet* of raised status, after Fokine (see pp. 8 and 79 above). (Other noteworthy performers were Carina Ari, a second prima ballerina of the company, and the Witzansky brothers, one of whom, Axel, had by February 1921 become a *premier danseur*.) Again, this principle projects through dance an idea central to Ravel's orchestration: the presence of an instrumental duo as a dynamic focus for the chamber ensemble. And while Ravel varies the instrumental personnel of his interacting 'couples', there must surely have been a sense of Börlin personifying the oboe line.

It is a reasonable assumption that two photographs relate to the 'Menuet'. The first is a close-up of Börlin and Hasselquist adopting a stately pose, full of foppish affectation, coquettishness and mannered detachment (Figure 6.6).[40] Both have exaggeratedly made-up eyebrows and lips, with faces powdered to a rather ghostly pallor. A dandyesque Börlin stands, arching slightly backwards, with his lady to his right, the fingers of their raised right arms elegantly meeting over Hasselquist's head. This conjoined gesture is arch-like, echoing the tree boughs of the set. A second photograph, from a general programme,[41] shows Laprade's set in action: six couples are spaced across the back of the stage, adopting the same arch-like handholding pose; the men are most likely turning the ladies. Slightly in front are positioned the central couple, distanced as if in a courting tiff; the lady is backing away

---

[39] Häger, *Ballet Suédois*, 17–18. For a video on eighteenth-century music and dance, demonstrating typical minuet and rigaudon steps, see *Baroque Dances and Baroque Music* (New York: Insight Media, 1997; [NSTC] 55AF2687).

[40] A similar, posed studio photograph is reproduced in Häger, *Ballets Suédois*, 100.

[41] *Le Tombeau de Couperin* (Photo Isabey) in programme, *Les Ballets Suédois (1920–24)*, n.p. PRO.F.94 (3) (B-MO). The programme includes an introduction to de Maré, photographs of four artists, with a pensive M. Laprade and bespectacled M. Bonnard (the designer for Debussy's *Jeux*), a two-page Avant-propos on the Ballets Suédois, a feature on Börlin and a staged photograph of Inghelbrecht's *El Greco*.

Figure 6.6   Jean Börlin and Jenny Hasselquist in *Le Tombeau de Couperin*
(Ballets Suédois, 1920). By permission of the DansMuseet,
Stockholm.

towards stage right, while the man looks rather put out and bemused, clutching a handkerchief in his left hand.

Another photograph appears to be a curtain-call shot at the end of the 'Rigaudon', showing the *corps de ballet* with graceful arm movements and one foot placed slightly in front of the other.[42] Dancers are arranged symmetrically, with three groups of two ladies positioned left, right and centre, adopting curtsey-like gestures. Between the female groups are positioned two lines of three men, centre left and centre right, with arms outstretched. Their effete, even vacuous, poses are faithful to those in Laprade's sketches and could not contrast more strongly with the peasant-like rusticity of the Ballets Suédois's costumed dancers in a traditional folkdance at Stockholm's historically preserved village, Skansen.[43]

Even if the composer was less directly involved in this ballet than in most others, de Maré insisted that 'Ravel interested himself vigorously in the production of this project, and was present at numerous rehearsals … Our collaboration with Ravel was of the most pleasant.'[44] Where the product was concerned, he maintained that a 'perfect harmony' existed between music, designs and performers. That all had not been so smooth *en route* can however be gleaned from the memoirs of the company's conductor, Inghelbrecht.[45] When Inghelbrecht first met the troupe newly arrived from Sweden, he was horrified to discover that any fast repertory, as in *Iberia* or *Le Tombeau*, was performed 'au ralenti'. Everything was limited by the pianistic capabilities of a *répétiteur* whom Inghelbrecht dubs 'this brave son of the fjords [*sic*]'. To compound the problem, Börlin's choreography, having been devised to these speeds, could not easily be executed faster. Predictably, this created music–dance conflicts and, as with the Ravel–Fokine collaboration, language incompatibilities necessitated a good measure of 'divining'.

The Ballets Suédois premiere and its critical reception

And so, with a few challenges overcome out of the public eye, the premiere took place at the Théâtre des Champs-Elysées on 8 November 1920. Critical

---

[42] This photograph, captioned '*Tombeau de Couperin*. – Décor de Pierre Laprade, Photo Isabey', is reproduced in the plates of de Maré (ed.), *Les Ballets Suédois*.

[43] Undated Ballets Suédois photograph from Skansen, in ibid.

[44] De Maré, 'Ravel et les ballets', 15: 'Ravel s'intéressa vivement à la réalisation de ce projet, et assista à de nombreuses répétitions … Notre collaboration avec Ravel fut des plus agréables.'

[45] D.-E. Inghelbrecht, *Mouvement contraire, souvenirs d'un musicien* (Paris: Editions Domat, 1947), 129–30.

response to *Le Tombeau* was predominantly very positive, and it could hardly have harmed its case that it represented a welcome antidote to the controversial premiere of the expressionist *Maison de fous* (The Mad House), probing lunacy and hysteria, with music by a little-known young Swede named Viking Dahl. The point was well made by George Lapommeraye: 'What a joy it was then to hear *Le Tombeau de Couperin* of Maurice Ravel, whose recent orchestration ... was so nicely brought out by the excellent direction of M. Inghelbrecht!'[46] (According to José Bruyr, *Le Tombeau* was followed by *Iberia*[47] – a three-act extravaganza showcasing three of Albéniz's pieces orchestrated by Inghelbrecht, interspersed with Debussy's *Ibéria*, which had been premiered on the company's opening night in Paris, 25 October 1920.)

Musically, Ravel's contribution was a known quantity, but Louis Schneider felt it helpful to remind his reader about the archaizing concept of the title: 'In bygone times they called the collecting of homages in prose, verse or music in tribute to a person deceased or even still living a *tombeau*',[48] offering the instance of Louis Couperin, uncle of François 'Le Grand', composing *Le Tombeau de Mr. Blancrocher* for his lute teacher. Further relating past and present, Hahn, more even-handed than on *Ma Mère l'Oye*, declared that *Le Tombeau* was 'a delicious musical entertainment composed of a brisk fast-moving introduction, nimbly and sharply executed, and full of coquetry, and of three dances, a forlana, a minuet and a rigaudon, traditional steps exquisitely dressed up in "modern" garb.'[49] The 'Menuet' was 'mischievous' and the 'Rigaudon' both 'impudent' and 'robust'. For Adolphe Boschot, the music was also 'a delightful little thing: sharp and subtle, prettily poetic, witty, even mocking'.[50] Boschot's slightly patronising tone is unfortunate, but his mention of mockery hints at a more serious dimension to the work that is absent from Hahn's assessment.

On choreography and dance, comments were more variable, but generally favourable. Even Hahn had to admit that 'M. Börlin has arranged for M. Ravel's music some very pleasing "figures", which were elegantly executed, in a very attractive setting.' Similar anodyne platitudes (partly reflecting the

---

    [46] George Lapommeraye, 'La Semaine musicale. – Théâtre des Champs-Elysées. – (Ballets Suédois 2ᵉ spectacle)', *Le Ménestrel* (19 November 1920), 446. 'Quelle joie ce fut d'entendre ensuite *Le Tombeau de Couperin*, de Maurice Ravel, dont l'orchestration récente ... fut si joliment mise en valeur par l'excellente direction de M. Inghelbrecht!'

    [47] Bruyr, *Maurice Ravel ou le lyricisme et les sortilèges*, 165.

    [48] Louis Schneider, 'Musique, Théâtre des Champs-Elysées – Le 2ᵉ Spectacle des Ballets Suédois', *Le Gaulois* (15 November 1920). 'On appelait autrefois *tombeau* la réunion des hommages en prose, en vers ou en musique adressés en hommage à une personnalité disparue ou même vivante.'

    [49] Hahn, trans. Häger, *Ballets Suédois*, 102.

    [50] Adolphe Boschot, *L'Echo de Paris* (10 November 1920), trans. ibid.

mannered proceedings themselves) emerged from Schneider's pen; Boschot, on the other hand, probed a bit deeper, viewing the dances as 'imbued with a dream-like languor, a whimsical grace, a mysterious and enchanting softness'.[51] Apart from the dancing of Hasselquist and Börlin, Lapommeraye highlighted the gracefulness and light-footed work of the male dancers generally. In his *Echo de Paris* review, Boschot offered more detail on figures 'who come and go, adopting precious, elegant and nonchalant poses. They dance in groups of eight, four and two'. Laloy, ever perceptive, considered that Börlin's danced 'accompaniment' adopted a rather exaggerated 'measured prose'.[52] And while parody was at some level intended, terms such as 'measured' and 'languor' imply a legacy from the tempo tensions raised by Inghelbrecht. Laloy concluded that this must be a Swedish characteristic since it recurred in the folkdances of Hugo Alfvén's *Nuit de Saint-Jean*, but he also felt that efforts to secure a North European identity should be encouraged. This unusually enlightened view was shared by Charles Tenroc, with some qualification on upholding the merits of aesthetic beauty over eccentricity.[53]

Laprade's French garden setting worked well: for Lapommeraye, 'The well-lit park décor, which framed the dances, made a pleasing effect'. Regarding costumes, Hahn, Boschot and Lapommeraye concurred about the prominence of the *Directoire* style. Nonetheless, Ravel would surely have defended Laprade's decisions on the basis that the work's tribute was to the eighteenth century in general, rather than exclusively to the era of Couperin. Roland-Manuel goes so far as to claim that Laprade's leaning towards 'Marie-Antoinette' style was precisely 'in deference to the wish of the composer'.[54] And while Lapommeraye enjoyed the costumes' 'sparkling' colours, Laloy was bothered by the ballerinas' skimpy dresses (including Laprade's risqué necklines?), 'whose clinging skirts make one long for panniers' – an eighteenth-century hoop device designed to stretch out a skirt.

For French critics, comparison with the Russian troupes inevitably sprang to mind. Milhaud later recalled: 'These dancers had not the virtuosity of the Russians, but their sincerity and love of the art were very captivating.'[55] For the nationalistic Hahn, it was perversely the fact that *Le Tombeau* felt so very French which clinched the Swedish evening. (De Maré perceived such

---

[51]   Boschot, *La Liberté* (17 November 1920), trans. ibid., 18.

[52]   Laloy, trans. ibid., 102.

[53]   Charles Tenroc, 'Théâtre des Champs-Elysées: Ballets Suédois', *Le Courrier musical*, 22 (15 November 1920), 304. By contrast, Tenroc's response to the *Maison de fous* was uncompromising, and best savoured in its French vernacular: 'Hyperguignolesque. Inepte. Hideux … Pas de musique. Cacophonie'.

[54]   Roland-Manuel, *Maurice Ravel*, 88.

[55]   Milhaud, *My Happy Life*, 92.

prejudices as a more general public lack of understanding and was grateful to open-minded supporters such as Ravel.)[56] More subtly, Tenroc perceived a synaesthetic 'perfumed emulsion': 'pavanes and menuets upon the delicate pages of the French composer who declined the cross. The music, costumes and dance were applauded.'[57]

The under-represented aspect in this criticism concerns interplay between the light-hearted and the serious (or even tragic). Apart from Schneider's reminder about a *tombeau*, there is no awareness of a twentieth-century war memorial, primarily because Ravel's private remembrance of his friends did not figure in the public face of the ballet, or in his orchestral score. This is one sense in which the ballet could not do full justice to the intimate, complex piano original. Nonetheless, the popular balletic success of *Le Tombeau* is evidenced by an impressive 167 performances, including tours in Sweden, Italy and elsewhere.[58] The opening season alone saw 102 performances, with the remainder following across the next two seasons.[59] Ravel was presented with a special 'banderole', or small banner, on the occasion of the 'Centième du *Tombeau de Couperin*, Ballets suédois, 15.6.1921',[60] when he himself conducted the orchestra.

Other versions were created subsequently, such as the freely adapted Louis XIV extravaganza entitled *The Enchanted Grove* by Rupert Doone (1903–66), whose real name was Reginald Woodfield. Doone was a one-time dancer of the Ballets Suédois (and Cocteau's lover), who later joined Ida Rubinstein's troupe and danced in the 1928 premiere of *Boléro*. His arrangement of *Le Tombeau* in 1932, with designs by Duncan Grant, was produced for the Vic-Wells Ballet and showcased de Valois in the company of Dolin and Markova.[61]

Balanchine's geometric reading

This third Balanchine 'take' on Ravel should be viewed alongside his approaches to *L'Enfant* and *La Valse*. Ravel's four orchestrated movements,

[56] De Maré, 'Ravel et les ballets', 16.

[57] Tenroc, 'Théâtre des Champs-Elysées', 304. 'Une émulsion parfumée ... pavanes et menuets sur les pages délicates du compositeur français qui refusa la croix. On applaudit musique, costumes, danses.' (Tenroc was referring to Ravel's refusal to accept the French establishment's Légion d'honneur.) Further criticism on *Le Tombeau* is found in the FM.

[58] Extant programmes in the B-MO include Svenska Baletten 1920–22: PRO.F.94 and Balli Svedesi: PRO.F.94 (8).

[59] Statistics from Häger, *Ballets Suédois*, 292.

[60] Lesure and Nectoux (eds), *Maurice Ravel*, 44.

[61] Walker, *Ninette de Valois*, 120.

including the 'Prélude', were choreographed as part of the centennial extravaganza of the Ravel Festival in 1975. And this exquisite miniature proved in
danger of getting lost *en route*. Atypically, Balanchine had worked through
the piece in one burst of enthusiasm at the very start of the rehearsal schedule,
before moving on to other things. According to Buckle, the dancer Rosemary
Dunleavy became anxious that *Le Tombeau* might be overlooked altogether,
so she recalled the dancers and had them work it up again. Eventually,
Balanchine was persuaded to watch the performance, after which an uneasy
silence ensued. Having contemplated the matter at length, Balanchine reputedly announced to Dunleavy: 'You know, dear, I like it'.[62] Thus reprieved, the
work was premiered on 29 May 1975 by the New York City Ballet, conducted
by Robert Irving. And within the continuing Ravel celebrations, the interpretation was repeated in Paris later that year, with subsequent performances in
Geneva (1976), Amsterdam (1977) and Zurich (1981).

Like Börlin's original, Balanchine's *Tombeau* explored relations between
the eighteenth and twentieth centuries, tradition versus innovation, and questions of national identity. (Marilyn Hunt usefully emphasizes associated
power relations: court, aristocracy, privacy (inequality); democracy, public,
folk dance, *corps de ballet* (equality).)[63] It is fair to assert, however, that critical assessment of Balanchine's contribution has not always acknowledged
Börlin's prior achievement. Some of Balanchine's apparent originality should
be credited to Börlin – or at least, Ravel's musical subject-matter should be
seen, to use Gorbman's term (p. 31 above), to generate certain 'mutual implications' for the two choreographers. Interestingly, Balanchine too was at
some level attracted to the concept of remodelling: 'Just as composers occasionally base scores upon other composer's themes, so George Balanchine
choreographed ballets that were fantasias upon other ballets.'[64]

Balanchine extended Börlin's notion after Fokine of celebrating the *corps
de ballet*, accepting that this idea is also intrinsic to eighteenth-century
formal dance. He expanded the forces from one quadrille to two (one on the
left and one on the right), who could 'perform in geometric patterns, often
with identical steps and gestures, simultaneous or canonic',[65] and dispensed
with soloists altogether. His description raises two interesting matters:
firstly, the concept of imitative choreographic counterpoint, which in turn
may be perceived as a neat visual amplification of Ravel's instrumental

[62] Buckle, *George Balanchine*, 290.

[63] Marilyn Hunt, 'Balanchine's democratic aristocracy', *Dance Magazine* (May 1993),
43–4.

[64] Jack Anderson, 'Balanchine's musings on other ballets', *New York Times* (6 December
1984).

[65] [Balanchine,] *Choreography by George Balanchine*, 269. For a photograph showing
work in fours in 1975, see Buckle, *George Balanchine*, plate 66.

counterpoint, as in the 'Prélude' opening; secondly, the sheer fascination with patterning that mirrors Ravel's pursuit of the mechanistic. Both ideas have a strong source in eighteenth-century dance and Balanchine, like Ravel, was very taken by menuets, pavanes and so on. Kirstein's eyewitness account is especially evocative:

> The floor patterns, viewed hastily, seem to be primary squares or diamonds, but these melt into one another like angular fragments of glass in a kaleidoscope. The whole suite of dances is suffused by an air of mutual consideration from single pairs to quartets, to their doublings and resolution back into original quadrilles.[66]

With this foregrounding of abstract craft, Kirstein could refer to *Le Tombeau*, in Ravelian metaphor, as 'a piece of master cabinetwork',[67] while Claude Baignères considered that '*Le Tombeau* ... is constructed as a working drawing where the structures of the *Menuet* or *Rigaudon* are shown.'[68] The phrase 'working drawing' calls to mind eighteenth-century numerical dance notation. While these formations are intricate, the steps on the ground are more straightforward, with much use of the classic daisy-chain formula.[69] Similarly, the humanizing gestures embrace eighteenth-century codes: 'The dancers bow to each other, ceremoniously join hands ... They walk on half-toe and settle into demi-plié as in the Minuet.'[70] In both the 'Prélude' and 'Forlane', large-scale dance repetitions correspond with those of the music and its formal structure. As Jordan comments, 'The formality and simplicity of the of the big repeats seem appropriate to the formal, "social" style, the court dance reference of the piece.'[71] The reconstructed social mores are such that the idea of detachment continues to be important: the dancers, absorbed in their private world, are seemingly unaware of the onlooking public.

Balanchine's interpretation thrives too on an eclecticism (and complex, paradoxical layerings) with which Ravel might readily identify. He avoids the problem of exact eighteenth-century allusion, not to mention expense, by utilizing simple twentieth-century rehearsal clothing. As Marilyn Hunt points out, in its 'four-sided floor patterns', this *Tombeau* owes a debt to the popular square dance: in this way, Balanchine redefines national (and class)

---

[66] Kirstein, *Thirty Years*, 259.

[67] Ibid., 268.

[68] Claude Baignères, 'Hommage à Maurice Ravel: un rêve de perfection', *Le Figaro* (15 December 1975). '*Le Tombeau* ... est bâti comme une épure où apparaissent les structures du *Menuet* ou du *Rigaudon*.'

[69] See Hunt, 'Balanchine's democratic aristocracy', 43, and Alexander Bland, *Observer of the Dance 1958–1982* (London: Dance Books, 1985), 163: review (1 February 1976) of the New York City Ballet in Paris.

[70] Hunt, 'Balanchine's democratic aristocracy', 43.

[71] Jordan, *Moving Music*, 148.

boundaries through the inflections of his adopted America. He had previously choreographed an official *Square Dance* (1957) to the music of Corelli and Vivaldi. Interestingly, another feature of this *Tombeau* viewed as a square-dance characteristic by Hunt, 'the women's turning under the men's hands', may also have a source in Börlin's choreography, as the Ballets Suédois photographs that most likely relate to the 'Menuet' suggest. Recourse to the repertory of square dancing provides Balanchine with a vernacular equivalent to Börlin's Swedish folkdances.

Although the light-hearted/serious opposition tends to become sidelined in the balletic dimension, Baignères perceived increased wit in the work's time travel through the twentieth century; for the 'Menuet' or 'Rigaudon', 'their original solemnity is readily tinged with humour, in a wink to dances of today'.[72] Conversely, the piece has been viewed as a *tombeau* for the ageing Balanchine himself: 'it is tempting to regard it as the first of Balanchine's "last ballets" – something for his company to dance by his grave after he was dead'.[73] Ironically, for a piece that was almost forgotten, *Le Tombeau* turned out to be amongst the most popular and enduring products of the Ravel Festival. It is still listed among 'Ballets in Active Repertory' by the George Balanchine Foundation and was performed again in the New York City Ballet's 2004 season.

Postscript: *L'Eventail de Jeanne* (Jeanne's Fan) and Ravel's 'Fanfare'

Ravel was the biggest name involved in another *tombeau* or tribute, this time to someone living: the Parisian artistic patroness Jeanne Dubost, wife of René Dubost. Mme Dubost was a postwar socialite who still hosted soirées that harked back to the carefree, lavish prewar gatherings of Mme René de Saint-Marceaux. Various stories persist regarding the origins of *L'Eventail*. One version asserts that in spring 1927, Dubost 'capriciously presented ten of her composer friends with leaves from her fan, asking each of them to write a little dance for her pupils'; according to Levinson, the resulting tribute was 'as opportunist as justified!'[74] Conversely, Milhaud, a contributor, recalled the project not as a commission but as a surprise for Dubost '[a]s a token of our thanks for all she had done for us',[75] while

---

[72] Baignères, 'Hommage à Maurice Ravel': 'leur solennité originelle se teinte volontiers d'humeur, de clins d'œil aux danses d'aujourd'hui'.

[73] Buckle, *George Balanchine*, 290.

[74] Edward Johnson, CD notes (n.p.), *French Ballet Music of the 1920s*: *L'Eventail de Jeanne* and *Les Mariés de la Tour Eiffel*; Philharmonia Orchestra, cond. Geoffrey Simon (London: Chandos Records, 1985; CHAN 8356). Levinson, *Les Visages de la danse*, 119: 'aussi opportun que légitime!'

[75] Milhaud, *My Happy Life*, 156.

Poulenc signed the manuscript of his 'Pastourelle' 'avec une bien fidèle amitié' ('in really true friendship'). Poignantly, a decaying black fan remains on display in Ravel's little house.

Either way, *L'Eventail* represented the ultimate collective ballet produced by the Ballets Suédois in 1927, outdoing, if only superficially, Cocteau's zany, surrealist *Les Mariés de la Tour Eiffel*, with five contributing composers. Like *Le Tombeau*, *L'Eventail* was fashioned as a neoclassical dance suite of separate numbers, embracing early dances such as the bourrée, sarabande and rondeau, as well as a polka and waltzes, as shown in the original programme (Figure 6.7). Inevitably, with such a great number of collaborators, the artistic result is a mixed bag stylistically and qualitatively: as Levinson pointed out, 'The differences in workmanship and style extend to the point of disparity, and sometimes, Watteau passes his brushes to the [popular] painter of the Epinal'.[76] Apart from Ravel's parodistic contribution, of

---

L'ÉVENTAIL DE JEANNE

BALLET EN UN ACTE

Chorégraphie de
Mlles Yvonne FRANCK et Alice BOURGAT

Danses
Mlle Alice BOURGAT
Mlles Odette, Léone, Rolande, Micheline, Simone
Raymond TROUARD

Décors et Éclairage de
MM. Pierre LEGRAIN et René MOULAERT

Costumes de Mme Marie LAURENCIN

FANFARE : MAURICE RAVEL

I. MARCHE	P. O. Ferroud.	III. CANARIE	Roland-Manuel.
II. VALSE	J. Ibert.	IV. BOURRÉE	M. Delannoy.

FANFARE : MAURICE RAVEL

V. SARABANDE	A. Roussel.	VII. PASTOURELLE	F. Poulenc.
VI. POLKA	Darius Milhaud.	VIII. ADIEU-BALLET	G. Auric.

FINAL : FLORENT SCHMITT

Orchestre sous la direction de M. Roger DÉSORMIÈRE.

Figure 6.7   *L'Eventail de Jeanne*: programme showing the repetition of Ravel's 'Fanfare' (salon of Jeanne Dubost, 1927). By permission of the Bibliothèque Nationale de France.

---

[76] André Levinson, *Les Visages de la danse*, 119: 'Les différences dans le travail et le style vont jusqu'à la disparate et, parfois, Watteau passe ses pinceaux à l'imagier d'Epinal.' Comparison with Jean Antoine Watteau (1684-1721) was made by Paul-Sentenac, 'Les Ballets Russes et les Ballets Suédois', 258 and recurred in Kirstein's criticism of Balanchine's *Le Tombeau* (*Thirty Years*, 268). 'The vernacular *image d'Epinal*' – the primitivist woodcuts from Lorraine that were viewed as a French primordium – reconnects with *Les Mariés*; see Glenn Watkins, *Pyramids at the Louvre: Music, Culture and Collage from Stravinsky to the Postmodernists* (Cambridge, MA: Harvard University Press, 1994), 300.

greatest interest are two further essays on the waltz: Florent Schmitt (1870–1958) recycled his richly scored prewar *Carnival-Waltz* (1903) for the rustic finale with sixteen young dancers, entitled 'Kermesse-Valse', and the 'Valse' by Jacques Ibert (1890–1962) put Ravel on the receiving end of parody, with a witty caricature of *La Valse*. As James Harding nicely put it, 'Ibert's little joke assumed an incestuous tinge.'[77] Mention should also be made of the 'Bourrée' by Marcel Delannoy (1898–1962), whose music 'carries its own reminiscences and inhabits the same sound-world as Ravel's *Le Tombeau*'.[78]

Neoclassicism apart, *L'Eventail* links up with two earlier themes (Chapter 2). Firstly, as a children's ballet, it reveals a continuing child-related dimension to Ravel's œuvre after *L'Enfant*; secondly, its choreographers, Alice Bourgat and Yvonne Franck, offer a point of connection with the eurhythmic experimentation that emerged briefly apropos Caryathis in *Ma Mère l'Oye*. Both these dancer-choreographers were part of the pre-1925 'classe de rythme' championed by Rouché that had briefly co-existed with more traditional balletic approaches at the Opéra.[79] On the children's costumes, Milhaud recounts how tasteful fairytale 'organdie costumes and plumed headdresses' were created by Marie Laurencin.[80] Laurencin's beautiful materials and designs are preserved in a 16-piece dossier that includes tracing-paper sketches and coloured drawings as well as pink and blue cloth samples with blue mesh gauze. An attractive drawing depicts a young girl on points, a bow in her hair, wearing a fancy blue dress with green-laced edging to her petticoat skirts, sporting a large red bow on her left shoulder and holding a bouquet, or fan.[81] Meanwhile, boldly constructivist motivic décor, enhanced by mirrors, was produced by MM. Pierre Legrain and René Moulaert. Following the success of this whimsical *ballet-divertissement*, presented for private guests in Dubost's drawing room on 16 June 1927 (Figure 6.7), Rouché undertook to produce the work at the Opéra. Consequently, the public premiere of 'this Lilliputian chamber ballet', in Levinson's words, was given by junior pupils of the Opéra school on the vast stage of the Palais Garnier, with music conducted by J. E. Szyfer, on 4 March 1929.

---

[77] James Harding, *The Ox on the Roof* (London: Macdonald, 1972), 208.

[78] Johnson, CD notes (n.p.), *French Ballet Music of the 1920s*.

[79] See Garafola, 'Forgotten interlude', 73, 75, 77, and LAS Nijinska, 1: a letter (11 December 1925) in response to Rouché on 'les classes de danse' at the Opéra. Nijinska thinks two different 'schools' an impossibility, but sees a case for major reform to create a single, complete curriculum.

[80] Milhaud, *My Happy Life*, 156.

[81] Opéra Rés. A. 775. A photograph of the costume design for a young female and a male figure is referenced as Cliché: 79 A 41778 Opéra, Rés. A. 775. For more on Laurencin, see Elizabeth Kahn, *Marie Laurencin: une femme inadaptée in Feminist Theories of Art* (Aldershot: Ashgate, 2003).

Levinson admired the entrusting of choreographic interpretation to children, applauding the 'spiritual discoveries' and 'well-composed groups', even if occasionally he found the movement sequences to be over-condensed – 'trop puérile'.[82] A Russian child prodigy, Mlle Tamara Toumanova, was the lead-dancer, exuding technique and confidence that were 'astonishing' and 'frightening' in equal measure. The cast also included the young Odette Joyeux, who starred in Poulenc's 'Pastourelle', a piece that would became popular out of all proportion and, as with Ravel and *Boléro*, threaten to overshadow Poulenc's serious work. For her part, Joyeux later produced memoirs of her time as a 'petit rat' at the Opéra, including her involvement in the Franck–Bourgat project.[83]

This captivating event was not a 'one-off': *L'Eventail* enjoyed some twenty-three performances in this run, most unusually being subsumed within the Opéra repertory.[84] Later in 1937, the year of Ravel's death and of an International Exhibition with much innovative dance, there is evidence of a revival. *The Dancing Times* carries a photograph of the young Tania Stepanova, in classic white tutu, floral 'Alice' band and ballet shoes, *sur les pointes*, captioned 'A Preobrajenska pupil in *L'Eventail de Jeanne* at the Opéra'.[85] In the same journal, Franc Scheuer worried that the Opéra was becoming a 'museum for past repertory',[86] but conceded that the revived *Eventail* had a 'perennial and unfailing appeal'.

The illustrious Ravel composed the shortest piece of all: a miniature 'Fanfare' to commence the proceedings.[87] The neoclassical musical economy is echoed by Ravel's neat, pencil notation in the three-page orchestral manuscript.[88] The composer does not usually bother to write in rests or, on occasion, a clef. Conversely, unexpected added markings indicate a certain mechanistic quality: division of the music into eight numbered segments, generally of three bars' duration, starting at Fig. 1; their meaning remains

---

[82] Levinson, *Les Visages de la danse*, 120.

[83] Odette Joyeux, *Côté jardin: mémoires d'un rat* (Paris: Gallimard, 1951), 163–6, 169.

[84] Harding, *The Ox on the Roof*, 209; Garafola, 'Forgotten interlude', 76.

[85] L. Franc Scheuer, '*La Vie de la danse*: our Paris letter', *The Dancing Times* (October 1937), 31.

[86] Scheuer, 'Paris in 1937: a retrospective view of the year', *The Dancing Times* (December 1937), 317–21: 318.

[87] Ravel's music lasts a mere 1'22" in the Simon/Philharmonia Orchestra recording of 1985. See n. 74.

[88] Ravel's MS, signed but not dated, is item 11 of the complete autograph collection of 18 items (Opéra Rés. A. 775), contained in large pink folders, each decorated with a stylized fan motif. The full score of *L'Eventail* was published by Heugel in 1929 and is available on hire. A piano four-hand MS (2 pp.) of the 'Fanfare', signed by Ravel, is held in the Archives of Heugel et Cie and was also published in 1929. This version too is decorated with the fan motif.

obscure. The manuscript also reveals some alterations to extend the ending by a bar and to achieve a lightening of orchestral texture. Originally the trumpet had continuing triplets at Fig. 1^{+1} (as at bar 12) and the bassoon joined with flute, oboe and clarinet in the three bars before Fig. 3 (bars 19–22). This latter effect must have been too heavy against the pizzicato double-basses and string harmonics. A non-specific 'Tempo giusto' in the manuscript and published four-hand version is modified to 'Allegro moderato' in the full score.

The orchestral score designates 'rideau' straight after Ravel's arresting, mock dramatic drum-roll, yet there is no evidence of any dance activity during this first number. This fanfare's role is to rouse the audience, create excited anticipation – and, seemingly, to draw attention to the stage: in the final declamatory three bars of his manuscript, Ravel underlines the requirement for 'Timbres. Sur la scène' ('Glockenspiel. On the stage'). Interestingly, Ravel's 'Fanfare' was also to articulate the second group of four dances midway through the act, as indicated in the programme (Figure 6.7). (The occurrence of more than one fanfare to cue programme subdivisions is reminiscent of the practice in Trouhanova's prewar *Concerts de danse*.) With Ravel among its performers, the piece was apparently so successful at its premiere that it was encored at the end of the work.[89]

This postwar 'Fanfare' may be compared with that of fifteen years earlier in the 'Prélude' to *Ma Mère l'Oye*, appreciating that the light-hearted and serious moods are in contrast (Examples 6.5 and 2.5, p.45). Important

Example 6.5 *L'Eventail de Jeanne* (ballet score, 1929): 'Fanfare' (bars 1–5)

---

[89] Johnson, CD notes (n.p.), *French Ballet Music of the 1920s*.

common features suggest that Ravel harboured a sonic image of the fanfare, as he did for the waltz. This further example of Ravel's internal remodelling also hints at what might have been heard in the lost fanfare for *Adélaïde*. Shared features or signifiers include extensive triplets, favouring anacrusic groupings and the use of contrasting durations (semiquavers/quavers in 1927; demi-/semiquavers in 1912). Triadic figures predominate: in the astringent, neoclassical *L'Eventail* these are arpeggiated and inverted in ascent, including a rising perfect fourth; in the lush, exotic *Ma Mère l'Oye* they incline to arpeggiated pentatonic fragments in descent with a falling fourth, although block triads are also present. Woodwind voices enter in counterpoint: in *L'Eventail* these are disparate at the tritone (piccolo/oboe), whereas in *Ma Mère l'Oye* they are imitative at the fifth (muted horns). Both loci confound the stereotypical in incorporating quiet sonorities, especially string harmonics in rhythmic unison, to increase tension and expectancy. Common ground exists too between Ravel's 'Fanfare' and the tiny *Frontispice* (1918), *Le Tombeau* and *Boléro*, which promote the mechanistic in their construction: thematic/harmonic repetition rather than development, clichéd figurations and collage-like juxtaposition of material. Like *Boléro*, this 'Fanfare' contains no crescendos, simply block terracing of dynamics.

Ravel also enjoys remodelling other composers' material. It is hard to hear the tritonally opposed opening voices – B and F majors – without being reminded of the bitonal superimposition in Stravinsky's *Petrushka*, although a later 'wrong-note' juxtaposition of C and B majors (Example 6.6a) finds a semitonal precedent in the F and F♯[7] at the end of 'Les Entretiens' from *Ma Mère l'Oye*. In *Le Tombeau*, allusion to Couperin was reverential; in the 'Fanfare', unusually explicit reference to Wagner is part of an irreverent game within a French tradition of such spoofs. From Fig. 1 onwards, the dotted triplet triadic figure, repeated with a sense of building, inevitably hints at the famous leitmotif from *Die Walküre* – or is it another 9/8 figure from *Siegfried*, or even Verdi's 'Triumphal March' from *Aïda*?[90] Three bars before Fig. 3, Ravel's four-hand piano score is marked 'Wagneramente' for a pompous, cadential C major moment (Example 6.6a). For Roland-Manuel, this piece was 'a lilliputian flourish which begins like the buzzing of troops of insects and rises to its climax in the style of the *Twilight of the Gods* [*Götterdämmerung*]'.[91] But the closest resemblance is surely that of the horn theme (Fig. 3) to a triadic leitmotif representing gold that first appears in *Das Rheingold* (Example 6.6b). Use of the Swiftian analogy by both Levinson and Roland-Manuel is apt. Ravel's neoclassical miniaturizing and

---

[90] I am grateful to Nicholas Baragwanath for additional suggestions: possible allusion to the Entry of the Gods into Valhalla (final bars of *Das Rheingold*) as early as bar 4 and to *Parsifal* in the rising B major (G♯ minor) triadic material on trumpet shortly after Fig. 3.

[91] Roland-Manuel, *Maurice Ravel*, 97.

Example 6.6 Comparison of Ravel and Wagner
      (a) *L'Eventail de Jeanne*: 'Fanfare' (Fig. 3⁻³, reduction)
      (b) Triadic leitmotive from *Das Rheingold*

choice of shrill voices such as piccolo matches so appropriately the little performers for whom he was writing; it is also the perfect vehicle for a mischievous deflating of the Wagnerian epic. The piece ends with an expectant focus on the stage created by the high-pitched ringing of the '[jeu de] timbres'. Most likely, this was the glockenspiel struck by mallets, used in *Daphnis*, as opposed to the piano-action version employed in Debussy's *La Mer*. Given the Wagnerian allusions and wish to project sound from the stage, Ravel may have had in mind an open glockenspiel with 'tube resonators', such as those 'patented in the early 1900s by Messrs J. C. Deagan and Co. of Chicago ("Deagan *Parsifal* Bells")'.[92] This bell-like B major triad melds, blues-like, with a G major triad in strings and is capped by a huge crash on tam-tam. Rather as with Ravel's reordering of *Le Tombeau*, an opening marks the end.

---

[92] James Blades and James Holland, 'Glockenspiel', in Stanley Sadie (ed.), *The New Grove Dictionary of Music and Musicians*, 29 vols (London: Macmillan, 2/2001), vol. X, 16–17: 16.

Chapter 7

Spain, machines and sexuality: *Boléro*

A deep affection for Spain – influenced by his mother's Basque heritage and by the time his father spent working as a railway engineer in that country – was a constant across Ravel's creative life from his early 'Habanera' in *Sites auriculaires* (1895–7), through *Rapsodie espagnole* (1907–8) and *L'Heure espagnole* (1907–9), to the late *Don Quichotte à Dulcinée* (1932–3). Spain also inspired two of Ravel's ballet projects: the powerfully obsessive *Boléro*,[1] envisaged initially as a simple orchestration of Albéniz's *Iberia*, for his friend Rubinstein in 1928; and a less important undertaking in 1918–19 for Diaghilev's Ballets Russes, comprising orchestrations of his own *Alborada del gracioso* from *Miroirs* of 1905 and Chabrier's *Menuet pompeux*, together with Fauré's *Pavane*, originally to be collectively entitled *Les Jardins d'Aranjuez*.[2]

This chapter maintains the by now familiar poietic–esthesic approach, but interwoven through the text are three new characterizing threads: Spanishness, the machine and sexuality. For *Boléro*, under things Spanish might be included images of Spain by Goya or Velázquez, bullfighting, orientalism (Arab/Moorish influence), bolero, flamenco dancing,[3] melody, rhythmic castanets, guitar, powerful colours (red, black), expression, obsession, humanity and death. Readings of machine could embrace factory, automation, mechanism, circularity, rhythm, repeated chords, order, suppression, drudgery, shackles, inhumanity, breakdown.[4] Sexuality might be associated with gender, role-play, flirtation, promiscuity, desire,

---

[1] Although the heading of Ravel's score does not include the acute accent, French commentary invariably does, including Ravel's letters. For consistency the accent has been maintained.

[2] The intended ballet did not happen. Polunin received Diaghilev's orders to stop painting the back-cloth for *Les Jardins* in favour of that for *La Boutique fantasque* (*The Continental Method of Scene Painting*, 56). *Menuet pompeux* and *Alborada* have, however, enjoyed an existence as short, stand-alone pieces. The orchestral premiere of *Alborada* was given on 17 May 1919, with Rhené-Baton and the Orchestre Pasdeloup.

[3] For background on Spanish music, see Claus Schreiner (ed.), *Flamenco* (Portland, OR: Amadeus Press, 1985) and Marina Grut, *The Bolero School* (London: Dance Books, 2002).

[4] On Ravel's machinist aesthetic as a particular concern with the 'object', see Mawer, 'Musical objects and machines', 47–67: 57–67.

215

suppression, circularity, goal-direction, tension and orgasm.[5] As is already becoming apparent, this chapter marks the compositional conclusion of Ravel's dance–destruction trajectory that first appeared in *Daphnis* and continued under the guise of *La Valse*. Attention is given to three very different balletic interpretations of *Boléro*: the initial flamenco-inspired Rubinstein productions of 1928–34; the 1941 Leyritz/Lifar realization inspired by Ravel's ideas; and the abstract, sexually-charged and re-gendered creations of Béjart, dating from 1961 onwards. Their success refutes a sensational claim of 'Le *Boléro*, tombeau des chorégraphes',[6] and proves the interpretative versatility of Ravel's music in its most famously packaged and disseminated form.

Genesis and evolution

In his reminiscences of the prewar years, Benois recalled enthusiastically that 'Ravel, a magnificent composer and a charming man, was an ardent admirer of our performances and dreamed of creating a ballet with me.' Ravel and Benois had first met earlier in the preliminary negotiations for *Daphnis*, and by 1914 had become strong friends when they holidayed together near Ravel's birthplace of Ciboure – even bringing their respective mothers with them; see Benois's delightful sketch of an effete Ravel (Figure 7.1).[7] The designer explained that the details of a joint project had yet to be established, but its essential Spanish nature had already been agreed: 'Ravel had a genuine cult for Spain, which I shared. We did not hurry ourselves. We had the whole summer in front of us and decided to spend it together at St-Jean-de-Luz.'[8] All plans were however put on hold by the outbreak of the First World War, less than a month later.

The collaboration eventually materialized fourteen years later, in spring 1928, when it transpired that Ravel's new brief for the Ballets Ida Rubinstein would be to produce an orchestration of some movements from *Iberia* (1906–9) by Isaac Albéniz (1860–1909), so as to create 'an impressionistic ballet with a Spanish flavour'.[9] Having returned on various occasions in the interim, Ravel then went back again to St-Jean-de-Luz in early summer

---

[5] On circularity versus goal-directed motion, see Hélène Cixous and 'l'écriture féminine', as considered for instance by Renée Cox, 'Recovering *Jouissance*: an introduction to feminist musical aesthetics', in Karin Pendle (ed.), *Women and Music: A History* (Bloomington: Indiana University Press, 1991), 331–40.

[6] J. B., 'Le *Boléro*, tombeau des chorégraphes', *Action Française* (24 November 1954).

[7] See too Benois's photograph of both families at the beach, reproduced in Larner, *Maurice Ravel*, 144–5.

[8] Benois, *Reminiscences of the Russian Ballet*, 365.

[9] Cossart, *Ida Rubinstein*, 127.

Figure 7.1   Alexandre Benois's sketch of Ravel after bathing, 'croquant son plasir' (St-Jean-de-Luz, July 1914). By permission of the Bibliothèque Nationale de France. © ADAGP, Paris and DACS, London 2004.

1928, presumably to rekindle his happy memories and acquire some further inspiration close to the Spanish border.[10]

This original plan could not be implemented, however, because a rather obscure Spanish musician, Enrique Fernandez Arbós (1863–1939), had already been contracted to arrange such an orchestration for a ballet to be staged by the phenomenal dancer La Argentina, with exclusive rights via the publishers Max Eschig. As late as the end of June 1928, Joaquín Nin recalled a casual conversation in which 'I remarked to Ravel that unfortunately this project was not viable because Albéniz's pieces had already been orchestrated by Arbós for a ballet destined for La Argentina (it was *Triana*, given

[10] See P. B., 'Le *Boléro* revient à l'Opéra', *Paris-soir* (12 November 1941), which mentions Ravel's spending time leisurely on the slopes of La Rhune, near Ciboure.

the following season with great success).' To this, Ravel responded in flippant and then more anxious tones: 'So who is this Arbós? ... And what to say to Ida? She'll be furious!'[11] Of course Ravel must in any case have been well aware of Inghelbrecht's orchestration of three pieces from the collection ('El Puerto', 'El Albaicín' and 'El Corpus en Sevilla'), which had been presented together with *Le Tombeau* by the Ballets Suédois in 1920.

By early August, Ravel had hatched a second plan, to compose a fandango. Jacques Durand was grateful since he had rightly regarded Ravel's recomposing of Albéniz as not fully worthy of his talents: 'You announced that you are occupied with a *Fandango* of your own devising – I applaud it in advance, while blessing Arbós! Only, you'll have to put on a huge spurt.'[12] Durand also outlined the financial arrangements, involving a three-year restriction on any other productions and a one-year embargo on concert performance imposed by Rubinstein, for which the publisher campaigned for generous compensation on behalf of his artist. In contemporary correspondence with Robert Casadesus, Ravel expressed his own anxieties about the schedule, realizing that he would need to be in two places at once: this new ballet was to be staged at the Opéra concurrently with Ravel's concert tour of, among other places, Spain.[13] Some two months later, Ravel's piece had assumed its familiar title and its machinist influence was already being articulated: 'I will return to complete a *Boléro*, using the same material [ostinatos] that you assured me Prokofiev employed in *Le Pas d'acier*.'[14] By mid-October, Ravel had with impressive speed completed the work,[15] although he was still needing to dash around through to the end of the year to fulfil his numerous commitments, including the award of his honorary degree from the University of Oxford. Thus *Boléro* was produced as planned

---

[11] Joaquín Nin, 'Comment est né le *Boléro* de Ravel', *La Revue musicale*, 19 (December 1938), 211–13: 211–12: 'je fis remarquer à Ravel que ce projet n'était malheureusement pas viable par le fait que les pièces d'Albéniz étaient déjà orchestrées par Arbós en vue d'un ballet destiné à La Argentina (c'étaient le ballet *Triana*, donné la saison d'après avec le succès que l'on sait) ... Qui est-ce donc cet Arbós? ... Et quoi dire à Ida? Elle sera furieuse!'

[12] Letter from Durand (13 August 1928), in Lesure and Nectoux (eds), *Maurice Ravel*, 66. 'Vous m'annoncez que vous vous occupez d'un *Fandango* de votre crû. J'y applaudis d'avance en bénissant Arbós! Seulement il vous faudra mettre les bouchées triples'.

[13] Letter to Casadesus (10 August 1928), in Orenstein (ed.), *A Ravel Reader*, 296.

[14] Letter to Roland-Manuel (4 October 1928), in ibid., 298.

[15] The MS (37 pp.), dated July–October 1928, is held in the ROLC; a pencilled first draft (31 pp.) was famously purchased by the French State at a cost of 1.8 million francs for the BNF in 1992: MS. 21917. ('Ravel, le manuscrit du *Boléro* revient en France', *Le Parisien* (9 April 1992)). A photograph of a very brief sketch of the main theme down to the first low C may be viewed as Cliché B 68369 (BNF Mus). The MS (15 pp.) of the four-hand version is held by the BL: Zweig MS 74. Orchestral and piano duet versions were published by Durand in 1929.

on 22 November 1928; it was originally to be coupled with *La Valse* and was presented by the same collaborative team as its sister project (see Chapter 5): Nijinska, Benois and Rubinstein, to whom Ravel's score is affectionately dedicated.

Ravel's aesthetic and compositional approach

Traditionally, the bolero may be defined as a moderately slow music–dance form in triple metre, often featuring a triplet on the second beat. It is performed by a single dancer or couple, to the accompaniment of voice, castanets and guitar. Ravel's obvious, yet enigmatic, *Boléro* has engendered more comment than most of his other works: correspondence, articles, and interviews with the composer provide copious information to consult and evaluate. A useful starting-point is *Une esquisse autobiographique*, a commentary contemporaneous with *Boléro*, where Ravel states that 'It [*Boléro*] is a dance with a movement that is very measured and consistently uniform, as much through the melody as the harmony and rhythm, this latter marked unceasingly by the side-drum. The only element of diversity is afforded by the orchestral crescendo.'[16] This description points up the intrinsic nature of dance and the importance of a controlling abstract form, which already implies some kind of mechanical experiment. Five years later, he revealed that 'My own *Bolero* owed its inception to a factory. Some day I should like to play it with a vast industrial works in the background.'[17] The work is thereby firmly placed within Ravel's machinist purview: a notion that may be traced back through the craftsman's fascination with compositional mechanisms in *L'Heure* and *Frontispice* (1918), although the more pronounced mechanicity of *Boléro* has led some to suspect the influence of Ravel's encroaching terminal illness.[18]

Several of Ravel's early comments on *Boléro* discuss it in negatives. In communication with Nin during its composition, the piece had 'No form properly speaking, no development, no or almost no modulation'; and later, in an interview with Calvocoressi, it achieved the ultimate negation: 'orchestral tissue without music'.[19] Manuel Rosenthal's reminiscences refer similarly to

---

[16] [Roland-Manuel,] 'Une esquisse autobiographique', 23. 'C'est une danse d'un mouvement très modéré et constamment uniforme, tant par la mélodie que par l'harmonie et le rhythme, ce dernier marqué sans cesse par le tambour. Le seul élément de diversité y est apporté par le crescendo orchestral.'

[17] Maurice Ravel, 'Finding tunes in factories', *New Britain* (9 August 1933), 367.

[18] John Whitfield, 'Brain disease shaped *Boléro*', *Nature* (22 January 2002) [online journal].

[19] Nin, 'Comment est né le *Boléro*', 213: 'pas de forme proprement dite, pas de développement, pas ou presque pas de modulation'; M.-D. Calvocoressi, 'M. Ravel discusses his own work: the *Boléro* explained', *Daily Telegraph* (11 July 1931).

'a score without music';[20] to distance the work in this way became almost a point of honour for Ravel, not least since its effortless popularity threatened to eclipse his other music. Gustave Samazeuilh gleaned other information on the work in progress: the formal plan, with a reiterated thirty-six-bar double melody (AABB) whose internal repeats are subsequently removed late in the piece to emphasize the climax, had all been mapped out in advance, and Ravel confirmed this idea of a premeditated exercise to Calvocoressi. The composer later confided that this was the one piece in which he had fully realized his aims, but that his achievement was qualified because 'it is too facile a genre'.[21]

So far, emphasis has been on the machinist aesthetic, arguably the most important aspect for Ravel, but the Spanish dimension was also taken up with ease, if more stereotypically than in other loci. Ravel talked topically of a rather vulgar theme in the style of José Padilla (1889–1960), the Spanish composer of the overexposed song *Valencia* for the revue *Moulin rouge* of 1925, and on another occasion of 'impersonal' stock themes, 'folk tunes of the usual Spanish-Arabian kind'.[22] When asked what sort of orchestration one should consult for Spanish sonority, Ravel also distanced himself from the real thing, suggesting Rimsky, Debussy, his own, even Meyerbeer, but definitely not d'Indy or Wagner.[23] The most colourful account and one which fuses the machinist concept with Spanishness (and sexuality) is René Chalupt's:

> he [Ravel] saw *Boléro* not between four walls but in the open air; he wanted to insist upon something of the Arab in the obstinate repetition of two unchanging themes. Then … he uncovered an analogy between the alternation of these two themes riveted one to the other just like the links of a chain and a factory production-line ["chaîne"]. Now, for this, it was necessary to make space for a factory within the décor to allow a troupe of male and female workers, coming out of workshops, to join together in general dancing. Finally, he wished to evoke bull-fighting in introducing a clandestine affair between Marilena and a bullfighter whom the jealous duped lover, turning up unexpectedly, stabs beneath the unfaithful one's balcony.[24]

---

[20] Manuel Rosenthal, 'Maurice Ravel: souvenirs', *Radio Classique* (December 1995), 26–7: 26.

[21] Nino Frank, 'Maurice Ravel entre deux trains', *Comœdia* (5 May 1932): 'c'est un genre trop facile'.

[22] Nin, 'Comment est né le *Boléro*', 213; Calvocoressi, 'M. Ravel discusses his own work'.

[23] Nin, 'Comment est né le *Boléro*', 212.

[24] René Chalupt and Marcelle Gerar, *Ravel au miroir de ses lettres* (Paris: Laffont, 1956), 237–8: 'il voyait le *Boléro* non pas entre quatre murs mais en plein air; il désirait insister sur ce qu'il y avait d'arabe dans la répétition obstinée des deux mêmes thèmes. Puis … il découvrait une analogie entre l'alternance de ces thèmes rivés l'un à l'autre ainsi que les anneaux

Here is Ravel at his most surprisingly melodramatic, complete with sexual connotation and violent, bloodthirsty outburst – just the explosive cocktail that Fokine had wanted to encourage in *Daphnis*. It is Bizet's *Carmen* 'with bells on': evident similarities include the mountainous Spanish setting, the factory, the girl's affections for a bullfighter and the climactic stabbing. While it might be hard to avoid humour in such a realization, there are anyway distinct echoes of the fully intentional humour of *L'Heure*. And whatever the rusticity of such a scenario, Chalupt was a trustworthy source in offering insights into how Ravel heard and saw his music. Such faithfulness to Ravel's intentions was to become evident in Leyritz's wartime production (see p. 233ff).

Musical essence: construction/destruction

'[I]n the later part of his life many of Ravel's compositions show that he had a feeling for a dramatic death – the *Boléro*, for instance'.[25] Death, mechanical explosion, or orgasm: the *raison d'être* of *Boléro* is its cataclysmic destruction as the culmination of an extended trajectory on closure in dance that had existed since Ravel had struggled with the ending of *Daphnis*. End-on to the E major climax, the irrevocable, dissonant rupture occurs six bars from the finish (Example 7.1), as a starker version of the impotent stutterings that denote the collapse of *La Valse*. The ear focuses on the desperate human crying or animal braying of saxophones and trombones (Example 7.1a), the only instruments not already subsumed by the monstrous mechanism with its relentless side drum(s) – now hit 'colla bacchetta', with the hardest sticks (Example 7.1b).[26] Is this the death of the bullfighter, the bull, or both?

As with comedy, the success of Ravel's formula depends upon discipline and timing, yet the power of the music brings this situation much closer to tragedy. The ultimate gesture only works because the preceding order has been so rigorous and its time-span so over-extended. For the final bars of release, there are over 300 bars of increasing tension to enjoy/endure – some seventeen maddening minutes in Ravel's favoured slow tempo.

---

d'une chaîne et une "chaîne" d'usine. Or, pour cela, il faillait faire place à une usine dans le décor afin de permettre à une troupe d'ouvriers et d'ouvrières, sortant des ateliers, de se mêler à la danse générale. Enfin, il souhaitait évoquer la tauromachie en introduisant une idylle clandestine entre Marilena et un torero que le jaloux berné, survenant à l'improviste, poignarde sous le balcon de l'infidèle.'

[25] Manuel Rosenthal in conversation with Nichols: *Ravel Remembered*, 62.

[26] For an introductory reading, see Mawer, 'Ballet and the apotheosis of the dance', 155–61.

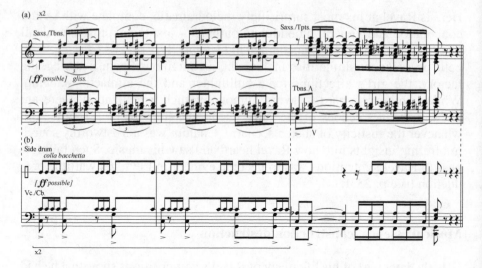

Example 7.1 *Boléro* (ballet, 1929): point of rupture (Fig. 18⁺⁸, reduction)
    (a) Saxophone/trombone cries
    (b) Composite ostinato: side drum and bass-line mechanism

Sexual allusions to foreplay and gratification are not hard to find, and although Ravel in his apparent naivety was initially surprised at the piece's popularity, he was sufficiently aware to attribute it in conversation with Jourdan-Morhange to this 'musico-sexual' phenomenon.[27] To use ideas from Cook's 'Theorizing musical meaning', this phenomenon may be regarded as an 'inherent' musical meaning which yet underwent further socio-cultural development in the sexually liberated era of the 1960s, as Béjart's production demonstrates.

Ravel's predetermined plan, clearly projected in a first draft (MS. 21917; see p. 218), necessitates four complete revolutions of his industrial assembly-line (opening, Figs. 4, 8, 12), essentially in C major, but with some later polytonal infiltration. In his draft, visual emphasis is given to the changing instrumentations for the double melody, while the ostinato background is blocked in with shorthand repeats. From a very sparse first page, the writing becomes increasingly dense. The ostinato mechanism is gradually foregrounded, by recruiting more instrumentalists – rather as Fokine had choreographed the finale of *Daphnis*. (A choreographic interpretation by Oswald Lemanis, given on 10 December 1936 by the Riga Ballet (Latvia), closely paralleled Ravel's technique of defining and expanding instrumental

---

[27] Jourdan-Morhange, *Ravel et nous*, 166.

blocks.)[28] In the struggle to maintain balance, reinforcements augment the melody, which around the fourth rotation (Fig. 13) comprises seventeen instrumental lines. But the entry of a second side-drummer clinches the ostinato's advantage, cueing a rendition without repeats (Figs. 16–18) – a temporal 'fast-forward' in halved time that propels the piece up a fatal major third to E (Fig. 18), in quartered time, thence to immediate breakdown. The basic formula may be summarized as 32 (× 8): 16 (× 2): 8 (× 1): 0. Playing with time was a feature of *Daphnis* and *La Valse*, the former using a subtle speeding up within a swift tempo and the latter interpolating a revelatory 'slow-motion' flashback prior to collapse; here, the bulk of the exercise is conducted in calculated slow motion.

Such is Ravel's machine, but of course Spanish flamenco techniques share this rhythmic discipline, creating an inherent tension between the percussive foundation (castanets, guitar, hand-clapping, heel-stamping) and the expressive vocal melody trying to break free. The first part of Ravel's melody (A) is repressively diatonic (Example 7.2), yet its desire not to conform is evident through frequent emphasis upon the second beat of the triple metre. Its hypnotic fixation with C, scalic meanderings and minor thirds also hints at something quasi-Arab. Stylized Spanishness and 'jazz' traits are displayed in the second part (B), with dissonantly piquant sevenths and ninths, portamentos, grace-notes, accentuations, syncopation and the 'vocal' use of saxophones and trombone (Example 7.3). Ravel utilizes a basic phrygian modality (C, D♭, E♭, F, G, A♭, B♭, C), with flexibility at the third and sixth (E♭/E, A♭/A), as a cunning intervallic alter ego or dark side of the initial C major scale. All this offers strong evidence to support Jordan's

Example 7.2 *Boléro*: opening of melodic material A (bars 5–12)

---

[28] See Georgs Brants, 'New ballets in Riga', trans. W. G. Hartog, *The Dancing Times*, 317 (February 1937), 620–21. 'He [Lemanis] makes use of a technique which consists in treating each group separately, while incorporating them one after the other into the general movement, while at the same time accenting the values of each in the same way as Ravel proceeds with its orchestral units. This technique enables him to present a picture which harmonizes with the music in astonishing fashion.'

Example 7.3 *Boléro*: opening of melodic material B (Fig. 6^{+2})

observation that 'Even the formal device of tonality has narrative implications.'[29] Moreover, the very moderate tempo, which was to cause such ruc-
tions with Arturo Toscanini and the New York Philharmonic in the early
1930s,[30] is explicitly a 'Tempo di Bolero', a more reserved cousin of the
fandango courtship dance, albeit a deliberately artificial application.

The premiere and further Rubinstein performances (Spanishness)

Rubinstein had confirmed the run of performance dates with Rouché in a letter
of 17 June 1928: 22, 27, 29 November and 4 December. She knew the December
date would involve Rouché in complications,[31] though fortunately the final
performance did happen since it was the only one that Ravel could attend. The
premiere of *Boléro* took place upon the huge stage of the Opéra (Figure 7.2),
on the opening night of the winter season. Its positioning as the final item of a
programme that also premiered Milhaud's *La Bien-aimée* Op. 101 simulated,
on a larger scale, the waiting game employed in the work itself. Sir Francis
Rose declared this enterprise to be the talk of the town: 'Everyone was excited
and it was whispered that the money would run out before the extravagant
curtain for the stage had been made.'[32] Rubinstein, as usual, adopted the star-

---

[29] Jordan, *Moving Music*, 66.

[30] On the Toscanini furore, see Alexandre Tansman quoted in Nichols (ed.), *Ravel
Remembered*, 48–9; 'he [Ravel] went back stage and told Toscanini, "It's too fast", and
Toscanini said, "It's the only way to save the work"'. This again raises interesting questions
as to where the composer stops being a composer and begins to be merely the first of many
interpreters. *Boléro* has been presented with tremendous variety of tempo, from 13 to
(Ravel's) 17 minutes. As recent examples, the Cleveland Orchestra (cond. Dohnányi) moves
briskly for a 14′10″ performance (Ultima, 1991; 0630-18959-2), against the notably extended
span of the CRS Symphony Orchestra of Bratislava (cond. Kenneth Jean), lasting 16′03″
(Naxos, 1991; 8.550173). For more, see Ronald Woodley, 'Style and practice in the early
recordings', in Mawer (ed.), *The Cambridge Companion to Ravel*, 213–39: 235–9.

[31] LAS Rubinstein, 9 (B-MO).

[32] Cossart, *Ida Rubinstein*, 129.

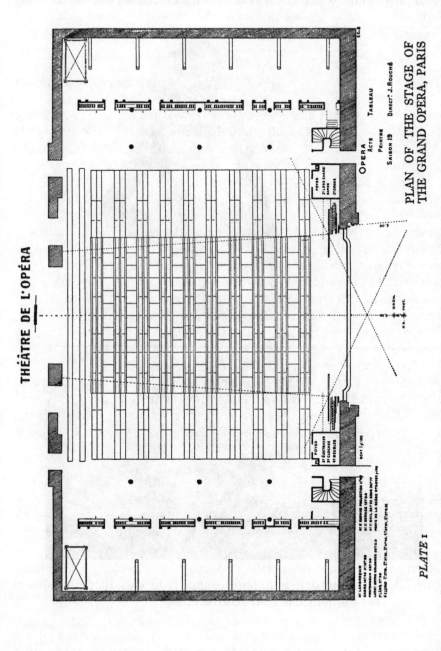

Figure 7.2   Stage plan of the Paris Opéra (from Vladimir Polunin, *The Continental Method of Scene Painting*, 1927).

ring role of 'The Dancer'; her costume, fashioned by la Maison Mirande, is depicted in a photograph where she poses with her pet (Figure 7.3).[33] The general programme, with a cover price of 5 francs, reveals that the admiring

Figure 7.3   Ida Rubinstein in *Boléro* costume (with cat). By permission of the Bibliothèque Nationale de France.

---

[33] Programme: *Madame Ida Rubinstein* (May 1929), Carton 2238 (B-MO); photo d'Ora, B de l'A, Fonds Rondel, Ro 12744.

male entourage of twenty was led by Anatole Vilzak, who would later partner Rubinstein in *La Valse*, and also included Alexis Dolinoff and the young Englishmen Ashton and William Chappell.[34] The Orchestre de l'Opéra was supposed to be conducted through its ballet season by Ernest Ansermet; however, a joint letter of 24 October 1928 from Ravel, Honegger, Milhaud, Sauguet and Auric to Rouché expressed grave concern over information from Rubinstein that the orchestra was refusing to play under him.[35] Seemingly, a resolution was not forthcoming since the first performances of *Boléro* were conducted by Walther Straram.

Despite the fact that Rubinstein and Ravel were professional allies and – especially during Ravel's later traumatic illness – platonic friends,[36] the simple scenario devised by Rubinstein (and Nijinska) and printed in the programme was quite different from that envisaged by Ravel. 'Inside a tavern in Spain, people dance beneath the brass lamp hung from the ceiling. [In response] to the cheers to join in, the female dancer has leapt onto the long table and her steps become more and more animated.'[37] Even within notions of Spanishness, the work already exhibited multiple identities that were due not least to differing French and Russian perceptions: Rubinstein sought a more literal evocation of flamenco, in contrast to Ravel's abstraction of obsessive thematic and rhythmic materials[38] (the latter was more akin to Nijinska's typical angularity, though ironically the choreographer softened her approach in *Boléro*). Meanwhile, the illustrious Benois had created a set that 'represented a hovel in the Paralelo', with Nijinska's idea of a stage within a stage erected 'in the centre of a vast room',[39] or, according to the contemporary opinion of Henry Prunières, 'a tableau in the manner of Goya: Interior of a huge barn, used for *baile* [flamenco dance]'.[40] Certainly, there is the same grandeur of scale as in Benois's contemporane-

---

[34] Programme: *Les Ballets de Madame Ida Rubinstein*, Académie Nationale de Musique et de Danse (November 1928), Carton 2238 (B-MO). For more on Chappell and the awe with which Rubinstein was regarded, see Nichols, *The Harlequin Years*, 168, 171–2.

[35] LAS Ravel, 13 (B-MO).

[36] Ravel kept Rubinstein's details in his address book at Montfort-L'Amaury.

[37] Programme: *Madame Ida Rubinstein* (May 1929). 'Dans une taverne d'Espagne, on danse sous la lampe de cuivre au plafond. Aux acclamations de l'assistance, la danseuse a bondi sur la longue table et ses pas s'animent de plus en plus.' The scenario appears verbatim in the programme: *Ballets Ida Rubinstein* (April–May 1934), Carton 2238 (B-MO).

[38] See José André, 'Maurice Ravel y su *Bolero*', *La Nación* (15 March 1930).

[39] Chalupt, *Ravel au miroir de ses lettres*, 237: 'un plateau' may translate as 'a stage' or 'a [table] top'. Tikanova makes clear that credit for the large table should go to Nijinska rather than to Rubinstein or Benois (or indeed Béjart): *La Jeune Fille en bleu*, 95.

[40] Henry Prunières, 'La Musique en France et à l'étranger', *La Revue musicale*, 91 (January 1929), 242–5: 244: 'un tableau à la manière de Goya: Intérieur d'une grange immense, servant au *baile*'. Benois's model of the décor for *Boléro*, a watercolour (43 × 63 cm), formed part of the private Collection André Meyer.

ous conception of *La Valse*, albeit transferred to a distinctly rustic setting. Ravel's instrumental crescendo – more strictly a terracing – was matched by Nijinska's choreography: from languorous beginnings the solo dancing was to become more accentuated and frenzied, balanced by increasingly lustful reactions from the male onlookers. For Ravel, however, who had dashed back in high spirits from Spain to the Opéra 'just in time for the final performance of my ballet, [it was] an excellent performance, but picturesque, which wasn't appropriate'.[41]

Despite not winning the composer's full approbation, Rubinstein's flamenco cabaret created a sensation that produced abundant newspaper coverage in French and English, not just for the premiere but also for subsequent performances in 1929, 1931 and 1934. The extensive review by Prunières, the respected editor of *La Revue musicale*, provides a good place to begin, aptly synthesizing music and dance in line with Ravel's pre-compositional mapping:

> One was immediately taken captive, transported by an art which partakes of magic. Ravel has doubtless written works with a greater musical richness, [but] he has done nothing more successful ... Mme Rubinstein understood that the strength of the score was such that dance must appear as a kind of visual projection of this radiant music ... on a platform, she performed a type of very stylized bolero, amid the encouragement and impassioned quarrels of the spectators.[42]

Comparison between musical and choreographic domains is also evident in Willi Reich's recollection of a supposedly less picturesque performance on tour at the Vienna Opera House in spring 1929: 'With an almost demonic indifference, Ida Rubinstein rotated ceaselessly, in this stereotyped rhythm, on an immense round tavern table, whilst at her feet the men, expressing an

---

[41] Letter to Roger Haour (4 December 1928), in Orenstein (ed.), *A Ravel Reader*, 299. Again, note each collaborator's desire to claim sole ownership. That little love was lost between Ravel and Nijinska is implicit in Ravel's dismissive reference in a letter to Lucien Garban (24 September 1929): Dossier d'artiste, Maurice Ravel (B-MO). Amongst score corrections, Ravel notes removing the 'Curtain' indication, 'which only interests Mme [*sic*] Nijinska'.

[42] Prunières, 'La Musique en France', 243–4. 'On est pris tout de suite captivé, emporté par un art qui tient du sortilège. Ravel a sans doute écrit des œuvres d'une plus grande richesse musicale, il n'a rien fait de mieux réussi ... Mme Ida Rubinstein a compris que la force de la partition était telle que la danse devait apparaître comme une sorte de projection sur le plan visuel de cette musique irradiante ... sur une estrade, elle exécute une sorte de boléro très stylisé, au milieu des encouragements et des disputes passionnées des spectateurs.' Conversely, J. B., 'Le *Boléro*, tombeau des chorégraphes' argued à la Diaghilev that the synaesthetic music was already an aural transposition of the image and feel of a bolero: 'Il est déjà la *Danse*'.

unleashed passion, beat themselves until the blood came.'[43] Reich's emphasis is upon the obsessive circularity inherent in the music, but apparent too in Rubinstein's almost robotic movements. Such haughty detachment was doubtless well suited to Rubinstein's considerable skills as a mime artist-cum-actress. Noting a practice slightly divergent from the programme scenario as theory, Reich's review endorses what he sees as a limited 'uncoupling' between music and solo dance whereby, as the dynamic intensity of the music and onlookers increases, Rubinstein's presence unsettles because of her seemingly indifferent repetition. (There may of course only be a fine interpretative line between emphasis through suppression, to paraphrase Jacques Derrida, and straightforward absence. After all, in 1931, Dominique Sordet considered that 'the choreography does not rediscover the dynamic *crescendo* of the score and rather diminishes the effect of it, in place of accentuating it', so creating an unintended or ineffective dissonance.)[44] In addition to emotional suppression, Reich's reading suggests a closely related, smouldering sexual suppression, together with a streak of masochism.

A brief interpretative aside is useful at this juncture to highlight an already implicit theme that will become explicit in Béjart's postwar explorations: sexuality, gender relations and role-reversal. The Rubinstein/Nijinska scenario indicates that the men take the initiative in urging the female dancer to adopt the stage and that she becomes the focus with her increasingly animated steps: potentially, a mere object of sexual desire. In Reich's reading, it is the woman who directs the proceedings, winding the score of male onlookers around her fingers and ultimately driving them to a physically painful state of ecstasy. The pain was real: according to Keith Lester, who danced in the 1934 performances, 'We all crept round and round, crouched over the rim of the table till at last the music ended and the descending curtain released us from what must have looked like a procession of lumbago sufferers.'[45] The image of a dominant female presence offers an apt metaphor for Rubinstein in real life. Her retinue included Ravel, but also female admirers and would-be lovers, notably Ravel's pianist friend Marguerite Long and the formidable feminist writer Natalie Barney, for whom Rubinstein was the perfect slender embodiment of androgyny.[46] Although

---

[43] Willi Reich, 'In memoriam Maurice Ravel', *La Revue musicale*, 19 (December 1938), 275: 'avec une indifférence quasi démoniaque, Ida Rubinstein tournoyait sans arrêt, dans ce rythme stéréotypé, sur une immense table ronde d'auberge, cependant qu'à ses pieds les hommes, exprimant une passion déchaînée, se frappaient jusqu'au sang'.

[44] Dominique Sordet, 'La Musique, Les Galas Ida Rubinstein', *Action française* (26 June 1931): 'la chorégraphie ne retrouve pas le *crescendo* dynamique de la partition et en diminue plutôt l'effet, au lieu de l'accentuer'.

[45] Keith Lester, 'Rubinstein revisited', *Dance Research*, 1/2 (Autumn 1983), 21–31: 29.

[46] See Cossart, *Ida Rubinstein*, 150–51, where the connection with Barney is first made (though not in the context of *Boléro*).

Rubinstein's role in *Boléro* was an archetypically female one, she enjoyed much cross-dressing, as in the title role of *David*, which she had commissioned from Henri Sauguet. A nice final touch, inverting Rubinstein's customary dominance, is provided by a wonderful curtain-call photograph in the May 1929 programme (see p. 160): it shows a diminutive Ravel, dapper in full evening dress but with hands casually in his pockets, holding centre stage amid the admiring entourage of his costumed performers (Figure 7.4). Rubinstein is seated on the floor at Ravel's feet.

Boléro also represented a coup for Benois and Nijinska, both of whom realized the presentation 'in the most remarkable manner'.[47] Benois's achievement was hailed as a masterpiece by Robert Dézarnaux and by Georges Pioch;[48] similarly, Gaston de Pawlowski thought these designs amongst his most successful.[49] Like Prunières, Dézarnaux related the style to that of Goya, with its black, brown, pale gold and flame colours creating a tableau 'en clair obscur'; interestingly Pioch noted this same quality in Ravel's orchestration: 'at once very dense and very clear'. Others applauded Benois as 'the grand master of ceremonies' by comparison with the immediacy of effect achieved by Velázquez or Rubens.[50] As for the choreography, Vuillermoz considered that 'Mme Nijinska, whose style was generally more harsh, delighted us with choreographic finds of a charming elegance',[51] and Pawlowski concurred that she had 'marvellously regulated' the whole programme. Straram was praised by Vuillermoz for his 'musical intelligence', which enabled Ravel's rich and varied instrumental timbre to come across so effectively, as an additional dimension equivalent to lighting. (According to Sordet, this contrasted with Gustave Cloez's rather poor conducting in summer 1931, which suffered especially from balance problems.)[52] Even if one grumpy reviewer thought that La Argentina or the Gomez Trio could have provided the audience with the same sensation of 'throbbing vertigo',[53] most critics conceded that the premiere had

---

[47] Emile Vuillermoz, 'La Musique', *Excelsior* (26 November 1928).

[48] Robert Dézarnaux, 'A l'Opéra, un nouveau ballet de Maurice Ravel', *La Liberté* (November 1928); Georges Pioch, 'Les Ballets de Mme Ida Rubinstein', *Soir Dimanche* (25 November 1928).

[49] Gaston de Pawlowski, 'Les Ballets de Mme Ida Rubinstein', *Le Journal* (24 November 1928). This view was shared by P.-B. Gheusi, 'Les Ballets de Mme Ida Rubinstein à l'Opéra', *Le Figaro* (25 November 1928).

[50] Henry Malherbe, review in *Le Temps* (28 November 1928).

[51] Vuillermoz, 'La Musique': 'Mme Nijinska, dont le style était généralement plus âpre, nous a ravis par de trouvailles chorégraphiques d'une grâce charmante.'

[52] Sordet, 'La Musique'.

[53] Louis Schneider, 'Le *Gaulois* au théâtre, les premières', *Le Gaulois* (24 November 1928). Gheusi also makes comparison with 'une Argentina' (Gheusi, 'Les Ballets de Mme Ida Rubinstein').

Figure 7.4   Ravel surrounded by his dancers in *Boléro* (programme, 1929). By permission of the Bibliothèque Nationale de France.

produced a first-rate collective entity: 'a sumptuousness of costumes, a harmony of colours, a Russian quality, and an incomparable frenzy of dance.'[54]

Apart from the French press, there were special interest groups with markedly partial views. Especially revealing are assessments of Rubinstein by Diaghilev and Stravinsky (who in 1928 was collaborating with Ida on *Le Baiser de la fée*). Diaghilev's severely jaundiced view was in reality the pathetic, defensive response of an artist in decline. In a letter to Lifar of 25 November 1928, Diaghilev – who on his English tour had rushed back from Manchester to Paris to check out the competition – declared: 'The evening was as dull as any provincial show. Everything went on too long, even the Ravel, and that only lasts fourteen minutes ... Benois is dull and colourless, the same as he was thirty years ago ... Bronia [Nijinska] is quite unoriginal.'[55] He felt particularly threatened by Rubinstein herself, and directed his venom accordingly: 'But the worst of all was Ida ... still with the inevitable red coiffure, she spent a quarter of an hour clumsily turning on a table as large as the whole stage of the Monte Carlo Opera.' Although Diaghilev's biased view inevitably held some sway, Prunières was adamant that in her creative originality as a director Rubinstein had already surpassed those she had sought to emulate and that therefore she had no purpose in trying to prove herself as a classical ballet dancer.[56] Typically contradictory responses were evinced from Stravinsky, who praised Rubinstein sycophantically to her face, but apparently subsequently disparaged the proceedings in private to Diaghilev.[57] Stravinsky's strategy seemed to be to please whomever he was in contact with, whilst safeguarding his own collaborative interests.

A further perspective upon Rubinstein's productions is afforded by the contemporary English press's coverage of the Spanish dance phenomenon. The generic bolero was very popular in England, as evidenced by the inclusion in *The Dancer* of a 'Bolero' arranged by 'Espinosa' of The Espinosa School, London, with music composed by a T. E. Atkins: 'The poise and carriage must be haughty and full of Spanish grandeur; the arm movements must be broad and deliberate but there should be great freedom in the hips.'[58] The contemporary phenomenon, La Argentina, alluded to somewhat disparagingly in French criticism, was featured in an extended article for *The Dancing Times*,[59] while the same journal reported the following year that the

---

[54] Pawlowski, 'Les Ballets': 'une somptuosité de costumes, une harmonie de couleurs, une qualité russe, une frénésie de danse hors de pair.'

[55] Letter from Diahilev to Lifar, in Serge Lifar, *A History of Russian Ballet*, trans. Arnold Haskell (London: Hutchinson, 1954), 270–71.

[56] Prunières, 'La Musique', 245.

[57] Lifar, *A History of Russian Ballet*, 271.

[58] *The Dancer* (September–October 1928), 617–19: 617.

[59] Cyril Rice, 'La Argentina, the Pavlova of Spain', *The Dancing Times* (December 1928), 285–90.

'*Bolero*, by M. Ravel, proved, as regards music and choreography, the best of the first programme and perhaps of the entire series. Theme, music, decor are of the simplest.' Tribute was paid on this side of the Channel also to Ravel's 'sonorous intensity'.[60] Despite its enthusiasm, English criticism was fully cognizant that Rubinstein – well into her forties for the UK premiere at Covent Garden on 7 July 1931 – had her limitations: 'while the movements of her arms are graceful and her poses well conceived, she seems to be a mime rather than a dancer'.[61] Indeed, William McNaught regarded the staged *Boléro* seen on the London tour as an anticlimax:

> That crescendo of music spells a crescendo of human passion, and all that the ballet gave us was human movement ... Madame Rubinstein merely executed Spanish gestures that any slim Carmen could emulate, while the onlookers worked up a formal dance that consisted largely of beating [a] slow three-in-a-bar with their bodies and extremities ... It seemed too uneventful a scenario, in these days of popular bloodshed, for such melodramatic music ... *Bolero* was deficient in gore.[62]

This view of less than passionate 1931 performances chimes with that of Sordet. Perhaps Ravel's melodramatic vision of bullfighting and stabbing was precisely what McNaught required! More seriously, there was a strong case for a production that supported more overtly Ravel's machinist aesthetic, with its factory allusion.

The Leyritz/Lifar wartime production (machines)

Ravel's good friend Léon Leyritz (1888–1976) was just the person to create an image of *Boléro* that was closer to the composer's intentions, but sadly Ravel did not live to see this production staged at the Opéra late in 1941. Leyritz had various detailed discussions with Ravel in his last years and had already produced a model of his intended décor by about 1936, which was exhibited at the Salon des Artistes Décorateurs and reputedly received Ravel's approval.[63] As early as summer 1928, he had produced the striking

---

[60] 'Paris notes', *The Dancing Times* (January 1929), 569–70: 569.

[61] Anon., 'Mme Rubinstein's Ballets', *The Times* (8 July 1931), 12.

[62] McNaught, 'Ida Rubinstein Ballet', *The Musical Times* (1 August 1931), 745. See too press coverage quoted in Woolf, *Dancing in the Vortex*, 125–7. On 1930s *Boléro* revivals by Nijinska, with Gontcharova's designs, and by Fokine, following Nijinska's departure for the Teatro Colón, Buenos Aires, see Tikanova, *La Jeune Fille en bleu*, 109–25. See too LAS Nijinska, 13 (letter to Rouché, 4 October 1932).

[63] Chalupt, *Maurice Ravel au miroir de ses lettres*, 237–8. According to Lesure and Nectoux (eds), *Maurice Ravel*, 66, this was a gouache model (29.5 × 35 cm).

stone bust of the composer that fittingly graces the foyer of the Opéra;[64] he had also designed Ravel's apartment inside his brother's house in the Parisian suburb of Levallois. Despite Leyritz's close association with Ravel, others involved in the new production, especially the conductor Gaubert and the ballet-master Lifar, were not properly convinced about the factory/ machinist angle to the work and protested to Rouché.[65] Having entrusted the project to Leyritz following Ravel's death, Rouché felt obliged to seek reassurance from Ravel's younger brother, Edouard (1878–1960), but he need not have worried. Edouard's reply of 19 February 1940 confirmed that

> My brother admired everything which was mechanical, from simple tin toys to the most intricate machine tools. He would thus spend entire days … in front of street vendor's stalls, and was delighted to come with me to factories or to expositions [exhibitions] of machinery. He was happy to be in the midst of these movements and noises. But he always came out struck and obsessed by the automation of all these machines.[66]

Following in their father's profession, Ravel's brother was visiting factories in his capacity as an engineer, and Ravel clearly shared this family fascination – yet while he 'admired' the machines, he was also 'obsessed' by their oppressive inhuman power. Edouard goes on to explain that Ravel did not discuss scenario plans with him, yet, when passing through the heavy industrial suburb of Le Vésinet, west of Paris, he often pointed out 'the *Boléro* Factory'. Importantly, Edouard also upholds Leyritz's credentials: 'Personally, knowing Leyritz's integrity, and his admiration for my brother, I have no doubt that the ideas expressed in the model and the scenario derive from the conversations they had during their trip to Morocco and Spain.' Rubinstein had generously financed this inspirational voyage in February–March 1935; it included visits to Madrid and Cordoba and three weeks in Marrakesh, during which the ailing Ravel made a very modest addition to brief sketches for his next intended project for her on the Arabian tale of *Morgiane*.[67] Furthermore, Chalupt claims that Edouard threatened to remove his authorization if his brother's wishes were not adhered to – a point not made explicit in the letter.[68]

As a way of appreciating the rationale behind Leyritz's décor, costumes and scenario, a document from around November 1940, entitled 'Leyritz

---

[64] See photograph of a model in Orenstein (ed.), *A Ravel Reader*, plate 12, or the cover illustration of Ivry, *Maurice Ravel*.

[65] Chalupt, *Maurice Ravel au miroir de ses lettres*, 238.

[66] Orenstein (ed.), *A Ravel Reader*, 328.

[67] Orenstein, *Ravel: Man and Musician*, 107. For more, see Chapter 8.

[68] Chalupt, *Maurice Ravel au miroir de ses lettres*, 238.

parle de ses décors', proves very enlightening.[69] Although this set of notes, with some alterations and deletions, constitutes a retrospective theorizing of artistic practice roughly contemporary with the scenario, it offers an apt place to begin. Its essential contents may be organized into a number of pertinent issues. The first involves a relative downplaying of Spanishness: Leyritz's view of *Boléro* and Spain is not so much Spanish as Arab or Moorish, marrying closely with Ravel's stance on his thematic material.[70] For set design, this means a central feature of archways, or arcades, intrinsic to Arab architecture and thereby to the grandeur of southern Spain, as in the gateways of Cordoba or terraces of Granada: 'I have placed within my set design model some Moorish archways as a principal motif.'[71] These arches also allow access, at least figuratively, to hostile desert terrain beyond. Furthermore, Leyritz is adamant that he wants no Spanish clichés: no more Goyaesque Spain, no guitars, pompoms, fringed shawls, or evocations of Triana (in the style of La Argentina).

A second notion is that of two different things being associated by a common quality, and so exhibiting a kind of equivalence. Large spiky desert cacti as background landscape and the ceremonial of bullfighting as human activity are linked by the quality of cruel magnificence; the toughness of the cactus has a counterpart in a harsh factory.[72] The 'Le Vésinet' location is now transmuted into the set's generic Arab/Spanish factory, whose significance to Ravel is confirmed by Leyritz: 'It is there to underline the mechanical aspect of the construction of the music.'[73] Again this stance upholds equivalence in Ravel's approach: chains connecting between a factory assembly line and the linked musical themes, one in the major key opposed by one in the 'minor' – more strictly the phrygian mode. For Leyritz, this then implies further 'chains' within dance, pursued in his scenario from the opening onwards when young girls begin dancing the popular classic of the bolero, followed by the entry of the bullfighters.

A related issue concerns symbolism: the bull, for instance, acts as a symbol for abstract passion. In addition to the leading pair of characters, Marilena and the handsome bullfighter, Le Matador, a third character, Le Spontané (The Impetuous One), is a personification of youthful folly and

---

[69] 'Leyritz parle de ses décors': a mimeograph copy coupled by the scenario, signed and dated November 1940, in Dossier d'œuvre, *Boléro* (B-MO). Some extended quotations from these papers are given in Elisabeth du Closel, 'De l'usine à la messe, qu'est devenu le *Boléro?*' (28 April 1986): Dossier d'œuvre, *Boléro*. Extracts are translated below.

[70] '[L]'atmosphère musicale du BOLERO n'est pas tant espagnole qu'arabe tout comme l'atmosphère de l'Espagne elle-même.'

[71] 'J'ai mis dans ma maquette de décor des arcades mauresques en motif principal.'

[72] '[L]a végétation de cactus s'imposera, cruelle et magnifique, elle aussi, comme le spectacle de taureaux ... Au dur cactus, répond une dure usine.'

[73] 'Elle est là pour souligner le côté mécanique de la construction de la musique.'

'unchained', unleashed passion, with whom Marilena becomes infatuated. So emerges the classic love triangle, as used in Ravel's scenario for *Adélaïde*. As a further manifestation, the Spanish colours of red and black (a pairing maintained by Béjart) are regarded as having tragic association: blood and death. Leyritz's buildings are rose-coloured with black balconies; the factory too is black and red. Alternating pairs of bright colours, as chain links, are featured in the costumes – with one colour on the front and another on the back. Through these means, Leyritz intends that the ballet-master should be able to effect visual accentuation in line with the rhythms and themes of Ravel's music.

Even if more incidental here, the sexuality/gender agenda is evident in a clichéd note, later crossed out, about the phallic symbolism of 'an aggressive cactus', together with an observation that the principal role taken by the male dancer is to underline the masculine aspect of the music.[74] Returning to the tragedy implicit in the colour-palette, Leyritz observes that the piece could well culminate in a 'villainous melodrama' – a ruinous 'spoiling', as in Ravel's destruction of the musical dance. But despite Leyritz's labelling The Matador parenthetically as 'the slayer' (whose prey is suitably ambiguous: bull or man?), specifics of the intrigue are perhaps wisely avoided in the accompanying scenario. Leyritz explains how just in time the bull appears, with his attached firework and no shortage of phallic symbolism, to circumvent the dangerous triangular situation by representing and so dehumanizing the passion.

The accompanying scenario is carefully cross-referenced to musical rehearsal figures, with numbered repetitions of the theme in its major and 'minor' presentations. Ravel's oboe d'amore entry is marked, as is the bitonal play with fifths (Figs. 4 and 13). Leyritz's thoughtful approach is also evidenced by three footnotes on lighting and costumes. In maintaining his Spanish-Arab balancing act, he adopts a present-day setting in a terraced courtyard (outside a factory) that may be located either in the Sierra Nevada just south of Granada, or in the Atlas Mountains of Morocco, above Marrakesh. A photograph of this oriental set with assembled *corps de ballet* (and Le Spontané prostrate in front?) confirms the large courtyard, whose castellated, towered walls enclose three sides, punctuated by prominent archways: two to the left, with the highest, impressive three-quarter circle arch in the back centre (Figure 7.5).[75] The inclusion in the scenario of the bolero character dance and bullfighting pageantry, complete with capes and

---

[74] '[L]e livret ... donne le rôle principal au danseur, ce qui marque le côté essentiellement masculin de la musique.'

[75] Lifar, *Lifar on Classical Ballet*, plate 13. A photograph of the staged décor (Cliché Harcourt) is also held in the Ravel Estate. For Leyritz's set painting, see Cogniat, *Les Décorateurs de théâtre*, 89.

Figure 7.5 Staged set with *corps de ballet* for Léon Leyritz/Serge Lifar, *Boléro* (1941) (from Serge Lifar, *Lifar on Classical Ballet*).

'flashes',[76] clearly resonates with southern Spain, yet Ravel's machinism is also embedded to create a unique inflection.

As the curtain rises, the dancers' chain-like movements are already in progress, winding around a pivoting dancer. They continue throughout, like Ravel's ostinato, or perhaps like the geometric patterns of Arab mosaics. Reference is made to other abrupt and jerky mechanical movements near the opening and close, while a Spanish–machinist fusion results from the constant rhythmic play of fans. Leyritz does not dwell on the machinations of the love triangle, but his scenario details entrances of girls, bullfighters, Marilena on her balcony and later Le Spontané. The white bullfighter, now named Ricardo, features in his own central 'pantomime' (Fig. 9), handing Marilena his ceremonial cape, as the dancing becomes more accentuated. Subsequently, Le Spontané, as if engaged with a charging bull, launches himself into an acrobatic dance, whereupon the predictably fickle Marilena discards the cape and joins in his frenetic dance (Figs. 11–12). Twilight falls (Fig. 16). In an uncoupling of music and stage action, attention is then focused on the impending musical catastrophe. Leyritz's exciting ending (Figs. 17–18), albeit dramatically off at a tangent, features the bewildered bull dancing incoherently, followed by fireworks, including the bull's 'rocket', and finally dead of night.

Leyritz's signed costume designs are beautifully preserved in a huge scrapbook, together with other designs for 1941 productions, including *Le Roi d'Ys*, *Sylvia*, *Jeux d'enfants* and *L'Or du Rhin*.[77] Marilena adopts a classic pose with left hand on hip and right hand waving a black fan, tipped with pink. She sports a small hat, a black and pink shawl over her left shoulder and a white dress adorned with red and black diagonal fringes: not so far from the fringed shawls that Leyritz was keen to avoid.

Lifar's outfit for the role of Ricardo features a white jacket, decorated dramatically with shocking pink epaulettes, broad wavy braid at the cuffs and horizontal flashes of colour across the front. A long, black tie and pink cummerbund accompany a white shirt, with breeches enlivened along the vertical seam by more pink braid, and finished with white stockings and black shoes. An elegant cloak, predominantly white, is adorned with a gold, blue and pink image, seemingly a haloed Madonna and Child. A contemporary photograph of Lifar shows him holding the cape over his left arm, with hand on hip. In a nod to Morocco, he wears a fez-like bullfighting cap.

---

[76] Ravel too enjoyed alluding to capes: his letter to Roger Haour (4 December 1928) talks of changing swiftly from 'toga' to 'cape' in reference to his honorary Oxford degree and Spanish concert tour (Orenstein (ed.), *A Ravel Reader*, 299).

[77] See D. 216, 96, B-MO (previously classified as D. 216, 99 in Lesure and Nectoux (eds), *Maurice Ravel*, 67, which refers also to a design for a costume by Leyritz, in crayon and watercolour, heightened with gold).

Enjoying his athletic physique, Lifar adopts a confident, relaxed pose with knees slightly flexed and the weight on his left foot, ready to demonstrate a deft step backwards to the right (Figure 7.6).[78] Lastly, Le Spontané is depicted in a brash, ostentatious manner, alluring with his open arms and

Figure 7.6   Serge Lifar in Léon Leyritz/Lifar, *Boléro* (1941) (from Serge Lifar, *Lifar on Classical Ballet*).

---

[78]   See Lifar, *Lifar on Classical Ballet*, plate 34, to illustrate an 'écarté en arrière'.

bared chest, dark hair and stereotyped oriental slanting eyes. He sports a small pink waistcoat, lavender blue cummerbund, purple breeches and a pendant on a leather thong (an early medallion man?).

Additionally, the collection illustrates male and female factory-workers and one of Marilena's sophisticated girlfriends wearing a haughty, cockerel-like red headpiece, a lemon yellow dress with black trimmings and matching parasol. Meanwhile, bullfighters are shown in black and pink (rather than the standard red), with flashes and frills down the breech seams; their backs feature reversed colour images. The *pièce de résistance* is the 'toro de fuego', a man with bull's head and hooves for shoes: half-man half-beast, with a sexual connotation by now – post-*L'Après-midi* – inevitable. His appearance matches those final bestial cries in Ravel's music. Long pink and black ribbons criss-cross his arms and torso, marked with pink rosettes, and fly in the air. Explosive gold rays radiate from the horned head of this apparition, newly mutated into a dangerous, exciting animal; the man's arms clasp his huge head as though in disbelief.

Leyritz is clearly the lead partner in this production, having devoted much energy to realizing Ravel's vision, but there is little information on Lifar's role, despite his writings. Lifar mentions his obligation to *Boléro* in a letter of autumn 1941 to André Jolivet, with whom he was to collaborate on another ballet. He explains that 'The death of our dear Philippe Gaubert has turned everything upside down and Rouché isn't there [at the Opéra], therefore no definite projects – one must be patient as in all things. I know only that presently I am redoing *Oriane* and am putting on *Boléro*.'[79]

So in the middle of the Second World War, on 29 December 1941, the Leyritz/Lifar production was given at the Opéra; Lifar choreographed and danced the lead role of The Matador (see Figure 7.6), with Suzanne Lorcia as Marilena. Serge Peretti played Le Spontané: his name appears in Leyritz's costume designs, and he is credited as the one who will adopt this role in a preview.[80] Following the death of Gaubert (who despite being an early doubter of Leyritz's *Boléro* had successfully conducted much Ravel, including the 1921 reprise of *Daphnis*), the Opéra orchestra was conducted by Louis Fourestier.

As for the reception of this *Boléro*, most reliance has to be placed upon a review of Yann Loranz, early in 1942.[81] This critique furnishes some

---

[79] Autograph letter from Lifar to Jolivet (3 October 1941): 'La mort de notre cher Philippe Gaubert a tout renversé et Rouché n'est pas là, donc pas de projets précis – il faut patienter comme en toutes choses. Je sais seulement que actuellement je reprends *Oriane* et je monte *Boléro*.' Access to this letter was kindly provided by Christine Jolivet-Erlih; Jolivet's correspondence is now deposited in BNF Mus.

[80] P. B., 'Le *Boléro* revient à l'Opéra', *Paris-Soir* (12 November 1941).

[81] Yann Loranz, 'Danse sur la glace de Raymonde du Bief; *Boléro* à l'Opéra', *La Gerbe* (22 January 1942).

information on Lifar but also demonstrates how reality may become distorted. Almost all credit is given to Lifar, with Leyritz mentioned only *en passant* and even then negatively. Loranz considers Lifar to have put down a most engaging choreography beneath Ravel's score; furthermore, 'Lifar has approached Ravel's idea sensitively in seeing in the *Boléro* only the mechanical aspect of the score and in creating an obsessive dance rhythm'.[82] Given Lifar's protestations to Rouché about Leyritz's approach, this is highly ironic, yet it confirms a unity of aesthetic practice in maximizing the mechanical. For the reviewer, Lifar supported the concern with obsession and machine in deftly juxtaposing the dance and musical entries; more accurately, Lifar visualized the intentions expressed in Leyritz's notes. This accentuation of musical entries sounds similar to Lemanis's basic approach for the Riga Ballet in the mid-1930s, although Lifar does not augment the number of dancers in line with the instruments.[83] Loranz considers appropriately that the love story grafted onto this mechanical framework was not essential for the ballet's success since 'All the genius of the choreography was concentrated upon the increasing exaltation, upon the fever of the rhythm.'[84]

Loranz expresses reservation regarding décor and costumes, whose colours clashed (presumably reds against pinks), and thinks the 'canary' yellow dresses in dubious taste. Equally, he doubts, surely rightly, that Ravel would have approved Fourestier's concluding accelerando though 'it is true that the orchestra had to serve a ballet and that one was not at a concert'.[85] Such an observation again raises issues of autonomy versus balletic integration. Specifically, modification of tempo recalls the Toscanini episode: the question of how much scope a conductor or performer should enjoy in developing ideas while still respecting the original authorship.[86] An accelerando is of course legitimate in theory, but here it merely gilds the lily since the necessary momentum is built into the musical structure.

Despite such qualifications, this 1941 production was received enthusiastically; in short, according to Chalupt, 'Thus *Boléro* had itself its factory, and its bullfighter and the success was complete.'[87]

---

[82] Loranz, '*Boléro* à l'Opéra': 'Lifar s'est sensiblement rapproché de l'idée de Ravel en ne voyant dans le *Boléro* que la partie mécanique de la partition et en créant un rythme de danse obsédant'.

[83] See n. 28.

[84] Loranz, '*Boléro* à l'Opéra': 'Tout le génie du chorégraphe s'est concentré sur l'exaltation croissante, sur la fièvre du rythme'.

[85] Ibid.: 'il est vrai que l'orchestre avait à servir un ballet et que l'on n'était pas au concert'.

[86] See n. 30.

[87] Chalupt, *Maurice Ravel au miroir de ses lettres*, 238: 'Ainsi, *Boléro* eut-il son usine, et son torero et le succés fut complet.'

Béjart and beyond (gender and sexuality)

Love it or loathe it, the iconoclastic showman's art of the uncompromising Marseillais Béjart has brought *Boléro* and Ravel into the modern era, demonstrating the interpretative scope afforded by the music and the potential benefits of not being pinned down by one definitive scenario. This said, the main slant of Béjart's various readings is towards gender-cum-sexuality. After his 1961 original which maintained Rubinstein's formula of one woman and many men, Béjart explored reversed gender roles: one man with many female onlookers, and then his all-male homoerotic version where the lead dancer arguably displays more femininity than did Rubinstein herself. Such re-gendering is a hallmark, first employed in 1959 in a dramatic re-interpretation of Stravinsky's *Le Sacre* that rejoiced in and ritualized the fertility of sexual union between a chosen man and woman.[88] Of course the original *Le Sacre* of 1913 viewed the Chosen One as a victim, and this sacrificial aspect also has a resonance in *Boléro*, both musically and in Béjart's reading.

Béjart's first *Boléro* 'experiment' was given by his Ballets du XXe Siècle, with the female star Douchka Sifnios, at the Théâtre Royal de la Monnaie in Brussels on 10 January 1961. In addition to choreography, Béjart designed décor and costumes, creating a one-man show somewhat reminiscent of Rubinstein's one-woman original. One of Béjart's founding principles for his set of *Boléro* variations was here established: an identifying of the central role of melody with the solo dancer, and that of the ostinato rhythm with the massed group of dancers.[89] This created an effective personification of musical parameters: La Mélodie, 'feminine symbol', danced in November 1961 by the celebrated Bolshoi Ballet star Maya Plisetskaya (alternating with Angèle Albrecht), and Le Rythme, 'masculine symbol', danced by Francky Aras and by seventeen other men. In Ravel's terms, such personification nicely echoes, for instance, that in *L'Enfant*.

Predictably, early reactions were very mixed. Reviewing a performance at the Théâtre des Nations in May 1961, Dinah Maggie was horrified: 'the *Boléro* is a monstrosity, an unpardonable crime of lèse-Ravel'. Maggie felt that the gestural style and movements without meaning did little to respect the composer's thoughts, that the 'dissonance', to use Albright's concept, between dance and music was too great. Ironically, given its evident sexuality, 'Never does the spectacle bring out the atmosphere of

---

[88] See online database 'Stravinsky the Global Dancer', compiled by Stephanie Jordan and Larraine Nicholas, and hosted by the Centre for Dance Research, Roehampton University (www.roehampton.ac.uk/stravinsky/).

[89] See 1961 programme in Dossier d'œuvre, *Boléro*, and the official website for Béjart Ballet Lausanne: www.bejart.ch/fr/home (accessed 25 February 2003).

warm sensuality produced by the music. It is a long way from a voluptuous ambience to gestures that are sometimes stamped with a puerile obscenity.'[90] Interestingly, her male counterpart, Baignères, writing for *Le Figaro*, felt very differently: 'For the first time, without doubt, it [*Boléro*] benefits from a choreography which respects both its rhythmic and its melodic obsession.' Baignères noted Béjart's 'visual translation', especially a developing pulsation in the dance as the orchestration grew richer, and applauded the knowing relationship: 'There is a kind of magnificent complicity between dance and music, whose interests are so often taken to be contradictory.'[91]

Measured English reaction to later performances gives more hints about the expression of sexuality. In 1971, Buckle's facetious take was that 'Stunningly as Béjart presents it, with his girl writhing and stamping on her huge vermilion table, surrounded by nine million panting men, I cannot surrender.'[92] Meanwhile, for Alexander Bland nearly five years later, 'This apotheosis of randiness is a bit of cabaret kitsch (in anticipation, one might venture, of lap- or pole-dancing). The ageing Plisetskaya was by now more commanding than alluring, very much as Rubinstein had been in the 1930s, but nonetheless 'she performed the table-top routines with a cold, angular menace which invited a masochistic response'.[93] More recent performances with a seductive female soloist include those of Sylvie Guillem on tour with Béjart Ballet Lausanne in 2000.

The second Ballets du XXe Siècle version of 1979 featured the now-celebrated Jorge Donn, surrounded by some fifty women. In a balanced French review, Maurice Fleuret reckoned that for those who had not seen the first version, the gender inversion contained little that could really shock. More importantly, it made visible 'the insistent virility of the rhythmic theme' by dancing out the music rather than dancing indirectly upon it. Once more, Béjart's way of working between disciplines merited special comment: 'And the choreographic work, instead of being a puerile compromise between the storyline-as-pretext and the music-as-filler, becomes a

---

[90] Dinah Maggie, 'Le Ballet du XXe Siècle au Théâtre des Nations', *Combat* (31 May 1961): 'le *Boléro* est une monstruosité, un crime impardonnable de lèse-Ravel ... Jamais le spectacle ne dégage l'atmosphère de chaude sensualité que produit la musique. Il y a loin d'une ambiance voluptueuse aux gestes parfois empreints d'une obscenité puérile'.

[91] Claude Baignères, 'Au Théâtre des Nations – Le Ballet du XXe Siècle', *Le Figaro* (31 May 1961). 'Pour la première fois sans doute, il bénéficie d'une chorégraphie qui respecte à la fois son obsession rythmique et mélodique ... Il y a une sorte de complicité magistrale entre la danse et la musique dont les intérêts passent si souvent pour contradictoires.'

[92] Richard Buckle, *Buckle at the Ballet* (London: Dance Books, 1980), 309 [review, 20 June 1971].

[93] Bland, *Observer of the Dance, 1958–1982*, 162 [review, 1 February 1976].

reading through movement, an exploration and exaltation of the musical sense.'[94]

A third version was given in the same year at the Opéra, with Donn still as soloist. For its 1985 filming,[95] Béjart provided a perceptive commentary, a variant on his 1961 programme-note, acknowledging that *Boléro* is not primarily Spanish music. Indeed, Ravel had questioned whether it was music at all, claiming wryly to Honegger that 'I've only written one masterpiece – *Boléro*. Unfortunately, there's no music in it.'[96] Analogously, for Béjart there is no plot:

> It is an abstract work, a work of violence and emotion, portraying the struggle between a melody – an oriental melody – and a remorseless rhythm ... Forty boys on chairs in a circle rise in turn and reinforce the power of the music, following the rhythm. On the central table a single boy dances the melodic line – with his torso, his arms, his body.[97]

So Béjart maintains explicitly Nijinska's table-platform as minimal staging and, like Leyritz, he multiplies the number of onlookers while remaining sensitive to the oriental exoticism of the melody and relentless machinist circularity. (He has always had a particular affinity with ideas of the orient, culminating in his setting up a Hindu-named performance research centre, *Mudra*.)[98] Béjart also replicates Leyritz's bold tones of black, red and white. What is interesting about Béjart's statement is that which remains implicit: for 'body' read unashamedly erotic exploration.

Out of darkness emerge Donn's rotating hands, twisting and turning as if delicately depicting birds through shadow-play, or musing on the female gestures of Indian classical dance. As the melody expands from an initial pitch on C, so too these moving shapes develop form and grow, through the arms and torso to the feet, drumming upon the fiery red pedestal. Although Béjart regards the *corps de ballet* as his main rhythm section, gradually expanding its forces à la Ravel, Donn's repeated footwork also constitutes a

---

[94] Maurice Fleuret, 'Béjart, ni ange, ni bête – Le Ballet, c'est aussi un opéra où le corps remplace la voix', *Nouvel Observateur* (18 February 1979). 'Et l'œuvre chorégraphique, au lieu d'un compromis puéril entre l'argument-prétexte et la musique-bouche-trou, devient lecture par le mouvement, exploration et exaltation du sens musical.'

[95] For the commercial video, see Maurice Béjart, *The Art of the 20th-Century Ballet*: Ravel's *Boléro*, Jorge Donn and Ballet du XXᵉ Siècle (Philips Video Classics [PAL VHS], 1985; 070 134-3). Its duration is a moderately swift 14'51".

[96] Arthur Honegger, *Incantation aux fossiles* (Lausanne, 1948), 91–2; trans. Nichols (ed.), *Ravel Remembered*, 50.

[97] Béjart, *The Art of the 20th-Century Ballet*: Commentary, 2.

[98] See Noël Goodwin, 'Maurice Béjart: the sensual style', in Béjart, *The Art of the 20th-Century Ballet*, 1–2: 2. On the early years, see Stengele, *A la recherche de Béjart*, 'Béjart et l'Orient', n.p.

compelling dance ostinato, analogous to Ravel's one-bar units. As the right foot placed flat in front of the left marks the main beats, the left on toe behind (with knee slightly bent) counterbalances with the off-beats.

At a mechanical level, this interpretation creates a multi-dimensional circularity (which has a precedent in Béjart's *Le Sacre*). Three musical circles or cycles (two ostinatos and the two-part rotating melody) are mirrored and amplified by as many as five choreographic ones, the first four interpreted by both soloist and *corps de ballet* (hands, arms, feet, bodies, plus group patterns), in turn supported by simple staging and lighting. The basic point is illustrated diagrammatically in Table 7.1. As to the meaning of such circular mechanics softened by more irregular writhing, the sexual underpinning is hardly in doubt. Here is teasing flirtation, soft-porn style, as the feminine-looking male soloist with dramatic eye make-up smooths his hands down his glistening torso, sometimes preening and blowing kisses (although his expression remains serious and aloof). That he is an object of desire is confirmed by the symbolism of the colour red; but more than this, he acquires a god-like status as a chosen one. His perfect body, capable of

Table 7.1 Béjart's *Boléro* (video 1985): multi-dimensional circularity

Dimension	Nature of circularity	Detail
Music	Harmony: circularity in repeated I–V formula	Two ostinatos in operation: 1- and 2-bar rotations
	Melody: larger-scale circularity	36-bar cycle (18 + 18)
Dance	Hands	Solo and group: rotating formations
	Arms	Solo and group: arms raised to outline semicircles
	Feet	Solo: repeated 4th position *croisé* device analogous to 1-bar ostinato (i.e. circular through time); group: less ornate equivalent without 'crossed' element
	Body	Solo: clockwise rotations of body on round pedestal; group: individual rotations, plus hip circles and later reiterated thrusts
	Group patterns	Circling around pedestal (group alone)
Staging and lighting	Pedestal and positioning	Round pedestal centre-stage
	Circular light 'spots'	Highlighting device, especially of solo dancer
Camera work (supporting element)	Aerial view	Bird's-eye-view of body rotation
	Panorama	To show whole-group rotations
	Close-up	To highlight hand, feet rotations

impressive acrobatic leaps, is to be worshipped by his entranced followers who replicate some movements – a provocative mixture of the sacred and profane. As Judith Hanna puts it in no-nonsense terms, 'Forty [young] men pant and pace, circle nervously and generally cream over a beautiful bare-chested man undulating above.'[99] The *corps de ballet* present varying states of upper-body (un)dress: some with black T-shirts, others lewdly sporting ties alone. So rotations and repeated gestures, circular through time, denote primitive sexual display (hip circling and reiterated thrusting), frustratingly extended foreplay, attempts at masturbation and release. Other accompanying expressions of manhood include 'he-man' gestures and Cossack-like arm-linking formations – another Ravelian chain.

To turn once again to the theme of Ravel's endings, especially in relation to his destructive agenda, the various-sized circles *en route* might connote female 'jouissance': non-progressive or non-hierarchic cycles, circles and mandalas as emblematic of the diffusion of female sexual experience.[100] But closure in Béjart's interpretation has to capitalize on the large-scale goal-directed motion: simulated male orgasm. At the music's breaking-point six bars from the end, the soloist is felled, down on his right knee, with his arms pounding the air, like some proud being destined for sacrifice. As in Leyritz's reading and Ravel's music, man and beast come together: Donn's imposing mane of hair suggests a lion-like majesty. His mouth falls open to utter the music's ambiguous cry or orgasmic roar. The men encircle him around the pedestal also on their knees, with arms extended. From his position with arched back as if to be catapulted, at the final beat the soloist snaps exhausted into the middle of the circle. Orgasm, or death, has been achieved.

This might be seen as a rather different image of Marrakesh from the one Ravel had experienced near the end of his life, but is it really a crime of 'lèse-Ravel', as Maggie had claimed of its first incarnation? Again, issues of interpretative freedom arise. One may speculate that the essentially conservative Ravel would not have approved, but then this further evolution of his work-concept exists within a post-Second World War age of which he could have no experience. Admittedly, Béjart probably shows more love than respect for Ravel's music; it is imperative, however, that he has sufficient scope to establish his creative space, workable too within his own aesthetic. Beyond the 'consonance' of shared circularity and the overall tension–resolution 'energy pattern',[101] the stylistic effect might still be perceived as somewhat 'dissonant' in Albright's terms, but it is nevertheless highly effective.

---

[99] Judith Lynne Hanna, *Dance, Sex and Gender* (Chicago: University of Chicago Press, 1987), 234.

[100] See for instance Cox, 'Recovering *Jouissance*', 334–6.

[101] Jordan, *Moving Music*, 78.

These three selected productions, highlighting in turn Spanishness, machines and sexuality yet also blending these notions, show how contrasting interpretations can each enjoy success. All three work. Up to a point, they reflect contemporary trends in ballet conception. And this is not the end; the sophisticated simplicity of *Boléro* has the potential to sustain multiple interpretations: serious and light-hearted, within and beyond ballet. (A downside of this is that the work may fall victim to its own popularity, and to some extent this has already been borne out.) Blake Edwards's infamous film *10* (1979), a satire on the male midlife crisis starring Dudley Moore and Bo Derek, brought *Boléro* a whole new set of associations and listeners. Then came the Ice Dance Championships at the Sarajevo Olympics (1984): finally embracing on their knees upon the ice, Jayne Torvill and Christopher Dean danced a tragic *Romeo and Juliet*-inspired version, of superlative choreographic invention, in which a couple's love could endure only in death.[102] For Torvill and Dean, *Boléro* secured the Olympic gold medal; it also brought unprecedented success – as indeed it had for Ravel, whose attempt to attribute that success to the work's lack of musical content does not quite ring true.

Value judgements aside, there appear to be no limits to rethinking *Boléro*. In March 2001, the composer Marc-Olivier Dupin created an orchestral transcription, one of many in existence, to enable 2,000 amateur musicians and forty different instrumental families (including fifty-one African drums) to participate in an extraordinary outdoor performance at the Parc de la Villette in Paris.[103] Such treatment serves to underline the universality of the work. As one extreme, or to illustrate a progression from the sublime to the faintly ridiculous, in October 2002 a finale at Blackpool Tower Circus, itself an emulation of the Tour Eiffel, with mock Moorish gilded décor and famous sinking ring, featured an aquatic *Boléro*.[104] The set was a water-filled, circular pit with a central rotating podium, to which were attached six radiating seahorses arranged as a kind of snowflake design, ridden by mermaids – echoes of the Nijinska/Rubinstein early 'aquatic' version of *La Valse*. A central figure, scantily clad in a white and silver leotard, gradually descended to the podium in acrobatic fashion, via a long drape suspended from the roof-space.

---

[102] See Jayne Torvill and Christopher Dean, with John Man, *Facing the Music* (New York: Simon & Schuster, 1995) and 'Christopher Dean: Online interview' (17 July 2003), at www.goldenskate.com (accessed 17 December 2003). For a commercial VHS video, whose cover features the ending shot of *Boléro*, see Torvill and Dean, *Path to Perfection* (Hbo Studios, 1991; ASIN 630 1934628).

[103] Frédérique Jourdaan, 'A La Villette, ce soir en plein air: un *Boléro* de Ravel joué par 2,000 musiciens' (30 March 2001): Dossier d'œuvre, *Boléro*.

[104] Materials relating to Blackpool Tower are held in the Jack Hylton Archive, Lancaster University.

Boléro's status as a masterpiece is not in question, but Ravel's apparently flippant explanation of its success belies his highly perceptive insight. The piece does contain music and masterly orchestration, yet it is, as he readily admitted, a self-limiting experiment – a compelling formulaic device. Its 'less is more' philosophy works superbly well in this case; as a critic who experienced Rubinstein's 1931 production in London observed: 'the less expression is put into the performance, especially in the matter of *tempo*, the more effective it becomes'.[105] Here is further support for not succumbing to an accelerando. 'Less is more' also means more space for dance. Even if one does not concur with this same critic's reasoning that 'spectacle provides an antidote to its mechanical monotony', there is no doubting his conclusion: 'It [*Boléro*] gains enormously from performance as a ballet'.

---

[105] Anon., 'Mme Rubinstein's ballets', *The Times* (8 July 1931), 12. The London premiere was conducted by Ravel himself.

Chapter 8

'Danse générale': Ravel's œuvre as ballet

And so to a final 'Danse générale', that *sine qua non* of extended classical ballet, to conclude this choreographing of Ravel and the genre. Through the preceding chapters, an attempt has been made to enhance our historical and interpretative understanding of Ravel's ballets, with various ideas presented as to how the six main pieces might work in the context of the other balletic elements. Nonetheless, the picture is inevitably still incomplete. This last chapter seeks to provide an overview and a means of consolidating, and sometimes resolving, issues raised *en route*. The reasons for Ravel's collaborations and the strengths and weaknesses of his interpersonal relations are summarized; the overall nature of relations in the resulting ballets is also established. Additional repertory is brought into the frame: plans, sketches and orchestrations, as well as the balleticizing by others of Ravel's music from other genres. The importance of performance as the means by which to realize this repertory is underlined, with emphasis on special performance events. Ravel's practice of compositional remodelling is also brought into the final argument. Throughout this chapter, an underlying notion is developed: that of Ravel's full œuvre as ballet.

Motivations and collaborative relations

One might reasonably ask why Ravel collaborated in ballet projects. The answer ranges from the mundane to the more sublime. In almost all the works under discussion, and many in other genres, Ravel was commissioned by an impresario figure, or 'catalysed' by his publisher, to produce music for the ballet. Rouché commissioned *Ma Mère l'Oye* and *L'Enfant*; Diaghilev commissioned *Daphnis*; Jacques Durand and de Maré encouraged the orchestration and balletic development of *Le Tombeau*. The only partial exceptions to this rule are *La Valse* and *Boléro*: *La Valse* existed, at least in Ravel's mind, long before its association with Diaghilev; similarly, although Rubinstein had commissioned a Spanish orchestration from Ravel, the precise concept of *Boléro* was very much Ravel's own. As Calvocoressi was keen to point out, for the most part these were purely pragmatic beginnings

249

with no great mystery: 'All these were straightforward commissions, entailing no special conditions or problems.'[1]

Another part of the answer concerns financial incentive: after all, composers must live. This perspective is revealed by Ravel's letter to the librettist George de Feure – the pseudonym of Georges van Sluijters (1868–1928) – regarding a possible project for the Alhambra Theatre, London. The letter was written in 1914 just before Ravel left for his summer break at St-Jean-de-Luz, where he spent time with Benois. Ravel lays down his terms to de Feure:

> This contract ... would stipulate the general terms, including the schedule of payments and the delivery of the ballet ... The premium which the Alhambra will reserve for me should be representative of my royalties in England ... and it seems to me that its sum should not be less than Fifteen Thousand francs.[2]

On this occasion, he perhaps set his price too high, maybe because he was not convinced of the calibre of Sluijters; in any event, nothing appears to have come of this project. Certainly, a couple of years later, Ravel asked only for 10,000 francs for another scheme mooted with Diaghilev;[3] conceivably this higher-profile project held greater potential appeal. Such pragmatic factors apart, Ravel's motivation was directed by a long-term aesthetic commitment to ballet and theatrical art that is strongly evidenced by his writings (Chapter 1). His natural affinities with visual art and French literature and his confidence to express opinions on them are beyond doubt.

What of the overall nature of Ravel's poietic, or collaborative, relationships? As Christopher Best concedes, this method of fashioning art-works is a risky business: 'Making an artistic statement by committee requires either complete mutual trust or a strong hierarchy. The end result can be compromised by weaknesses in either the music or the dance or indeed simply the non-compatibility between otherwise strong components.'[4] Additionally, it is not always possible for the researcher to glean sufficient information to reconstruct definitive personal relationships.

Ironically, given the irretrievable breakdown of the Ravel–Diaghilev team in 1920 over *La Valse*, the most frequently repeating collaborations were with the Ballets Russes, if one also includes works that Ravel orchestrated: Musorgsky's stage work *Khovanshchina* (with Stravinsky), Chabrier's *Menuet Pompeux*, plus parts of Schumann's *Carnaval* and Chopin's music within *Les*

---

[1] M.-D. Calvocoressi, 'When Ravel composed to order', *Music & Letters*, 22 (January 1941), 54–9: 55.

[2] Letter from Ravel to de Feure (19 June 1914), in Orenstein (ed.), *A Ravel Reader*, 148. The fee is underlined by Ravel.

[3] Letter from Ravel to Diaghilev (12 January 1917), in ibid., 179.

[4] Best, 'Why do choreographers and composers collaborate?', 29.

Sylphides for Nijinsky's breakaway troupe. Even *L'Enfant* maintained an indirect Diaghilev connection. Happier Russian relations were those with the Ballets Ida Rubinstein, especially with Rubinstein herself and Benois, even if Ravel appears to have been more distanced from Nijinska. Ravel's compatriot Rouché was intimately connected with three projects, *Ma Mère l'Oye*, *Adélaïde* and the 'Fanfare' for *L'Eventail* (together with *L'Enfant*), the first two of which also involved Drésa. By extension, the quality of Ravel's contribution is evidenced not least by the company he kept – the sheer stature of many of his fellow collaborators. Similarly, this quality is attested to by the stature of many subsequent figures inspired to recreate his ballets, especially after his death: Ashton/Craxton/Fonteyn, Lifar/Leyritz, Skibine/Chagall, Balanchine/Karinska, Massine/Derain, Béjart and Murphy.

Ravel's collaborative relations were variable; they were influenced and at times compromised by his private and somewhat unyielding personality. But such relationships were not Ravel's sole responsibility: as with any marriage, they depended equally on the other individuals involved and the resulting psychological chemistry; and personal attributes that might be construed as weaknesses in some contexts proved to be strengths in others.

At some level, there certainly was within Ravel's make-up what might be termed the Peter Pan Syndrome, especially evident in his difficulties with strong, overtly heterosexual women. This phenomenon seems to have applied in Ravel's limited collaboration with Colette: the distance or contrast between them was picked up by Roland-Manuel as early as 1928.[5] Conversely, Ravel's relationship with another strong woman, Rubinstein, was much closer, but then she herself was arguably more interested sexually in women than men. Another character witness well versed in the composer–conductor collaboration of musical performance was Ansermet. Unlike Calvocoressi, Ansermet saw a mysteriously self-contained and perhaps shy man: 'He was very eccentric, very original, and also – how do you say? – secret. He would not externally express his feelings at all.'[6] Part of Ravel's self-consciousness seems to have related to body image. Consider the dismissive language of the American satirist Dorothy Parker–'Ravel? Sexless' – and Kennicott's ensuing assessment: 'The persnicketiness with which he dressed, hid and gussied up his body seems at first glance to be incompatible with the temperament required to compose dance music.'[7] (Nonetheless, Kennicott would have to concede that there has been no shortage of successful, dandyesque choreographers.) Furthermore, this was not just other people's image of the composer; Ravel himself expressed doubts

---

[5] Roland-Manuel, *Ravel et son œuvre dramatique*; see too a review of this book by M.-D. Calvocoressi in *The Musical Times* (1 June 1929), 517–18.

[6] Dummond, *Speaking of Diaghilev*, 218.

[7] Kennicott, 'Ravelation', 68.

about his collaborative reliability; even if in jest, he declared to Georgette Marnold: 'I've finally found my vocation: I was made to be a hermit.'[8] Nevertheless, this ability to thrive in circumscribed solitude was an essential for Ravel's own compositional processes.

But there is an alternative view of the composer. De Maré speaks highly of Ravel, and wants 'to show the great musician from the point of view of an enthusiastic and friendly collaborator'.[9] Equally, according to Prunières, 'There is nothing solitary about Ravel, he is the most sociable of men'.[10] Indeed, Prunières explains Ravel's need to move to the retreat of Montfort-L'Amaury precisely as a consequence of the fact that he could never bear to shut the door on his Paris friends. For Massine too, Ravel was 'a witty and erudite conversationalist', who discussed balletic ideas in detail.[11] No doubt any 'truth' resides between these extremes.

Another Ravel trait concerns the strength and clarity of his artistic convictions, which may again be both an asset and, at times, a hindrance. In respect of *Ma Mère l'Oye*, Ravel seemingly enjoyed significant leadership within a collaboration that he found very satisfying, although this kind of directorship – Best's 'strong hierarchy' – probably excluded other viable solutions that might have strengthened the dance dimension. Conversely, despite the prominent aesthetic common ground in Ravel's collaboration with Fokine in *Daphnis*, the strength – even stubbornness – of both individuals appears to have compounded difficulties, most obviously in creating the scenario (a limited instance of Best's 'non-compatibility'). Later on, Ravel's strength and absolute dignity in harrowing, humiliating circumstances was evident in his response to Diaghilev's rejection of *La Valse* when he silently walked out of the room.

Evidently the tension between collaborators as flexible team players and as representatives of autonomous disciplines was real, and was complicated by Ravel's ability to embrace choreography within the musical fabric of *La Valse*, *Daphnis* and even *Boléro*; yet, ironically, this is part of ballet's very appeal. Ravel's synaesthetic pursuit, discernible to varying degrees in these works, embodies an intriguing paradox. It emphasizes a possible musical self-sufficiency, while clearly not precluding the successful interpolation of dance and design. Acute conflicts between practitioners may be resolved by

[8] Letter to Georgette Marnold (8 December 1919), in Orenstein (ed.), *A Ravel Reader*, 194.

[9] De Maré, 'Ravel et les ballets', 15: 'pour montrer le grand musicien sous l'aspect d'un collaborateur enthousiaste et amiable'.

[10] Henry Prunières, 'Trois silhouettes de musiciens – César Franck, Saint-Saëns, Maurice Ravel', *La Revue musicale*, 7 (October 1926), 225–40: 237. 'Ravel n'a rien d'un solitaire, c'est le plus sociable des hommes.'

[11] Massine, *My Life in Ballet*, 112. For more on Ravel's character, see Orenstein, *Ravel: Man and Musician*, 110–14, and Larner, *Maurice Ravel*, 219ff.

judicious negotiation, but this does not always work: one comes to understand Ravel's error of judgement in allowing the First Suite from *Daphnis* to be performed before the ballet premiere, and Nijinska's mistaken insistence on dance autonomy in *La Valse* (which seriously compromised the cohesiveness of the 1929 production). Equally, the fact that Chagall's design for the 1958 *Daphnis* had emerged from a large-scale autonomous lithographic project explains why the designs overpowered Skibine's dancers on stage, even though they complemented the rich, impressionist musical sounds.

The poietic–esthesic approach has facilitated interaction between process and product, capturing some fascinating polarities: severe collaborative tension yet an exquisite resulting work for *Daphnis*; happier collaborations yet less enduring products for *Ma Mère l'Oye* and *Le Tombeau*. Furthermore, Ravel's variable levels of communication seem not to have affected the quality of the resulting work: a curious telepathic, or at least instinctive, aesthetic rapport connected Ravel with Fokine, Colette and others.

Balletic relations in and across productions of works

This study has witnessed various theoretical ideas (Chapter 1) in action (Chapters 2–7), concerning both small-scale facets and larger-scale relations across productions of works. But again, especially with less well-documented interpretations, it is not always possible to establish definitive relations. Snippets of information from one or more angles provide insight into part of the experience. Particular views need, where feasible, to be deconstructed, since the French press in Ravel's case tended to be polarized into supporters (including Vuillermoz, Laloy, Malherbe, Prunières and Schneider) and detractors (Lalo and Pougin, and on occasion Vuillemin and Levinson).

Playing with time in music and dance was found in portions of works: compression through overlap in the 'Danse du rouet' of *Ma Mère l'Oye*; the slow-motion 'flashback' near the revelatory close of *La Valse*. Fokine talked of judicious 'freezing' of dance time (see p. 92); the idea recurred in Ashton's 1951 *Daphnis* and, more idiosyncratically, in Gallotta's reading of 1984. From the 1912 original onwards, dramatic time was treated episodically in relation to Chloé's abduction and Daphnis's dream. Localized 'uncoupling' of time between music and dance appeared to have been part of Leyritz's strategy in the 1941 *Boléro* and at a more fundamental level in Murphy's *Daphnis*. Time can be conjured with: musical middles can become endings and endings can become middles. Ravel's reordering of movements in the orchestrated *Le Tombeau* created an ending from the middle, and Balanchine caused the end of *Valses nobles* to become the middle of his conjoined production of *La Valse*. Design too exists within extended temporal notions. In the case of *Ma Mère l'Oye*, Ravel, Drésa and Leyritz all had ideas about the various cloths to be pulled down in front of the main backdrop to mark time and scenic change, while the alternation of Bakst's sets or Chagall's backdrops for *Daphnis* fulfilled a similar function. Nor does scenario have to subscribe to a linear temporal progression: Ravel's scenario for *Ma Mère l'Oye* interpolated episodes from other sources ('Le Petit Poucet' and 'La Belle et la Bête') within its *Sleeping Beauty* story.

Varied dimensions of space were apparent. Ashton's playing with fixed and moving space in *La Valse* was especially noteworthy. In some of Balanchine's realizations of *L'Enfant*, music partook visibly of physical space with singers present on stage. In *Daphnis*, the wordless chorus and offstage fanfares, which from initial distant positions seemed to get ever closer, added a spatial dimension to the sonic and dramatic effect. From a visual perspective, space in musical scoring was a striking feature of Ravel's *Boléro* draft (see p. 222). While dance emphasizes the body moving through space, art sometimes complements with painted figures fixed in space, as occurred with Bakst's main backdrop for *Daphnis*.

Also important was musical meaning: 'objets sonores' with common signifiers (and up to a point common 'signifieds') were found in fanfares and waltzes; chromaticism in *Ma Mère l'Oye*, *Daphnis* and elsewhere invariably signalled dramatic instability; more contrarily, *Le Tombeau* used mechanistic signifiers to connote poignant emotion. From a broader balletic perspective, some meanings were obvious through association with their respective subject-matters; others proved more elusive, either because the full story was lacking, or because such meanings were deeply encoded in disciplines beyond music.

Despite these latter difficulties, interesting topics emerged, especially regarding *La Valse* and *Boléro*. Mediation between inherent 'attributes' and external, socially constructed, 'emergent' meaning (broadly along Cook's lines of a 'conceptual integration network') enables a useful reconciliation in *La Valse*. Ravel argued that the 'whirling' was intrinsic to the work's origin in pure nineteenth-century dance, but others perceived socio-cultural baggage relating to the fall of the Habsburg Empire. Such differing views can be partially accommodated via the nineteenth-century literature to which Ravel was strongly attracted (Baudelaire's 'Correspondances' and Poe's destructive prose) and his own traumatic experience during the First World War. It is partly because of its symbolism and Poe-like grotesquery that Balanchine's *La Valse* works so well. Similarly, Ashton's production might be seen in terms of Abbate's narrative fissure, or an 'unsung' dissonant voice: from initially close music–dance relations, an increasing crack appears as paths or meanings deviate and threaten to rupture the work. Other productions of *La Valse* that did not quite gel seem to have compromised the music into appearing tame or dull (Massine's 1950 version) or even slightly silly – passionately 'worked up' for no reason (Nijinska's 1929 premiere, perhaps). One may relate to the phenomenon whereby a given colour may appear enhanced, merely neutral, or sullied by that with which it is juxtaposed.

Where *Boléro* is concerned, even if Ravel considered the 'musico-sexual' meaning intrinsic to its restricted and tense tonal structuring, this meaning has undoubtedly undergone socio-cultural development through the sexually permissive 1960s before being codified choreographically by Béjart. In relating to gender theory of the 1990s, one may – à la McClary – perceive small cyclical patterns of 'jouissance' that are ultimately obliterated by goal-directed thrusting in what for Ravel was still a patriarchal, male-dominated society.

In relation to the ideas of Albright and Jordan, there were instances of strong verticals, working synchronically, that could be interpreted as 'transmediating chords' as with the approaches of Ravel and Bakst to *Daphnis* (see p. 97). But although Ravel's contemporaries, such as de Maré on the subject of *Le Tombeau*, talked metaphorically of states of harmony, the relating of 'lines' through time, as well as to each other, generally proved more relevant. Equally, the idea of 'consonant' music breeding 'dissonant' overall relations and vice versa had some application (with implicit layering or levels, after Cook),[12] but it was clearly less a matter of strict consonance/dissonance than of tension/resolution, or stability/instability – notions also considered by Jordan. In the opening of Ashton's *La Valse*, unstable music is in consonant relation with dance, appearing as close mimetic counterpoint. In these terms, the problematic ending arises because the music becomes increasingly dissonant, whereas dance is locked in a time warp and does not follow suit. Ravel might have declared this visualization too 'picturesque', as he had the premiere of *Boléro*. Similarly in *Boléro*, the music if not strictly dissonant is still very tense. And as Jordan has noted, there can be a 'reflection of tonal tension in the structuring of dance material' and a pursuit of similar large-scale 'energy-patterns':[13] these are the means by which Béjart achieves a music–dance consonance, but his modern dance also exhibits a certain stylistic 'dissonance' with Ravel's music.

As remarked on by Best (Chapter 1), when balletic elements truly function sympathetically, one is hardly aware of the effect of one upon the other. Albright expresses a similar ideal, relating also to the time–space agenda above: 'Certain collaborations seem to possess such an intimate integrity

[12] Cook, *Analysing Musical Multimedia*, 124–6.
[13] Jordan, *Moving Music*, xi, 78–9.

that all consciousness of the constituent arts vanishes. The arts that pertain to time, such as poetry and music, seem to acquire a new dimension in space; the arts that pertain to space, such as painting, seem strangely temporalized.'[14] This is perhaps the special quality of oneness that Ravel also perceived. Examples where almost inexplicable synthesis seems to have occurred, even from dissonant ingredients, include the gripping drama of Balanchine's composite *Valses nobles/La Valse*, Nijinska's 1931 *La Valse*, the audio-visual fantasy of Kylián's *L'Enfant* and, up to a point, Leyritz's *Boléro* and Ashton's *Daphnis*. In such circumstances, one might propose a 'symbiotic' relationship between elements as a modification of Jordan's 'interdependence'. Whereas in a study that focuses upon dance in ballet the relationship with music is one of need, the argument for a study that focuses upon music, acknowledging in Benois's words its central 'gravity', is that whilst music can stand alone, it is undoubtedly for the most part enhanced when it chooses to evolve in sympathetic, reciprocal relations with dance and design. 'Symbiosis' expresses this positively as sharing, mutually beneficial relationships, and the word's biological origin emphasizes that within the relevant time-frame these are dynamic, 'living' kinships.

Additional Ravel ballet repertory

Apart from the wealth of established repertory, there are other plans and orchestrations that further point up Ravel's natural affinity with ballet and in turn suggest part of the reason for his success. These additional materials also contribute to an argument for overviewing Ravel's œuvre as ballet. An interesting find in the Bibliothèque Nationale de France is an unpublished early manuscript in Ravel's musical hand.[15] Annotations in another hand entitle this piano score *La Parade* and indicate that this was ballet music to a scenario by 'Mlle Antonine Meunier de l'Opéra'.[16] There is no need to detail this music: it is formulaic, practice-type dance music firmly founded in D major, seemingly too utilitarian for Ravel to put his name to, but interesting in providing an instance, long before *L'Eventail*, of Ravel operating in Parisian salons. A boisterous 'Mouvt. de marche' in accented duple metre

---

[14] Albright, *Untwisting the Serpent*, 5.

[15] Maurice Ravel, MS. autogr. 16939 (17 pp.), BNF Mus. Orenstein favours the later 1890s for a likely compositional date, contemporary with the overture *Shéhérazade*, and this seems plausible given the largely diatonic writing: Orenstein, *Ravel: Man and Musician*, 22, 243.

[16] Amid superimposed scrawling at the head of the MS is Ravel's name and a curious note that appears to read 'sous le pseudonyme de Jacques Dream', together with the qualification, 'élève de Dalier, organiste-compositeur'.

leads to 'Scène I' (p. 3), cued by melodramatic rising scalic flourishes on B within an A major key signature – a relationship later pursued on the large scale in *Daphnis*. Various dances ensue, including another 'Mouvt. de Valse', in F♯ major (pp. 9 and 13) and a 'Tempo di Mazurka' in a balancing six flats. Undoubtedly the handwriting is that of Ravel, yet it contains uncharacteristic amounts of crossing-out (p. 4) and was clearly written at speed. The style is simple, with sparse dynamic indications and no choreographic indications, and the construction of this medley of dances is highly traditional, utilizing a *da capo* form.

Poignantly, at the other end of Ravel's life were plans and brief sketches of melodies supported by figured bass, seen by Rosenthal, for *Morgiane*.[17] *Morgiane* was intended as a third project with Rubinstein; again, it used an exotic theme, this time derived from *Les Mille et une nuits* (The Thousand and One Nights), of which several leather-bound volumes may be found at Ravel's house. Rubinstein's papers confirm the intention for 'Morgiane de Ravel', together with Stravinsky's *Perséphone*, to be presented in 1934, in an undated listing of 'Nouveaux Ballets'.[18] In a prophetic way, Ravel reputedly viewed the work-concept in the same destructive vein as *Boléro*: 'There will be blood, desire and death.'[19] His letter to Marie Gaudin mentions the ballet as scheduled to be mounted at the Opéra in March 1934, but his deteriorating state is painfully evident from the failing handwriting.[20] Gathering apt inspiration was supposedly still part of the *raison d'être* for his 1935 Moroccan trip with Leyritz (Chapter 7), though with his progressive brain condition the project advanced hardly at all.[21]

Between these extremes were other mooted ballet projects that for less obvious reasons remained unrealized (except that, even before his final illness, Ravel found a challenge in bringing his creative impetuses to fruition). What can be gleaned of these plans tends to reinforce previously observed traits. Significantly, Ravel's preferred topics for the projected ballet with de Feure discussed in 1914 were of either an exotic or an eighteenth-century (French or Italian) nature. On the other hand, it was an Italian futurist, Francesco Cangiullo, who was chosen to write the scenario for a 1917 Diaghilev scheme, interestingly very much contemporary with Ravel's mechanized *Frontispice* to Ricciotto Canudo's poem. Ravel's claims that the piano score would be completed in 1917 and the orchestration by April

---

[17] Orenstein, Ravel: *Man and Musician*, 209.

[18] Rés. Pièce 78: fols 76–7 (B-MO).

[19] Ravel quoted in Marnat, *Maurice Ravel*, 664: 'Il y aura du sang, de la volupté et de la mort'.

[20] See facsimile of letter (2 August 1933) in Larner, *Maurice Ravel*, 214.

[21] See R. A. Henson, 'Maurice Ravel's illness: a tragedy of lost creativity', *British Medical Journal*, 296 (4 June 1988), 1585–8.

1918 provide another illustration of a work growing in stages towards its balletic culmination, and of unrealistic schedules in his wartime crisis.[22]

A supplementary way in which Ravel expanded ballet (and concert) repertoire was through orchestrations of nineteenth-century Romantic works. The most celebrated, while not a ballet, does have a distinct pictorial element: the orchestration of Musorgsky's *Tableaux d'une exposition*, completed in 1922. These transcriptions were not always unmitigated successes, however: Taruskin went so far as to refer to Ravel's orchestrations of *Carnaval* and *Les Sylphides* as 'unaccountably clumsy'.[23] More successful products included those of Debussy's *Sarabande* and *Danse* in 1922, choreographed for instance by Jacques d'Amboise for the 1975 Ravel Festival.[24] Happier too was Ravel's orchestration of his beloved Chabrier's *Menuet pompeux* (1881) in 1919 for Diaghilev, which, as various writers have noted, was mediated by his own early *Menuet antique*. Ravel adds to Chabrier's original through textural development with more complex layering, and through distinctive, especially percussive, sonorities. Both the *Menuet pompeux* and Ravel's own *Alborada* (orchestrated in 1918; see Chapter 7) were intended for incorporation in a Spanish ballet, *Les Jardins d'Aranjuez*; the two works are mentioned in Ravel's letter to Godebska of 24 May 1919.[25] An earlier letter of 7 May from Ravel to Diaghilev concerning an unidentified work surely also refers to the orchestration of *Menuet pompeux*.[26] Interestingly, a bizarre 'throw-away' line at the close of this letter, 'I'm dreaming of football – musically speaking' ('Je songe au football – musicalement s'entend'), anticipates Honegger's enthusiasm for rugby in his *Mouvement symphonique no. 2* of 1928. The comment must relate to another projected ballet of the later war years, this time with Massine and Robert Delaunay. Ravel was apparently intrigued by football moves and how these might be translated, choreographically, into modern ballet. For Massine, images of a football being thrown among the dancers promised exciting new dance moves and group formations. Sadly, this project too remained unrealized.[27]

During and after Ravel's lifetime, ballet repertory has been enriched by choreographies of much of the composer's remaining non-ballet music,

---

[22] Ivry mentions two other projects: *Le Portrait de l'Infante* (c. 1920), partially completed, and *Les Violons de Paris* (c. 1927), an idea explored with Léon-Paul Fargue: *Maurice Ravel: A Life*, 110, 144.

[23] Taruskin, *Stravinsky and the Russian Traditions*, vol. II, 1526. For the opening page of MS of 'Préambule' from *Carnaval*, see Jankélévitch, *Ravel*, 139.

[24] Kirstein, *Thirty Years*, 384.

[25] Orenstein (ed.), *A Ravel Reader*, 190–1.

[26] This letter was rediscovered by Lifar: see Serge Lifar, 'Correspondances, II', *La Revue musicale*, 20 (January–February 1939), 13–14: 14.

[27] Massine, *My Life in Ballet*, 112.

including the celebrated *Pavane pour une infante défunte* (see below), the song collection *Shéhérazade*, the *Introduction et allegro*, the *Rapsodie espagnole* and the Concerto in G.[28] That this varied music has become popular and enjoyed success in its new context again indicates the extent to which Ravel foregrounds dance within music; as Lifar rightly remarked, 'The dancing element abounds in Ravel's music'.[29] But what is its particular lure for choreographers? Attributes that make Ravel's music so suitable for extended classical dance include the underlying tonality-cum-modality with beautifully drawn, expressive melodies (important to Ashton), the regular yet subtly sophisticated rhythmic–metrical layering and the luxuriant orchestral sound-world (important to Balanchine), as well as the more elusive qualities of elegance, sensibility and nostalgia. Major choreographic names have chosen to work with Ravel's wider œuvre, often retitled and reinterpreted (e.g. MacMillan, *La Fin du jour* and Robbins, *In G Major*, both to Ravel's Concerto), from as early as the 1930s (Ashton and Catherine Littlefield), through the 1950s and 1960s (Glen Tetley, John Cranko and Roland Petit), 1970s (Balanchine, Robbins, MacMillan and Murphy) and on to the new millennium. Additionally, choreographers have combined Ravel's scores in new works: Kylián's *Un Ballo* (the 'Menuet' from *Le Tombeau* and the *Pavane*), or Yuri Possokhov's *Damned* for the San Francisco Ballet (the *Pavane* and the Concerto for the Left Hand). Whether the practice works musically depends very much on individual context.

Early English illustrations of this trend include Andrée Howard's *The Mermaid* of March 1934. Howard's creation worked mainly with Ravel's *Introduction et allegro* (1905) plus – for the fourth scene on a seaside terrace – *Alborada*. These works were coupled with a fairytale scenario after Hans Christian Andersen's poignant story of the *Little Mermaid* of which Ravel might have approved. According to Marie Rambert, the title role was danced to moving, melancholic effect by Pearl Argyle, who also starred in Ashton's *Valentine's Eve*, to the music of *Valses nobles*.[30] One does not need to be a balletomane to appreciate that this process may foster new musical meanings: thus Ravel's implicitly fluid *Introduction* was attractively developed by an imaginative underwater visualization, but the interpolation of *Alborada*, albeit contemporary, was more questionable. In the postwar era

---

[28] For an extensive listing, see Noël Goodwin, 'Ravel', in Bremser (ed.), *The International Dictionary of Ballet*, vol. II, 1180–82: 1182.

[29] Serge Lifar, 'Maurice Ravel et le ballet', *La Revue musicale*, 19 (December 1938), 74–80: 74: 'L'élément dansant abonde dans la musique de Ravel'. One would hardly concur with Lifar's initial judgement that Ravel composed merely one ballet, *Daphnis*; but, to be fair, he later conceded that *La Valse* and *Boléro* were 'eminently danceable': see Lifar, *Serge de Diaghilev*, 239.

[30] Marie Rambert, *Quicksilver: An Autobiography*, 159–60.

too, MacMillan's *La Fin du jour* (1979) for the Royal Ballet created additional meaning for Ravel's Concerto in G. Ravel's music, first performed in January 1932, was employed as a nostalgic, jazz-based symbol in a commentary on the fashionable but fragile years that led to the Second World War – fitting too in respect of the end of Ravel's life. In Ian Spurling's art deco set, the female figures, including Merle Park and Jennifer Penney, appeared carefree, yet curiously automated – even ghost-like. More recently Ravel's music has been used, if not entirely successfully, in Lila York's *Sanctum* (1997) for the Birmingham Royal Ballet: exemplifying a 'dreamy' old world, it was juxtaposed starkly with that of the American composer Christopher Rouse as a tyrannical, machinist new world, in the manner of Charlie Chaplin's *Modern Times*.

Ravel ballet productions: highlights of time and place

As is already evident, performance is always more than implicit: it is impossible to talk of a work without relating to its realization in performance. Although, as pointed out in the Introduction, staged performances appear much less frequently than concert ones, musicians should also make more effort to seek them out. Overall, Ravel's ballets have enjoyed a relatively busy, but far from properly acknowledged, reception history, with many subsequent productions across international territory. (See Appendix, especially entries for *Daphnis*, *La Valse* and *Boléro*.)

Ravel's ballets have been produced and toured widely in Europe (France, Monaco, Belgium, Italy, the United Kingdom, Germany, Austria, Switzerland, the Netherlands, Scandinavia, the Czech Republic and Baltic States), as well as in the United States (especially New York), Latin America (Argentina) and Australia (especially Sydney). In Paris alone, they have graced the Opéra, the Opéra-Comique, the Théâtre du Châtelet, the Théâtre des Arts (Théâtre Hébertot) and the Théâtre des Champs-Elysées; provincially, they have been acclaimed in Lyon and his native Ciboure. In the United Kingdom, they have enjoyed a long association with Sadler's Wells Ballet, which became The Royal Ballet and with Sadler's Wells Theatre Ballet, now the Birmingham Royal Ballet, as well as being experienced in smaller locations such as the Festival Theatre Cambridge, the Mercury Theatre Colchester, the Royal Court Theatre Liverpool and the Abbey Theatre Dublin. Even early on, these works had travelled impressive distances to surprising destinations: to the Teatro Colón, Buenos Aires for Nijinska's interpretation of *Daphnis* after Fokine in 1927; to the Riga Ballet, Latvia for Lemanis's interpretation of *Boléro* in 1936.

The various premieres of *L'Enfant* offer a typical itinerary: after its Monte Carlo outing in March 1925, the work appeared at the Opéra-Comique on

1 February 1926, then in Brussels (11 February), Prague (17 February), Leipzig (6 May) and Vienna (14 March 1929). Later productions included the Italian premiere in Florence (2 May 1939), followed finally by admittance to the hallowed ground of the Opéra on 17 May 1939. Where productions of the not unproblematic *Daphnis* are concerned, one may note at least twelve different versions. These tend to be clustered in small groups, with at least two versions appearing in each of the following seasons: 1951, 1958–9, 1962, 1972 and 1975. Most European countries (especially Germany and Italy), plus the United States, have produced their own versions of *Daphnis*, with the work having been staged in Stuttgart, Berlin and Frankfurt; Rome and Milan; Amsterdam; Philadelphia and New York. Given that one factor militating against its staging is the static quality of the scenario (and the extensive portions of music in relation to action), Buckle was elated in the mid-1970s to discover in van Manen's plotless choreography of the Second Suite 'At last a sixteen-minute *Daphnis and Chloë*!'[31] Certainly, this represents one way of capitalizing on the popularity of the orchestral suites. With *La Valse*, similar clusters are revealed: 1929/31; 1934; 1940; 1950–1; 1955; 1958–9. Some periods coincide with those for *Daphnis* productions, suggesting a more general resurgence of appreciation for Ravel's ballets beyond precise anniversaries, especially in the early and late 1950s.

Even small works not originally construed as ballet have undergone complex evolutions. Despite his reservations about its form, Ravel's evocative, highly melodic *Pavane* (Fauré-like), composed for piano in 1899 and orchestrated in 1910, provides a good example (see Appendix). Again, dance may create new inflections of meaning: it can intensify the musical gravity by visualizing Ravel's fictional image of the princess or, alternatively, lift the melancholic musical mood. By 1928, Bolm had choreographed the *Pavane* in association with the Chamber Music Society of Washington,[32] and early versions for what would become Ballet Rambert included those by Anthony Tudor presented on New Year's Day 1933 and Bentley Stone in 1937. It is however Ashton's early reading of May 1933 for the Ballet Club, decorated by Stevenson and danced by the young Markova and Stanislas Idzikowski,[33] that one tends to focus upon in the interwar years. Evolution continued with productions by Frank Staff (1941; also for Rambert) and Lifar (1944), leading to further interpretation in the 1960s, such as that by Robert North (1967). But one of the best-known postwar choreographies, still in the repertory, is that of Balanchine, premiered on 29 May 1975 by the New York City Ballet, and presented as a soulful, dreamed 'lament, choreographed for a single dancer [Patricia McBride] and

---

[31] Buckle, *Buckle at the Ballet*, 332; review of 31 March 1974.
[32] Beaumont, *The Complete Book of Ballets*, 787.
[33] Information from Frederick Ashton, Dossier d'artiste (B-MO).

a piece of chiffon she holds.'[34] The work's reinterpretation continued through the millennium with, for instance, Jan Van Dyke's stark solo rendition, re-titled *Slow Embrace*, at the North Carolina Dance Festival early in 2002.

Although Ravel's music has been successfully interpolated within mixed dance programmes for many years, the biggest impetus has come from ded-icated commemorative festivals on both sides of the Atlantic from the late 1930s onwards that found a special place for ballet. Thus the exact first anniversary of Ravel's death saw a 'Soirée Ravel à l'Opéra de Paris' under Lifar on 28 December 1938, featuring *Adélaïde*, *Daphnis* after Fokine and *L'Heure*. The 'Festival Ravel' at the Opéra-Comique in May 1950 cele-brated the seventy-fifth anniversary of the composer's birth, as well as offer-ing homage to Colette on the fiftieth anniversary of her literary début, with productions of *L'Enfant* and *La Valse*. Recent anniversary events have included those of 1997 and 2000: summer 1997 saw The Royal Ballet's *A Ravel Evening* on tour in California (May) and New York (July) with a four-work extravaganza comprising Ashton's *La Valse* and *Daphnis*, MacMillan's *La Fin du jour* and the young Christopher Wheeldon's *Pavane*; May 2000 saw the Opéra National de Lyon production of *Ma Mère l'Oye*, coupled with *L'Enfant*.[35] Anniversaries apart, the cause of Ravel's ballets was further promoted in 2002 by two troupes: the Pascal Rioult Dance Theatre and the Opéra-Ballet de Lyon, producing all-Ravel touring programmes in the United States and Europe, both of which included a new *Boléro*. But anni-versaries returned for 2004 with the centenaries of Ashton and Balanchine, as marked in March of that year by Birmingham Royal Ballet's gala 'Sir Fred and Mr B', and the promise of more exciting showcasing of Ravel.

Fittingly, the most ambitious celebrations to date were those for Ravel's centenary masterminded by Balanchine in his 'New York Ravel Festival' at the New York State Theater, Lincoln Center, with four programmes across 14–31 May 1975. The audacious undertaking was to choreograph Ravel's main œuvre as ballet, including some sixteen new creations, half of which were by Balanchine, with emphasis upon dance rather than lavish visual effects. The 1972 Stravinsky centenary evidently acted as a model for the Ravel enterprise: Kirstein, who had founded the New York troupe with Balanchine, was adamant that, Stravinsky apart, 'Ravel left the most considerable body of Western music suitable for theater (apart from opera)

---

[34] [Balanchine,] *Choreography by George Balanchine*, 269. The work was still being per-formed most effectively in January 2003; for Kyra Nichols in the role in 1994, see Garafola, 'Dance for a city', 42.

[35] The home response to *A Ravel Evening* at Covent Garden was rather muted, though *Daphnis* fared well: Debra Craine, 'Mixed fortunes', *The Times* (21 October 1996). The year 2000 also saw publication of Ivry, *Maurice Ravel* and Mawer (ed.), *The Cambridge Companion to Ravel*.

... there was no other contemporary composer available whose body of work, as a whole, could serve as a possible source of repertory'.[36] Not all were so convinced, however, believing that Ravel's repertory was less suitable for this treatment and that, *Daphnis* excepted, 'Ravel's contribution to dance is distinctly lightweight', while for Buckle the occasion yielded 'a bizarre crop of ballets'.[37]

Nonetheless the Festival witnessed Balanchine's highly successful versions of *Le Tombeau* and the *Pavane*, both still in NYCB repertory,[38] the third version of *L'Enfant* and Robbins's *Mother Goose*. Other contributions included Balanchine's *Sonatine* as a lightly danced duo, Robbins's *Introduction et allegro* and *Concerto en sol* (later retitled *In G Major*), Jacques d'Amboise's version of *Alborada* and John Taras's *Daphnis*, which unfortunately did not quite work. For Buckle, Balanchine's 'most outrageous essay' in dance translation was *Gaspard de la nuit*.[39] Other creations from non-balletic sources numbered Robbins's reading of *Chansons madécasses*, whose striking visualization as two black plus two white dancers was compelling[40] – a literalism à la Ravel (see p. 52ff. above), and Balanchine's version of Ravel's rhapsodic *Tzigane*, composed in 1924 and still in NYCB repertory, for the superb Suzanne Farrell coupled by Peter Martins, with the violinist Lamar Alsop. The solo violin was balanced by a female solo dancer in a deconstructing of clichéd Hungarianisms that echoed the treatment of Spanish music in *Boléro*: 'Farrell did not impersonate a "gypsy"; her body played with theatricalized elements of wildness, caprice, longing.'[41] Some months later Balanchine presented a centennial offshoot, 'Hommage à Ravel', at the Opéra; and for his services to French music he was awarded the Légion d'Honneur that Ravel had earlier declined.

One main aim has been to establish that Ravel's ballet music is generally enhanced by its companion arts; nevertheless it would be perverse to ignore Ravel's success as a classical 'best-seller' of audio recordings and ballet music scores for Durand/BMG. Kennicott argues that the 'self-contained' quality of Ravel's art means that 'his music works extremely well with and without its choreography'.[42] And the point is surely that one can enjoy strong audio recordings in addition to, rather than instead of, an appreciation of the

---

[36] Kirstein, *Thirty Years*, 255–6.

[37] Bland, *Observer of the Dance*, 162; Buckle, *George Balanchine*, 289. See also Robert Irving's view in Jordan, *Moving Music*, 109.

[38] See 'Ballets in Active Repertory', The George Balanchine Foundation, url:http://balanchine.org/01/activerep.html (accessed 1 October 2004).

[39] Buckle, *George Balanchine*, 289.

[40] Livio, 'New York', 6: a French perception of American interpretation of French music.

[41] Kirstein, *Thirty Years*, 258.

[42] Kennicott, 'Ravelation', 69. Goodwin also champions selected audio recordings of Ravel's ballets.

inter-arts dimension, with new technology serving Ravel's subtle sonic art particularly well. Kennicott rightly endorses the revivified first-rate recordings of Monteux and Charles Dutoit. Monteux especially offers artistic continuity from the 1912 premiere of *Daphnis* through to the late 1950s. Similarly, Ravel's success is attested to by music score sales from the early years onwards: the 500 printed copies of *Ma Mère l'Oye* in its 1910 four-hand version were sold by 1912, and, astonishingly, the 2,000 copies of the equivalent edition of *Boléro* sold out in the year of issue, 1929.[43]

The challenge of endings: no perfect cadence

Although Ravel's younger compatriot Milhaud developed an enviable reputation with *L'Homme et son désir* and *La Création* and one would be foolish to ignore Satie's *Parade* and *Relâche*, where the significance of Ravel's balletic output is concerned, its quality-cum-quantity is exceeded only by Stravinsky. And in this genre of ballet, Ravel was certainly a very active and versatile figure, producing dedicated music (*Daphnis*, *La Valse*, *Boléro*, plus *L'Enfant*), refashioning music with new material (*Ma Mère l'Oye* and the lost fanfare for *Adélaïde*), writing scenarios (*Ma Mère l'Oye*, *Adélaïde*, *La Valse* and input for *Daphnis*), getting involved in staging (*Ma Mère l'Oye* and ideas for *Boléro*), producing his own design (frontispiece for *Le Tombeau*) and showing real appreciation of choreographic and artistic details, especially in *Ma Mère l'Oye* and Bakst's tableaux for *Daphnis*.

Paradoxically, even if this book is ostensibly a study of just one medium, it is also about Ravel's music more broadly because of the composer's predilection for internal remodelling. For Ravel, the act of creating ballet music was one that necessarily engaged with piano writing – either as a starting-point or subsequent reduction – just as much as orchestral writing.[44] Ballet thus opens a window onto Ravel's most significant contributions to musical repertory; indeed, it was in the triumphant and sensitive achievements, against the odds, of *Daphnis* and *L'Enfant* that his largest-scale orchestral writing was to emerge. (*Daphnis* was always an emotive work for Ravel and, following a first-rate performance in July 1937 by Inghelbrecht and the Orchestre National, a tearful Ravel declared to Jourdan-Morhange that he had not yet said anything musically and there was still so much inside his

---

[43] Records of Durand printed in Arthur Honegger, *I am a Composer*, trans. Wilson O. Clough with Allan A. Willman (London: Faber & Faber, 1966), 47. I am grateful to my former research student Jess Stokoe for this reference.

[44] On Ravel's composition, orchestration and remodelling, see too Kelly, 'Maurice Ravel', 868–9.

head.)[45] Thus, from another angle, Ravel's wider œuvre may be seen as invoked by his ballets, themselves the ultimate embodiment of his artistic conceptions and a noteworthy proportion of his overall output. The importance for Ravel of dance in music, as noted by Lifar (see p. 259), leads him to extend his boundaries to ballet itself, a notion consonant with the image of the composer offered by Prunières, as one 'sacrificing above all to the lord of the Dance'.[46] Ravel's process of internal remodelling or organic growth, in a symbiotic relationship with dance and design, results in a multi-faceted work-concept, or pehaps better a composite artistic being, energized or reified through performance.

And here a second paradox comes into play. In dealing with such multi-faceted creations, it is still necessary not to lose track of Ravel's aesthetic of oneness: 'For me, there are not several arts, but one alone.'[47] And the desirability of wholeness, or cohesiveness, within an artistic entity is hardly in doubt. Certainly, the notion of the whole as greater than the sum of its parts holds true for specific realized work-concepts of *Boléro*, *La Valse*, *Daphnis* and *L'Enfant*. By extension, in this unusual possibility of an œuvre as ballet, both through Ravel's own accomplishments and those of subsequent chore-ographers, there is also a sense of the whole as more special than the sum of many individual works. Yet to overplay consonance, similarity or synthesis can be problematic (Chapter 1); moreover, in various ways it is not a matter of oneness, but of diversity, or plurality.

When trying to experience the creation of Ravel's ballets there is definitely no single truth: contrast Fokine's positively portrayed experience of collaboration with Ravel in *Daphnis* with the composer's troubled account, or de Maré's claim of absolute 'harmony' for *Le Tombeau* in relation to Inghelbrecht's more frank revelations. What remains are multiple positions, although some sort of consensus may reduce the options. So too, in interpreting early productions of works, one cannot experience them as a whole; it is crucial not to be deceived into thinking one has found the thing itself. Most of the time, the researcher is left with an imprint, fossil-like, in the sand of where the work once was, or one side of a mould that used to surround the work. There is striking common ground between this present quest and that embraced by Lowenthal, a historian previously introduced in conjunction with *Daphnis*:

> To span the mental gulf between past and present, to communicate convinc-ingly, and to invest historical accounts with interpretive coherence requires

---

[45] Hélène Jourdan-Morhange, 'Mon ami Ravel', 195.

[46] Prunières, 'Trois silhouettes', 240: 'sacrifiant par-dessus tout au dieu de la Danse'.

[47] Ravel, 'Mes souvenirs d'enfant paresseux', 1: 'Pour moi, il n'y a pas plusieurs arts, mais un seul.'

their continual reshaping. No absolute historical truth lies waiting to be found; however assiduous and fair-minded the historian, he can no more relate the past "as it really was" than can our memories. But history is not thereby invalidated; faith endures that historical knowledge casts some light on the past, that elements of truth persist in it.[48]

Similarly, multiplicity operates in respect of productions through history, or through stylistic progression, so that any ballet art-work is not a fixed object but a fluid, varying or evolving concept.[49] Indeed, one might imagine a continually extending family tree of beings, accepting that sometimes a branch may die out, become extinct, and that conversely a new branch may begin. Such an image would extend 'vertically' as generations through time (poietically) and might involve contemporaneous siblings, but no one production is theoretically superior to another (esthesically). Clearly there must be a beginning, and such sources are special, but it does not follow that this represents the definitive realization of a work: the 1921 production of *Daphnis* seemingly worked better than the premiere, as did the 1931 production of *La Valse*. Furthermore, for *La Valse* and *Boléro* especially there are several strong productions across the generations and no single ideal representation. Thus this image is not hierarchical or canonic; various productions may be of equal, 'horizontal',[50] ontological status or artistic value within a parallel present.

Close physical resemblance to ancestors may occur in descendants, especially with productions of a given ballet company, or those after a particular choreographer – productions of *Daphnis* 'after Fokine' for example – and in this way one may emphasize a fragile historical lineage to a ballet that began its performed existence in 1912. As June Layson notes, 'a current performance of a ballet such as *Swan Lake* is but the latest presentation of a work that originated in 1877'.[51] By extension, some family trees may be closely associated with others, within and outside Ravel's œuvre: childhood fantasy, exoticism (Greek, Spanish), dance forms (*Boléro*, *La Valse*), Greek-inspired Ballets Russes ventures (*Daphnis*, *Narcisse*, *Cléopâtre*) and so on. Conversely, kinships between productions of a work may be much less apparent, with markedly new choreography, design and even scenario, to the extent that a family tie is broken and a new tree generated. In any given production, each danced and musical performance is different and any individual will only ever gain phenomenological experience of a fraction of a potentially limitless whole.

[48] Lowenthal, *The Past is a Foreign Country*, 235.

[49] See Lydia Goehr, *The Imaginary Museum of Musical Works* (Oxford: Clarendon Press, 1992) and more recently Butterfield, 'The musical object revisited'.

[50] See Cook, 'Between process and product', 17.

[51] Layson, 'Dance history source materials', 21.

There is no final, perfect cadence; like *Le Tombeau*, this story leaves off in the middle. Although Ravel's dance–destruction trajectory reaches inexorable closure, as in the rupture of *Boléro*, the process of reinterpretation is not end-stopped, but continuous. There must be scope for powerful future productions, unlocking aspects of the music as yet unexplored, rather as Murphy's *Daphnis* pointed up the incipient machinist element within Ravel's compositional technique. And the listener can enjoy a range of interpretations: there is no obligation to arbitrate finally between the Ashton and Balanchine versions of *La Valse*. One can take on board the strengths of each and learn from what does not quite succeed. Equally, as the critic Brunel believed, writing on *La Valse* in 1931,[52] there may be occasions when one does want to leave the visual dimension to the imagination. Admittedly harder to achieve once a strong choreographic reading has been experienced, this wish too can be satisfied at least in theory. Inevitably, the best symphony orchestras can bring a refinement that is harder to realize in the theatre, for reasons of rehearsal scheduling, acoustics and so on. But imaginative modern ballet companies can have it both ways, as did Kylián in his prize-winning video recording of *L'Enfant*, which confected an international coupling of the Nederlands Dans Theater and the Orchestre National. This surely offers one attractive future model, although there is still no substitute for 'being there' and experiencing the spontaneity, risk and excitement of unique live performances. In this way, one may enjoy a work in its varied facets across time as – to extend that concept of Gorbman's – a 'multiplex of expression' (see pp. 31 and 169–70 above).

Ravel was a supremely successful composer of ballet music for all the reasons offered above, and his achievement is of an exceptional order. His music appeals to classicists and modernists of many nationalities, and the extent of choreographing and designing to his music illustrates its versatility, even universality. The special quality of working with this music is attested to enthusiastically by a current practitioner, the choreographer Pascal Rioult: 'Over time, Ravel's genius becomes self-evident, giving one the sense of being on a journey of discovery that somehow feels familiar. I have found a natural match with Ravel.'[53] Ravel is also a composer's composer. Hugh Wood remarks on 'Ravel's marvellous feeling for tranforming a piano piece into an orchestral piece, or vice versa'. He talks of the sheer pleasure of listening to Ravel's orchestration ('like eating chocolate'), of the brilliant, huge forces of *Daphnis* (and the exquisite timbres of *Shéhérazade*); conversely, he singles out the pianistic virtuosity of *Le Tombeau*. Those who

---

[52] Brunel, 'Les Ballets de Mme Rubinstein'. See Chapter 5.

[53] Quoted from website: www.frenchculture.org 'The Ravel project' (accessed 20 April 2004).

are snobbish about Ravel are but 'pseuds'; in short, Wood freely admits, 'I adore Ravel'.[54]

As outlined in the Introduction, this book has aimed to demonstrate that the musician is missing out on the potential for intensified experience if Ravel's ballet music is only ever heard in isolation from its 'kindred arts', that the act of performance can be crucial to musicology and that there is considerable scope for future interdisciplinary scholarly research. Despite escalating costs for theatrical productions, there are strong grounds for encouraging more Ravel and less *Giselle* at the Opéra; further experimentation to secure the most dynamic *Daphnis*; and more ballet recordings that capitalize on the best danced and musical performances after the example of Kylián.[55] May Ravel's ballets continue to be performed, recorded, studied and enjoyed through to his 150th anniversary in 2025.

---

[54] Personal communication with the composer (30 April 2002).

[55] Currently, the few Ravel ballets available on DVD include Kylián, *L'Enfant* and Ashton, *La Valse*.

Appendix

Overviewing the feast: selected productions of Ravel's ballets

Abbreviations

SMI	Société Musicale Indépendante
OP	Opéra, Paris
O-CP	Opéra-Comique, Paris
ROH	Royal Opera House, Covent Garden
TC	Théâtre du Châtelet, Paris
TC-E	Théâtre des Champs-Elysées, Paris
NYCB	New York City Ballet

M	Music
C	Choreography
D	Design
Sc	Scenario
L	Lighting
Co	Conductor
Da	Dancers

In the case of *L'Enfant et les sortilèges*, it has not always been possible to ascertain which roles were sung; where known, singers and singer-dancers are identified by asterisks and daggers.

Entries are presented in three columns, giving the date of performance; the venue/auspices; and the creators/performers.

Main ballets (including *L'Enfant*)

1 *Ma Mère l'Oye* (ballet orch. 1911, pub. Durand 1912; from pf. duet 1908–10)

20 April 1910 (piano duet premiere)	SMI, Salle Gaveau, Paris	Jeanne Leleu, Geneviève Durony
29 January 1912 (ballet premiere)	Théâtre des Arts/ Rouché, Paris	Maurice Ravel (M/Sc), Jeanne (Jane) Hugard (C), Jacques Drésa (D), Gabriel Grovlez (Co), Ariane Hugon (Florine), Henriette Quinault de l'Opéra (La Belle), Djemil Anik (La Fée), Geneviève Delaunay (Le Prince Charmant), Caryathis (Le Serpentin Vert), Couperant (Laideronnette), Piere Sandrini (La Bête)
11 March 1915	Opéra (Académie Nationale de Musique et de Danse), Palais du Trocadéro, Paris	Léo Staats (C), Gabriel Grovlez (Co), Mlle Schwarz (Florine), Mlle Barbier (La Belle), Mlle Léa Piron (La Fée), Mlle G. Franck (Le Prince Charmant), Mlle Delsaux (Le Serpentin Vert), Mme Aveline (Laideronnette), M. Raymond (La Bête)
30 January 1928 (as *Beauty and the Beast*)	Abbey Theatre, Dublin	Ninette de Valois (C), Kathleen Dillon (costumes), Ursula Moreton (Beauty), Mary Tree (The Beast)
31 January 1928 (as *Beauty and the Beast*)	Festival Theatre, Cambridge	
26 November 1928 (as *Beauty and the Beast*)	Royal Court Theatre, London	
11 June 1942	O-CP	Constantin Tcherkas (C), Léon Leyritz (D), Roger Désormière (Co)
1 November 1948 (as *Mother Goose Suite*)	NYCB, City Center, New York	Todd Bolender (C/Da), André Derain (costumes), Leon Barzin (Co), Marie-Jeanne (The Young Girl), Beatrice Tompkins (The Spectator), Una Kai, Dick Beard, Francisco Monción (Da)

Date	Venue	Credits
20 December 1949 (as *Beauty and the Beast*)[a]	Sadler's Wells Theatre Ballet, London	John Cranko (C), Margaret Kaye (D), Patricia Miller (Beauty), David Poole (The Beast)
22 May 1975 (as *Mother Goose*)	NYCB, 'New York Ravel Festival', New York State Theater	Jerome Robbins (C), Stanley Simmons (costumes), Muriel Aasen (Story Teller and Princess Florine), Delia Peters (Good Fairy), Tracy Bennett (Bad Fairy), Daniel Duell (Prince Charming)
21–23 March 2000	Opéra National de Lyon, Lyon	Stanislav Wisniewski (C), Vincent Lemaire (décor), Jorge Jara (costumes), Philippe Sireuil (staging/L), Louis Langrée (Co), Emile Béjar, Gaël Bovio, Florent Ottello, Cécile Pegaz, Crystelle Pierron (Da)

2 Adélaïde ou Le Langage des fleurs; orig. Valses nobles et sentimentales (orch. 1912, pub. Durand 1912; pf. 1911, pub. Durand 1911)

Date	Venue	Credits
9 May 1911 (piano premiere as *Valses nobles*)	SMI, Salle Gaveau, Paris	Louis Aubert
22 April 1912 (ballet premiere)	Troupe of N. Trouhanova, TC	Maurice Ravel (M/Sc/Co), Ivan Clustine (C), Jacques Drésa (D), Orchestre Lamoureux, Trouhanova (Adélaïde), M. Bekefi (Lorédan), M. Vandeleer (The Duke)
15 February 1914 (concert premiere)	Société des Concerts Populaires ('Concerts Pierre Monteux'), Salle du Casino de Paris	Pierre Monteux (Co), Orchestre de Paris

[a] Excerpts from *Mother Goose Suite*.

2 Adélaïde (cont.)

4 February 1935 (as *Valentine's Eve*)	Ballet Rambert, Duke of York's Theatre, London	Frederick Ashton (C), Sophie Fedorovitch (D), Pearl Argyle, Maude Lloyd (Da)
28 December 1938 (as *Adélaïde*)	'Soirée Ravel à l'Opéra de Paris', OP	Serge Lifar (C/Da), Maurice Brianchon (D), Yvette Chauviré (Da)
1 October 1947 (as *Valses nobles*)	Sadler's Wells Theatre Ballet (Repertory), London	Frederick Ashton (C), Sophie Fedorovitch (D), Anne Heaton, Donald Britton, Michael Boulton, Michael Hogan, Kenneth MacMillan, Peter Darrell (Da)
20 February 1951 (as *La Valse* [*Valses nobles/La Valse*])	NYCB	George Balanchine (C)
1966	German Opera Ballet, Berlin	Kenneth MacMillan (C)
1975	New London Ballet	Ronald Hynd (C)
17 April 1975 (as *Noble et Sentimentale*)	Nederlands Dans Theater, Amsterdam	Hans van Manen (C)
15–17 May 1975 (as *La Valse* [*Valses nobles/La Valse*])[a]	NYCB	George Balanchine (C)

[a]. Revised version (1974).

272

3 *Daphnis et Chloé* (ballet score 1909–12; pub. Durand 1913; from pf. 1910, pub. 1910; orch. suites, 1911, 1913)

2 April 1911 (as Orchestral Suite No. 1)	'Concerts Colonne', Paris	Gabriel Pierné (Co), Orchestre Colonne
8 June 1912 (ballet premiere)	Ballets Russes/ Diaghilev, TC	Maurice Ravel (M/Sc), Michel Fokine (C/Sc), Léon Bakst (D), Pierre Monteux (Co), Vaslav Nijinsky (Daphnis), Tamara Karsavina (Chloé), Adolph Bolm (Dorcon), Mme Frohman (Lyceion)
9 June 1914 (London premiere)[a]	Theatre Royal, Drury Lane, London	Michel Fokine (Daphnis), Tamara Karsavina/Vera Fokina (Chloé)
20 June 1921 (restaging)	Ballets Russes, OP	Michel Fokine (C/Da), Léon Bakst (D), Philippe Gaubert (Co), Vera Fokina (Chloé), M. Ryaux (Dorcon), Mlle Bos (Lyceion), M. Raymond (Le Chef des pirates)
1 January 1924 (revival after Fokine)	Ballets Russes, Théâtre de Monte Carlo	Sergei Grigoriev (régisseur), Juan Gris (Daphnis's costume), Anton Dolin (Daphnis), Lydia Sokolova (Chloé), Serge Lifar (Brigand, Greek)
1927 (after Fokine)	Teatro Colón, Buenos Aires	Bronislava Nijinska (C)
31 March 1937	Philadelphia Ballet	Catherine Littlefield (C)
28 December 1938 (after Fokine)	'Soirée Ravel, à l'Opéra de Paris', OP	Serge Lifar (C), Lifar (Daphnis)
1946	Berlin State Opera Ballet	Tatiana Gsovsky (C), Gert Reinholm, Sybill Werden (Da)

a. Non-choral version.

3 Daphnis et Chloé (cont.)

February 1951	Rome Opera Ballet, Rome	Aurel Milloss (C), E. Prampolini (D)
5 April 1951 (after Fokine)	Sadler's Wells Ballet, London	Frederick Ashton (C), John Craxton (D), Michael Somes (Daphnis), John Field (Dorcon), Margot Fonteyn (Chloé), Violetta Elvin (Lyceion), Alexander Grant (Bryaxis)
8 July 1958 (new version)	Opéra-Ballet de Paris, Brussels	Serge Lifar (C), Marc Chagall (D)
4 June 1959	OP	George Skibine (C/Daphnis), Marc Chagall (D), Claude Bessy(Chloé)
15 July 1962	Stuttgart Ballet, Stuttgart	John Cranko (C), Nicholas Georgiadis (D), Georgina Parkinson, Erik Bruhn, Egon Madsen (Da)
21 December 1962 (after Fokine)	Teatro alla Scala, Milan	Serge Lifar and Nicholas Zverev (C)
2 January 1972	Frankfurt Ballet	John Neumeier (C), Jürgen Rose (D)
14 December 1972 (Suite No. 2 only)	Dutch National Ballet, Amsterdam	Hans van Manen (C), Jean-Paul Vroom (D), André Presser (Co), Dutch National Orchestra, Hans Ebbelaar (Daphnis), Alexandra Radius (Chloé)
March 1974 (Suite No. 2 only)	Sadler's Wells, London	
17 May 1975	Stuttgart Ballet, Stuttgart	Glen Tetley (C), Willa Kim (D), Richard Cragun (Daphnis), Marcia Haydée (Chloé)
22 May 1975	NYCB, 'New York Ravel Festival', New York State Theater	John Taras (C), Joe Eula (D), Peter Martins (Daphnis), Nina Fedorova (Chloé)

January 1984	Théâtre de la Ville, Paris	Jean-Claude Gallotta (C/Pan), Pascal Gravat (Daphnis), Mathilde Altaraz (Chloé)
First performed 1980; video 1989, produced by Philippe Charluet (ScreenSound Australia: Title no. 257075)	Sydney Dance Company/ Australian Ballet	Graeme Murphy (C/Sc), Kristian Fredrikson (D), John Drummond Montgomery (L), Vicki Attard, Paul Mercurio, Ross Philip, David Prudham, Janet Vernon, Kim Walker (Da)
8–25 May 2004 (revival after Ashton)[a]	The Royal Ballet, ROH	John Craxton (D), Christopher Carr and Grant Coyle (staging), Barry Wordsworth (Co), Federico Bonelli (Daphnis), Jaimie Tapper (Chloé), Martin Harvey (Dorcon), Marianela Nuñez (Lyceion), Bennet Gartside (Bryaxis)

4 Le Tombeau de Couperin (orch. 1919, pub. Durand 1919; from pf. 1914–17, pub. 1917)

11 April 1919 (piano premiere)	SMI, Salle Gaveau, Paris	Marguerite Long
28 February 1920 (orchestral premiere)	'Concerts Pasdeloup', Paris	Rhené-Baton (Co), Orchestre Pasdeloup
8 November 1920 (ballet premiere)	Ballets Suédois/Rolf de Maré, TC-E	Jean Börlin (C/Da), Pierre Laprade (D), D.-E. Inghelbrecht (Co), Jenny Hasselquist, Carina Ari[b], Margareta Johanson[b], Margit Wåhlander[b], Dagmar Forslin[b], Axel Witzansky[b], Holger Mehnen[b], Kaj Smith[b], Paul Witzansky[b] (Da)
February 1921		Börlin, Carina Ari, Mlles Klara Kjellblad[b], Johanson[b], Wåhlander[b], Forslin[b], MM Axel and Paul Witzansky[b], Smith[b], Holger Mehnen[b] (Da)

[a.] 13 May performance observed by author.

[b.] Quadrille dancers.

275

4 Le Tombeau de Couperin (cont.)

11 March 1932 (as *The Enchanted Grove*)	Vic-Wells Ballet, London	Rupert Doone (C), Duncan Grant (décor), Ninette de Valois, Anton Dolin, Alicia Markova (Da)
29 May 1975[a]	NYCB, 'New York Ravel Festival', New York State Theater	George Balanchine (C), Robert Irving (Co), Judith Fugate[b], Jean-Pierre Frohlich[b], Wilhelmina Frankfurt[b], Victor Castelli[b], Muriel Aasen[b], Francis Sackett[b], Susan Hendl[b], David Richardson[b], Marjorie Spohn[c], Hermes Condé[c], Delia Peters[c], Richard Hoskinson[c], Susan Pilarre[c], Richard Dryden[c], Carol Sumner[c], Laurence Matthews[c] (Da)
13 December 1975	NYCB, OP	George Balanchine (C)

5 L'Enfant et les sortilèges (fantaisie lyrique en deux parties, 1920–25, vocal/orch. score pub. Durand 1925)

21 March 1925 (opera-ballet premiere)[d]	'Les Artistes des Ballets Russes'/Raoul Gunsbourg, Opéra de Monte Carlo	George Balanchine (C), Alphonse Visconti (décor), Georgette Vialet (costumes), Vittorio de Sabata (Co), Marie-Thérèse Gauley* (L'Enfant), Mme Orsoni* (Maman)
1 February 1926 (French premiere)	O-CP	George Balanchine (C), Mme Virard (ballet director), Raymond Deshayes, Armand (D), Albert Wolff (Co), Marie-Thérèse Gauley* (L'Enfant), Mlle Calvet*, Mlle Féraldy*, Sibille*, Réville*, Prazères*, Ducuing*, Kamienska*, MM Guénot*, Bourdin*, Génin*, Hérent*
14 March 1929	Vienna Opera	George Balanchine (C), Eugene Gustave Steinhof (D)

a. All four movements ('Prélude', 'Forlane', 'Menuet', 'Rigaudon') were choreographed.
b. Left quadrille.
c. Right quadrille.
d. For full cast listing see Orenstein, *Ravel: Man and Musician*, 236–7.
* Singer

Date	Venue	Personnel
17 May 1939	OP	Serge Lifar (C), Paul Colin (D), Philippe Gaubert (Co)
20 November 1946 (as The Spellbound Child)	Ballet Society, Central High School of Needle Trades, New York	George Balanchine (C), Aline Bernstein (D), Barbara Karinska (costume production), Leon Barzin (Co), Joseph Connolly[†] (The Child), Elise Reinman (Fire), Tanaquil LeClercq (The Princess), William Dollar (Black Cat), Georgia Hiden (White Cat)
15 May 1975 (as The Spellbound Child)	NYCB, 'New York Ravel Festival', New York State Theater	George Balanchine with Jerome Robbins (C), Kermit Love (D), Manuel Rosenthal (Co), Paul Offenkranz[†] (The Child), Marnee Morris (Fire), Christine Redpath (Princess), Jean-Pierre Frohlich (Black Cat), Tracy Bennett (Grey Cat)
25 May 1981 (as The Spellbound Child)	NYCB, School of American Ballet (Broadcast for PBS TV series Dance in America)	George Balanchine with Kermit Love (C/costumes), David Mitchell (D), Ralph Homes (L), Manuel Rosenthal (Co), NYCB Orchestra
1984; video 1986, directed by Hans Hulscher (Virgin Classics); DVD 2001 (RM Arts/BBC/WDR)	Nederlands Dans Theater/Kylián	Jiří Kylián (C/staging), John Macfarlane (D), Lorin Maazel (Co), Orchestre National, Chœur et la Maîtrise de la RTF, Marly Knoben (L'Enfant)
21–23 March 2000	Opéra National de Lyon, Lyon	Patrick Azzopardi and Moira Delattre (régisseurs), Vincent Lemaire (décor), Jorge Jara (costumes), Philippe Sireuil (staging/L), Louis Langrée (Co), Marie-Belle Sandis* (L'Enfant), Hélène Jossoud* (Maman)

[†] Singer-dancer
* Singer

277

5 *L'Enfant et les sortilèges* (cont.)

24 October 2001 (reprise of November 1998)	OP	Richard Jones and Anthony McDonald (D/direction), James Conlon (Co), Gaële Le Roi* (L'Enfant), Désirée Rancantore* (La Princesse/Le Rossignol), Felicity Palmer* (Maman)
May–June 2002[a]	Opera North, Leeds (and UK tour)	Amir Hosseinpour (C), Nigel Lowery (D/staging), Emmanuel Plasson (Co), Claire Wild* (The Child), Fiona Kimm* (His Mother)

6 'Fanfare' for *L'Eventail de Jeanne* (one-act children's ballet 1927; 'Fanfare', pf. 4-hand version pub. Heugel 1929)

16 June 1927 (private premiere)	Salon of Jeanne Dubost, Paris	Alice Bourgat (C/Da), Yvonne Franck (C), Marie Laurencin (costumes), Pierre Legrain and René Moulaert (décor/L), Roger Désormière (Co), Odette Joyeux, Léone[b], Rolande[b], Micheline[b], Simone[b], Raymond Trouard (Da)
4 March 1929 (public premiere)	OP/Rouché	Alice Bourgat (C/Da), Yvonne Franck (C), Pierre Legrain and René Moulaert (décor), M. Tisserand (régisseur), Olga Goldenstein (rehearsals), M. J.-E. Szyfer (Co), Mlles Tamara Toumanova, Marcelle Bourgat, Joyeux, Chauviré, Goullouaud, Robe, MM Decarli, Storms (Da)

7 *La Valse* (orch. 1919–20, pub. Durand 1920; also pf. and 2pfs)

12 December 1920 (concert premiere)	'Concerts Lamoureux', Paris	Camille Chevillard (Co), Orchestre Lamoureux
8 December 1925 (as *The Art of the Theatre*)	Queen's Theatre, London	Ninette de Valois (C/'Painting'), Kathleen Dillon (D), Dorothy Coxon ('Music'), Molly Lake ('Dancing'), Margaret Craske ('Comedy'), Ursula Moreton ('Tragedy')
20(?) October 1926	Royal Flemish Opera Ballet, Antwerp	Sonia Korty (C/Da), Jean Vanderborght (costumes)

* Singer

a. 21 June performance at The Lowry, Salford Quays observed by author.
b. No surnames are available for these young dancers.

278

12 January 1929	Ballets Ida Rubinstein, Théâtre de Monte Carlo, Monte Carlo	Bronislava Nijinska (C), Alexandre Benois (D), Ida Rubinstein, Anatole Vilzak (Da)
23 May 1929 (French premiere)	Ballets Ida Rubinstein, OP	Bronislava Nijinska (C), Alexandre Benois (D), Gustave Cloez (Co)
25 June 1931 (new production)	Ballets Ida Rubinstein, OP	Bronislava Nijinska (C), Alexandre Benois (D), Gustave Cloez (Co)
8 July 1931 (UK premiere)	Ballets Ida Rubinstein, Covent Garden Theatre, London	Bronislava Nijinska (C), Alexandre Benois (D), Maurice Ravel (M/Co)
30 April 1934[a]	Ballets Ida Rubinstein, OP	Michel Fokine (C)
25 January 1940	Royal Danish Ballet, Copenhagen	Harald Lander (C/Da), Svend Johansen and Axel Bruun (D), Lis Fribert (costumes), Egisto Tango (Co), Hujgaard (Da)
17–24 May 1950	'Festival Ravel et Hommage à Colette', Réunion des Théâtres Lyriques Nationaux, O-CP	Léonide Massine (C/Sc/Arbénine), André Derain (costume design), H. and A. Mathieu (costumes), Roger Durand (décor), André Clutyens (Co), Mlle Solange Schwarz (Nina), Mlle Geneviève Kergrist (Baronne Schiral), M. Paul Goubé (Prince Zwedzich), M. Michel Gevel (Un Inconnu)

a. Probably based on 25 June 1931 production.

7 La Valse (cont.)

20 February 1951 (incorporating *Valses nobles*)	NYCB, City Center of Music and Drama, New York	George Balanchine (C), Jean Rosenthal (D), Barbara Karinska (costumes), Leon Barzin (Co), Tanaquil LeClercq, Diana Adams, Nicholas Magallanes, Francisco Monción (Da)
13 August 1955	Les Ballets Janine Charrat, Santander	Janine Charrat (C)
24 January 1958	'Festival' (20th anniversary of Ravel's death), OP	Harald Lander (C/Sc), Jean-Denis Maillart (D), R. Blot (Co), Claire Motte, Alexandre Kalioujny (Da)
31 January 1958	Teatro alla Scala, Milan	Frederick Ashton (C), André Levasseur (D)
6 March 1958	Finnish Opera Ballet, Helsinki	George Gé (C)
10 March 1959 (restaging of 31 January 1958 production) film (video) c. 1963: *An Evening with the Royal Ballet* (London, BHE); DVD 2002	Royal Ballet, ROH	Frederick Ashton (C), André Levasseur (D)

Date	Company/Venue	Credits
October 1973 (incorporating *Valses nobles*)	Reiner Moritz Productions, Berlin (German TV production)	George Balanchine (C), Barbara Karinska (costumes), Ghislaine Thesmar[a], Jean-Pierre Franchetti[a], Birgit Keil[b], Vladimir Klos[b] (Da)
15–17 May 1975 (revised version from c. 1974)	NYCB, 'New York Ravel Festival'	
December 1975–January 1976	OP	
28 November 1976	Stuttgart Ballet	
1–3 September 2005[c] (after Balanchine)	Dutch National Ballet, Edinburgh Festival	George Balanchine (C), Karinska (costumes), Martin Yates (Co), Royal Scottish National Orchestra

8 Boléro (ballet 1928, pub. Durand 1929; also 2 pf. version 1929, pub. 1929)

Date	Company/Venue	Credits
22 November 1928 (ballet premiere)	Ballets Ida Rubinstein, OP	Bronislava Nijinska (C), Alexandre Benois (D), Walther Straram (Co), Mme Ida Rubinstein (La Danseuse), MM. Anatole Vilzak, Alexis Dolinoff, Lapitzky, Ungerer (Les Hommes)
11 January 1930 (concert premiere)	'Concerts Lamoureux', Paris	Maurice Ravel (M/Co), Orchestre Lamoureux
7 July 1931 (UK premiere)	Ballets Ida Rubinstein, Covent Garden, London	Bronislava Nijinska (C), Alexandre Benois (D), Maurice Ravel (M/Co), Ida Rubinstein (Da)

a. In Paris.
b. In Stuttgart.
c. 1 September performance observed by author.

281

8 *Boléro* (cont.)

Date	Company/Venue	Personnel
Summer 1932 (new production)	Théâtre de la Danse, Paris	Bronislava Nijinska (C), Natalia Gontcharova (costumes)
6 December 1932	Sadler's Wells Theatre (Repertory), London	Anton Dolin (C/Da)
April–May 1934	Ballets Ida Rubinstein, OP	Michel Fokine (C), Alexandre Benois (D), Ida Rubinstein, Anatole Vilzak (Da)
1934	Theatre Royal, Copenhagen	Harald Lander (C), Svend Johansen (D)
10 December 1936	Riga Ballet, Riga, Latvia	Oswald Lemanis (C), Mlle Grikis (Da)
29 December 1941	OP	Serge Lifar (C/Da), Léon Leyritz (Sc/D), Louis Fourestier (Co), Suzanne Lorcia, Serge Peretti (Da)
10 January 1961	Ballets du XXe Siècle, Théâtre Royal de la Monnaie, Brussels	Maurice Béjart (C), Douchka Sifnios[a], Maya Plisetskaya/Angèle Albrecht[b], Francky Aras (Da)
November 1961	Ballets du XXe Siècle, OP	
October 1970		Maurice Béjart (C), Claude Bessy[c], Maya Plisetskaya/Florence Clerc/Josyane Consoli[d]
June 1971	Coliseum, London	

a. On 10 January 1961.
b. In November 1961.
c. In Paris 1970 and London 1971.
d. In Paris 1976.

282

14–30 January 1976	'Soirée de Ballets en Hommage à Ravel', OP	Maurice Béjart (C), Jorge Donn (Da)
1979 (new version: gender inversion)	Ballets du XXᵉ Siècle	Maurice Béjart (C), Jorge Donn (Da), Jean Martinon (Co), Orchestre de Paris
1979 (new version: 'men only'); video 1985, directed by Eric Bastin: Maurice Béjart, *The Art of the 20th-Century Ballet* (Philips Video Classics)	Ballets du XXᵉ Siècle, OP	
14 February 1984	Ice Dance Championships, Winter Olympics, Sarajevo	Jayne Torvill and Christopher Dean (C/Da)
15 February 2002	Pascal Rioult Dance, Theatre, USA tour	Pascal Rioult (C)

Additional items (including orchestrations and *Pavane*)

1 Musorgsky, *Khovanshchina* **(orch. Rimsky-Korsakov, partly reorch. Ravel and Stravinsky, 1913)**

5 June 1913 (opera premiere)	TC-E	Ballets Russes

2 Schumann, *Carnaval* **(orch. for Vaslav Nijinsky, 1914; four pieces extant: 'Préambule', 'Valse allemande', 'Paganini', 'Marche des "Davids-bündler" contre les Philistins')**

2 March 1914 (premiere with no. 3 below)	Palace Theatre, London	Troupe of Vaslav Nijinsky

3 Chopin, *Les Sylphides* **(orch. for Vaslav Nijinsky, 1914: autograph not traced)**

2 March 1914 (premiere with no. 2 above)	Palace Theatre, London	Troupe of Vaslav Nijinsky

4 Ravel, *Alborada del gracioso***, from** *Miroirs* **(orch. 1918, from pf. 1904–05)**

17 May 1919 (orchestral premiere)	'Concerts Pasdeloup', Paris	Rhené-Baton (Co), Orchestre Pasdeloup
18 July 1919 (intended ballet premiere within *Les Jardins d'Aranjuez* (aborted))	Ballets Russes, Alhambra Theatre, London	Léonide Massine (C), José-Maria Sert (D)

24 August 1930	Opening of Quai Maurice Ravel, Ciboure	Choreographic interpretation
4 March 1934 (as *The Mermaid* [*Alborada* and *Introduction et allegro*])	Ballet Club (Rambert), Mercury Theatre, London	Andrée Howard and Susan Salaman (C/Sc/D), Pearl Argyle (Da)
22 May 1975	NYCB, 'New York Ravel Festival', New York State Theater	Jacques d'Amboise (C/Da), John Braden (costumes), Suzanne Farrell (Da)

5 Chabrier, *Menuet pompeux*, from *Pièces pittoresques* (orch. for Ballets Russes, 1919)

| 18 July 1919 (intended ballet premiere within *Les Jardins d'Aranjuez* (aborted)) | Ballets Russes, Alhambra Theatre, London | Léonide Massine (C), José-Maria Sert (D) |
| 21 March 1936 (concert premiere) | 'Concerts Pasdeloup', Paris | Albert Wolff (Co), Orchestre Pasdeloup |

6 Ravel, *Pavane pour une infante défunte* (1899, pub. E. Demets (Eschig) 1900; orch. 1910, pub. E. Demets (Eschig), 1910)

| 5 April 1902 (piano premiere) | Société Nationale, Salle Pleyel, Paris | Ricardo Viñes |

285

6 Ravel, *Pavane* (cont.)

Date	Venue	Credits
27 February 1911 (orchestral premiere)	'Gentlemen's Concerts', Manchester	Henry J. Wood (Co)
1928 (ballet presentation)	Chamber Music Society of Washington	Adolph Bolm (C)
1 January 1933	Ballet Club (Rambert)	Anthony Tudor (C)
7 May 1933	Ballet Club (Rambert)	Frederick Ashton (C), Hugh Stevenson (D), Alicia Markova, Stanislas Idzikowski (Da)
12 August 1937	Ballet Rambert	Bentley Stone (C)
29 June 1941	Ballet Rambert	Frank Staff (C)
31 December 1944	OP	Serge Lifar (C), Léon Leyritz (D)
29 May 1975	NYCB, 'New York Ravel Festival'	George Balanchine (C), Patricia McBride (Da)
18 October 1996	Royal Ballet, ROH	Christopher Wheeldon (C), Darcey Bussell, Jonathan Cope (Da)
January 2002 (as *Slow Embrace*)	North Carolina Dance Festival	Jan Van Dyke (C/Da)

Select bibliography

Manuscript (and other unpublished) sources

Archives Nationales, Paris

Archives Nationales, AJ^{13} 1208 (Bakst): letter from Bakst to Rouché (17 May 1921).

Bibliothèque-Musée de l'Opéra, BNF

Archives Internationales de Danse

AID, Mus. 646: annotated piano score, *Valses nobles/Adélaïde*.

Costume design

D. 216, 76. Bakst costume designs for *Daphnis et Chloé* (1921).
D. 216, 93. Brianchon costume designs for *Adélaïde* (1938).
D. 216, 96. Leyritz costume designs for *Boléro* (1941).
D. 216, O.C. 4. Leyritz costume designs for *Ma Mère l'Oye* (1942).
D. 216, O.C. 13. Derain costume designs for *La Valse* (1950).

Dossier d'artiste

Dossier d'artiste, Trouhanowa: 'Ordre des répétitions', 'Interprètes'.
Dossier d'artiste, Grovlez: autograph letters to Rouché.
Dossier d'artiste, Ravel: copy of autograph letter to Lucien Garban (24 September 1929).
Also 'Dossier d'artiste' files for Ashton, Balanchine, Béjart, Börlin, Clustine, Lifar, de Maré, Massine, Rouché, Ida Rubinstein.

Dossier d'œuvre

Dossier d'œuvre, *Boléro*: typescript, 'Leyritz parle de ses décors', coupled with scenario (November 1940).

Also 'Dossier d'œuvre' files for *Daphnis et Chloé* (including Muelle costume invoices for 1921 production), *L'Enfant et les sortilèges*, *Ma Mère l'Oye*, *Le Tombeau de Couperin*, *La Valse*, *Valses nobles/Adélaïde*.

Fonds Rouché

Th. des Arts, Arch. R4: fols 13, 14 ('Lettres de lancement–programmes 1910–13'), 16 ('Théâtre des Arts, saisons 1912 et 1913'), 18 (1912–13 performance listing: *Ma Mère l'Oye*, *Les Aveux indiscrets*, *Le Feu*).

Th. des Arts, Arch. R8 (4), Pièce 19: fols 4 (letter from Drésa to Rouché, 9 February 1912), 5 (letter to Rouché, 2 February 1912 [LAS Drésa Saglio, 3; see below]).

Th. des Arts, *Spectacles de danse de Natalia Trouhanowa, 1911–12*. Pièce 74 (21 fols): fols 2 (letter to Rouché, 30 January 1912), 5 (letter to Rouché, March 1912), 13 (invoice, Marie Muelle) and 15 (invoice, 19 April 1912).

Th. des Arts, *Tournées de danse de Natalia Trouhanowa*. Pièce 75: fols 5 (*La Péri, Salomé, Thamar, Istar* (aide-mémoire), n.d.), 7 (accounts).

Th. des Arts, *Concerts de danse de Natalia Trouhanowa, Th. du Châtelet 1912*. Pièce 98. 'Correspondance relative aux décors et aux costumes' (19 fols): fol. 7.

Th. des Arts, *Concerts de danse de Natalia Trouhanowa, Th. du Châtelet, 1912*. Pièce 99. 'Correspondance entre N. Trouhanowa et Jacques Rouché' (46 fols): fol. 7 (letter from Trouhanova to Rouché, 11 December 1911).

Th. des Arts, *Concerts de danse de Natalia Trouhanowa Th. du Châtelet, 1912*. Pièce 100. 'Contrats et comptes' (17 fols): fol. 4 (letter from Trouhanova to Rouché, 11 February 1912).

Th. des Arts, *Concerts de danse de Natalia Trouhanowa, Th. du Châtelet, 1912*. Pièce 113. 'Arguments et distribution pour: *Salomé, La Péri, Adélaïde, Thamar*' (12 fols).

Th. des Arts, Pièce 268 (letter from Clustine to Rouché, 1 January 1912).

LAS (autograph letters)

LAS Drésa/Saglio, 1–5: 3 (see Pièce 19 (5) above), 4 (4 fols; undated letter to Rouché regarding Molière, *Le Sicilien ou L'Amour peintre*).

LAS Grovlez, 1–4, undated letters to Rouché: 1, 4 (c. January 1912).

LAS Inghelbrecht, 1–10.

LAS Nijinska, 1–15, letters to Rouché: 1 (11 December 1925), 9 (4 May 1928), 13 (4 October 1932).

LAS Ravel, 1–14, correspondence with Rouché: 1 (*Ma Mère l'Oye*: undated letter, scenario, notes), 2 (9 February 1912), 5 (16 March 1921), 13 (letter from Ravel et al. to Rouché, 24 October 1928), 14 (*Adélaïde*: undated letter, scenario).

LAS Rubinstein, 1–27, letters to Rouché: 9 (17 June 1928), 10 (24 June 1931), 13 (6 March 1933), 16 (27 July 1934).

Manuscripts (on reserve)

Rés. Pièce 78 (Rubinstein, I), fols 1–92: fols 10 (telegram to M. Blondot, 25 November), 14 (accounts May 1929), 15 (letter to confirm Opéra bookings: 16, 21, 23, 30 May 1929), 16–18 ('Théâtre National de l'Opéra' [May 1929]), 59–60 (letter, 1 May 1931), 76–7 ('Nouveaux Ballets').
Rés. 1093 (2), 'Ravel analyse sa propre musique'.
Rés. 2249, Maurice Ravel, *Valses nobles et sentimentales*: undated autograph annotations on piano score (Paris: Durand, 1911).
[Opéra] Rés. A. 775, MS score *L'Eventail de Jeanne* (18 items): item 11, Ravel, 'Fanfare'; 16-piece dossier of Laurencin costume designs.

Département de la Musique, BNF

Ravel manuscripts

MS. 16939, *La Parade* (17 pp. n.d.).
MS. 17140, *La Valse* (70 pp.), rough copy of orchestral score notated in pencil (provenance: Roger Désormière).
MS. 21917, *Boléro* (31 pp.), first orchestral draft notated in pencil.

Annotated scores

[BN Mus.] Vm. Casadesus 000489 (7), Robert Casadesus, annotated piano score, *Valses nobles*.
[BN Mus.] Vmg. 039507, Yvonne Loriod, annotated piano score, *Valses nobles*.

Autograph letters

[BN Mus.] N.L.a. 26 (082, 599), postcards from Trouhanova (and Dukas) to Robert Brussel (26 January 1911, 3 September 1912).
[BN Mus.] N.L.a. 37 (612, 613), letters from Nijinska to Poulenc (24 March 1926, 9 March 1932).

Fonds Montpensier

France–Compositeurs: Ravel.

Royal Opera House Archives (ROHA)

Ashton Collection

Benesh movement notation scores for Ashton, *Daphnis et Chloé* and *La Valse*.
Music vocal score of *Daphnis*, with Ashton's annotation.

Published sources

Abbate, Carolyn, 'Outside Ravel's tomb', *Journal of the American Musicological Society*, 52/3 (Fall 1999), 465–530.

Adshead-Lansdale, Janet and Layson, June (eds), *Dance History: An Introduction* (London and New York: Routledge, 2/1994).

Albright, Daniel, *Untwisting the Serpent: Modernism in Music, Literature and Other Arts* (Chicago and London: University of Chicago Press, 2000).

Alexandre, Arsène and Cocteau, Jean, *The Decorative Art of Léon Bakst*, trans. Harry Melvill (London: The Fine Art Society, 1913; facsim. reprint New York: Dover, 1972).

Aulnoy, Marie-Catherine, Comtesse d', *Serpentin vert*, in *Les Contes des fées* (Paris, 1697–8).

[Balanchine, George,] *Choreography by George Balanchine: A Catalogue of Works*, ed. Leslie George Katz, Nancy Lassalle and Harvey Simmonds (New York: Eakin Press Foundation/Viking, 2/1984).

Beaumont, Cyril W., *Michel Fokine and His Ballets* (London: Dance Books, 1996; orig. pub. London: C. W. Beaumont, 1935).

———, *The Diaghilev Ballet in London, A Personal Record* (London: Putnam, 1940, 2/1945; A. & C. Black, 3/1951).

———, *Ballet Design: Past and Present* (London: Studio, 1946).

———, *The Complete Book of Ballets* (London: Putnam, 1937; rev. edn 1949).

Beaumont, Marie Leprince de, 'Les Entretiens de la Belle et de la Bête', in *Magazin des enfants, Contes moraux* (Paris, 1757).

Benjamin, George, 'Last dance', *The Musical Times*, 135 (July 1994), 432–5.

Benois, Alexandre, *The Russian School of Painting* (New York, 1916).

———, *Reminiscences of the Russian Ballet*, trans. Mary Britnieva (London: Putnam, 1941).

———, *Memoirs*, trans. Moura Budberg, 2 vols (London: Chatto and Windus, 1964).

[————,] *Alexandre Benois, 1870–1960, Drawings for the Ballet* [exhibition catalogue] (London: Hazlitt, Gooden & Fox, 1980).

Bernard, Robert, 'La Valse de Maurice Ravel', *La Revue mensuelle, variétés littéraires art, science, philosophie*, 239 (July 1921), 14–21.

Bertelin, Albert, 'L'Art de la danse', *Le Courrier musical* (15 January 1912), 38–41.

Best, Christopher, 'Why do choreographers and composers collaborate?', *Dance Theatre Journal*, 15/1 (1999), 28–31.

Bizet, René, '*Ma Mère l'Oye*: c'est un petit ballet très original de M. Maurice Ravel', *L'Intransigeant* (28 January 1912).

Bland, Alexander, *The Royal Ballet: The First Fifty Years* (London: Threshold Books, 1981).

————, *Observer of the Dance 1958–1982* (London: Dance Books, 1985).

Boll, André, 'Le décor de ballet', in *Les Spectacles à travers les âges: musique, dance* (Paris: Editions du Cygne, 1932).

Bowden, Jill Anne, 'John Craxton, *Daphnis and Chloé*, and Greece', *The Dancing Times*, 981 (June 1992), 851–3.

Brants, Georgs, 'New ballets in Riga', trans. W. G. Hartog, *The Dancing Times*, 317 (February 1937), 620–21.

Bréant, Pierre G., 'Le Fantastique comme attirance', *Musical*, 4 (June 1987), 52–61.

Bremser, Martha (ed.), *International Dictionary of Ballet*, 2 vols (Detroit and London: St James's Press, 1993).

Brinson, Peter and Crisp, Clement, *Ballet and Dance: A Guide to the Repertory* (London: David and Charles, 1980).

Bruyr, José, *Maurice Ravel ou le lyricisme et les sortilèges* (Paris: Editions Le Bon Plaisir/Librairie Plon, 1950).

Buckle, Richard, *Buckle at the Ballet* (London: Dance Books, 1980).

Buckle, Richard with Taras, John, *George Balanchine, Ballet Master: A Biography* (London: Hamish Hamilton, 1988).

Butterfield, Matthew, 'The musical object revisited', *Music Analysis*, 21/3 (October 2002), 327–80.

Calvocoressi, Michel-Dimitri, 'M. Ravel discusses his own work: the *Boléro* explained', *Daily Telegraph* (11 July 1931).

————, *Musicians Gallery: Music and Ballet in Paris and London* (London: Faber & Faber, 1933).

————, 'When Ravel composed to order', *Music & Letters*, 22 (January 1941), 54–9.

Carter, Alexandra, 'The case for preservation', *Dance Theatre Journal*, 14/2 (1998), 26–9.

Casella, Alfred, 'L'Harmonie', *La Revue musicale*, 6 [special issue] (April 1925), 28–37.

Chagall, Marc, *Daphnis and Chloe* (Munich, London and New York: Prestel Publishing, 1994).

Chailley, Jacques, 'Une première version inconnue de *Daphnis et Chloé* de Maurice Ravel', *Mélanges d'histoire littéraire offerts à Raymond Lebègue* (Paris: Nizet, 1969), 371–5.

Chalupt, René, 'La Féerie et Maurice Ravel', *La Revue musicale*, 19 [special issue] (December 1938), 128–34.

Chalupt, René and Gerar, Marcelle, *Ravel au miroir de ses lettres* (Paris: Laffont, 1956).

Clarke, Mary and Crisp, Clement, *Design for Ballet* (London: Studio Vista, 1978).

Cogniat, Raymond, *Les Décorateurs de théâtre*, Cinquante ans de spectacles en France (Paris: Librairie Théâtrale, 1955).

Cohen-Lévinas, Danielle, '*Daphnis et Chloé* ou la danse du simulacre', *Musical*, 4 (June 1987), 88–95.

Colette et al., *Ravel par quelques-uns de ses familiers* (Paris: Editions du Tambourinaire, 1939).

Compton, Susan, 'Marc Chagall', in *The Dictionary of Art*, ed. Jane Turner, 34 vols (London and New York: Macmillan/Grove, 1996), vol. VI, 383–6.

Cook, Nicholas, *Analysing Musical Multimedia* (Oxford: Clarendon Press, 1998).

———, 'Theorizing musical meaning', *Music Theory Spectrum*, 23/2 (October 2001), 170–95.

———, 'Between process and product: music and/as performance', *Music Theory Online*, 7/2 (2001), 1–31.

Cossart, Michael de, 'Ida Rubinstein and Diaghilev: a one-sided rivalry', *Dance Research*, 1/2 (Autumn 1983), 3–20.

———, *Ida Rubinstein (1885–1960): A Theatrical Life* (Liverpool: Liverpool University Press, 1987).

[Diaghilev,] *Catalogue principally of Diaghilev Ballet Material* (London: Sotheby & Co., 1968).

Depaulis, Jacques, *Ida Rubinstein, une inconnue jadis célèbre* (Paris: Honoré Champion Editeur, 1995).

Doris, Hubert, 'Some thoughts on Balanchine and the waltz', *Choreography and Dance*, 3/3 (1993), 49–57.

Drummond, John, *Speaking of Diaghilev* (London and Boston: Faber & Faber, 1997).

Durand, Jacques, *Quelques souvenirs d'un éditeur de musique*, 2 vols (Paris: Durand, 1924).

Flood, Philip, 'In the silence and stillness', *Dance Theatre Journal*, 13/4 (1997), 36–9.

Fodor, Nandor, 'The riddle of Nijinsky', *The Dancing Times*, 333 (June 1938), 268–9.

Fokine, Michel, *Memoirs of a Ballet Master*, trans. Vitale Fokine (London: Constable, 1961).

[Fonteyn, Margot,] *The Art of Margot Fonteyn*, photographed by Keith Money (London: Michael Joseph, 1965).

Frank, Nino, 'Maurice Ravel entre deux trains', *Comœdia* (5 May 1932).

Garafola, Lynn, *Diaghilev's Ballets Russes* (New York: Oxford University Press, 1989).

————, 'Ten years after: Peter Martins on preserving Balanchine's legacy', *Dance Magazine* (May 1993), 38–42.

————, 'Forgotten interlude: eurhythmic dancers at the Paris Opéra', *Dance Research*, 13/1 (Summer 1995), 59–83.

————, 'Dance, film and the Ballets Russes', *Dance Research*, 16/1 (Summer 1998), 3–25.

Garafola, Lynn and Baer, Nancy Van Norman (eds), *The Ballets Russes and its World* (New Haven, CT: Yale University Press, 1999).

Garafola, Lynn with Foner, Eric (eds), *Dance for a City: Fifty Years of the New York City Ballet* (New York: Columbia University Press, 1999).

Goddard, Scott, 'Maurice Ravel, some notes on his orchestral method', *Music & Letters*, 6 (1925), 291–303.

Goehr, Lydia, *The Imaginary Museum of Musical Works* (Oxford: Clarendon Press, 1992).

Goléa, Antoine, *Esthétique de la musique contemporaine* (Paris: Presses Universitaires de France, 1954).

Gorbman, Claudia, 'Narrative film music', *Yale French Studies*, 60 (1980), 189–90.

————, *Unheard Melodies: Narrative Film Music* (Bloomington: Indiana University Press, 1987).

Griffiths, Paul, *Modern Music: A Concise History from Debussy to Boulez* (London: Thames & Hudson, 1978, repr. 1986).

Grigoriev, Sergei L., *The Diaghilev Ballet, 1909–1929*, trans. Vera Bowen (Harmondsworth and Baltimore, MD: Penguin Books, 1960).

Gross, Valentine, *Nijinsky on Stage*, introduced by Richard Buckle (London: Studio Vista, 1971).

Guest, Anne Hutchinson and Preston-Dunlop, Valerie, 'What exactly do we mean by dynamics?', *Dance Theatre Journal*, 13/2 (Autumn–Winter 1996), 28–38.

Guest, Ivor, *Le Ballet de L'Opéra de Paris*, trans. Paul Alexandre (Paris: Théâtre National de L'Opéra, 1976).

Häger, Bengt, *Ballets Suédois*, trans. Ruth Sharman (London: Thames & Hudson, 1990).

Hanna, Judith Lynne, *Dance, Sex and Gender* (Chicago: University of Chicago Press, 1987).

Hansen, Robert C., *Scenic and Costume Design for the Ballets Russes* (Ann Arbor, MI: UMI Research Press, 1985).

Harding, James, *The Ox on the Roof* (London: Macdonald, 1972).

Harris-Warrick, Rebecca, Goodwin, Noël and Percival, John, 'Ballet', in *The New Grove Dictionary of Music and Musicians*, ed. Stanley Sadie, 29 vols (London: Macmillan, 2001), vol. II, 565–96.

Harrold, Robert, *Ballet* (Poole: Blandford Press, 1980).

Henson, R. A., 'Maurice Ravel's illness: a tragedy of lost creativity', *British Medical Journal*, 296 (4 June 1988), 1585–8.

Hodson, Millicent, *Nijinsky's Crime against Grace: Reconstruction Score for the Original Choreography of Le Sacre du printemps* (Stuyvesant, NY: Pendragon Press, 1996).

Honegger, Arthur, *Je suis compositeur* (Paris: Editions du conquistador, 1951); *I am a Composer*, trans. Wilson O. Clough with Allan A. Willman (London: Faber & Faber, 1966).

Howat, Roy, 'Modes and semitones in Debussy's *Preludes* and elsewhere', *Studies in Music*, 22 (1988), 81–91.

Hugard, Jane, 'Du ballet classique: le caractère et l'évolution classique', in *Les Spectacles à travers les âges: musique, danse* (Paris: Editions du Cygne, 1932).

Hunt, Marilyn, 'Balanchine's democratic aristocracy', *Dance Magazine* (May 1993), 43–4.

Inghelbrecht, Desiré-Emile, *Mouvement contraire, souvenirs d'un musicien* (Paris: Editions Domat, 1947).

Ivry, Benjamin, *Maurice Ravel: A Life* (New York: Welcome Rain Publishers, 2000; repr. 2003).

Jackson, Sheila, *Costumes for the Stage: A Complete Handbook for Every Kind of Play* (London: A. & C. Black, 2/2001).

Jankélévitch, Vladimir, *Ravel* (Paris: Editions Rieder, 1939; Editions du Seuil, ed. Jean-Michel Nectoux, 3/1995).

Jordan, Stephanie, *Moving Music: Dialogues with Music in Twentieth-Century Ballet* (London: Dance Books, 2000).

Joseph, Charles M., *Stravinsky and Balanchine: A Journey of Invention* (New Haven, CT and London: Yale University Press, 2002).

Jouhandeau, Elise, *Joies et douleurs d'une belle eccentrique: l'altesse des hasards* (Paris: Flammarion, 1954).

Jourdan-Morhange, Hélène, 'Mon ami Ravel', *La Revue musicale*, 19 [special issue] (December 1938), 192–7.

———, *Ravel et nous: l'homme, l'ami, le musicien* (Geneva: Editions du Milieu du Monde, 1945).

Joyeux, Odette, *Côté jardin: mémoires d'un rat* (Paris: Gallimard, 1951).

Kahane, Martine, *Les Artistes et l'Opéra de Paris: dessins et costumes* (Paris, 1987).

Kalinak, Kathryn, *Settling the Score: Music and the Classical Hollywood Film* (Madison, WI: University of Wisconsin Press, 1992).

Karsavina, Tamara, *Theatre Street: The Reminiscences of Tamara Karsavina* (London: Heinemann, 1930; rev. edn Constable, 1948).

Kavanagh, Julie, *Secret Muses: The Life of Frederick Ashton* (London: Faber, 1996).

Kelly, Barbara L., 'Maurice Ravel', in *The New Grove Dictionary of Music and Musicians*, ed. Stanley Sadie, 29 vols (London: Macmillan, 2/2001), vol. XV, 864–78.

Kennicott, Philip, 'Ravelation', *Dance Magazine* (April 1990), 68–9.

Kiley, Dan, *The Peter Pan Syndrome: Men who Have Never Grown Up* (New York: Dodd and Mead, 1988).

Kilian, Hannes, *Stuttgarter Ballett* (Weingarten: Kunstverlag Weingarten, 1981).

Kirstein, Lincoln, *Thirty Years: Lincoln Kirstein's The New York City Ballet* (New York: Knopf, 1973, 2/1978; London: A. & C. Black, 1979).

Kramer, Lawrence, *Classical Music and Postmodern Knowledge* (Berkeley: University of California Press, 1995).

Kristeva, Julia, *Les Mots: Colette, ou la chair du monde* (Paris: Fayard, 2002; Eng. trans. Jane Marie Todd (New York: Columbia University Press, 2004).

Laloy, Louis, 'Wagner et les musiciens d'aujourd'hui: opinions de MM. Florent Schmitt et Maurice Ravel – Conclusions', *La Grande Revue*, 13/9 (10 May 1909), 160–64.

———, 'Maurice Ravel' in *Histoire du théâtre lyrique en France, depuis les origines jusqu'à nos jours*, 3 vols (Paris: Poste National Radio, 1939), vol. III, 229–33.

Larner, Gerald, *Maurice Ravel* (London: Phaidon, 1996).

Lenormand, René, *Etude sur l'harmonie moderne* (Paris: Le Monde Musical/Eschig, 1913).

Lester, Keith, 'Rubinstein revisited', *Dance Research*, 1/2 (Autumn 1983), 21–31.

Lesure, François and Nectoux, Jean-Michel (eds), *Maurice Ravel* [Catalogue de l'exposition] (Paris: Bibliothèque Nationale, 1975).

Levinson, André, *Ballet Old and New*, trans. Susan Cook Summer (orig. pub. St Petersburg: Svobodnoe iskusstvo, 1918; New York: Dance Horizons, 1982).

———, *Bakst, The Story of the Artist's Life* (London: Bayard, 1923; repr. New York: Benjamin Blom, 1971).

———, *Les Visages de la danse* (Paris: Editions Bernard Grasset, 1933).

Lifar, Serge, 'Maurice Ravel et le ballet', *La Revue musicale*, 19 [special issue] (December 1938), 74–80.

————, *La Danse: les grands courants de la danse académique* (Paris: Denöel, 1938); rev. edn, *Lifar on Classical Ballet*, trans. D. M. Dinwiddie (London: Allan Wingate, 1951).

————, *Histoire du ballet russe* (Paris: Nagel, 1950); *A History of Russian Ballet*, trans. Arnold Haskell (London: Hutchinson, 1954).

————, *Serge de Diaghilev: sa vie, son œuvre, sa légende* (Monaco: Editions du Rocher, 1954).

Livio, Antoine, 'Dans le monde: New York', *dp* (October 1975), 6.

————, 'Balanchine et Stravinsky: 40 ans d'amitié', *Ballet Danse, L'Avant-scène, Le Sacre du printemps* (August–October 1980), 124.

Long, Marguerite, *Au piano avec Maurice Ravel* (Paris: Julliard, 1960, 2/1971); *At the Piano with Ravel*, ed. Pierre Laumonier, trans. Olive Senior-Ellis (London: Dent, 1973).

Longus, *Les Pastorales de Longus ou Daphnis et Chloé*, trans. Jacques Amyot, rev. Paul-Louis Courier, ill. Pierre Bonnard (Paris: A. Vollard, 1902).

————, *Daphnis and Chloe*, trans. G. Thornley (London: Heinemann, 1916).

Lowenthal, David, *The Past is a Foreign Country* (Cambridge: Cambridge University Press, 1985).

Mackrell, Judith, *Reading Dance* (London: Michael Joseph, 1997).

Maré, Rolf de (ed.), *Les Ballets Suédois dans l'art contemporain* (Paris: Editions du Trianon, 1931).

Maré, Rolf de, 'Ravel et les ballets', *La Revue musicale*, 20 (January–February 1939), 15–16.

Marnat, Marcel, *Maurice Ravel* (Paris: Fayard, 1986; 2/1995).

Massine, Léonide, *My Life in Ballet*, ed. Phyllis Hartnoll and Robert Rubens (London: Macmillan, 1968).

Mawer, Deborah (ed.), *The Cambridge Companion to Ravel* (Cambridge: Cambridge University Press, 2000).

McClary, Susan, *Feminine Endings: Music, Gender, and Sexuality* (Minnesota and Oxford: University of Minnesota Press, 1991.)

Messing, Scott, 'Polemic as history: the case of neoclassicism', *Journal of Musicology*, 9/4 (Fall 1991), 481–97.

Milhaud, Darius, *Ma vie heureuse* (Paris: Belfond, 1987); *My Happy Life: An Autobiography*, trans. Donald Evans, George Hall and Christopher Palmer (London and New York: Marion Boyars, 1995).

Morris, Geraldine, 'Dance partnerships: Ashton and his dancers', *Dance Research*, 19/1 (Summer 2001), 11–59.

Morrison, Simon, 'The origins of *Daphnis et Chloé*' (1912), *19th Century Music*, 28/1 (Summer 2004), 50–76.

Narmour, Eugene, *The Analysis and Cognition of Basic Melodic Structures: The Implication–Realization Model* (Chicago: University of Chicago Press, 1991).

Näslund, Erik, *Les Ballets Suédois 1920–1925* [Exhibition] (Paris: Bibliothèque Nationale de France/Louis Vuitton, 1994).

Nattiez, Jean-Jacques, *Music and Discourse: Toward a Semiology of Music*, trans. Carolyn Abbate (Princeton, NJ: Princeton University Press, 1990).

Nichols, Roger, *Ravel* (London: Dent, 1977).

—————— (ed.), *Ravel Remembered* (London and Boston: Faber & Faber, 1987).

——————, *The Harlequin Years: Music in Paris*, 1917–1929 (London: Thames & Hudson, 2002).

Nijinska, Bronislava, 'Reflections about the production of *Les Biches* and *Hamlet* in Markova–Dolin ballets', trans. Lydia Lopokova, *The Dancing Times*, 317 (February 1937), 617–20.

Nijinsky, Romola, *Nijinsky* (London: Victor Gollancz, 1933; repr. 1937).

Nijinsky, Vaslav, *The Diary of Vaslav Nijinsky*, trans. Kyril Fitzlyon, ed. and introduced by Joan Acocella (London: Penguin Books, 2000).

Nin, Joaquín, 'Comment est né le *Boléro* de Ravel', *La Revue musicale*, 19 [special issue] (December 1938), 211–13.

Nugent, Ann, 'Valedictory fare well', *Dance Theatre Journal*, 17/1 (2001), 34–8.

Orenstein, Arbie, *Ravel: Man and Musician* (New York: Columbia University Press, 1975; Dover, 2/1991).

Orenstein, Arbie (ed.), *Maurice Ravel: lettres, écrits, entretiens* (Paris: Flammarion, 1989); trans. *A Ravel Reader* (New York: Columbia University Press, 1990).

Parnac, Valentin, 'Notation de danses', *La Revue musicale*, 9 (March 1928), 129–32.

Perrault, Charles, 'La Belle au bois dormant', 'Le Petit Poucet', in *Histoires ou contes du temps passé des moralités*, in *Contes*, ed. Gilbert Rouger (Paris: Editions Garnier, 1967).

Polunin, Vladimir, *The Continental Method of Scene Painting*, ed. Cyril W. Beaumont (London: C. W. Beaumont, 1927; repr. Dance Books, 1980).

Porter, Andrew, 'Frederick Ashton, 1960–1970', *About the House*, 8 (Summer 1970), 65–70.

Poulenc, Francis, *Moi et mes amis* (Geneva: La Palatine, 1963).

Prunières, Henry, 'Trois silhouettes de musiciens – César Franck, Saint-Saëns, Maurice Ravel', *La Revue musicale*, 7 (October 1926), 225–40.

Rambert, Marie, *Quicksilver: An Autobiography* (London: Macmillan, 1972).

Ravel, Maurice, 'Concerts Lamoureux', *Revue musicale de la S.I.M.*, 8/3 (March 1912), 50–52.

——————, '*La Sorcière* à l'Opéra-Comique', *Comœdia illustré*, 5/7 (5 January 1913), 320–23.

——————, '*Fervaal*', *Comœdia illustré*, 5/8 (20 January 1913), 361–4.

————, 'Au Théâtre des Arts', *Comœdia illustré*, 5/9 (5 February 1913), 417–20.

————, '*Boris Godounoff*', *Comœdia illustré*, 5/17 (5 June 1913), n.p.

————, '*Parsifal*', *Comœdia illustré*, 6/8 (20 January 1914), 400–03.

————, 'Les Nouveaux Spectacles de la saison russe', *Comœdia illustré*, 6/17 (5 June 1914), 811–14.

————, 'Take jazz seriously!', *Musical Digest*, 13/3 (March 1928), 49–51.

————, 'Contemporary music', *The Rice Institute Pamphlet*, 15 (April 1928), 131–45.

————, 'Mes souvenirs d'enfant paresseux', *La Petite Gironde* (12 July 1931), 1.

————, 'Finding tunes in factories', *New Britain* (9 August 1933), 367.

————, 'Les Aspirations des moins de vingt-cinq ans: la jeunesse musicale', *Excelsior* (28 November 1933).

[————,] *Catalogue de l'œuvre de Maurice Ravel* (Paris: Fondation Maurice Ravel, 1954).

Reade, Brian, *Ballet Designs and Illustrations, 1581–1940* [catalogue raisonné, Victoria and Albert Museum] (London: HMSO, 1967).

Reich, Willi, 'In memoriam Maurice Ravel', *La Revue musicale*, 19 [special issue] (December 1938), 275.

Reynolds, Nancy, *Repertory in Review: Forty Years of the New York City Ballet* (New York: Dial, 1977).

Robbins, Lee N. and Rutter, Michael (eds), *Straight and Devious Pathways from Childhood to Adulthood* (Cambridge: Cambridge University Press, 1990).

Roland-Manuel, Alexis, *Maurice Ravel et son œuvre* (Paris: Durand, 1914).

————, *Ravel et son œuvre dramatique* (Paris: Librairie de France, 1928).

[————,] 'Une esquisse autobiographique de Maurice Ravel [1928]', *La Revue musicale*, 19 [special issue] (December 1938), 17–23.

——, *A la gloire de Ravel* (Paris: Nouvelle Revue Critique, 1938; Paris: Gallimard, 2/1948); *Maurice Ravel*, Eng. trans. Cynthia Jolly (London: Dobson, 1947).

Rose, Jacqueline, *The Case of Peter Pan, or the Impossibility of Children's Fiction* (London: Macmillan, 1984, rev. 1992).

Rosenthal, Manuel, 'Entretiens avec Rémy Stricker', *France Culture* (April 1985).

————, 'Maurice Ravel: souvenirs', *Radio Classique* (December 1995), 26–7.

Rouché, Jacques, *L'Art théâtral moderne* (Paris: Cornelly, 1910; Bloud et Gay, 2/1924).

Russell, Douglas A., *Stage Costume Design: Theory, Technique and Style* (New York: Appleton-Century-Crofts, 1973).

Scholl, Tim, *From Petipa to Balanchine: Classical Revival and the Modernization of Ballet* (London and New York: Routledge, 1994).

Schouvaloff, Alexander, *Léon Bakst: The Theatre Art* (London and New York: Sotheby's Publications, 1991).

————, *The Art of Ballets Russes: The Serge Lifar Collection of Theater Designs, Costumes and Paintings at the Wadsworth Atheneum* (New Haven, CT and London: Yale University Press, 1997).

Scheuer, L. Franc, 'Paris in 1937: a retrospective view of the year', *The Dancing Times* (December 1937), 317–21.

Scott, Derek B. (ed.), *Music, Culture, and Society: A Reader* (Oxford: Oxford University Press, 2000).

Segal, Robert A., *Theorizing about Myth* (Amherst, MA: University of Massachusetts Press, 1999).

Silverman, Kaja, *The Acoustic Mirror: The Female Voice in Psychoanalysis and Cinema* (Bloomington and Indianapolis: Indiana University Press, 1988).

Sokolova, Lydia, *Dancing for Diaghilev*, ed. Richard Buckle (London: John Murray, 1960).

Stengele, Roger, *A la recherche de Béjart* (Brussels: J. Verbeeck Editeur, 1968).

Straus, Joseph N., *Remaking the Past: Musical Modernism and the Influence of the Tonal Tradition* (Cambridge, MA: Harvard University Press, 1990).

Taper, Bernard, *Balanchine* (London: Collins, 1964; rev. edn Berkeley: University of California Press, 1996).

Taruskin, Richard, *Stravinsky and the Russian Traditions: A Biography of the Works through Mavra*, 2 vols (Oxford: Oxford University Press/ University of California Press, 1996).

Thieffry, Jeanne (ed.), *Alfred Cortot, cours d'interprétation* (Paris: Legouix, 1934).

Thurman, Judith, *Secrets of the Flesh: A Life of Colette* (London: Bloomsbury, 1999).

Tikanova, Nina, *La Jeune Fille en bleu, Pétersbourg–Berlin–Paris* (Lausanne: L'Age d'homme, 1991).

Troussevitch, Alexandrine, 'La Chorégraphie et ses rapports avec la musique', *La Revue musicale*, 15 (May 1934), 340–48.

Vaillat, Léandre, *Ballets de l'Opéra de Paris* (Paris: Compagnie Française des Arts Graphiques, 1943).

van den Toorn, Pieter C., *Music, Politics and the Academy* (Berkeley: University of California Press, 1995).

Vaughan, David, *Frederick Ashton and his Ballets* (London: A. & C. Black, 1977).

Walker, Kathrine Sorley, *Ninette de Valois: Idealist without Illusions* (London: Hamish Hamilton, 1987).

———, 'Ashton ballets: post-mortem performance', *Dance Now*, 3/3 (Autumn 1994), 45–51.

Watkins, Glenn, *Pyramids at the Louvre: Music, Culture and Collage from Stravinsky to the Postmodernists* (Cambridge, MA: Harvard University Press, 1994).

Welker, David, *Theatrical Set Design: The Basic Techniques* (Boston and London: Allyn & Bacon, 1979.)

Williams, Peter, *Masterpieces of Ballet Design* (Oxford: Phaidon, 1981).

Wolff, Stéphane, *L'Opéra au Palais Garnier (1875–1962)* (Paris: Slatkine, 1983).

Woolf, Vicky, *Dancing in the Vortex: The Story of Ida Rubinstein* (Amsterdam: Harwood Academic Publishers, 2000).

Yaraman, Sevin, *Revolving Embrace: The Waltz as Sex, Steps, and Sound*, Monographs in Musicology No.12 (Hillsdale, NY: Pendragon Press, 2002).

Index

The index includes names, works and themes. 'Names' includes some collective names of ballet companies, orchestras, and concert societies. 'Works' includes selected writings of Ravel and others. Some discretion has been exercised in the inclusion of material from the Appendix and footnotes. The major ballets are indexed under their titles, with the definite article ignored in the alphabetical ordering, but not inverted. *Le Tombeau de Couperin* will therefore be found under 'T'. Cross-references are made to collaborative artists, such as principal dancers, or set designers, in the form *see also under*. Illustrations are referenced in **bold**, and music examples in *italics*. This index was prepared by Tom Norton.